THE USEFUL COBBLER

THE USEFUL COBBLER

EDMUND BURKE AND THE POLITICS OF PROGRESS

JAMES CONNIFF

STATE UNIVERSITY OF NEW YORK PRESS

Portions of text throughout this book were taken from
The Correspondence of Edmund Burke, originally published
by the Syndics of the Cambridge University Press
as well as the University of Chicago Press,
© 1958–1978.

Portions of text throughout this book were reprinted with the permission
of Macmillan Publishing Company from *Reflections on the Revolution
in France* by Edmund Burke and edited by H. D. Mahoney. Copyright © 1955
by Macmillan Publishing Company.

The cover photo entitled "Edmund Burke, M. P. (1729–1797), Statesman and
Writer" by Joshua Reynolds, is courtesy of the National Gallery of Ireland.

Published by
State University of New York Press, Albany

Printed in the United States of America

For information, address State University of New York
Press, State University Plaza, Albany, N.Y., 12246

Production by Diane Ganeles
Marketing by Dana Yanulavich

Library of Congress Cataloging-in-Publication Data

Conniff, James, 1942–
The useful cobbler : Edmund Burke and the politics of progress /
James Conniff.
p. cm.
Includes bibliographical references and index.
ISBN 0–7914–1843–X (alk. paper). — ISBN 0–7914–1844–8 (pbk. :
alk. paper)
1. Burke, Edmund, 1729–1797—Contributions in political science.
I. Title.
JC176.B83C55 1994
320′.01—dc20 93–16994
CIP

10 9 8 7 6 5 4 3 2 1

CONTENTS

PREFACE

My interest in Edmund Burke's political thought developed early. It was the topic of my first undergraduate term paper in political theory, and it is over fifteen years since I first published on the topic. This book, however, has been in progress for considerably less time. Early in my professional career, I turned my attention to questions involving the origins and development of modern representative democracy. It was only after I studied a number of other eighteenth century thinkers, particularly David Hume and James Madison, that it dawned on me that most of the paths taken by political thought in that time eventually led to Burke and that the early history of representative theory was one of the most important of those paths.

As might be expected over the course of such a long intellectual odyssey, I have compiled a substantial list of obligations. To mention them all, however, would dilute the value of the most important. These fall into three classes: my teachers, my colleagues, and my family. At Rutgers University, I had the good fortune to be assigned to introductory political science with Eugene Meehan. I probably owe to him my choice of career and whatever ability I have developed as a writer. I doubt if I could have survived the doctoral program at Columbia University without the encouragement and support of Julian H. Franklin and, in a somewhat different way, the late Herbert A. Deane. For over twenty years, I have been a member of a fine political science department. My colleagues have been consistently interested and supportative. In particular, I would like to mention Ed Heck, Bill Schultze, Dwight Anderson, Bob Keiser, Brian Loveman, Dick Hofstetter and Harlan Lewin. Finally, but most importantly, I must thank my family. My father has always been my principal model and my best teacher, and my mother a source of comfort and support. My wife, Francine, and my daughters, Colleen and Elizabeth, form the foundation on which all else is built.

Portions of this work have appeared in modified form elsewhere. Chapter five is an expanded version of my article, "Burke on Political Economy: The Nature and Extent of State Authority." *The Review of Politics,* Vol. 49, No. 4 (fall 1987), pp. 490–514. Chapter seven draws heavily on "Burke, Bristol, and the Concept of Representation," *Western Political Quarterly,* Vol. XXX, No. 3 (September 1977), pp. 329–341. The discussion of Irish politics in chapter ten is based on "Edmund Burke's Reflections on the Coming Revolution in Ireland," *Journal of the History of Ideas,* Vol. XLVII, No. 1 (January–March 1986), pp. 37–59.

I would also like to express my gratitude to the following:

The University of Chicago Press for permission to quote from: Edmund Burke, *The Correspondence of Edmund Burke,* 10 Volumes, Chicago: University of Chicago Press, 1963–1978.

Dover Publications for permission to quote from: John Locke, *An Essay Concerning Human Understanding,* II Volumes, New York: Dover Publications, 1959.

The University of Notre Dame Press for permission to quote from: Edmund Burke: *A Philosophical Enquiry into the Origin of Our Ideas of the Sublime and Beautiful,* edited by James T. Bolton. Copyright 1968 by University of Notre Dame Press.

The Macmillan Publishing Company for permission to quote selections from: *Reflections on the Revolution in France* by Edmund Burke and edited by H. D. Mahoney. Copyright 1955 by Macmillan Publishing Company.

1

INTRODUCTION: THE SIGNIFICANCE OF EDMUND BURKE

The reputations of some political thinkers rise and fall with the times. Considered great in one period, they are largely ignored in another. Other thinkers, Edmund Burke among them, seem always to be of interest and significance. Ever since his own day, Burke's writings have been studied with great care—both as a guide to the politics of the late eighteenth century and as a program for action in subsequent periods. Thus, at first glance, it might appear odd that scholars cannot seem to agree on an assessment of Burke. In fact, in the nearly two hundred years since his death, his thought has been characterized in a bewildering variety of ways. In the nineteenth century, the dominant interpretation of Burke, advanced by writers like Leslie Stephen and John Morley, saw him as a politician-philosopher, who grounded a cautious reformism on a combination of Humean skepticism and pre-Benthamite Utilitarianism.[1] However, in the twentieth century and increasingly since World War II, the utilitarian approach has given way to a natural law interpretation.[2] As exemplified by Peter Stanlis, this school holds that "in every important political problem he ever faced . . . Burke *always* appealed to the natural law. What is more, by Natural Law Burke always meant essentially the same thing . . ."[3] To the objection that Burke rarely explicitly mentioned natural law, these writers reply that Burke considered natural law to be imminent in history, and, therefore, held that "Natural Law can enter our cognition only so far as it is embodied in social prescription or character."[4] The political implications of this interpretation are, of course, profoundly conservative, for it suggests that the measure of what is good is to be found in what is established. For this reason, the natural law school somewhat neglects the more reformist and empirical aspects of Burke's thought. Therefore, some advocates of the approach, Burleigh Wilkens, for example, offer a softer version of the thesis, or even, as in the case of Michael Freeman, seek to combine it with the utilitarian view.[5] Outside the framework of the utilitarian-natural law debate, still other interpretations have developed. C. B. Macpherson, for example, deemphasizes the discussion of Burke's philosophical roots and insists that Burke should be understood as a defender of early capitalism. Macpherson thus attributes the continuing interest in Burke to his being the first major British thinker to recognize that the traditional intellectual defense of elitism could be adapted to capitalist use.[6] Alfred Cobban, on the other hand, sees Burke not as a modernist, but as the principle early spokesman for the Romantic "revolt" against the Enlightenment.[7]

If the students of Burke's thought cannot agree, those who study his political career do little better. Frank O'Gorman largely rejects the claims for Burke as a profound thinker, preferring instead to think of him as a defender of the material interests of the aristocratic Rockingham Whigs.[8] However, John MacCunn, though agreeing with O'Gorman's emphasis on Burke as a practical politician, sees considerable merit in Burke's political philosophy.[9] Indeed, MacCunn identifies Burke as one of the major sources of late nineteenth century liberalism. MacCunn's attempt to link Burke to liberalism brings us to the source of much of the confusion about his significance, for the modern consensus that Burke was a founder of conservatism was not shared by his immediate heirs. In fact, even the earliest apologists for twentieth century conservatism paid little attention to him.[10] Only when Hugh Cecil hit on the tactic of linking Burke's denunciation of the French Revolution to his own opposition to the dangers of creeping socialism did Burke become a popular conservative source. Along this line, Irving Babbitt, for instance, contrasted Burke to Rousseau, whom Babbitt saw as a political extremist and intellectual godfather to the French Revolution.[11] According to Babbitt, Burke defended the two cornerstones of European civilization, the spirit of Religion and the spirit of the Gentleman, against the radical leveling of the Revolution and advocated instead an ethic of moderation and humanistic control. Still more recently, Burke achieved virtually paradigmatic conservative status. Thus, Anthony Quinton writes, "Edmund Burke is plainly the first of English conservative thinkers in influence and importance."[12] Yet even now the conversion remains incomplete. In his important study of the history of the English Conservative party, Lord Robert Blake scarcely mentions Burke and begins, instead, with Disraeli and Derby's organization of right-wing Tories into an opposition to Robert Peel's move to repeal the Corn Laws.[13] In Blake's opinion, Burke is no more than a vaguely sympathetic precursor of modern Conservatism.

Why is there such controversy about Burke? Quinton makes a useful point when he distinguishes between two different conservative traditions: the first, religiously-based, draws its inspiration from the doctrine of original sin and stresses the mutual support of Church and State, while the other is more secular, skeptical, and pragmatic.[14] In this interpretation, Burke can thus be seen as an important fount of one form of Conservatism, the more religious line, but relatively uninfluential with the other school. From a slightly different perspective, Fair and Hutcheson explain the modern conservative's ambivalence toward Burke by suggesting that the radical branch of the movement finds it difficult to reconcile his many liberal views with his reputed Conservatism, while more moderate Conservatives see that very liberalism as his primary appeal.[15] In this study, I will go a step further. I will suggest that Burke's appeal lies in his Whiggism. That is, I believe that Burke sought to reconcile a generally conservative outlook with an acceptance of the need for change through reform. Burke's accomplishment was to recognize that the past could be a guide to the future, and, therefore, need not be set in opposition to it. However, before I attempt to present yet another interpretation of Burke's political thought, I should perhaps make clear why I think it worthwhile—indeed, necessary—to do so. In the next section of this introduction, I will explain the approach I have taken to Burke, and attempt to clarify some of the assumptions about his thought and about its intellectual and political context which I have made. I will also try to offer a reason for reading Burke beyond an antiquarian interest in the eighteenth century. In my view, there is good and ample reason to study Burke in the insight that study provides into the development and nature of modern Western politics. This book as a whole will be concerned with making that argument, but, as an inducement to read further, I will briefly anticipate it here. Thus, in the last section of the introduction, I will offer a brief outline of the remainder of the book. I will describe how Burke's argument develops, how its various components fit together, what role it played in the politics of its day, what strengths and, perhaps more importantly, what weaknesses it contained, and how adequate, both as a description and a prescription, it was to the politics of his, and our, day.

I

R. G. Collingwood suggested sometime ago that all history, expecially the history of ideas, is, in a fundamental sense, "present" history.[16] We go to the past, he said, not in a disinterested attempt to discover how things actually were, but to seek answers to questions which concern us in the present. We seek to discover the origins and to plot the development of those factors which shape our own time in the hope that such a search will give us understanding of and, if we are especially fortunate, a degree of control over our world. The purpose of history, then, is self-knowledge. We wish to know what we are and what we should do, but to do so we must know how we got where we are: "knowing yourself means knowing what you can do; and since nobody knows what he can do until he tries, the only clue to what man can do is what man has done. The value of history, then, is that it teaches us what man has done and thus what man is."[17] As we do not approach history blind, we begin with some ready-made set of assumptions, indeed prejudices, about the nature of the past and about how to recover it. Moreover, these "pictures" of the past, formed out of our concerns in the present, are the very bases of the questions we ask, determine the nature of our research, and provide the grounds for assessing whatever conclusions we come to. In addition, as the problems of contemporary society change, so do the questions we ask and the solutions we seek. Thus, there is an inherent element of indeterminateness in the study of ideas, for "each historian sees history from his own centre, at an angle of his own: and therefore he sees some problems which no other sees, and sees every problem from a point of view, and therefore under an aspect, peculiar to himself. No one historian, therefore, can see more than one aspect of the truth; and even an infinity of historians must always leave an infinity of aspects unseen."[18] Political theory, then, even in its historical dimension, has an immediacy which many other disciplines lack, for it is oriented to action in circumstances which are both difficult and urgent. John Dunn has put it well: "Unlike history or moral philosophy, political theory cannot select a subject matter for its apparent epistemological tractability. It cannot confine itself to detached explanation or abstract prescription but has to set itself, as best it can, to judge how human beings now have good reason to act, both in the light of modern politics and within modern politics."[19] Against this constantly shifting background, there can be no final or fully completed explanation of any of the major historical thinkers or ideas. Each generation of scholars must reexamine its intellectual traditions in the light of its own needs and concerns.

My interest in Burke stems from a desire to understand the nature of modern representative government. It is relatively clear, I think, that, while many of the ideas, practices, and institutions associated with representative government were anticipated by the Ancient Greeks, and even the European Middle Ages, its earliest development was primarily in Great Britain and the United States. I would further argue that this growth occurred in three broad stages.[20] First, in the sixteenth and seventeenth centuries came the idea that government rests on the consent of the governed, and an attempt to embody that idea in constitutional devices intended both to render government responsible to the people, however defined, and to limit its power. Yet, the political conflicts of the seventeenth century also taught that purely formal limitations on government were insufficient in the real world of politics. Something more was needed, and that something was often perceived as a measure, again usually rather narrowly defined, of popular participation in ruling. Thus, the eighteenth century witnessed the second stage of the process—the growth of representative institutions.[21] This growth brought with it a host of problems, both theoretical and practical, and was accompanied by a major transition in the way people viewed politics. At the most abstract level, it introduced changes in the way both the public and private spheres were conceived, and in the manner in which conflict within the community was conceptualized. For example, Kishlansky has suggested that in England the meaning of so basic a feature of representative institutions and practices as parliamentary elections changed extensively during the seventeenth century, as a process of "selection," in which "patrons and peers, civic dignitaries and officeholders, community leaders and community neighbors were designated members of Parliament without opponents, competition, or votes," gradually, and under the pressure of revolutionary developments, was replaced by something like elections in our modern sense.[22] Similarly, J. H. Plumb has argued that the period of one-party Whig rule in the early eighteenth century was vital to the growth of representative government, for it provided a context of social and political stability in which conflict over office and policy could be domesticated and accepted as normal and safe.[23] Finally, in the third stage, once a functioning representative system was fully implemented, the issue of democracy came to the front. In the nineteenth and early twentieth centuries, it became obvious that the logic of consent and participation tends toward universalism, but not everyone was happy with that conclusion. Thus, a major political debate developed around the question of who was entitled to participate in the political process. At first, control of the representative parts of the political system was preserved for members of various elites determined by class and gender. Eventually, however, universal suffrage came to prevail as the idea of the "people" constantly expanded.

Though marked by important differences in detail, a very similar process took place in America. This was not by coincidence. As Ian K. Steele has indicated, "the North Atlantic united that empire more than it divided."[24] Americans saw representative institutions, in this case their own colonial legislatures, as a means of gaining control of local affairs and of limiting their dependence on the mother country.[25] Moreover, as in the British case, these changes in institutions and practices were accompanied by shifts in outlook and theory. Gordon S. Wood, among others, has written extensively of the changes in American political thinking in the eighteenth century.[26] He notes that one of the most important of these was in the concept of representation. In the years leading up to the Revolution, the American radicals rejected those theories which characterized representatives as relatively independent trustees of the public interest, and instead asserted that they were merely delegates required to enact the will of their constituents.[27] Some thinkers went even further. They asked why, if all political authority is derived from the people, are not the people capable of governing themselves? Thus, especially among elements of the Antifederalists, all representation became suspect, and it was claimed that the people constituted the only legitimate authority. Along this road, of course, lies mass democracy.[28] Still, the story is both complex and ambiguous. On the one hand, for instance, the recognition and acceptance of political conflict was an important step in the movement toward modern pluralistic democracy. On the other, the suspicion of both politicians and parties undermined confidence in representative institutions and discouraged participation in them. John Taylor, one of the first to decry the seamy side of legislative politics, wrote: "knaves or fools only, surrender their duties and rights to party despotism. Knaves, to get a share in its acquisitions; fools because they are deceived. Can an honest man of sound understanding think himself bound by wisdom or duty, to give or sell himself to one of two parties, prompted by interest and ambition to impair the public good? Are men bound by wisdom or honour to take sides with one of two competitors, if both are robbers or usurpers?"[29] Even in his own day, Taylor was considered something of an extremist, but his questions continue to concern us.

In my view, Burke played a vital role in this process. I believe that Burke's greatest contribution to modern politics lies in his role as a theorist and practitioner of representative government. In my opinion, his key contribution was his formulation of a conception of politics which identified political change as the central issue of the day and which defined representative government as the appropriate mediator of that change. In his advocacy of a political model which saw society as a corporation suspended in history and evolving over time, in his acceptance of political controversy as an appropriate device for driving that process, and in his characterization of the professional politician as responsible for directing evolution into progress, Burke provided a defense of representative institutions which also rendered change safe. Here, it seems to me, we have an explanation for the continuing interest in Burke, while earlier conservatives like Bolingbroke seem more appropriately consigned to a hazy pre-history of modern thought. One of the principal points of difference between Burke and Bolingbroke is their respective conceptions of history. Where Burke took a generally progressive view of history, arguing that civilization develops slowly over time, Bolingbroke was much more radically conservative. He insisted that a study of history reveals a decline from the excellence of the past (chiefly, that is, from the glorious days of Queen Elizabeth), and that, therefore, the proper politics for his own time was a suspension of conflict and a return to old forms. England's past success, Bolingbroke maintained, was due to her maintenance of a balance by which "our free constitution of government hath been preserved so long inviolate, or hath been brought back . . . to its original principles, and been renewed, and improved too, by frequent and salutary revolutions."[30] Bolingbroke's position was, perhaps, minimally cogent in the early eighteenth century, but it had little appeal in the period of the American and French Revolutions. In the late twentieth century, his Ancient Constitutionalism is merely quaint. Burke, on the other hand, with his message of moderated progressivism, still speaks effectively to our concern with the politics of change. Burke meets the test for relevancy proposed by Isaiah Berlin: ". . . the ambition of those who wish to know how we, the present generation, came to be what we are, who our ancestors have been, what they have done, what were the consequences of their activities, what were their hopes and fears and goals, and the natural forces with which they had to contend; for it seems obvious that only barbarians feel no curiosity about the sources of their own forms of life and civilization, their place in the world order as determined by the antecedent experiences of their ancestors, which alone can give a sense of identity to their successors."[31] While Burke, then, was one of the most important contributors to the intellectual synthesis, based on the acceptance of interest-based politics and a conflict-resolution model of government, which underlay the development of modern representative democracy, Bolingbroke has little to offer—save, perhaps, a sense of the starting-point—to the interested student.[32]

For purpose of introduction, Burke's contribution to the theory of representative government can be summarized in seven propositions. The first four provide a means of conceptualizing change. First, Burke argued that all abstract or "metaphysical" styles of political reasoning, including natural law theories, are inherently unsatisfactory. The complexity and variety of politics is so great, according to Burke, that little can be said without reference to particular circumstances. In the *Reflections,* he contrasted the French reformers unfavorably to ancient law-givers: "the legislators who framed the ancient republics knew that their business was too arduous to be accomplished with no better apparatus than the metaphysics of an undergraduate, and the mathematics and arithmetic of an exciseman."[33] The results of such efforts are at times merely ludicrous, but more often, as indeed in France, they are disastrous.[34] Second, a rejection of abstractions did not, for Burke, require a denial of all reasoning in politics, but was, rather, part of a turn to principles solidly based on the dictates of experience and history. As he put it, "the science of constructing a commonwealth, or renovating it, or reforming it, is, like every other experimental science, not to be taught *a priori.*"[35] Third, Burke's conception of history led him to view society as a corporate entity developing through time. For Burke, this proposition has two important subheadings. First, contrary to much of the commentary on Burke, he clearly denied any analogy between society and a living organism. Society is, he said, based on "a permanent standing covenant," and, therefore, "the idea of a people is the idea of a corporation. It is wholly artificial, and made, like all other legal fictions, by common agreement."[36] Second, Burke held that history is broadly, though not uniformly, progressive; that is, history is the story of a gradual evolution from primitive barbarism to modern commercial civilization. Therefore, he argued that at all times a balance must be maintained between the need to adapt society to changing circumstances and environments and the equally strong need to preserve its essence for those who are to come. Fourth, Burke believed that social change may be controlled and directed by human intelligence and effort. Thus, he maintained both the possibility and desirability of political reform. In a kind of eighteenth century Aristotelianism, Burke conceived of such reform as a gradual perfecting of the ongoing system. As he explained to the North American colonists in January 1777, "this constitution has therefore admitted innumerable improvements, either for the correction of the original scheme, or for removing corruptions, or for bringing its principles better to suit those changes which have successively happened in the circumstances of the nation or in the manners of the people."[37] Both sides of this equation must be kept in mind if Burke is to be properly understood. The key is balance; one must preserve and improve as well.

The remaining propositions deal with the way society handles change. The fifth is that, as change is natural and reform necessary, the proper role of the politician, according to Burke, is to serve as the agent and mediator of social and political progress. Further, for reform to be effective, it must be both acceptable to the people and practical as well. Burke maintained that a politician is, in some sense, a public trustee. "It is," he said, "of the essence of every trust to be rendered *accountable;* and even totally to *cease,* when it substantially varies from the purposes for which alone it could have a lawful existence."[38] Burke recognized that this role was not easy to play. Thus, he thought that education and training are essential to a good politician, and defended the leadership role of the landed aristocracy. Sixth, a good ruler, in Burke's opinion, must subscribe to certain political values. For example, he must support a politics based on the reconciliation of interests. Burke wrote of the English constitution: "there is a perpetual treaty and compromise going on, sometimes openly, sometimes with less observation," and, therefore, "the whole scheme of our mixed Constitution is to prevent any one of its principles from being carried as far as, taken by itself, and theoretically, it would go."[39] Moreover, good politicians are also prudent, for prudence is the virtue which adjusts general principles to practical concerns. Burke felt that the practical reason of the politically-active must, almost intuitively, recognize the necessary exceptions and modifications of applied morality.[40] Finally, Burke defended the various devices and weapons, such as political parties, which a politician finds useful in performing his function. As he wrote early in his career, "I find it impossible to conceive, that any one believes in his own politics, or thinks them to be of any weight, . . . refuses to adopt the means of having them reduced into practice."[41] For Burke, it was never enough to know what is right; one must also seek some means of implementing that truth.

There is, of course, more to Burke than concern with the growth of representative government. I make no claim to have discovered the "real" Burke. What I seek to do is to present Burke from a certain point of view, against a particular background, and in the light of my own theoretical and political interests. No single perspective can exhaust all that Burke has to say, and any approach must remain aware of at least some of the other aspects of his thought. I believe that among these additional factors, three are of sufficient importance that they will have to receive considerable attention in the following pages. To begin with, I think it important to keep in mind that the development of eighteenth century philosophy was marked by a dual crisis of knowledge and values. With the religious conflicts and scientific revolution of the seventeenth century, philosophers began to consider the traditional scholastic and scriptural sources as inadequate guides to truth about the world around them.[42] On the one hand, they wanted to break the hold of the old views by employing scientific methods, but, on the other, they also attempted to prevent those methods from leading to skepticism. They sought, in short, a middle ground between dogmatism and agnosticism. In this battle, John Locke was a key figure. Barbara J. Shapiro notes, "the ultimate spokesman of this generation was John Locke, who voiced the shared concerns of scientists, theologians, historians, and lawyers . . . For Englishmen, the central intellectual phenomenon of the second half of the seventeenth century was the peculiar interaction between efforts to establish a rational basis for a historically based, nondogmatic, Protestant Christianity and comparable efforts to achieve a probabilistic basis for the factual assertions of scientists, historians, and lawyers."[43] In the realm of moral philosophy, the problem was simple: if nothing can be known for certain, how can values be established and defended? While the question was clear, the answer was not. Locke's own philosophy, though widely accepted, did not solve the difficulty, and, indeed, in some ways left matters worse than before. In my opinion, it is no accident that Burke's initial writings sought to provide an empirical psychological basis for values, and, when that effort failed, petered out into incoherence. Burke's characteristic attacks on abstractions, and his embracing of experience and history are, I further believe, also responses to this crisis.

In addition, Burke's political heritage and role are of particular importance. Simply put, it makes a difference that Burke thought of himself as a Whig. That meant, among other things, that when he turned to history, he saw it from a certain perspective. The Whig party had developed at the time of the Exclusion Crisis in the 1670s. As Jones argues, its participation in that crisis largely defined its early character: "the first Whigs were, and had to be, a party, something more highly organized and disciplined than a mere alliance or coalition of small and autonomous groups. They possessed, and required, organization in both Parliament and country, effective discipline, and a wide popular appeal, stimulated and maintained by a large-scale propaganda machine."[44] Moreover, unusual for that time, the Whigs had something of a general philosophy and program. They saw themselves as defenders of the constitution, and as the natural spokesmen for the people. Yet, the Whigs were often unable to agree on the details or the implementation of that program. In fact, over the next century, the party split into so many branches and groups that some scholars question whether the label meant anything at all by the time of the American Revolution. My point is, however, narrower. I argue simply that Burke thought that it did, for he often identified Whiggism in general with the interests and ideas of his own faction within the larger movement. He saw himself and his allies as the natural descendants of the men who had made the Revolution and ruled England for a century thereafter. Burke thus felt obliged to defend the Revolution and to justify the existing political system which had grown out of it. He was, in the language of the time, an "Old Whig," and, in his view, an heir to the politics and philosophy of Robert Walpole and his associates. H. T. Dickinson describes the position well: "the Court or establishment Whigs were anxious to sustain a social system in which a small minority possessed wealth and status and a political system which represented property rather than people."[45] There is, in short, some considerable truth to the jibe that Burke attempted something nearly impossible—a conservative defense of a revolutionary settlement.

Lastly, I hope to give full recognition to those interpretations of Burke, such as that put forward by Frank O'Gorman, which insist on the importance of his activity as a practical politician.[46] Although I do not agree with O'Gorman's contention that Burke's arguments are often little more than a rationalization of the interests of the Rockingham party, I do think that concerns of the political moment figure prominently in his works. For example, most of Burke's major early political works were, in fact, produced during two waves of party activity. The first, in the late 1760s and early 1770s, saw many of Burke's most radical statements about parliamentary politics. As he attempted to explain the Rockingham Whigs' loss of power in terms of an attempt by George III and his supporters to subvert parliamentary government, Burke was driven to embrace advanced positions on ministerial accountability and the rights of electors. Thus, while most modern scholars believe that Burke's charges were largely mistaken, his theoretical efforts, nonetheless, bore great fruit in his theories of trusteeship, representation, and party government.[47] The American War and the struggle for power at its end was a second important contributor to Burke's thought. Indeed, it stimulated his formulation of ideas on imperial matters, the means of creating and expressing opposition to royal policy, and the importance of representation as a control on government. At the same time, in the various Petitioning Movements, the Whigs, and Burke, learned to work in league with other parties, and also learned something of the limits of such cooperation. Indeed, O'Gorman himself suggests that the Rockingham Whigs' experience with the reformers biased them against working with later radicals: "the success of Wyvill and his friends in beating off the Rockinghamite bid for control of the movement, and the quickening of the reformist impulse which led its leaders to embrace a Plan of Association with its attack on the rotten boroughs, ended Rockingham's brief flirtation with parliamentary reform."[48] Even Burke's major writings of the period around the French Revolution were produced with one eye on party advantage. Much of what he said then was intended to drive the radicals out of the Whig fold, and, that accomplished, to rebuild the party as an antirevolutionary but still reformist force. In short, while even in his most partisan moments Burke sought to go beyond the immediate issues to a deeper level of understanding, and exhibited a desire to discover broader principles at work, it would be a serious error to ignore the immediate altogether.

II

It will, of course, require the remainder of this book to present my argument in full detail, but an outline of that argument would, perhaps, not be remiss here. I believe that the place to begin a study of Burke's political thought is with his early writings on aesthetics and psychology, for it is there that one best sees his response to the crisis he perceived in normative philosophy. As I have already indicated, the effect of work in the tradition of empirical philosophy since Locke had been, Burke believed, to undermine all attempts to establish objective moral values. Thus, in chapter 2, I will discuss Burke's early concern with psychology, his growing frustration at its moral indetermination, and his turn to history. I will argue that Burke's first major published work, *A Philosophical Enquiry into the Origin of Our Ideas of the Sublime and Beautiful,* was primarily intended as an attempt to establish a purely associationalist psychology.[49] However, because the discussion of psychology had come to be framed as an adjunct of a much broader concern with the nature of human understanding and its limits, Burke's *Enquiry* also had profound implications both for the study of human behavior and for moral philosophy as well. The discussion of human understanding moved toward an increasingly subjective basis, and therefore, had the effect of relativising both aesthetics and morals. When Burke began to study the topic, he soon found that his criticism of the classical standards of taste and his attempt to build a consistent sensationalist psychology only served to worsen matters. Moreover, he also found that proposals, like those of Hutcheson and Hume, to solve the problem by postulating the existence of a moral sense also failed. Hence, in the *Vindication of Natural Society,* written before the *Enquiry* but revised and published after, Burke sought to block the extension of the new relativism from psychology to social theory by demonstrating the dangerous consequences for society of rejecting all standards of judgment outside the passions of the individual.[50]

In light of Burke's doubts about the possibility of establishing either an objective aesthetics or absolute moral standards, it appears to me that it is quite unlikely that he can be classified as a natural law thinker. Rather, in chapter 3, I will suggest that Burke's failure to create an objective morality led him to abandon psychology for history. If, he reasoned, one cannot establish rational absolutes, perhaps values can be discovered through the study of historical experience. I will argue that Burke used history in two ways. First, he saw history as a means of understanding society. With his conception of society as an evolving corporation, Burke found the form for expressing some of his most characteristic ideas. For example, that conception underlay his rejection of social contract theory and his arguments on prescription and presumption. Moreover, it provided a dynamic element to his thought and, therefore, a means of conceptualizing and domesticating social and political change. Burke saw change, as such, as relatively neutral: some changes were good, but others were not. Those changes which benefited society were those which perfected the ongoing social order. Second, Burke's understanding of progress as a fragile but real process which could be controlled to some degree by men led him to the opinion that the essence of sound politics was the careful management of political reform so as to insure improvement while avoiding the pitfalls of radicalism. Thus, Burke used history to explain and defend his political party—the Rockingham Whigs. Burke claimed that the Whigs were the descendants and representatives of a traditional governing aristocratic class in English society, and, in his more directly political writings of the time, sought to show that the party, over the course of its one hundred or so years of involvement in British government, had always operated on a "correct" appreciation of the historical process.

Chapter 4 considers Burke's position on the British political institutions of his time. Burke's adoption of the model of society as a corporation which develops through time, of course, had important consequences for his theory of politics. He saw British government as both a product of historical evolution, therefore deserving of defense on the basis of prescription, and as a set of institutions which served to facilitate further reform. As to its forms, Burke held that English government was not, in fact, a mixed government but rather a limited monarchy, whose chief virtue was the preservation of the rule of law. Thus, he saw the king as the effective focus of government, but also thought it essential that the power of the king be checked in two ways: by the participation in administration and in the House of Lords of the aristocracy, and by the negative requirement that royal policy not be rejected by the people as represented in the House of Commons. Finally, Burke's conception of history also provided the basis of his defense of a Church establishment. That defense was couched in the same language of prescription and reform as his ideas on state and society. Burke saw important social and political reasons for an established church. In his view, a religious establishment served as a major repository of culture, an important educator, and a civilizer of manners. However, along with his support for a religious establishment, Burke also was willing to recognize the right of the individual to form his own relationship with God. Thus, he also followed the more advanced currents of his time in accepting a broad degree of religious toleration. In fact, following John Locke, the only limitations Burke would place on religious expression flowed from political rather than religious considerations. Chapter 5 will round out the discussion of the formation and nature of Burke's theoretical system with a consideration of Burke's views on the role of government in society. In light of the broad agreement among Burke's contemporaries that government could, and indeed should, play only a very limited role in society, I will ask whether Burke believed that the state had adequate authority to carry out the kind of reform he thought necessary. I believe that he did. In my opinion, Burke was prepared to accept a broad range of governmental action and was, in fact, neither a laissez-faire ideologue nor an advocate of natural-rights limitations on the state. Rather, he took a position quite close to that of his friend, Adam Smith; that is to say, that while Burke usually favored free trade and limited government involvement in the economy, he did so as a matter of policy choice and not of principle. Burke believed that governmental social and economic policy should be based on pragmatic and prudential considerations and not on some concept of economic "laws."

Chapters 6 and 7 form the pivot of my argument as a whole. In chapter 6 I will suggest that Burke's theory of trusteeship is the cornerstone of his thought, for it was meant to link together the Whig aristocrats and politicians and the public as a whole in a reformist political party. I will maintain that Burke's theory, which I describe as a form of defensive trusteeship, was intended to promote freedom for the representative to pursue responsible reform from above, while also providing a measure of popular control of that representative. A representative, Burke held, was to give all his talent and experience to his constituents' service and interest, and therefore, to act on the basis of his own judgment rather than their instructions when the two conflicted. Still, Burke believed that the question of whether the representative was performing his role effectively was one for the electorate to decide. While the voters should give the representative broad leeway in the performance of his responsibility, it was, he said, in the final analysis, their right to remove him for any reason they felt sufficient. However, I will also hold that, because Burke's theory of trusteeship sought to combine effective and responsible government with limitations on the people's right to participate in politics and to control the party, that theory contained a serious internal contradiction. In chapter 7, I will claim that Burke's contradiction became manifest in internal politics when he attempted to apply his theory of party to the affairs of the 1780s. I will first detail Burke's attempts to frame a consistent theory of political party as a force to unify men of goodwill. Burke was not the first thinker to attempt to justify parties. Rather, his contribution was to provide a theoretical defense of party as a permanent institution which is neither part of administration nor of the opposition, but which moves from one to the other, to examine the consequences of the acceptance of party—that is, to see party as an instrument for accomplishing political purposes, to analyze some of the tools and tactics which could be employed to make party effective, and, through his association with a party, to bring the theory and practice of party into a balanced consistency. I will conclude the chapter with an examination of Burke's attempts to forge an alliance between the Rockingham Whigs and various other reform groups in the period near the end of the American Revolution and just after. I will argue that those efforts failed because the Whigs were willing to act for the people but not with them or their more radical leaders. In my view, this refusal deprived the Whigs of the popular support which would have been necessary to counterbalance the power of the Crown and its allies.

Chapters 8 through 10 will trace the breakdown of Burke's conception of politics. In chapter 8, I will consider a relatively successful example of Burkean politics. I will follow the development of Burke's position on American affairs from the Stamp Tax Crisis, which the Rockingham Whigs sought to end by combining the repeal of the tax with the passage of the Declaratory Act, to his support for American independence some fifteen years later. In my opinion, contrary to the claims of many of the students of his thought, Burke did have a coherent theory of the Empire. As his speeches on American Taxation and Conciliation with the Colonies make clear, that view was essentially federalist.[51] Burke argued that the English Parliament was both the local Parliament of England and the governing body of the Empire. However, he believed that its imperial powers should be exercised only sparingly and that, for most purposes, the more mature branches of the Empire, such as the American Colonies, should be allowed to govern themselves through their local assemblies. Burke's initial theory of the Empire proved inadequate, for he could not reconcile his vindication of the sovereignty of the English Parliament with the need to conciliate the Americans. Nonetheless, Burke persevered. He reformulated his position, and eventually came to believe that only American independence could end the struggle. While Burke's approach to the American issue was a success at the political level, for the Rockingham Whigs found allies, rose to power in coalition with Shelburne, and ended the war, it raised serious questions about the internal consistency of his political thought. With the end of the war and the death of Rockingham, the Whigs were unable to hold their coalition together. They broke with Shelburne and his supporters and allied with Lord North. This move allowed them to regain power but otherwise cost them dearly, for it alienated them from the radicals without reconciling them with the King. Consequently, the opposition of the King to their Indian policy prevented the Whigs from winning within the existing parliamentary system, and the election of 1784, highlighted by Pitt's smashing victory, showed that they were both unwilling and unable to go outside it.

Chapter 9 will examine Burke's response to the French Revolution. Once again, Burke sought to rally the English people behind a reformist Whig party, but in this far more dangerous case it was the leadership, the trustees of the people, who failed him. In Burke's view, the Revolution required a new political understanding and a new form of politics. He believed that the key to that understanding was a recognition that the revolution demanded responses at three levels: within France, where it threatened the destruction of the old regime; in the whole of Europe, where the spread of French ideas endangered modern civilization, itself; and, finally, in England, where France might serve as an example for the English radicals. Burke's reply, therefore, was equally multi-faceted. First, he believed that the defense of European culture required that the as yet uncontaminated nations of the continent form an anti-revolutionary coalition. Second, Burke argued that those nations should then launch a crusade to destroy revolutionary France, and to restore a reformed constitutional monarchy at the center of the continent. Finally, he undertook a campaign to discredit radicalism in England, and to build national unity on a patriotic basis. Burke's basic message was that the Old Whig faith of reform in detail combined with stability in essence was still valid. However, while he found that most of the English people were willing to support the counter-revolutionary cause, the split in the Whig party between radical and conservative elements, the indecisiveness of the Pitt Administration, and the efforts of demagogues like Paine frustrated his campaign. In the end the country was unified, but in a common resistance to all reform: the leaders would not propose it, and the people would not accept it. Moreover, Burke's campaign destroyed the Whig party, his chosen vehicle of progress. All of his best efforts to recreate it, to build a new third force, or to form a coalition of all the parties failed.

Chapter 10 will deal with the consequences of that failure, and with the deep pessimism that it introduced into Burke's thought. Indeed, Burke's efforts to deal with Ireland offer both a counterpoint and a confirmation to his reflections on French politics. Ireland offers a counterpoint because, while the French Revolution accelerated and hardened Burke's opposition to reform in England, it seems to have had the opposite effect on his views on Irish politics. From the early 1770s to the mid-1790s, Burke argued a consistent reformist position in regard to Ireland. He insisted that Ireland's problems originated in Ireland and not in England, and maintained that the primary issue was the social and economic one of the exclusion of the Catholic majority from participation in government. The solution, therefore, was the incorporation of the native Irish into the political community of the nation and of the British Empire. A central part of this solution was the vote, and Burke soon found himself advocating reforms in Ireland which he rejected in England. Burke's Irish writings of the mid-1790s reveal a sense that he was in a race against time, for Burke believed that Ireland had to be reformed before repression led to the radicalization of the Irish masses and consequent civil war. It is here that Burke's thought on Ireland represents a confirmation of his thought on America and France: the same internal contradiction in his theory of trusteeship which plagued his attempts to generate reform in those situations led him to failure in Ireland. In all three cases, Burke was unable to combine strong aristocratic leadership, reform, and popular support.

2

BURKE AND THE SEARCH FOR THE PSYCHOLOGICAL BASIS OF HUMAN ACTION

An interesting insight into Burke's political thought can be obtained by placing it in the context of the eighteenth century search for an objective standard of judgment. The problem of judgment developed out of John Locke's work on human understanding and his attempt to provide a basis in natural law for a standard of right which could be enforced by government. However, Locke's effort failed, for it floundered on the rocks of scepticism and relativism, and his adoption of an empiricist methodology led to a new emphasis on the probabilistic nature of truth. The importance of the difficulty he confronted and the prestige of his writings on psychology insured that Locke's dilemma would quickly become general. Attempts to solve the problem of judgment soon spread into fields ranging from aesthetics to sociology. As a careful student of mid-eighteenth century English literature, philosophy, and culture, Burke joined in the effort. In his first major published work, *The Vindication of Natural Society,* he demonstrated his awareness of the problem, a sense that none of the existing solutions—including Locke's—truly worked, and a perception that the consequences of that failure, intellectual and social anarchy, were serious indeed. In his next work, the *Enquiry into the Origin of our Ideas of the Sublime and Beautiful,* Burke presented his own answer. Unfortunately, as Burke's proposal took Locke's empiricism to even greater lengths, it also suffered from an inability to place effective normative limits on the practical diversity of human opinion. Burke himself recognized this weakness, but none of the other major schools of thought, including moral sense philosophy and natural law theory seemed acceptable either. In fact, the most attractive alternative lay, Burke found, in another direction. The work of David Hume, while it did not solve the value problem, suggested that one could operate without an objective truth. Hume argued that standards, adequate for actual living, could be developed through a process of probabilistic reasoning based on the data provided by practical experience. In addition, Hume maintained that a record of such experience could be found in historical study. Thus, Burke, following Hume, turned to history for a guide to morally sound political action.

I

John Locke's first foray into politics, the *Two Tracts on Government,* was undertaken in 1660 as part of an internal Oxford debate on the nature of the religious settlement of the Restoration.[1] His intention was to reply to an argument, made by Edward Bagshaw among others, that, since God and the Scriptures are silent on things indifferent for salvation, such matters should be left to each person's individual conscience. In Locke's opinion, similar assumptions about human nature and the Scriptures led, in fact, to an opposite conclusion. He began by holding that men are so depraved by sin and so partial to their own interests that, if they are not bound to a common order in society, chaos will follow. Given man's ignorance, Locke argued, there can be no viable subdivision between what is essential and what is indifferent, for any act can be variously claimed to be either essential or indifferent for salvation. Moreover, Locke insisted, nothing in Scriptures denies the magistrate the right to regulate indifferent matters. Christian liberty, he continued, though it is indeed vital, is a liberty of thought and belief, not of action. Based on these initial assumptions, Locke maintained that the magistrate may impose, and the citizen must obey, a system of religious discipline. He defended his position through a theory of law. Defining all law as the expressed will of a superior enforced by some sanction, Locke argued that there are four levels of authority: God and the divine law; human law enforced ultimately by the state; the fraternal law of Christianity; and, finally, the individual judgment of private law. According to Locke, each of these is competent to rule only in those matters which have not already been decided by a higher level. For example, a magistrate may overrule a decision of private conscience provided that no higher authority—in this case God or Scriptures—has acted.

So far, Locke was operating well within the confines of traditional political theory. The goal he set was the preservation of order, he assumed that order requires that moral truth be maintained, and natural law—along with Scriptures—provided him with a means of knowing the truth. At this point, all he had to do was reduce the role of government to the enforcement of the objectively valid moral law, and he was home free. Instead, Locke proceeded to add a second argument to his case, and this addition proved fatal to his own position. He now claimed that the magistrate's right to rule is also, in part, based on the prior authorization of the governed themselves. Moreover, as the magistrate is free to rule, he has need to do so as well. Men form society, Locke held, to secure peace and order, but if each is free to follow his own conscience in all matters, there can be no order and, consequently, little peace. As Locke put it, "no mutual obligation is possible unless each surrenders the competence of his own will over indifferences and invests some other, the magistrate, with a competence to decide for him and thus for all."[2] This argument is inadequate for two reasons. First, the theory of natural law cannot meet the requirements Locke placed on it. As Abrams notes, Locke's "theory of law rests on the assumption that certain general injunctions of divine law can be treated as matter of established knowledge."[3] Yet, that is the very point in dispute, for men clearly and openly disagree on the nature of divine and natural law. Even to determine what is indifferent or who is to regulate it requires a knowledge of the moral law that goes far beyond any Locke is able to claim for the magistrate. Second, Locke's use of consent theory only compounded the problem. He introduced the notion of consent as a means of overcoming the vagueness of the moral law. Men were bound, he said, to that law to which they had consented. The obvious questions for a critic to ask were how had that consent been expressed, and where was the charter which described the agreed-upon law. At this point in his intellectual development, Locke had no answer to these questions. What he lacked was a theory of judgment, a theory which would explain how one could come to know anything for certain.

Nearly thirty years later, in *An Essay Concerning Human Understanding,* Locke tried again. He began by sweeping the boards clean. Disclaiming any intention of seeking the ultimate sources of our sensations or ideas, Locke spent the entire first Book denying the existence of innate ideas.[4] If, he further admitted, we have no innate ideas, it is equally impossible for us to have innate moral principles: "since, if the *ideas* which made up those truths were not, it was impossible that the *propositions* made up of them should be innate, or our knowledge of them be born with us."[5] Where, then, do our ideas come from? Locke's answer was simple—from experience:

"our observation employed either about external sensible objects, or about the internal operations of our minds perceived and reflected on by ourselves, is that which supplies our understandings with all the *materials* of thinking."[6] Thus, all of our knowledge, Locke maintained, in any area, is based on sense perceptions, the rational comparison of mental images or ideas grounded in those perceptions, or a very limited range of direct intuitions.[7] However, this solution to the problem of knowledge left a large barrier in the path of the search for absolute truth. As Locke, himself, asked: "how shall the mind, when it perceives nothing but its own ideas, know that they agree with things themselves?"[8] Locke admitted in a number of places that we cannot know if our sensations accurately mirror the world or if our logic correctly reproduces it. While he believed that we can indeed know that there is an external reality, he denied that we can be certain of its properties. All that we can hope for is that our sensations are self-consistent; that is to say, we must assume that a given object will consistently reproduce the same internal reaction in us, and we must further trust that such consistency will suffice. In short, we cannot know that some item which we perceive as red is "really" red in an objective sense, but, so long as our various perceptions of that object's redness are consistent with one another, we can expect to function more or less satisfactorily in the world.

How, then, is the problem of grounding morality to be settled? Locke's handling of the issue, near the end of the *Essay,* was sophisticated.[9] He began by repeating the argument of the *Two Tracts* that morality is best considered as a subfield of law, and he now divided law into three categories: the divine law laid down and enforced by God; the civil law enforced by government; and the law of reputation regulated by public opinion. Locke next asserted that the defining characteristic of law is the presence of a lawgiver to decree and enforce it. Moreover, to fully legitimate the enforcement of law, it is essential that it be promulgated in some manner, so that the subject can be aware of it and conform his behavior to it. The issue of promulgation soon became especially serious because Locke again, as in the earlier sections of the *Essay,* denied the existence of innate ideas or moral principles: "moral principles require reasoning and discourse, and some exercise of the mind to discover the certainty of their truth."[10] Further, he also anticipated and rejected the moral sense school's belief in implanted moral faculties. The term is, he said, proper enough if it is used only metaphorically and not as a label for some real "beings in the soul that performed those actions of understanding and volition."[11] Used in the latter sense, Locke said, the concept has done much harm, for "this way of speaking of *faculties* has misled many into a confused notion of so many distinct agents in us, which had their several provinces and authorities, and did command, obey, and perform several actions, as so many distinct beings."[12] Viewed in this light, Hutcheson, Reid, and the moral sense school need never have written.

Locke did not seek to avoid the moral consequences of his analysis. Indeed, it was clear to him that, without innate ideas or a moral sense, man can not attain certainty in moral questions. For example, in rejecting religious enthusiasm, Locke insisted, "but how shall it be known that any proposition in our minds is a truth infused by God; a truth that is revealed to us by him, which he declares to us, and therefore we ought to believe? Here it is that enthusiasm fails of the evidence it pretends to."[13] Unfortunately, for Locke, the enthusiast's problem is that of all men. On the one hand, empirical observation, though a source of data about nature, is incapable of discovering laws about the world. We cannot, Locke admitted, prove the truthfulness of any general proposition from the evidence afforded by singular experiences, for no experience allows us to infer the content of some future experience. On the other hand, reason is equally limited. The only immediate objects the human mind has to work with, according to Locke, are its own ideas, and those tell it nothing about the world outside itself. As he put it, "those universal and self-evident principles [i.e., which are obtained comparing ideas] being only our constant, clear, and distinct knowledge of our own ideas . . . can assure us of nothing that passes without the mind."[14] Is one, then, obliged to give up hope for standards which are both demonstrable and universal? Locke did not think so. In the *Essay,* he rejected the views of both those who claim that there is an innate law and those who assert that there is no law at all: "I would not here be mistaken, as if, because I deny an innate law, I thought there were none but positive laws. There is a great deal of difference between an innate law and a law of nature; between something imprinted on our minds in their very original, and something that we, being ignorant of, may attain to the knowledge of, by the use and due application of our natural faculties."[15] Locke believed that moral principles, as instances of rational demonstrations, could be conclusively proven: "from self-evident propositions, by necessary consequences, as incontestable as those in mathematics, the measures of right and wrong might be made out, to anyone that will apply himself with the same indifferency and attention to the one as he does to the other of these sciences."[16] To be sure, these principles might not apply in the external world. That is a matter for actual experience to decide. In dealing with the physical world, we have only the evidence of the senses, and this is inherently uncertain.[17] Still, Locke felt that such probablistic knowledge was a long way from no knowledge at all.

Thus, according to Locke, moral rules, though not themselves empirical, are capable of being tested against experience. What seems to be true by logic may be confirmed by what occurs in nature, and, in this way, something like certainty may be attained in moral affairs.[18] Locke's confidence on this point was based on his belief that God has linked virtue and happiness by creating men so that they can determine what is naturally right out of a sense of utility. As he saw matters, from the human perspective, "things then are good and evil, only in reference to pleasure and pain. That we call *good,* which is apt to cause or increase pleasure, or diminish pain in us; or else to procure or preserve us the possession of any other good or absence of any evil."[19] In short, Locke argued that God has formed men so that by following the dictates of their own nature, dictates taught to them through a utilitarian process based on the experiencing of pleasure and pain, they are also following his will. It is not a matter of sense perception or of the possession of some trans-empirical faculty. Rather, Locke saw the question as one of biological structure. God, in his wisdom, has made man to operate a certain way. In so doing, man not only brings pleasure to himself, but also works God's will. In contrast, when man goes against God's intentions, he inflicts pain and suffering on himself. Therefore, if the predicted consequences, defined in terms of pleasure and pain, of an action actually occur, then the rationally established principle on which that action is based gains a measure of creditability. Locke maintained, "*experience here must teach me what reason cannot:* and it is by *trying* alone, that I can *certainly know,* what other qualities co-exist with those of my complex idea."[20] As I argued above, Locke did not hold that such information could claim to be certain knowledge; it is, at best, only probable.[21] However, probability is usually sufficient to live by and adequate to our needs, provided that we observe due humility and moderation: "it would methinks, become all men to maintain peace, and the common offices of humanity, and friendship, in the diversity of opinions; since we cannot reasonably expect that anyone should readily and obsequiously quit his own opinion, and embrace ours, with a blind resignation to an authority which the understanding of man acknowledges not."[22] Locke's political liberalism is, then, a consequence of his psychology and morality.

II

Since Locke raised the problem of judgment within the context of a discussion of human understanding as such, rather than within the framework of a particular area of study, his argument quickly became the focus of a wide-ranging debate. In the field of aesthetics, where the controversy first came to Burke's attention, Locke's influence was both great and complex. Perhaps the primary effect of Locke's work was to reinforce an already developing tendency toward subjectivity. Samuel H. Monk has argued that, against the prevailing classical standards, which judged a work by its adherence to universal abstract principles of taste, the early eighteenth century witnessed a gradual movement away from a concern with the external object, with what about an object causes a certain reaction, toward an emphasis on the individual's reaction to the object, that is, to the passions excited by it. As Monk explains in regard to sublimity: "sublimity as an aesthetic concept is made entirely subjective; it is not a quality residing in the object, but a state of mind awakened by an object."[23] Locke's argument also contributed to the emerging psychologization of the subject. As writers turned away from the works of art or literature themselves to the effects they created on their audience, it appeared obvious that the most immediate of those effects were mental and that the best way to explain them was to apply some theory of how the mind worked. Finally, though he was not completely successful, Locke had at least made some effort to keep his scientific study of human understanding separate from his interest in morality. Many of those who followed in his wake did not do so. Thus, they often hopelessly confused their discussions of the mechanics of perception and understanding with their efforts at moral persuasion.

Burke first attempted to deal with the problem of the nature of judgment in *A Philosophical Enquiry into the Origin of Our Ideas of the Sublime and Beautiful*. This was a work with a long period of gestation. Burke's letters and the records of his undergraduate Club at Trinity College indicate that most of the book was written in 1747 while he was a student, but the essay was not completed and published until April 21, 1757, some ten years later.[24] Burke's goal in the *Enquiry* was to provide a more or less scientific and dispassionate account of the working of the human mind without necessarily addressing normative concerns. As one of his friends wrote to another, this sharply distinguished Burke from such writers as Francis Hutcheson, who had written with avowedly moral purpose: "You ask about Hutcheson's book and what is the difference. A great deal my friend. One is a moral, the other a critical work. The moral piece corrupts and the critical enlarges the understanding. Hutcheson's treatise is an establishment of morals from the beauty, order, fitness and rectitude of actions, . . . but our friend anatomizes our passions and the objects of them, and thus teaches by sound logical principles how the arts are to be judged, and how the Artist or Writer is to operate if he would affect the soul with sublimity and beauty."[25] The work proved to be a great success. It was reprinted and read throughout the remainder of the eighteenth century and drew a considerable amount of commentary. As Monk points out, its arguments fit the time well, for it met the public taste both for a psychological approach to the issues of aesthetics and for a loosening of the straightjacket of neo-classicism.[26]

Students of eighteenth century aesthetics have generally agreed that the most significant aspect of the *Enquiry* is what Boulton refers to as Burke's "uncompromising sensationalism."[27] In fact, Burke's sensationalism was not new as such, for David Hume, among others, had adopted a similar approach, but Burke was far and away the most radical proponent of the new method.[28] He argued that to move the passions an object must excite either pleasure or pain in the observer.[29] For example, he said of beauty: "beauty is, for the greater part, some quality in bodies, acting mechanically upon the human mind by the intervention of the senses. We ought therefore to consider attentively in what manner those sensible qualities are disposed, in such things as by experience we find beautiful, or which excite in us the passion of love, or some correspondent affection."[30] Denying that beauty is associated with proportion, fitness, or perfection, Burke claimed that beautiful objects are those which are small, smooth, gradually varied in shape, delicate, and of clear and bright color.[31] In Parts II and III of the essay, Burke went on to categorize the various passions caused by the sublime and the beautiful and to attempt to explain the psychological mechanism by which the process works—that is, to discover what kind of sensory inputs are associated with each of the various passions. Thus, Burke held that the most powerful of the passions caused by the sublime is astonishment, and that the most effective cause of the sublime is terror.[32] Similarly, beauty is "that quality or those qualities in bodies by which they cause love, or some passion similar to it."[33]

In Part IV, Burke broke with those authors who sought to discover the final or ultimate cause of things. That, he said, is beyond the ability of science. Citing Isaac Newton, Burke wrote: "that great chain of causes, which linking one to another even to the Throne of God himself, can never be unravelled by any industry of ours. When we go but one step beyond the immediate sensible qualities of things, we go out of our depth."[34] Rather, he attempted to discover the specific physiological links between our sensations and our ideas and actions and thus to explain the efficient causes of the sublime and the beautiful. Burke found the link he sought in direct physical changes in the state of our nerves and muscles. Thus, after noting that we react to fear with such physical changes as hair standing on end, he suggested that "having considered terror as producing an unnatural tension and certain violent emotions of the nerves; it easily follows . . . that whatever is fitted to produce such a tension, must be productive of a passion similar to terror, and consequently must be a source of the sublime, though it should have no idea of danger connected with it."[35] In like manner, pain, according to Burke, can be a source of delight, for it exercises the muscles and organs associate with the sublime. As an example of his meaning, Burke cited darkness, which he believed is terrible because it causes excessive contractions of the fibers of the iris and strains the nerves that compose it beyond their usual norm.[36] By the same token, he asserted that our idea of beauty is stimulated by "relaxing the solids of the whole system," and therefore smoothness is considered beautiful because, on touching something smooth, the muscles of one's hand are relaxed.[37]

Yet, as Burke's argument stood in the first edition of the *Enquiry,* it was subject to the same difficulty concerning standards which had plagued Locke before him. Indeed, to the extent that Burke was more thoroughgoing in his sensationalism, the problem was even more acute for him, for he had reduced aesthetics to a derivative of psychology. As Burke admitted, the concern is that, if our ideas of the sublime and the beautiful, and by extension everything else, are consequences of our environment, senses, and our internal structure, how can agreement be attained in matters of taste? Will not taste, itself, vary as men's circumstances do? Moreover, because Burke's aesthetics were based on a logically prior theory of psychology, the threat that his psychology posed for aesthetic standards could easily be broadened to raise doubts about standards of all sorts—including those of morality. So long as the same psychological principles underlay all judgments, in whatever area, the same limitations would apply to them all. That Burke was aware of the difficulty is shown by his addition of a new introduction in the form of an "Essay on Taste" to the second edition of the *Enquiry*.[38] Burke began the "Essay" with a clear statement of the problem: "for if there were not some principles of judgment as well as of sentiment common to all mankind, no hold could possibly be taken either on their reason or their passions, sufficient to maintain the ordinary correspondence of life."[39] But, as human social life does in fact go on, Burke felt justified in asserting that standards do exist and that they are built into our very nature: "with regard to truth and falsehood there is something fixed. We find people in their disputes continually appealing to certain tests and standards which are allowed on all sides, and are supposed to be established in our common nature."[40] However, Burke distinguished his position from that of Hutcheson by denying that taste is either a moral sense or a faculty of the mind. As he put it, "to multiply principles for every different appearance is useless, and unphilosophical too in a high degree."[41] To postulate a sense or organ of taste is to invent a name which refers to no physical object.

What, then, is taste? Burke claimed that it is "that faculty, or those faculties of the mind which are affected with, or which form a judgment of the works of imagination and the elegant arts."[42] Taste, he maintained, is a compound of the primary pleasure of sense, of the secondary pleasure of imagination, and of the conclusions of the reason.[43] Since these are similar in all men, "there is a sufficient foundation for conclusive reasoning on these matters."[44] With the elements of taste so similar, how did Burke explain the variety we see in the real world? He offered two principal causes of conflicting judgments on taste. First, Burke admitted that different experiences and customs may reduce the area of agreement.[45] Still, he asserted that "there is in all men a sufficient remembrance of the original natural causes of pleasure, to enable them to bring all things offered to their senses to that standard."[46] Therefore, of greater importance is the second factor—the varying mixture of the basic elements among individuals: "but the degree in which these principles prevail in the several individuals of mankind, is altogether as different as the principles themselves are similar. For sensibility and judgment, . . . vary exceedingly in various people."[47]

Thus, minor individual variations in prejudice, ignorance, lack of attention, and a number of other qualities explain the diversity of standards among human societies. Unfortunately, these admissions by Burke put us back where we started. On one hand, the "Essay," by inventing a mental characteristic which functions much like Hutcheson's moral sense, provided a mechanism to unify and standardize judgment. On the other hand, Burke recognized that even this structural uniformity could not overcome the effects of the great diversity of human situations and histories.

In his *Vindication of Natural Society,* a work written after but published before the *Enquiry,* Burke turned to an examination of the potential consequences of extending the denial of universal standards from aesthetics to morality and religion.[48] Burke claimed that his intention was to satirize Bolingbroke's critique of organized religion by applying the rationalistic arguments of the latter to an analysis of society. As he explained in the preface which he added to the second edition, "the design was to show that, without the exertion of any considerable forces, the same engines which were employed for the destruction of religion, might be employed with equal success for the subversion of government; and that specious arguments might be used against those things which they, who doubt of everything else, will never permit to be questioned."[49] Burke believed, correctly I think, that Bolingbroke's philosophy was inconsistent with his politics. If, he asked, we are to model our religion on the dictates of nature and reason, why should we not do the same with our social theory? Bolingbroke wished to stop short; he sought to combine radicalism in religion with conservatism in politics. Burke considered this hypocritical: "we laid open the Foundations of society; and you feared, that the Curiosity of this Search might endanger the ruin of the whole Fabrick."[50] As he saw it, once reason was given its head, there would be no telling where matters would end. Moreover, if the standards provided by experience and established morality are called into question, the reasoning of each individual, however absurd, becomes the only guide. Burke made clear that there can be, on Bolingbroke's terms, no common basis of judgment when he has his anonymous author say "to know whether any Proposition be true or false, it is a preposterous Method to Examine it by its consequences."[51] We know from Burke's other writings that this is the very method of judging political proposals he most often used. If it is to be rejected, what is left? And that, of course, is precisely the point. John Morley maintains that "Burke foresaw from the first what, if rationalism were allowed to run an unimpeded course, would be the really great business of the second half of his century."[52] Viewed in this perspective, it is hard not to agree with him.

Burke's anonymous author began the *Vindication* with the ironical assertion that "the great error of our nature is, not to know where to stop, not to be satisfied with any reasonable acquirement; not to compound with our condition; but to lose all we have gained by an insatiable pursuit after more."[53] Thus, he argued, man gave up the advantages of natural society, with its glories of primitive existence, and entered political society. Advancing the very standard of judging by consequences which he had earlier denied, the author proceeded to criticize political society on both external and internal grounds. As for the external critique, he blamed political society for every war and every death in those wars from ancient times to the present. For example, he said of Alexander the Great that, "to form this hero no less than twelve hundred thousand lives must have been sacrificed; but no sooner had he fallen . . . than a thousand breaches were made for ruin to enter . . ." into the political system he established.[54] Internally, the writer continued, no matter what their specific forms, all governments ultimately degenerate into despotism. Of aristocracy, he noted, ". . . a people who are in general excluded from any share of the legislative, are, to all intents and purposes, as much slaves, when twenty, independent of them, govern, as when but one domineers."[55] Should the people, therefore, be given power? One is inclined to doubt, for the author spent more time denouncing democracy than he allowed monarchy and aristocracy put together. Nor did mixed government fare any better, for "the government is, one day, arbitrary power in a single person; another, a juggling confederacy of a few to cheat the prince and enslave the people; and the third, a frantic and unmanageable democracy.[56] In short, according to the author, artificial society destroys natural equality, creates arbitrary and unjust distinctions, and introduces poverty into the lot of man.[57] What is the answer to the problems created by society? Burke's social critic had a solution—anarchy. First, he said, we must "confess that the Cause of Artificial society is more defenceless even that that of Artificial Religion."[58] Indeed, he claimed: "if you say, that Natural Religion is a sufficient Guide without the foreign aid of revelation, on what Principle should Political Laws become necessary? Is not the same Reason available in theology and in Politics?"[59] If the artificial norms and standards of society cannot be maintained, we must simply return to those which are natural and rational. That such standards are individual rather than universal and cannot be discovered or enforced is beside the point. Men will cooperate willingly, their very natures will be transformed, and everyone will be at peace. Surely, he concluded, the elimination of all society, all art, and all civilization is a small price to pay for such progress.

III

Burke was not alone in his attempt to deal with the Lockean legacy. Many other writers, representing a wide variety of attitudes, also sought a means of grounding normative judgments. Though none of these efforts seemed completely satisfactory to Burke, a brief review of two of the most prominent positions is probably warranted in light of their significance for Burke's own intellectual development. The first of these is the moral sense school and its related offshoots, such as the common sense philosophy of Thomas Reed and the moral sympathy position of Adam Smith. That the problems left by Locke's analysis were widely perceived, led to considerable confusion in both psychology and aesthetics, and yet remained unsolved is perhaps best revealed by an examination of Francis Hutcheson's attempt to refute the empirical hedonism of Bernard Mandeville. Hutcheson divided *An Inquiry into the Origin of Our Ideas of Beauty and Virtue* into two treatises.[60] In the first, he sought to develop a fully empirical and sensationalist psychology and to employ that psychology to explain our ideas of beauty and order. All of our ideas, Hutcheson said, are based on our senses: "no Definition can raise any simple Idea which has not been before perceived by the Senses."[61] According to Hutcheson, the effects of these sensations are uniform among people, for "there does not seem to be any Grounds to believe such a Diversity in human Minds, as that the same simple Idea or Perception should give pleasure to one and pain to another, or to the same person at different times."[62] Thus, those perceptions or ideas which give us pleasure we call beautiful, and those which give us pain are called ugly. It was of central importance to Hutcheson that these judgments are not matters of reason, will, or training. Rather, he believed them to be immediate and intuitive and thus attributable to what he called an internal sense.[63] He claimed this capacity was a sense because "the Pleasure does not arise from any *Knowledge of Principles, Proportions, Causes, or of the Usefulness of the Object; but strikes us at first with the Idea of Beauty*," and he believed it to be internal because it plays a part in our perception of "*Theorems,* or universal Truths, in *general Causes,* and in some *extensive Principles* of Action."[64] Hutcheson further divided beauty into two types: the original beauty which strikes the mind without comparison to anything else and the comparative beauty which is based on an object's resemblance to something else.[65] In the remainder of the essay, Hutcheson went on to investigate the various qualities in objects which excite or occasion our ideas of beauty. As a rule, he held, "the Figures which excite in us the Ideas of Beauty, seem to be those in which there is *Uniformity amidst Variety.*"[66] For example, Hutcheson maintained that we believe the universe to be a thing of beauty because of the uniformity and order found among its varied constituent parts. Indeed, even scientific theories can be beautiful because they display a pleasing variety of corollaries all derived from some single proposition.[67]

Hutcheson was anxious to formulate a theory of virtue as well as one of beauty. Like many other writers of the Scottish Enlightenment, he was obsessed with discovering an answer to what he considered to be the socially destructive consequences of Mandeville's *The Fable of the Bees.*[68] Mandeville had made his intention quite clear: "to show the Impossibility of enjoying all the most elegant Comforts of Life that are to be met with in an industrious, wealthy and powerful Nation, and at the same time be bless'd with all the Virtue and Innocence that can be wish'd for in a Golden Age . . ."[69] Mandeville believed that a choice was necessary: society could continue to take virtuous Republicanism seriously or it could plunge ahead into the politics of selfishness, wealth, and world Empire. What, according to Mandeville, it could not do is have both traditional virtue and modern civilization. Put bluntly, "Great Wealth and Foreign Treasure will ever scorn to come among Men, unless you'll admit their inseparable Companions, Avarice and Luxury."[70] Moreover, he believed that the two forms of society are so incompatible that what serves as virtue in one is vice in the other. For instance, in contrast to ancient Republican simplicity, according to Mandeville, modern commercial society sees government, itself, as a matter of profit: "their Kings were serv'd; but Knavishly / Cheated by their own Ministry; / Many, that for their Welfare slaved, / Robbing the very crown they saved . . ."[71] And yet, Mandeville claimed, seen in its own terms, modern civilization works, for "To such a Height, the very Poor / Lived better than the Rich before."[72] In Mandeville's view, only hypocrites could wish to have both wealth and republican virtue: "I could swagger about Fortitude and the Contempt of Riches as much as *Seneca* himself, and would under-take to write twice as much in behalf of Poverty as ever he did, for the tenth part of his Estate."[73] Finally, Mandeville professed to be appalled by the inconsistency of his contemporaries. He insisted that, if they want the wealth, they must steel themselves to such logical consequences of their own greed as the suppression of the poor and the elimination of charity.[74]

For a more conventional moralist like Hutcheson, wealth gained at the price of the loss of virtue seemed too dear. In his opinion, to have the science without the morality was to achieve the means without the end. As Hutcheson was convinced that the central weakness of Mandeville's argument was its assumption of a psychology based on a view of man as self-interested, he believed that the best reply would be to formulate an alternative theory of human nature which stressed man's cooperative and social side. In the treatise on morality which accompanied that on beauty, Hutcheson modeled his discussion of virtue on the latter's explanation of aesthetics. He argued that, as in the case of the internal sense of beauty, God has endowed us with a moral sense which is structural rather than innate. Comparing this sense to both our external senses and our sense of beauty, Hutcheson argued that, as God gave us those other senses, so "in the same manner he has given us a moral sense to direct our Actions, and give give us still *nobler pleasures*."[75] According to Hutcheson, this moral sense functions as "*a Determination of the Mind, to receive any Ideas from the Presence of an Object which occurs to us, independent of our will.*"[76] He maintained that the moral sense manifests itself in a natural and disinterested affection, which he calls benevolence, toward all rational agents. Hutcheson believed that we desire the good of others, as well as our own, and therefore approve those acts which seem to us to flow "from *Love of others,* and a study of their Happiness . . ."[77] Thus, we call that virtue which serves others, and we admit as most virtuous that which gives the greatest pleasure to the largest number. In fact, Hutcheson claimed, our desire to benefit others is so strong that our moral sense underlies all of our most developed and complex moral ideas, including those of obligation, property, and individual rights.[78] Even our notion of physical beauty is based on our moral sense, according to Hutcheson, for we find attractive what we consider to be the physical representation or expression of such virtues as sweetness, mildness, or dignity.

Unfortunately, Hutcheson found it easier to disagree with Mandeville than to refute him. In fact, the same dilemma which had proven so difficult for Burke surfaced near the end of the Treatise on Virtue. If the moral sense is so powerful and is universal besides, why then, Hutcheson asked, do men differ on questions of morality? In part, his reply was that such disagreement is more apparent than real. Hutcheson held that the moral sense plays a greater role in life than most people think, and forms "the *most delightful Ingredient* in the ordinary Pleasures of *Life*."[79] Where differences do obtain, they are due, he suggested, to mistakes in judging the tendency of actions, to the violent passions outweighing men's judgment, to the different application of the same principles to different contexts, and to the prevalence of different, and often excessively narrow, moral and religious systems.[80] Further, though he held that benevolence is universal, Hutcheson also believed that we do not feel an equal measure of concern for all. We care, and properly so, said Hutcheson, most for those closest to us by birth or culture. Finally, Hutcheson insisted that association plays a role in morality as well as in psychology. We often, and at times even incorrectly, learn to think well or ill of those things which are present when we derive pleasure or pain from something else. Hutcheson's answer, of course, was no more adequate than Burke's: to admit that passion can frequently outweigh benevolence is to concede Mandeville's point about the relative strengths of the various forms of motivation, and to attribute moral variety to the prevalence of different moral systems is to explain diversity by citing diversity.

When faced with the relativistic consequences of the failure of the arguments offered by Hutcheson, most mid-eighteenth century moral and aesthetic writers were at a loss. One popular response was to attempt to solve the problem by fiat. Thus, Thomas Reid simply postulated the existence of a universally-shared common sense.[81] Reid argued that philosophers should give off quibbling and accept, as the common man does, the reality of nature and the truthfulness of conventional morality.[82] However, the difficulty could not be so simply waved away. The Common Sense proposal has about it the air of an *ad hoc* and philosophically inept attempt to get around Hume's inconvenient skepticism. As Leslie Stephen noted long ago, its theme seems to be "if our principles cannot be justified, we had better take them for granted."[83] On the other hand, Adam Smith advanced a somewhat more creative approach in his *Theory of Moral Sentiments*.[84] Smith's thrust was twofold. First, he made morality a largely empirical study by arguing that "men judge the opinions, perceptions or sentiments of each other by comparing them with their own; if they 'agree,' that is, if one man perceives that he shares the opinion, perception or feeling of another, then he judges it to be correct."[85] In an attempt to remove the normative problems associated with the theory, Smith further held that this sense of "sympathy" is implanted in us by God. Therefore, he believed that, to act morally, men must cooperate with the purposes of God, and in accordance with both the physical and moral laws of nature. Second, to explain variations in the moral standards of historical and existing societies, Smith postulated a theory of social evolution.[86] He maintained that each society goes through a series of four stages of development, ranging from primitive nomadic community to modern commercial nation. In Smith's view, then, the morality of societies will vary according to their respective level of progress and the conditions of their social and physical environment. Still, Smith's answer to the problem of judgment is little more convincing than Hutcheson's, for it rested on the arbitrary assumption of a God who coordinated the natural and human worlds in the formation of a divine harmony. All of the sociological and historical details of Smith's speculative history function only to confirm the essential goodness of God's plan for man.

Burke's attitude toward moral sense philosophy is complex. Indeed, a comparison of his argument in the "Essay on Taste" to moral sense doctrine offers several points of interest. Perhaps most important, it is clear that Burke's attempt at a solution to the problem of standards is, in a number of ways, quite close to the moral sense tradition—especially as it is reformulated by Smith. To begin with, Burke heartily endorsed Smith's intention to make morality an empirical science. In September 1759, he wrote to Smith, "I am not only pleased with the ingenuity of your Theory: I am convinced of its solidity and Truth; and I do not know that it ever cost me less trouble to admit so many things to which I had been a stranger before."[87] Burke continued, "a theory like yours founded on the Nature of Man, which is always the same, will last, when those that are founded on his opinions, which are always changing, will and must be forgotten."[88] Second, since Burke and the moral sense writers shared a belief that a theory of psychology was both logically and empirically prior to a theory of normative judgment, they further agreed that psychology, aesthetics, and morality were but different aspects of a single enterprise. As Burke noted in his review of Smith's *Theory of Moral Sentiments* in the *Annual Register* of 1759, "the author seeks for the foundations of the just, the fit, the proper, the decent, in our most common and most allowed passions: and making approbation and disapprobation of the tests of virtue and vice, and shewing that those are founded on sympathy, he raises from this simple truth one of the most beautiful fabrics of moral theory, that has perhaps ever appeared."[89] Third, Burke's theory of human nature, like that embedded in moral sense philosophy, led to a belief in human moral equality. For example, Burke's writings on the European settlements in North America are full of sympathetic references to both the native Americans and the black slaves.[90] Of the American Indians, he wrote, "whoever considers the Americans of this day, not only studies the manners of a remote present nation, but he studies, in some measure, the antiquities of all nations."[91] Fourth, Burke was prone to attribute much of the existing variation in moral standards to differences in historical development or social circumstances. Moreover, Burke held to this position throughout his life. As late as the 1790s, he could be found appealing to sympathy as an explanation for his concern for the victims of the French Revolution: "our sympathy with them under Such wrongs, are feelings implanted in us by our creator . . . They arise out of instinctive principles of self-defense and are executive powers under the legislation of nature, enforcing its first laws."[92]

Still, Burke differed in important respects from Hutcheson, Smith, and the other moral sense writers. Although he shared much of their framework of analysis, there were three issues on which Burke disagreed with at least some members of the school. First, Burke rejected the very term "moral sense" as a holdover from the pre-scientific search for final causes. He believed that the label referred to no empirical reality, and that its use simply confused the discussion of psychology and morality. Second, Burke believed that the postulation of a moral sense encouraged a further, and related, mistake: an attempt to infer the existence of a deity who was the author of both the natural order and of the senses by which we learn about that order. Thus, though most of the moral sense thinkers, including both Hutcheson and Smith, made substantial use of the assumption that God is the creater of the moral law and the ultimate reconciler of nature's and man's respective purposes, Burke usually did not speak of God in this way. I would suggest that this was a consequence of his acceptance of Hume's claim that the introduction of the Deity does little to improve the argument. On the other hand, Burke occasionally did refer to God because he, nonetheless, agreed with Hutcheson and Smith about the actual existence and role of God in the universe. He was, in short, more willing than Hume to merge the empirical and normative aspects of the theory, but less so than Smith or Hutcheson. Finally, Burke stood with the later proponents of a moral sense, such as Hume, Smith, and Ferguson, in emphasizing the historical and sociological elements of the theory. When Ferguson said, "if we are asked, therefore, where the state of nature is to be found? we may answer, it is here; and it matters not whether we are understood to speak in the island of Great Britain, at the Cape of Good Hope, or the Straits of Magellan," he undoubtedly struck a responsive chord in Burke.[93]

IV

A second approach to the problem of judgment that was available to Burke was natural law theory. In fact, a number of recent scholars have argued that his thought is best understood within that context. Perhaps the strongest version of this claim is to be found in the works of Peter J. Stanlis.[94] Stanlis grounds his argument in Leo Strauss's famous distinction between natural law and natural right. Following Strauss, Stanlis holds that, before Hobbes, it was almost universally agreed that God governs the natural order through laws, that these laws can be discovered by man through the use of reason, and that they are, therefore, binding on him.[95] On this view, then, the laws of nature are both empirical and normative. According to Strauss and Stanlis, Hobbesian natural right, on the other hand, is a product of the will or ego of the individual, and is not controlled by any sense of a prior law of nature or even of divine will. Therefore, unlike natural law, natural right is not based on rules laid down by God, and has nothing to do with a desire to properly perform one's function in the great scheme of things. It rests instead on the assertion that each individual has a right to anything which is necessary for his own survival. Moreover, given the uncertainty of survival in a world without law, the question of precisely what is necessary to the individual becomes a subjective and open-ended one. It follows for Strauss that talk of duty makes little sense in such an environment. Strauss asserts, "if, then, Natural Law must be deduced from the desire for self-preservation, if, in other words, the desire for self-preservation is the sole root of all justice and morality, the fundamental moral fact is not a duty but a right; all duties are derivative from the fundamental and inalienable right of self-preservation. There are, then, no absolute or unconditional duties; duties are binding only to the extent to which their performance does not endanger our self-preservation."[96] Thus, against the idealist, hierarchical, and duty-bound nature of natural law, natural right theory is, for Strauss, a radical, pseudo-scientific, disguise masking the naked self-assertion of the modern individual.

As for Burke, Stanlis maintains that Burke's writings were based on natural law, and intended as a refutation of the natural right theory of the radicals of his day. Stanlis writes, "in every important political problem he ever faced . . . Burke *always* appealed to the Natural Law. What is more, by Natural Law Burke always meant essentially the same thing . . ."[97] Since he sees Locke as a disciple of Hobbes, Stanlis denies that Burke could have been influenced by Locke. On the contrary, Stanlis insists that Burke's theory of human nature was grounded in a rejection of Lockean psychology. In Stanlis' view, Burke did not believe that man is born with his mind an isolated blank tablet, did not confuse sense impressions with the necessary principles of right reason, and never identified the pleasurable with the good. Indeed, he argues that, far from being an empiricist in psychology or morality, Burke believed that God's normative truths are embedded in nature, and that the human mind is equipped to discover those truths. The link between natural order and human knowledge, Stanlis argues, Burke found to lie in reason, for he believed that God structured nature to operate according to rational principles, and also gave man reason with which to discover the character of that order. Moreover, Stanlis suggests that Burke felt that historical continuity serves as yet another source of knowledge of God's will. Thus, in addition to its other functions, reason can also discover important normative truths in historical social forms.[98] That is to say, Burke saw prescription as a part of natural law: what has existed from time immemorial has generally done so through the sanction of God and his law. As Stanlis puts it, "since man in every state is by nature a political animal, the real natural rights of man are a matter of practical political reason, and are to be found only within the objectives and conventions of civil society."[99] In sum, according to Stanlis, there is no value problem in Burke's thought, for reason, nature, and history all join together to teach a single objective truth.

It seems to me that there are two major lines along which an evaluation of the natural law explanation of Burke's thought might be pursued. First, there is the question of whether Burke would have seen natural law as a viable answer to the questions he was concerned with. Second, there is the more empirical question of whether Burke actually adopted such an approach. As to the first point, it strikes me as distinctly odd that the natural law thesis has come to dominate Burkean studies, for there is every reason to think that Burke saw natural law theory as one of the sources of the difficulty, and not as a means of solving it. As we have seen, the problem which most concerned Burke in his early writings was the absence of a common standard of judgment. Burke was aware that this problem had originated within a natural law framework, as a result of Locke's psychology, which had destroyed the notion of innate ideas and greatly weakened reason as a tool for discovering truths about the world, and he also was familar with the failure of Hutcheson and the moral sense school to remedy the defect of Locke's theory. Moreover, it was clear that all of the moral sense writings shared key features of the natural law approach, and their failure was due to those features. Surely, in the light of these considerations, Burke can be assumed to have understood that his critique, in the *Vindication of Natural Society,* of Bolingbroke's radical natural law approach to morality also applied to his own ideas as outlined in the *Sublime and Beautiful.* To credit the natural law thesis, one would have to assume that, after identifying the major intellectual and moral problem of his time, after perceiving and acknowledging all of the defects of natural law theory as a solution to that problem, and without securing a remedy for any of those defects, Burke simply reverted to natural law as though nothing had changed since the days of Aquinas.

Even if Burke were not capable of making the connection himself, the work of David Hume, which was well known to Burke, would have drawn it for him. Hume vigorously attacked natural law theory, arguing that it was illogical, vague, and unhistorical. As Hume put it, for reason to be able to establish right and wrong, "the character of virtuous and vicious either must lie in some relations of objects, or must be a matter of fact, which is discovered by our reasoning."[100] However, in Hume's view, neither relationships nor facts are capable of bearing moral conclusions, and, therefore, whatever else may be said about them, human actions cannot be proven to be morally correct.[101] Similarly, the very diversity of interpretations of natural law among people of different times and places argued, for Hume, against any attempt to apply it to existing governments and societies. Burke knew all this. In fact, he frequently spoke Hume's language even in works like the *Reflections.* For instance, he wrote there of natural rights: "the pretended rights of these theorists are all extremes, and in proportion as they are metaphysically true, they are morally and politically false . . . The rights of men in governments are their advantages; and these are often in balances between differences of good, in compromises sometimes between good and evil, and sometimes between evil and evil. Political reason is a computing principle: adding, subtracting, multiplying, and dividing, morally and not metaphysically, or mathematically, true moral denominations."[102]

Another oddity in the interpretation of Burke as a natural law thinker is that its proponents refuse to admit that he had good reason to reject it as the solution to his problem. They simply assume, but do not demonstrate, that natural law generally, and their own version of it in particular, provides an objectively correct understanding of political morality. Thus, Stanlis dismisses Hume's critique as a "precaution carried to excess," and speaks of Burke as recognizing the natural law, as though he simply discovered something which is obviously true.[103] Such an approach ignores a considerable body of twentieth century writing on moral and political theory. If, rather, we accept the arguments of the mainstream of contemporary rights' theory, much of the natural law line of interpretation falls to the ground. For example, following the practice established by Wesley N. Hohfeld, Richard Flathman defines a right as "a warrant, provided by socially established rules, that holds against some at least loosely specified range of objections and that authorizes A, usually on his decision, to engage in a type of action that A judges to be advantageous to himself and that is often judged or can be expected often to be judged, disadvantageous to some B or B's."[104] Viewed from this perspective, rights are like trumps in a game of cards: they allow one to act against the opposition of other interested parties.[105] However, just as trumps have meaning only within the context of a game, so do rights have meaning only within some social structure of rules and authority. Flathman makes the point well: "the practice of rights is individualistic and individualizing but it is not fairly described as atomistic or atomizing . . . Thus there is a very important sense in which participation in the practice of rights enmeshes individuals in a network of social relationships and a social structure. The autonomy of action that rights warrant and protect is autonomy within that network."[106] Rights are intended to limit authority and to preserve an island of freedom for the individual, but, even as they limit authority, they also affirm it. In a very important sense, then, rights exist as part of a constitutional framework. As Joseph Raz notes, they "maintain and protect the fundamental moral and political culture of a community through specific institutional arrangements or political conventions."[107] In any society, rights, duties, and both individual and social goals are all interrelated. Where there are rights for some, there are duties for others to respect those rights; where there are duties to be obeyed, others have rights that correspond to the performance of those duties.

If we apply these considerations to Stanlis' argument, several conclusions follow. First, the very idea of a natural law, far from being obvious, is itself quite questionable. Writing in the tradition of Wittgensteinian language theory, Flathman expresses something like the consensus view: "contrary to the impression often given by natural rights theorists from Locke to Robert Nozick, rights are not natural, divine, primitive, or brute facts. Nor are they somehow self-justifying or self-evidently justified. Those who hold particular rights can perhaps be expected to favor the arrangement in respect to the rights they hold. But on what grounds can a society or polity expect those who are disadvantaged by those rights to accept the restrictions and interferences that they entail?"[108] Others are, of course, less emphatic. They argue, not that natural law does not exist, but rather that its content, if any, cannot be specified in a sufficiently unambiguous manner. Even those philosophers, like H. L. A. Hart, who maintain that at least some minimal principles of law can be derived from a natural right to equal freedom admit that those principles do not take us very far in the real political world.[109] Second, it is clear that the natural law versus natural right distinction is untenable. In fact, as Flathman points out, the notion of a Hobbesian natural right is incoherent. Indeed, Flathman says, "Hobbes' right of nature is not a right at all—whether in the Hohfeldian sense of a liberty or any other. It is a principle or precept that can be employed in reasoning about rights of the several kinds that have developed in our moral and legal practice."[110] A right is a warrant to act contrary to the will or interest of another. Therefore, to the extent that Hobbes' natural right is one of each individual to everything that individual deems necessary to his own survival it cannot provide such a warrant. It offers, at best, the beginning of an argument, a place to start, and not a set of practical conclusions. It follows, then, that to ground the study of Burke in a presumed contest between natural law and natural right is to employ a dilemma with an underdeveloped horn. A wide variety of conclusions can be built on a Hobbesian approach, and not all of them would have been of concern to Burke. The mere premise that men are self-interested, and even the consequent pronouncement that that is a good thing, would hardly have disturbed him. He often said as much himself. Third, like the concept of a battle between natural law and natural right, that of a contrast between rights and duties is hopelessly inadequate. To have meaning, concepts like right and duty must be placed in the context of some social and political theory. It is probably true that not every right has a correlative duty, and every duty a correlative right, but most do. Moreover, social rights and duties imply the existence of a system of authority to give them meaning. It simply does not make sense to contrast a system based on rights to one based on duties. Both are intrinsic features of any political system.

But is Burke a natural law thinker? The possibility remains that he may have been aware of its limitations and used it nonetheless. I, therefore, turn next to the question of to what degree Burke actually employed natural law in his writings. I think that it must be admitted that Burke did cite natural law in two ways. First, especially late in his career, and usually in regard to India, Burke used natural law as a response to his adversaries' claims that differences in cultural values or positive law permitted them to engage in activities which were immoral or illegal by English standards. Thus, for example, to Hastings' argument that Indian custom and law excused his disregard of European norms, Burke proclaimed a universal standard of justice rooted in natural law: "If, then, all dominion of man over man is the effect of the Divine disposition, it is bound by the eternal laws of Him that gave it, with which no human authority can dispense,—neither he that exercises it, nor even those who are subject to it; and if they were mad enough to make an express compact that should release their magistrate from his duty, and should declare their lives, liberties, and properties dependent upon, not rules and laws, but his mere capricious will, that covenant would be void."[111] Many of Burke's appeals to natural law in such contexts were, I think, probably quite sincere. Second, throughout his career, Burke often referred to nature as a short way of saying something like "the nature of things." This use was more of a recognition of brute fact than a normative argument. It may well have been modeled on Montesquieu's famous definition, in *The Spirit of the Laws,* of law as "taken in the broadest meaning, . . . the necessary relations deriving from the nature of things."[112] For Montesquieu, the paradigm of law was not traditional natural law but rather the discoveries of men like Isaac Newton. He illustrated his definition, for example, with planentary motion: "these rules are a consistently established relation. Between one moving body and another moving body, it is in accord with relations of mass and velocity that all motions are received, increased, diminished, or lost; every diversity is *uniformity,* every change is *consistency.*"[113] On the other hand, Montesquieu was somewhat uncertain as to how normative such rules were in the human arena: ". . . the intelligent world is far from being as well governed as the physical world. For, though the intelligent world also has laws that are invariable by their nature, unlike the physical world, it does not follow its laws consistently."[114] Similarly, Burke often argued that one must take natural reality and the circumstances of politics and social life into account when one acts. Like a barrier across our intended route, such obstacles are simply there; they are facts requiring attention and consideration but not always matters of moral concern.

Something more than examples of occasional rhetorical displays or references to modern science is necessary, if one is to argue seriously that natural law forms the central core of Burke's thought. Indeed, before Burke can be accepted as a natural law thinker, it seems to me that four points must be established. First, it must be shown that Burke actually believed in a law of nature created by God and binding on men. This requirement is, I think, met by the evidence. Burke clearly proclaimed the existence of natural law, and he occasionally made use of it in his political writings. In denouncing what he called Warren Hastings "geographical morality" Burke asserted "we are all born in subjection,—all born equally, high and low, governors and governed, in subjection to one great, immutable, pre-existent law, prior to all our devices and prior to all our contrivances, paramount to all our ideas and all our sensations, antecedent to our very existence, by which we are knit and connected in the eternal frame of the universe, out of which we cannot stir."[115] However, this admission comes to rather little, for Burke also argued that natural law can only rarely be directly applied to political matters. Thus, whenever a social right was claimed as a derivative of a presumed natural right, Burke usually rejected the implication on the grounds that natural law is too vague to be easily discovered or too abstract to be applied without regard to circumstances. When a group of Dissenters demanded the repeal of the Corporation Act because it interfered with their natural right to religious freedom, Burke responded, "as long as they continue to claim what they desire as a *Right;* so long will they find it difficult to obtain it. Parliament will not hear of an *abstract principle,* which must render it impossible to annex any qualification whatsoever to the capacity of exercising a public Trust; and I am myself much of the same Mind . . . This high claim of *Right,* leaves with Parliament no *discretionary* power whatsoever concerning almost any part of *Legislation;* which is almost all of it, conversant in qualifying, and limiting some *Right or other of man's original nature.*"[116] Even during the French Revolution Burke never wavered in his opinion. For example, in the "Appeal," he maintained that a good part of political wisdom lies in an avoidance of ultimate questions and a concentration on the mundane, for "political problems do not primarily concern truth or falsehood. They relate to good and evil. What in the result is likely to produce evil is politically false; that which is productive of good, politically true."[117] In short, Burke believed that it is not so much that there is no law of nature, as it is that natural law is simply not applicable to most political issues.

Second, since the natural law school claims that Burke made few explicit references to natural law because he believed its meaning to be clear beyond question, it must be shown that Burke held that natural law is easily known. However, such an assertion, it appears to me, not only violates Burke's psychological theory but also contradicts almost everything he said about the complexity of political issues, the consequent importance of the careful study of policy, and the need for moderation in its implementation. For example, when Burke criticized the French reformers in the *Appeal,* he was particularly upset by their dogmatism. Politics, he said, is not a matter of abstractions or of absolutes because "they admit of exceptions; they demand modifications. These exceptions and modifications are not made by the process of logic, but by the rules of prudence.[118] The English constitution, according to Burke, is built on a process of perpetual compromise and reconciliation; its very structure promotes reasoning and moderation.[119] Nor was Burke doctrinaire in matters of religion or morality. In his "Speech on the Acts of Uniformity," he rejected the proposal to substitute adherence to Scripture for acceptance of the 39 Articles in these words: "to ascertain Scripture, you must have one article more; and you must define what that Scripture is which you mean to teach . . . The Scripture is no one summary of doctrines regularly digested, in which a man could not mistake his way. It is a most venerable, but most multifarious, collection of the records of the divine economy: a collection of an infinite variety,—of cosmogony, theology, history, prophecy, psalmody, morality, apologue, allegory, legislation, ethics, carried through different books, by different authors, at different ages, for different ends and purposes."[120] It is quite clear that Burke did not think that the political truth was self-evident or a matter of simple deduction from first principles. He thought its discovery difficult at best and often impossible.

Third, partly to compensate for the infrequency of Burke's direct citations of natural law and partly to explain his emphasis on circumstances and actual practice, advocates of the natural law school maintain that Burke believed natural law to be embedded in existing social institutions. From this it follows, they insist, that Burke was no reformer. In a letter written at the time of the French Revolution, Burke unambiguously rejected such an awed view of structures. They are, he said, "but instruments at best."[121] In an earlier letter on the same topic, Burke further explained his de-emphasis of the importance of institutions: "I am not so narrow minded as to be unable to conceive, that the same Object may be attain'd in many ways, and perhaps in ways very different from those which we have follow'd in this County."[122] And, after praising all governments which reconcile liberty and order, he continued: "the Government whatever its name or form may be, that shall be found, substantially and practically, to unite these advantages, will most Merit the applause of all discerning Men."[123] It is equally certain that Burke did not hold that all that God caused to happen in the world was somehow desirable when viewed from a human perspective.[124] In fact, Burke's references to the intervention of the Divinity in politics were actually rather rare. He felt that political and social institutions are the work of men and are intended for human purposes and uses. There is, in his opinion, nothing sacred about them, and they might be reformed with impunity. As they were created by men, so they can be altered or abolished by men. In this regard, England is no different than any other country save perhaps in degree. It, too, has its sound laws and traditions, but it also has laws and practices which require reform or even elimination. In his great speech on conciliation with the colonies, for instance, Burke mocked those who argued for preserving the existing colonial system simply because it had served in the past: "then, Sir, you keep up revenue laws which are mischievious in order to preserve trade laws that are useless."[125] Similarly, in complaining of the semi-feudal nature of the Royal Household, he argued "but when the reason of old establishments is gone, it is absurd to preserve nothing but the burden of them."[126] Burke did, indeed, respect the accumulated experience of the past, but, when that experience was no longer relevant, he was ready to move beyond it.

Finally, the natural law thesis insists that Burke was no rationalist. If, the argument goes, Burke believed that natural law is embedded in existing institutions, and if he thought that abstract reason is inadequate in social affairs, then it follows that he must have held that any attempt to design political forms or practices is foolish. To begin with, it should be noted how truly remarkable it would be for Burke to have considered natural law to be immanent in both history and in existing social institutions. This is especially so when one considers that so many of the great natural law thinkers, men like Cicero, St. Thomas, and Locke, saw natural law as providing an external standard for judging worldly law and practice. For example, Cicero wrote "to invalidate this Law by human Legislation is never morally right, not is it permissible ever to restrict its operation, and to annul it wholly is impossible."[127] Likewise, Aquinas noted of human law ". . . in so far as it deviates from reason, it is called an unjust law and has the nature, not of law, but of violence."[128] However, just as Burke did not oppose all reform, he did not disparage reason. As he explained, he considered "government and legislation are matters of reason and judgment, and not of inclination."[129] Even as he opposed those extreme rationalists, the French Revolutionaries, Burke did not waver in his insistence on the importance of reason in politics, for he always believed that the strongest opponent of false reasoning was sound reasoning.[130] As Fennessy has pointed out, Burke's anti-rationalism was not intended as a rejection of all reason but only as a protest against the application of a crude *a priorism* to the study of society and the state.[131] Nor did Burke only appeal to reason as a critical tool; it often formed the basis of his own position. In defending his economic reforms, he asserted, "I proceeded upon principles of research to put me in possession of my matter, on principles of method to regulate it, and on principles in the human mind and in civil affairs to secure and perpetuate the operation."[132] He did, Burke said, nothing arbitrary, for "government is made for the very purpose of opposing that reason to will and to caprice, in the reformers or in the reformed, in the governors or in the governed, in kings, in senates, or in people."[133] Burke far preferred the coolness of logic to the heat of passion.

I have thus far sought to make my case without wrangling over specific citations and examples, but, before leaving the issue, something should be said about the abundance of and variety among the forms of the natural law argument and the extreme tenuousness of much of the evidence used to support it. One would think that, if Burke were a natural law thinker, the many proponents of that interpretation should be in some considerable agreement about the details of his position. Yet, it is quite clear that they are not. Marxists and conservatives make markedly different claims about Burke, and, even within the ranks of a single approach, individual writers differ considerably. Wilkens, for instance, rejects Strauss and Stanlis' distinction between natural law and natural right, and declares the fundamental consistency of Burke's thought against their insistence on a break between the *Sublime and Beautiful* and the rest of his work.[134] Moreover, each of the individual accounts can be subjected to detailed criticism. Stanlis, for instance, appears to rather overstate his case. In his four page Appendix of quotes drawn from the *Reflections* and the *Appeal,* there is hardly one which is undoubtedly an instance of a natural law argument and several which are obviously not. I cannot, to cite a single case, see what natural law has to do with the following statement drawn from the *Reflections:* "the old fanatics of single arbitrary power dogmatized as if hereditary royalty was the only lawful government in the world, just as as our new fanatics of popular arbitrary power maintain that a popular election is the sole lawful source of authority."[135] Taken in context, Burke's point was merely that there are many ways in which government originate. This is a good and worthy argument, but it is not obviously based on natural law.

Just as his citations don't always support his argument, Stanlis' arguments, themselves, are often unsound. He tells us that the quotations assembled in his Appendix are intended to prove that "Burke rejected popular sovereignty as the ultimate moral basis of politics; on such a principle the individual citizen counted for nothing and the state, as the expression of the 'general will,' became a popular tyranny."[136] Now there are three problems with this claim. First, as I have argued above, the evidence cited does not prove the case. It does not even bear on it. Second, the argument is illogical. Belief in popular sovereignty is consistent with a variety of positions, and does not necessarily lead to statist majoritarian tyranny. Hobbes, as is well-known, employed a contractually-based version of popular sovereignty as a part of the justification of an authoritarian, anti-democratic regime, while Locke used popular sovereignty to build a limited liberal state. Third, and most important, however, is the fact that Burke did not oppose popular sovereignty. His actual position was both complex and highly nuanced. In the course of a long and sophisticated discussion in the *Appeal,* Burke argued: "though civil society might be at first a voluntary act, (which in many cases it undoubtedly was,) its continuance is under a permanent standing covenant, coexisting with the society; and it attaches upon every individual of that society, without any formal act of his own."[137] Burke's argument is that popular sovereignty underlies all government, but, in practice, there are many ways of forming a state. Moreover, once created, states take on a life of their own, and are to be justified by their performance not their origins. Again, this is an interesting and respectable argument, but it is not a natural law argument.

V

If neither moral sense philosophy nor natural law provided a satisfactory solution to Burke's quest for a firm grounding of morality, where was he to turn? Fortunately, another alternative was available and appeared more attractive. David Hume's work suggested how one might operate in the world without an absolute truth. Adequate moral standards could be developed, Hume argued, through probabilistic reasoning based on experience. Viewed in this light, on the theory of the mechanics of human perception and understanding, Hume's role was to return the discussion to something close to Locke's original position. Hume disposed of all the theoretical "epicycles" of the moral sense school and the untenable claims of certainty of the proponents of natural law, and reverted to a more thorough-going empiricism. For instance, while Hume did, at times, use the term "moral sense," he generally meant by it nothing more that the biological structure of man. On the other hand, in the section of the *Treatise* dealing with morality, Hume undermined Locke's approach to values. Like Locke, Hume began by professing a confidence in the possibility of a determination of a uniform morality: "I am not, however, without hopes, that the present system of philosophy will acquire new force as it advances . . ."[138] However, after referring to "those who affirm that virtue is nothing but a conformity to reason; that there are eternal fitnesses and unfitnesses of things . . . ," Hume said, "to judge of these systems, we need only consider, whether it be possible, from reason alone, to distinguish betwixt moral good and evil . . ."[139] He concluded, of course, that it is not. According to Hume, morals excite passion and lead to action, but reason is "utterly impotent in this particular."[140] Reason is capable, Hume claimed, only of discovering the truth or falsehood of the relation of ideas and of determining the real existence of facts. However, "our passions, volitions, and actions are not susceptible of any such agreement or disagreement; being original facts and realities, compleat in themselves and implying no reference to other passions, volitions, and actions. 'Tis impossible, therefore, they can be pronounced either true or false, and be either contrary or conformable to reason."[141] Hume did not believe that morality could be a form of relationship. Citing his earlier discussion of the four basic forms of relationship—resemblance, contrariety, degree in quality and proportion, and number or quantity—he noted that morality is none of those.[142] Moreover, even if it were, Hume argued that we would still trip over the problem of cause and effect, for "all beings in the universe, consider'd in themselves, appear entirely loose and independent of each other. 'Tis only by experience we learn their influence and connexion; and this influence we ought never to extend beyond experience."[143] Nor can morality be a matter of fact. Morality involves statements of obligation while a fact is a statement of existence. They are simply two different kinds of terms.[144]

How, then, could Hume believe in a universal morality? How did he think that man could be free of relativism and social disorder? Hume sought to avoid relativism by employing three related concepts. First, he assumed that, as nature appears to be orderly and to operates according to uniform principles, similar causes will have similar effects. Thus, what nature teaches one set of men in one part of the world, and at one time, will be confirmed among other sets of men in other places at other times. Second, as Leslie Stephens notes, "the moral which Hume naturally drew from his philosophy was the necessity of turning entirely to experience. Experience, and experience alone, could decide questions of morality or politics; and Hume put his theory in practice when he abandoned speculation to turn himself to history."[145] In the *Treatise,* Hume wrote, "the only connexion [*sic*] or relation of objects, which can lead us beyond the immediate impressions of our memory and senses is that of cause and effect; . . . The idea of cause and effect is deriv'd from *experience,* which informs us, that such particular objects, in all past instances, have been consistently conjoined with each other: And as an object similar to one of these is suppos'd to be immediately present in its impression, we thence presume on the existence of one similar to its usual attendant."[146] If one would know what political objects have usually been conjoined with one another, one must, according to Hume, turn to the records of the human race—that is, to history. Third, Hume tried to counter the fanaticism of the enthusiastic few and the folly of the masses by appealing to a moral consensus which he supposed to exist among the knowledgeable. In his famous "Essay on Taste," Hume argued that aesthetic judgments are not really arbitrary, for the standards of the educated and refined are, in fact, superior to those of the common herd.[147]

Burke, for his part, developed a related but slightly different approach. Like both Locke and Hume, Burke saw the problem of morality as primarily one of knowledge: how is one to know what morality requires in any given case? Again like both Locke and Hume, Burke accepted that neither reason nor experience is capable of providing us with clear and objective truth.[148] In the *Reflections,* he wrote, "government is not made in virtue of natural rights, which may and do exist in total independence of it, and exist in much greater degree of abstract perfection but their abstract perfection is their practical defect."[149] Rather, he continues, "the science of constructing a commonwealth, or renovating it, or reforming it, is, like every other experimental science, not to be taught *a priori.*"[150] Men must do the best they can. They have, on some few occasions, the guidance of reason and natural law, but, most often, they must rely on their own accumulated experience and the considerations of utility.[151] Their calculations are not, and cannot, be always correct. Still, those calculations are all men have, and they usually suffice. However, at this point, Burke diverged from both Locke and Hume. On the one hand, he shared Locke's confidence that some loose standard of common judgment is possible. Burke never became a relativist to the degree that Hume did. On the other hand, he went further than Locke along the road toward Hume's greater skepticism about the possibility of objective knowledge and the absoluteness of social values. Leslie Stephen's comment about Hume is equally true of Burke: "though Hume affects to attack equally all reasoning which has to do with the external world, his skepticism is really directed against the superfluous hypothesis of an absolute substratum distinct from the world."[152] Like Hume, Burke was uncomfortable with the notion of final cause. He was, in the end, a believer, but he lacked Locke's optimism and faith in the ultimate victory of the good. Most importantly, Burke agreed with Hume on where the record of relevant human experience is to be found. It is, in my view, no accident that most of Hume's later writings concerned history or that Burke wrote history for a time after the *Sublime and Beautiful* and the *Vindication* were published.

The aesthetics debate kept lapping over into politics because it called all judgment, not just aesthetic judgment, into question. The significance of that debate for Burke was, therefore, that it forced him to redefine the nature of politics. If the goal of society is seen as the maintenance of order and the enforcement of morality, then government, as Locke recognized early on, becomes a device for the discovery and enactment of truth. However, Locke's psychology raised the question of whose truth is to be upheld. If no one's judgment can be established as superior to another's, then society must recognize a plurality of equally legitimate voices, for there are then many truths, not one, and we must learn to accept and deal with a degree of confusion and disorder. For Locke, the solution was to recognize the absence of certainty, to permit the expression of all views consistent with social order, to retreat into probability, and to render government the arbitrator of order and the resolver of conflict. However, Locke's answer would not work for Hume or Burke, in large part because of the rise of progressive radicalism. Radicals like Thomas Paine were not content with a politics of bargaining within the established framework; they believed that experience showed that the existing constitution was pernicious, and argued that it therefore must be changed. For Hume and Burke, Locke's theory was insufficiently dynamic to cope with the radical critique. In response, they added to Locke a time dimension which is of vital importance. For them, mutual political adjustments formed, or avoided, over time equal the record of experience, and that, in turn, is history. In Burke's opinion, one must seek to harness the wisdom embodied in such records: "if we do not take to our aid the foregone studies of men reputed intelligent and learned, we shall be always beginners."[153] As he put it, the radicals "being unacquainted with the conflict which has always been maintained between the sense and nonsense of mankind, know nothing of the former existence and the ancient refutation of the same follies they now indulge in."[154] With this move, Burke combined the radicals' emphasis on progress with two more conservative ideas: first, he redefined progress as the perfection of the ongoing social system; and, second, he made Locke's device for conflict resolution—mutual bargaining—the means of progress. Burke turned the radicals' own historicism against them. Moreover, along the way, he also developed a rationale for representative government. In his opinion, representative government is desirable because it provides an arena for the working out of the historical process. It allows the effective expression of the various views concerning the nature of the good, it provides a forum, in the legislature, for compromising and resolving disputes among those views, and, in the electoral process, it offers a means of legitimating the decisions achieved in the legislative process. Burke was, in a sense, a Humean philosopher in action. Where Hume was largely content to debate political issues, Burke acted on a very similar appreciation of the situation.

3

THE WHIGGISM OF HISTORY AND THE HISTORY OF WHIGGISM

An appreciation of the full meaning and complexity of Burke's turn to history is crucial to the study of his political thought, for, throughout his career, his politics were always grounded in his conception of the historical process. I believe that history plays three central functions in Burke's thought. First, in the eighteenth century, all history was political history. Conservatives and radicals alike used history to further their causes. On the one side, history was held to prove the folly of innovation and the value of traditional forms, while, on the other, it was proclaimed to demonstrate an unbroken line of progress toward the realization of the program of the moment. For that reason, Burke's very decision to write history, and his choice of what kind of history to write, involved an important political commitment. Second, in Burke's view, history was both a record of human experience and a process of development based on that experience. Therefore, he believed that it provided broad guidelines which, in part, limited the range of possible political action, and thus served as an effective brake on political chaos and anarchy. In a related but more positive manner, Burke, largely by employing the concept of society as an evolving corporation, was able to educe a series of principles to direct and justify reform. His understanding of history included a notion of the nature of society, a sense of the various factors which drive history, and a fairly clear idea of the goals a politician should seek and the means he could use to pursue them. Indeed, when one adds up all the reforms Burke favored at one time or another, the list is truly impressive. Third, by placing the Whig party at the center of recent British history, Burke accomplished several political purposes: he further domesticated radicalism, offered an effective justification of controlled evolution, and defended the aristocracy he meant to direct it. In his contrast between the Old and the New Whigs, Burke presented his branch of the Whig party as the agents of past historical change, and, therefore, as reliable trustees for the future. That is to say, Burke's treatment of the Revolution of 1688–90, the Sacheverall Trial, and the transition from Walpole to Rockingham was essentially an ideological defense of a certain kind of progressive Whiggism.

I

A survey of the major approaches available to Burke will make clear the intrinsically political nature of most eighteenth century history writing. The oldest of these models was the classical-humanistic school. As developed by such ancient writers as Caesar and Tacitus, and exemplified in Burke's day by Bolingbroke, this school had several leading characteristics. First, history was seen as having a moral or political purpose: by recording the deeds of great men of the past, it provided a model for modern men to copy. Tacitus, for example, introduced the *Agricola,* the story of his father-in-law's conquest of Britain, with a disclaimer: "famous men of old had their lives and characters set on record: and even our generation, with all its indifference to the world around it, has not quite abandoned the practice. An outstanding personality can still triumph over that blind antipathy to virtue which is a defect of all states, great and small."[1] Tacitus' purpose, then, was to reawaken the Roman spirit of virtue and glory, which he believed had been lost in his day. The moral purpose of classical-humanistic history gave form to its presentation. Generally, the historian began by describing the social and political circumstances of the hero's field of action. He then listed the various political opportunites and difficulties the protagonist faced, and discussed the factors which informed his choice of policy. Next came a detailed account of the events which ensued. Finally, the historian concluded with an assessment of the results and a pronouncement of any morals to be drawn from the story. The central assumption of classical-humanist history was that neither men nor circumstances changed so much over time as to render comparison between the past and the present impossible. In a letter praising Salust, written to Richard Shackleton early in his life, Burke revealed that he was quite familiar with the classical model: "he has I think a fine easy and diversified narration mixt [*sic*] with reflections moral and political neither very trite and obvious nor out of the way and abst[ract] which I think is the true beauty of Historical Observation."[2] Indeed, in Burke's *Abridgement of English History,* Tacitus was one of the most frequently cited sources.

An interesting variation on classical history was offered by Bolingbroke, whose *Letters on The Study and Use of History* was an important landmark in eighteenth century historiography. On one level, that of proclaimed method, Bolingbroke's view of history appeared to be a revival of classicism. Thus, of the purpose of history, Bolingbroke wrote, "an application to any study that tends neither directly nor indirectly to make us better men and better citizens, is at best but a specious and ingenious sort of idleness . . . and the knowledge we acquire by it is a creditable kind of ignorance . . ."[3] Indeed, he continued, true history is not to be confused with the writings of the Annalists and Antiquaries: "naked facts, without the causes that produced them, and the circumstances that accompanied them, are not sufficient to characterise actions or counsels."[4] Bolingbroke maintained, rather, that history is simply "philosophy teaching by example." That is to say, it is a field of instances which may be mined to provide illustrations and proofs of principles already taught to us by our religion and philosophy: "such is the imperfection of human understanding . . . that abstract or general propositions appear obscure or doubtful to us very often, till they are explained by examples."[5] As one might expect, Bolingbroke believed that this didactic use of history is made possible by the uniformity of both circumstances and human nature. Thus, he held that we should concentrate our concern on the generalizations and applications which can be drawn from history, not on the specific details of any given event, for "these are certain general principles, and rules of life and conduct, which always must be true, because they are conformable to the general rule of things."[6] Thus far, Bolingbroke was operating well within the classical-humanistic school, though he was, perhaps, somewhat more explicit about his methods than most exponents of the approach.[7] When, however, Bolingbroke turned to the actual writing of English history, another level of meaning presented itself. In these works, his organizing principle was to view English history as a constant struggle between those who would defend the traditional mixed constitution and those who would destroy it.[8] Thus, Henry VIII was viewed as evil, for he sought, according to Bolingbroke, to undermine the balance of government: "he who had been led, amused, governed by his minister, drives, overbears, tyrannizes; butchers his servants and his wives, his commons and his nobility."[9] On the other hand, the greatest of monarchs was Elizabeth I, for she "chose the sole expedient that remained, for making herself and her people happy; which was to place the whole strength and security of her government in the affections of her people, and in superior credit with them."[10] Therefore, Bolingbroke suggested that current and future rulers could do no better than follow the example of Elizabeth. They should attempt to unite the country by ruling in the general interest, and by establishing a single party composed of the entire people. In its time, Bolingbroke's history was subjected to severe criticism, for it was quite obviously partisan history of a rather clever kind. The political thrust of his writings was to argue that the Revolution of 1688 had reestablished the true constitution and had removed any need for political parties. He argued that the persistence of contemporary parties resulted, not from issues, which no longer mattered in politics, but from the Whigs' desire to maintain power. Moreover, he insisted that the Whig monopoly of office led to corruption and would eventually undermine the very constitution itself. Bolingbroke's solution was for the nation to unite in a general country party, to oppose the court politics of the Whigs, and, once the Whigs were defeated, to install a unity government under a patriot king.[11] Bolingbroke's contemporaries were quick to see him as the historian of neo-Toryism. As such, it seems clear that Burke would find little of interest or use in his writings.

The long-standing debate about the ancient constitution provided Burke with a second source of historical models. That discussion had grown out of attempts, particularly in France, to determine the nature of Roman Law and develop techniques for its study. When, in the early seventeenth century, the same methods were applied to the study of English history, Sir Henry Spelman, among others, noted a strong resemblance between early English and Germanic practices and usages.[12] This led Spelman to the concept of a unified European history and to the belief that feudalism was one of its stages. Spelman saw the central feature of feudalism as the system of dependence and consultation between the lord and his vassals. Thus defined, Feudalism, he argued, had been introduced into England by William the Conqueror. In his view, then, it followed that the English Constitution did not extend back beyond the Conquest and that it, in fact, had developed through a series of royal acts of concession. For instance, Spelman believed that Parliament had grown out of the King's Council, had been originally merely an advisory body, and possessed only those powers which various kings had chosen to bestow on it. From this, it further followed that what a king had given could be taken away by the same or another king. Spelman, however, did not fully pursue all of the implications of his position: that task was left to Robert Brady in the 1670s. For example, since neither Spelman nor Brady was willing to accept that historical development—that is, changing circumstances over time—could lead to legitimate changes in the constitution, Brady maintained that the original constitution was still binding on England in his own day. Moreover, he also suggested that the rights held by Englishmen in his own day were dependent on a continuing royal will for their very existence. In sum, not only was the ancient constitution absolutist, so must be the current constitution.

Among the political writers who built on Spelman and Brady, the best known is Sir Robert Filmer. Filmer's principal line of attack was rationalistic: he began with a theory of sovereignty similar to that of Jean Bodin's and deduced its consequences. As Filmer saw it, there must be as a matter of definition in every society some authority, which he calls the sovereign, competent to determine the law: "there can be," he said, "no laws without a supreme power to command or make them."[13] He further held that it is the very nature of such sovereign authority that it cannot be limited or controlled. "for every custom there was a time when it was no custom, and the first precedent we now have had no precedent when it began. When every custom began, there was something else than custom that made it lawful, or else the beginnings of all customs were unlawful. Customs at first became lawful only by some superior which did either command or consent unto their beginning."[14] According to Filmer, in England sovereignty lies with the King. It therefore follows that "all those liberties that are claimed in parliament are the liberties of grace from the king, and not the liberties of nature to the people."[15] Even such apparent exceptions as Magna Carta are not, properly speaking, checks on royal authority, for "we find that Magna Carta and the Charter of Forests, and many other statutes about those time, had only the form of the king's letters-patents, or grants under the great seal, testifying those great liberties to be the sole act and bounty of the king."[16] Finally, Filmer, like Brady and Spelman, believed that as things began so should they ever be. In his opinion, to prove that English government originated in conquest and absolute will was tantamount to proving that the current king is absolute.

In the context of eighteenth century politics, the Tory version of ancient constitutionalism was an important threat to Whig thought. In their attempts to counter the Tory arguments, Whig writers employed a number of different strategies. Perhaps the most interesting, that of John Locke, can be passed over quickly for it was not historically based. Locke perceived that the essence of Filmer's case was rationalistic rather than historical. In Locke's opinion, the basis of Filmer's argument was his claim that all men are born into political subjection and that all states must contain some final absolute authority.[17] Locke understood that, if this point were not refuted, no historical evidence would be sufficient to answer Filmer. Therefore, he presented an alternative paradigm of political obligation in which man was conceived as being born free, and was, on that basis, entitled to create government for himself. For those who felt a need for historical evidence, Locke merely recommended that they read the history of his Whig colleagues. Algernon Sidney, one of the most popular of those colleagues, employed a tactic similar to Locke's.[18] Sidney held that revelation, natural law, and history all teach the same truth. Substituting reason for history, he proceeded to create a kind of theoretical ideal-type history in which consent played a major political role. All government, said Sidney, is based on the consent of some previously free men, and any state formed through conquest is illegitimate. Moreover, the role of consent is so important that no lapse of time can ever replace it, and even the customary acceptance of a conquest does not make it morally acceptable. If correct, Sidney's argument would make the history of Spelman and Brady irrelevant, for if only rational consent can validate government, then the questions of who descended from whom or which king conquered which people mean nothing.

While distinctly a minority view, another Whig response to Tory ancient constitutionalism had an important future before it. Though he differed with the Tories on the nature of the original English constitution, Algernon Sidney usually agreed with them that change is degeneration and corruption. In claiming, for instance, that the increase of wealth is generally associated with a decline in virtue, he asserted, "he that could rise from the plough to the triumphal chariot, and contentedly return thither again, could not be corrupted . . . but when luxury was brought into fashion . . . the most virtuous men were exposed to scorn if they were poor: and that poverty which had been the mother and nurse of their virtue, grew unsupportable."[19] However, on occasion, Sidney treated history as progress and improvement. At times, Sidney stressed that man is a limited and weak creature, prone to error. Still, what he does not get right the first time can be improved with experience: "it is a rare thing for a city at the first to be rightly constituted: men can hardly at once foresee all that may happen in many ages, and the changes that accompany them ought to be provided for."[20] As men's circumstances and living conditions change, Sidney held, so should his institutions. Sidney noted that "he that should make war at this day as the best commanders did two hundred years past, would be beaten by the meanest soldier . . . Men were sent into the world rude and ignorant, and if they might not have used their natural faculties to find out that which is good for themselves, all must have been condemned to continue in the ignorance of our first fathers, and to make no use of their understanding to the ends for which it was given."[21] Of those who believe that we are bound to live under our society's original government, Sidney asked, "if men are not obliged to live in caves and hollow trees, to eat acorns, and to go naked, why should they forever be obliged to continue under the same form of government that their ancestors happened to set up in the time of their ignorance."[22] In the 1720s and thereafter, Whig historians, especially those around Robert Walpole, extended Sidney's argument to create a new model of English history.[23] They insisted that, while previous English history is the story of a struggle between absolutistic and popular conceptions of government, the Revolution of 1688 had introduced a new age of progress and ever-expanding freedom. To return to the past, the Walpolian apologists scoffed, would be to reject the good that generations had labored to produce.

Burke found a third type of history in the writings of various Scotch thinkers.[24] In their attempts to trace the origins of modern commercial society, writers like Lord Kames, Adam Smith, William Robertson, and Adam Ferguson developed the thesis that all societies follow a certain order of progress from primitive to modern. In the words of Ronald Meek, "in its most specific form, the theory was that society 'naturally' or 'normally' progressed over time through four more or less distinct and consecutive stages, each corresponding to a different mode of subsistence, these stages being defined as hunting, pasturage, agriculture, and commerce. To each of these modes of subsistence, it came to be argued, there corresponded different sets of ideas and institutions relating to law, property, and government, and also different sets of customs, manners, and morals."[25] While the primary intention of the Scotch writers was to establish a comparative sociology, their writings could also be used as an ideal-typical history in which the disparate events of an individual nation's past could be assigned universal significance.

Thus, for example, one could learn a great deal about European society by studying the American Indians, for, as modern day hunters, their practices and institutions parallel Europe's own past and are the prototypes of all more advanced nations. As Ferguson put it, "in these happy, though informal, proceedings, where age alone gives a place in the council; where youthful ardour, and valour in the field, give a title to the station of leader; where the whole community is assembled on any alarming occasion, we may venture to say, that we have found the origin of the senate, the executive power, and the assembly of the people; . . ."[26] The ideal history of the Scots was not necessarily a tale of unalloyed advance. They recognized a negative side to the growth of civilization. In Ferguson's opinion, the progress of the division of labor both "breaks the bands of society" and saps the virtue of the people.[27] To encourage the clerk and the accountant instead of the statesman and the warrior is, he wrote, "to separate the arts which form the citizen and the statesman, the arts of policy and war, is an attempt to dismember the human character, and to destroy those very arts we mean to improve."[28] Nonetheless, the Whig bias of most of the Scotch writers is rather obvious, and their practical politics brings them close to Whig ancient constitutionalism or progressivism.

The historical writings of David Hume offered an interesting variation on Scotch social history. Hume did not accept the strict confines of the four stages theory nor did he share its emphasis on changes in the means of subsistence as a causal factor. Still, he did write within a framework of progress from barbarism to civilization, and he did utilize many of the concepts and techniques of the school. As I suggested in the last chapter, Hume's interest in history was both a logical extension of his earlier works and a major factor in his philosophy as a whole. In the essay, "That Politics May be Reduced to a Science," Hume applied the skeptical analysis of his *Treatise* to politics by holding that many of the supposed axioms of politics are not in fact true at all.[29] Partly through ridicule and partly by revealing the complexity and uncertainty of political issues, he proceeded to demonstrate that sure political knowledge, either rational or scientific, is impossible. Therefore, in politics, as in philosophy generally, we are forced to rely on our passions, our desire for pleasure, and our sympathy with others. On this basis, we must calculate what is likely to be of utilitarian value in satisfying our purposes. As a practical matter, Hume claimed that it is history, with its record of man's accumulated experience and examples, which teaches us what has been of value in the past, and so serves us as a guide for the future. Hume asserted, "History, the great mistress of wisdom, furnishes examples of all kinds: and every prudential, as well as moral precept, may be authorized by those events which her enlarged mirror is able to present to us."[30] In Hume's view, then, the study of politics is necessarily based on history.

Hume's history is at once less rigid and more optimistic than that of his colleagues. He began by accepting the contention that the ancient Saxons did indeed value freedom above all else: "kingly government . . . possessed a very limited authority; and though the sovereign was usually chosen from among the royal family, he was directed in every measure by the common consent of the nation over whom he presided."[31] Still, their practices cannot be regulative for later ages, for it appears unlikely that they were capable of creating a firm constitution: "we must conceive that the ancient Germans were little removed from the original state of nature."[32] Nor were they possessed of a unique political genius: "these institutions are not peculiar to the ancient Germans. They seem to be the necessary progress of criminal jurisprudence among every free people, where the will of the sovereign is not implicitly obeyed," and the Greeks, the Irish, the Jews and others have similar institutions.[33] Gradually, change came, though at first the new forms were of little value to the majority of the people. After the Conquest, feudalism was introduced, and the government inclined to an aristocracy of warriors, in which the people suffered, and arts, commerce, learning, and trade declined. For a time: "the languishing state of commerce kept the inhabitants poor and contemptible; and the political institutions were calculated to render that poverty perpetual."[34] Eventually, however, things did improve: commerce grew, learning increased, and the arts and science progressed. Among these achievements was an increased regularity in the law:"when the German nations had been settled some time in the provinces of the Roman Empire, they made still another step toward a more cultivated life, and their criminal justice gradually improved and refined itself."[35] Hume argued that the increased regularity of the law made men secure, security led to curiosity, and curiosity to discovery. Once begun, advances in knowledge and economics became self-sustaining, and further progress ensued. Finally, after a long and bitter struggle, the high level of modern civilization was attained.

Hume meant his history to be non-partisan. He wrote to a friend, "I may be liable to the reproach of ignorance, but I am certain of escaping that of partiality . . ."[36] Instead, he was roundly criticized from all sides. The crux of the criticism concerned his treatment of the seventeenth century. On the one hand, Hume agreed with the Tories that the Stuart monarchs did not violate the ancient constitution. In Hume's view, there was no such constitution to violate. In addition, Hume felt a great deal of admiration for the character of the Stuart kings. On the other hand, he suggested that, in light of the progress of society, the leaders of the Commons had a valid point in their desire for a more settled and regular form of government. They may have been wrong about the nature of government in the eleventh century, but they were probably more nearly right than the King's supporters in their assessment of the needs of the seventeenth. As Hume put it, "though men knew not upon what principles they could deny that prerogative, they saw that, if they would preserve their laws and constitution, there was an absolute necessity for . . . abolishing it."[37] Yet, Hume continued, the parliamentary cause was undercut by its own extremism. Of the Puritans, he wrote, "learning itself, which tends so much to enlarge the mind and humanize the temper, rather served on this occasion to exalt that epidemical frenzy which prevailed. Rude as yet, and imperfect, it supplied the dismal fanaticism with a variety of views, founded it on some coherency of system, enriched it with different figures of elocution; advantages with which a people, totally ignorant and barbarous, had been happily unacquainted."[38] Hume believed, in short, that there was good and bad, right and wrong, on all sides. However, few of his contemporaries appreciated his moderation; they preferred to fault him for not siding with their own party.

II

Traces of all the historical models we have discussed can be found in both Burke's specifically historical writings and in his occasional comments on matters of historical concern in his other works. For example, the *Abridgement of English History* begins with a discussion of the Roman Conquest of England which sounds much like Tacitus, who is, in fact, cited in Burke's notes.[39] Similarly, a few pages into the work Burke stopped to assess Caesar's motivation and character in the best classical style.[40] On the other hand, the influence of Scotch stages of civilization sociology is also clear. In commenting on the attempt of the British leaders to apologize to Caesar for an attack by young British warriors, Burke compared the ancient British to the modern American Indians: "this is exactly the excuse which the savages of America, who have no regular government, make at this day upon the like occasions; but it would be a strange apology from one of the modern states of Europe that had employed armies against another."[41] As for ancient constitutionalism, Burke cited Spelman, one of the leading advocates of the royal concession school, to determine the status of the medieval aldermen.[42] Similarly, in the *Abridgement,* the *Appeal,* and in the *Reflections,* he did not scruple to employ Whig ancient constitutionalism when it suited his purpose.[43] Yet, Burke is truly of none of these schools, for he most often wrote history from a perspective I would call "Whiggish Progressivism."[44] That is, Burke generally argued from a rise of civilization perspective somewhat similar to Hume's. In Burke's case, the argument resulted from a synthesis. On one side, he pursued a Scotch stages-of-civilization-approach, though Burke did not explicitly force his story into the abstract categories of the sociological model. On the other side, he also employed a Whig notion of history as development, through struggle, toward a goal given content by the nature of the Revolutionary Settlement. The result was, as Whitney recognized some time ago, a highly sophisticated theory of progress: "to deny that Burke has reached the conception of progress is to follow him in his reasoning about the necessarily increasing complexity of a state without seeing that that very theory presupposes progress as its basis."[45] Examples abound in Burke's writings. In praising Edmond Malone's exposure of fraudulent Shakespearean manuscripts, Burke took an evolutionary view of the history of the English language: "our Language during that important period, . . . after being refined by Chaucer, . . . fell into the rudeness of civil confusion and then continued in a pretty even progress, to the state of correctness, strength and elegance, in which we see it in your writings."[46] In the *Popery Tract,* Burke spoke of the growth of religious toleration thusly: "in proportion as mankind has become more enlightened, the idea of religious persecution, under any circumstances, has been almost universally exploded by all good and thinking men."[47] Indeed, Progressivism dominated Burke's thinking on history even in the *Abridgement* where the other models of thought are best represented.

The most common focus of Burke's historical writing was a single society or nation, and against either individualist or organic interpretations, he usually viewed a society as a kind of corporation. A society is, Burke said, an institution based on consent and united by adherence to common rules, the most important of which may not be altered without destroying the association itself. As he wrote in the *Appeal,* "the idea of a people is the idea of a corporation. It is wholly artificial, and made, like all other legal fictions, by common agreement," and again, a little earlier, "though civil society might be at first a voluntary act (which in many cases it undoubtedly was), its continuance is under a permanent standing covenant, coexisting with the society; and it attaches upon every individual of that society, without any formal act of his own."[48] Thus, society, for Burke, is an artificial creation—not a natural biological creature. In fact, contrary to the frequent claims of scholars, Burke often rejected organic analogies: "I am not of the opinion that the race of men, and the commonwealths they create, like the bodies of individuals, grow effete and languid and bloodless, and ossify, by the necessities of their own conformation, and the fatal operation of longevity and time. These analogies between bodies natural and politic, though they may sometimes illustrate arguments, furnish no argument of themselves."[49] Moreover, the fact that society is an artifical creation has, for Burke, important consequences. As society was created by men to serve certain specific purposes, through a study of its history, those purposes can be recaptured and their logic reaffirmed. In addition, Burke's beliefs in the artificial origins of society and its corporate nature underlie many of his most characteristic arguments. For instance, they are the basis of his attack on the majoritarian arguments of the New Whigs in the *Appeal* and much of his criticism of the French Revolution. Thus, when Burke defends past abuses in France, he does so in terms of corporate law: "it is not very just to chastise men for the offences of their natural ancestors, but to take the fiction of ancestry in a corporate succession as grounds for punishing men who have no relation to guilty acts . . . is a sort of refinement in injustice belonging to the philosophy of this enlightened age."[50] Similarly, Burke's famous theory of trusteeship and virtual representation can perhaps be best understood in the same context. In his opinion, the representative stands in the same relation to the elector as the officer of a corporation stands to a stockholder.

Burke believed that a theory of progress implies some goal: before one can say that society is advancing, it is necessary to have a sense of what a finished society would be like. Thus, in Burke's classic definition of society, "society is indeed a contract . . . It is a partnership in all science: a partnership in all art; a partnership in every virtue, and in all perfection. As the ends of such a partnership cannot be obtained in many generations, it becomes a partnership not only between those who are dead, and those who are to be born," I would suggest that the key words are "partnership," "art," and "virtue."[51] As we have seen, Burke argued that society originated in some express act, but, at the same time, he also saw it as natural to man in certain respects. First, it is natural in the sense that it provides a necessary discipline which renders civilization possible. Second, society is natural in the further sense that it is inevitable. Where there are men, there will be society. Burke believed that the human race cannot exist without some form of association and, therefore, that, though its creation is a voluntary act, it is an act to which man's biological character will always lead him. Finally, Burke saw society as natural in the sense that, like Aristotle, he believed that it both has a purpose of its own, the promotion of the good life and the realization of all the arts and sciences, and it aids each individual in achieving his personal ends. In the *Appeal,* after defending aristocracy as a natural institution, Burke continued on to argue that the state of civil society, which generates such a class, is as natural to man as any primitive model: "we are as much, at least, in a state of Nature in formed manhood as in immature and helpless infancy."[52] Burke seldom expressed his thoughts on what a society should aspire to, for his mind was not prone to such abstract speculation, and he was unwilling to force his belief in progress on to perfectionism. Yet, the passage in the *Reflections* which describes the value of a landed class, both civil and ecclesiastical, came close to just that: "why should the expenditure of a great landed property . . . appear intolerable to you or to me when it takes its course though the accumulation of vast libraries . . . through great collections of ancient records, metals, and coins . . . through paintings and statues . . . through grand monuments of the dead . . . through collections of the specimens of nature which . . . open the avenues to science?"[53] Progress, in short, has a material component but it is principally, in Burke's opinion, moral in nature.

Ronald Meek has suggested that one of the weaknesses of the Scotch approach to history was its failure to specify how change occurred; in fact, most of its practitioners were content to merely designate and compare the various stages without attempting to suggest how one developed into another.[54] When they did make some attempt to discuss the mechanics of progress, they usually attributed it to the growth of commerce and the softening of manners. For his part, Burke's view of the factors which drive historical change was similar to that of the Scotch school, but it was also somewhat more precise. Burke generally accepted the civilizing influence of commerce, manufacturing, and the arts. In the *Reflections,* he asked: "if commerce and the arts should be lost in an experiment to try how well a state may stand without these old fundamental principles, what sort of a thing must be a nation of gross, stupid, ferocious, and, at the same time, poor and sordid barbarians, destitute of religion, honor, or manly pride, possessing nothing at present, and hoping for nothing hereafter?"[55] However, Burke believed that two other agents were even more important in the creation of the modern world. First, he suggested that the code of honor embodied in the concept of the "gentleman," was basic to modern society. As he put it, "it is this which has given its character to modern Europe. It is this which has distinguished it under all its forms of government, and distinguished it to its advantage, from the states of Asia and possibly from the states which flourished in the most brilliant periods of the antique world."[56] Second, Burke attributed much of the progress toward civilization to the medieval clergy and its preservation of learning. His argument was carefully qualified. He recognized that the political aspirations of the medieval church did great harm, and he was often quite critical of individual churchmen like Thomas Becket, whom Burke regarded as a religious fanatic and a political meddler. Nonetheless, he thought that the Church's contributions outweighed its abuses.[57] As a general rule, he said, "the introduction of Christianity, . . . under whatever form, always confers such inestimable benefits on mankind, (and) soon made a sensible change in these rude and fierce manners."[58] The clergy protected the poor, provided a refuge from war, offered examples of pure and pious living, and introduced learning and civility.[59] Moreover, Burke felt that the civilizing influence of the clergy, like that of the aristocracy, continued into the modern world. Just after his famous quote about the disappearance of the age of chivalry in the *Reflections,* Burke suggested: "this mixed system of opinion and sentiment had its origins in the ancient chivalry; and the principle, though varied in its appearance by the varying state of human affairs, subsisted and influenced through a long succession of generations even to the time we live in. If it should ever be totally extinguished, the loss I fear will be great."[60]

I suggested in the preceding chapter that Burke came to see historical experience as offering a basis for evaluating political proposals and actions. In his opinion, it could, therefore, afford a means of controlling and limiting change, and, by extension, provide a brake on the social anarchy which might result from the crisis in philosophical judgment. Burke drew several principles from his study of history which were meant to serve this purpose. First,in his works on the French Revolution, he advanced the opinion that, since they began in and evolved from a common core, all of the various states of Europe form a single commonwealth. Burke maintained, "the whole of the polity and economy of every country in Europe has been derived from the same sources. It was drawn from the old Germanic or Gothic Custumary,—from the feudal institutions, which must be considered as an emanation from that Custumary."[61] As a result, he claimed, "from all those sources arose a system in all this quarter of the globe,—and which softened, blended, and harmonized the colors of the whole."[62] Burke believed that this commonwealth of Europe and its civilization was based on values which should guide all would-be reformers. In seeking to overturn these values, the radicals of England and especially those of France were not truly idealists or perfectionists; rather, they were new barbarians, who, like those who destroyed Roman civilization, threatened to inaugurate a new Dark Age in all of Europe. In a letter to the Earl of Charlemont, Burke explained his opposition to the radicals in terms of his commitment to the common European culture: "I did not think that Europe reforming, or more properly meliorating itself, upon its ancient principles, which more or less it was throughout all its States almost without exception ought to be disturbed with violent convulsions which would precipitate a premature birth of reformation, and consequently render it distempered and short-lived."[63] Considerations of the same sort led Burke to call for a common European effort to destroy the French Republic. A threat to one state was, he argued, a threat to all. A shared history creates a body of experience which ought to teach the same lesson to all. Thus, the members of any individual society had, he insisted, no right to disregard the lessons derived by all others from their common experience. That the common judgment went against them should, he suggested, give them pause.

Second, as a reformer in his own right, Burke claimed that the study of history revealed a need to distinguish among three closely related concepts: change, progress, and reform. Change for Burke was simply the modification of the social environment caused by historical events. As such, it had no necessary moral dimension. That is, Burke contended that change, in itself, was neither good nor bad. He did not believe that all change is decline or degeneration, nor did he, like Pangloss, argue that some aspect of the modern world was good simply because it existed. For example, Burke praised Alfred as a great king, holding that "he revived, improved, and digested all the Saxon institutions, insomuch that he is generally honored as the founder of our laws and constitution."[64] Yet, according to Burke, the progress made by Alfred did not endure, for, under his successors, his improvements were undone, and the way was paved for the Danish and Norman Conquests. Burke based his argument on the moral neutrality of change on three considerations. First, he held that perfection in human affairs is impossible because man himself is flawed: "that man thinks much too highly, and therefore he thinks weakly and delusively, of any contrivance of human wisdom, who believes that it can make any sort of approach to perfection."[65] Second, Burke did not believe that change followed any plan or logic. While some students of his thought have argued that Burke saw God's hand at work in history, comments to that effect are actually rather rare in his writings. Much more typical was his insistence in the *Abridgement of History,* on discussing the progress of Christianity among the Saxons in purely secular terms. Indeed, he expressly denied any interest in considering claims that miracles were one of the causes of its spread.[66] Third, Burke felt that both medieval and modern history abound with examples of historical regression. His rueful comments, in a letter to James Boswell on the resurgence of religious intolerance in Scotland during the Gordon riots, furnish us with a case in point.[67] Similarly, his sense that the French Revolution represented not progress, but the end of an era of reform and the beginning of a new dark age is too well-known to require much comment.[68]

For Burke, change is endemic to life: "nothing in progression can rest on its original plan. We may as well think of rocking a grown man in the cradle of an infant."[69] That which lives must either advance or retreat, grow or decline, but whether any particular instance of change is good or bad can only be determined by an examination of the circumstances of the case. Progress, on the other hand, is change which is improvement; that is, it is movement toward some goal. Thus, much like Aristotle, Burke saw society through a teleological lens. As an acorn grows into a tree, a primitive society tends naturally to grow into a civilized one. I think, for instance, that it is clear that Burke considered the history of European society not to be merely a story of change, but to embody a normative import as well. In his opinion, Europe had not only changed over time, but had changed for the better. This belief, in fact, introduces an implicit bias in Burke's thought, for it led him to assume that those institutions which have endured for a long time have probably done so for good reason. It is, he argued, probable that they have fairly consistently passed the test of utility. Therefore, they ought not to be lightly discarded. Still, at times, Burke acknowledged that this presumption of merit could be defeated. For instance, in advocating economic reform, Burke warned, "there is a time when men will not suffer bad things because their ancestors have suffered worse."[70] When a practice has outlived its usefulness, no obligation to retain it continues. Similarly, Burke also held that, as the origin of a practice, law, or right should be legitimate, a claim based on long possession could be called into doubt by a demonstration of defective origins. In a speech opposing parliamentary reform, he admitted that his arguments would not convince everyone: "it is true that to say your Constitution is what it has been is no sufficient defense for those who say it is a bad constitution."[71] Such critics, Burke recognized, require more, and he could not fault them too much for doing so. Generally, proper origins may be assumed and long existence suggests satisfactory experience. Still, at times, he conceded, one is entitled to ask for a demonstration of moral legitimacy or political effectiveness.

By adding an emphasis on the importance of human agency to his theory of progress, Burke developed a sophisticated and coherent theory of reform. As I have noted, Burke believed that society has a natural end or purpose: the perfection of all the arts and sciences, and the well-being of its members. Movement toward that end he, therefore, held to be progress, and progress or improvement which is guided by human hands is reform. Burke maintained that, just as a good gardener prunes and shapes a growing plant with its ultimate purpose in mind, a good politician has an obligation to act within the parameters set by the end of society and in furtherance of its goals. Thus, the concepts of progress, prescription, and presumption combined to provide Burke with tests for distinguishing among proposals for reform. The first test was that reform should seek to preserve what has worked in the past. In the *Reflections,* Burke insisted that, "the temporary possessors and life-renters . . . should not think it among their rights to cut off the entail or commit waste on the inheritance by destroying at their pleasure the whole original fabric of their society, hazarding to leave to those who come after them a ruin instead of a habitation."[72] Burke did not intend this principle to be taken as a complete denial of the possibility of effective human action. He wrote, "it is an obvious truth that no constitution can defend itself: it must be defended by the wisdom and fortitude of men;" and "miserable works have been defended by the constancy of the garrison. Weatherbeaten ships have been brought safe to port by the spirit and alertness of the crew."[73] Burke's second rule was that one should be willing to search for new ways when the old ones no longer work. Burke always insisted that he was a reformer and that his opposition to the radicals grew out of his reformism.[74] Indeed, the list of innovations he supported over the years is both lengthy and impressive. It includes electoral and imperial reform, American conciliation and later independence, free trade, religious toleration, abolition of the slave trade, administrative reform, reform of the East India Company, restructuring of the Irish Administration and repeal of the Irish Popery Laws, the abolition of imprisonment for debt, revision of the marriage laws, and much more. Third, however, Burke believed that the lessons of history also suggest limits to reform. Experience, he said, shows that sound reform is consistent with what has gone before and seeks to build on it. Burke often used the analogy of a house or a shoe. When a roof leaks or a shoe rubs, one does not simply raze the house to the ground or throw out the shoe. One seeks a carpenter or a shoemaker to repair the damage. As he wrote to Sir Gilbert Elliot: "I know you love world-making—why not world mending and repairing—the first I admit is a Nobler Theory; but a Cobbler is of some use in political Society."[75] Burke thought that the mistake of the French radicals was to ignore experience and root up what had served in the past. In its place they sought to put faulty structures based on untried and visionary schemes. In failing to build on the existing structure, they were sure to build badly.

III

Burke was not only a Whig historian, he was also a historian of Whiggism. Whatever his abstract interest in history, Burke was primarily a practicing politician. Thus, yet another role played by history in his thought was as a device for orientating and defining himself within the broad outlines of Post-Revolutionary English politics. In his analysis of Whig history, Burke presented the Whig party as the agent of past historical change, and, for that reason, as reliable trustees for the future. At the same time, however, he defended an interpretation of Whiggism which narrowed, moderated, and domesticated it. The conceptual device by which Burke pursued these objectives was a contrast between the Old and the New Whigs, which he first clearly introduced in *The Appeal From the New to the Old Whigs,* but which was an important feature of his thought from the very beginning.[76] In the *Appeal,* Burke denied that the French Revolution was a party issue; that is, a matter on which all Whigs must stand together, and insisted that the title of current Whig legitimacy ought to go to those of his own day who most nearly adhered to the true doctrine of past Whiggism.[77] Moreover, in his opinion, the Rockingham Whigs, as an aristocratic reform party, were the sole authentic heirs of the Whigs of the days of the Revolution, of the time of the trial of Sacheverall, of Walpole, and of the Pelhams: "it is certainly well for Mr. Burke that there are impartial men in the world. To them I address myself, pending the appeal which on his part is made from the living to the dead, from the modern Whigs to the ancient."[78] According to Burke, only the Rockingham Whigs, or their remnants under the Duke of Portland and Earl Fitzwilliam, could offer that combination of elitist responsibility and sensitivity to the currents of change necessary to steer England through its difficulties.

Burke characterized the Old Whigs in two ways. First, sociologically, he saw them as the embodiment of the aristocratic interest in the state. In a letter of January 1792, Burke described his party thusly: "as an aristocratick Party . . . I understood it to be a Party, in its composition and in its principles, connected with the solid, permanent long possessed property of the Country; a party, which, by a temper derived from that Species of Property, and affording a security to it, was attached to the antient [*sic*] tried usages of the Kingdom, a party therefore essentially constructed upon a Ground plot of stability and independence; a party therefore equally removed from servile court compliances, and popular levity, presumption, and precipitation."[79] It should be noted that, in this description, Burke ran several points together. That is, he believed that the party represented a number of factors in the state. To begin, it stood for property, especially property in the land and property which has been in the same hands for a long time. In addition, it represented the interests of the traditional governing elite. These people, as Burke told the Duke of Richmond, spoke for the long-term interest of the country: "you people of great families and hereditary trusts and fortunes are not like such as I am . . . we are but annual plants that perish with our season and leave no sort of traces behind us. You, if you are what you ought to be, are the great Oak that shade a country and perpetuate your benefits from generation to generation."[80] According to Burke, as the local rulers of England, the landed class was to be looked to for the leadership their education and training had prepared them to exercise. As early as the late 1760s, Burke had insisted that such men had an obligation to engage in politics: "they who are legally invested with public trust, or stand on the high ground of rank and dignity . . . can hardly in any case remain indifferent, without the certainty of sinking into insignificance; and thereby in effect deserting that post in which . . . the laws and institutions of their country have fixed them."[81] Finally, the Whig party was not composed exclusively of aristocrats, but also included all those who were willing to defend the aristocratic interests as vital to the well-being of the state.[82]

Support for aristocratic principles was Burke's second criterion for membership in the Old Whigs. Burke always bitterly resented any accusation that he was inconsistent in his principles. In a letter to Fitzwilliam, he complained of Fox, "he then brought out . . . every action and every expression almost of my whole Life, whether publick or private, whether in jest or in earnest, wresting and misrepresenting them, with little Logick and less candour, to make me pass for an Apostate from my principles."[83] As to what the basic principles of true Whiggism were, it would be impossible to cull from Burke a short Creed, but some of the most important are fairly obvious. On the abstract level, Burke said, he believed that governments are not truly made but originate naturally, and that, while their logic is contractual, their actual origins are not always so. No state, he continued, is necessarily majoritarian, for it would require some specific act of the people to make it so. Moreover, any attempt to alter a state without such unanimous agreement would both destroy the state and violate the laws of nature. Similarly, Burke claimed, at a more applied level, that true Whigs were relativists in the manner of governmental forms, believed in regulated liberty, and opposed all excesses, either by government or by the people. Indeed, he made clear that one of the central points in his form of Whiggism was moderation in politics. As he counseled Fitzwilliam, moderation was built into the very nature of the party: it was "a party grave and moral, equally removed from popular giddiness and profligacy on the one hand and from servile Court compliances on the other."[84] He asserted the value of free elections, and of a Parliament controlled by the majority of its own members and led by those they choose, but he opposed parliamentary reform and instructions to representatives. On specific issues, Burke defended opposition to the American war, holding that if the Administration had succeeded, "the Americans could have no sort of security for their laws or liberties . . . and . . . the very circumstances of *our* freedom would have augmented the weight of *their* slavery."[85] He also endorsed the correction of abuses in India, economic reform, and opposition to the King's coup in 1784. In short, Burke saw the Whigs as responsible reformers: "it has been the business of his strength to reform abuses in government, and his last feeble efforts are employed in a struggle against them. Politically he has lived in that element; politically he will die in it."[86] Even the much vilified *Reflections* was, he maintained a reformist work: its very purpose was to make war with the excesses of both left and right.[87]

Burke contrasted what he believed to be the sound principles of the Old Whigs with what he believed to be the dangerous radicalism of the New Whigs. His analysis of the composition and character of the New Whigs was complex. Apparently, he believed the faction to have two centers. The first was within the ranks of the Dissenters. According to Burke, though traditionally allied with the Whigs, they turned against the true Whigs sometime after 1784. For example, he insisted that, during the Regency Crisis, the Dissenters "seized the opportunity of division amongst the great, to bring forward their democratick Notions; and the object against which they chiefly directed their seditious doctrines, and the passions of the Vulgar, was your Party . . ."[88] The second center of New Whiggism was Charles James Fox and his supporters. Especially after the death of Rockingham, an increasing number of young Whigs began to look to Fox for leadership and they soon were, according to Burke, prepared to follow where his ambition led. And that was to an alliance with any power which would help him replace William Pitt as Prime Minister. As Burke put it, "I travelled with him very cheerfully, as long as he appeared to me to pursue the same direction with those in whose company I set out," but around 1790 "the whole frame and fashion of his politics appear to have suffered . . . a very material alteration."[89] Burke argued that what united Fox to the Dissenters, to Paine, Priestley, Price, Mackintosh, and Christie, was their common support for the politics of the French Revolution: "when it came to that point . . . Mr. Foxes publick declaration in Parliament in favour of the French Whiggism was a condition of the support he was to meet with from the first abilities in this Kingdom . . ."[90] In terms of principles, Burke saw the essence of New Whiggism to lie in the doctrines of popular sovereignty, government by continuing expressed consent, and majority-rule.[91] On the practical level, therefore, the New Whigs supported parliamentary reform, disestablishment of the Church, the elimination of all inequality, whether functional or not, and adoption of a whole series of French-like radical reforms. Perhaps most important to Burke was not their principles but the nature of their commitment, for he felt that they were neither moderates nor reformers, but extremists and revolutionaries. The New Whigs, he said, "build their politics, not on convenience, but on truth; and they profess to conduct men to certain happiness by the assertion of their undoubted rights. With them there is no compromise.[92] As outrageous as their tactics and actions were, Burke argued that the New Whigs were merely being consistent: "on their ideas, the New Whig party have, in my opinion, acted as became them."[93]

Burke's version of eighteenth century Whig history centered on three events: the Glorious Revolution, the Sacheverall trial, and the transmission of Whig leadership from Robert Walpole, through the Pelhams, to the Marquis of Rockingham. In each case, Burke sought to make two points: first, that the mainstream of Whiggism was moderate in its thought and responsible in its policy; and, second, that it led to his, and Rockingham's party. Thus, in his treatment of the Revolution, Burke set narrow limits for legitimate resistance to authority. He asserted that only the replacement of great evil by great good can justify rebellion: "without attempting, therefore to define, what never can be defined, the case of a revolution in government, this, I think, may be safely affirmed,—that a sore and pressing evil is to be removed, and that a good, great in its amount and unequivocal in its nature, must be probable almost to certainty, before the inestimable price of our own morals and the well-being of a number of our fellow-citizens is paid for a revolution. If ever we ought to be economical even to parsimony, it is in the voluntary production of evil. Every revolution contains in it something of evil."[94] Indeed, he insisted, when the English praise the Revolution of 1688, they mean to commend not only the subversion of the old government but also the settlement of the new.[95] Moreover, Burke also maintained that only limited changes were introduced into government by the Revolution. For example, he specifically denied that the revolutionaries claimed a right to cashier governments or to alter their forms. In his interpretation, the English people did not overturn hereditary monarchy. Burke argued, "unquestionably, there was at the Revolution . . . a small and a temporary deviation from the strict order of a regular hereditary succession; but it is against all genuine principles of jurisprudence to draw a principle from a law made in a special case and regarding an individual person . . . If ever there was a time favorable for establishing the principle that a king of popular choice was the only legal king, without all doubt it was at the Revolution. Its not being done at that time is a proof that the nation was of opinion it ought not to be done at any time."[96] Burke went even further: he held that, if the nation had ever possessed the right to choose kings, the makers of the Revolution, in actual fact, renounced and abdicated that right by affirming the hereditary right of the Stuart line.[97]

Having determined that the revolutionaries neither claimed nor exercised a right to establish a new government, Burke proceeded to consider whether their actions constituted a legitimate interruption of the usual norms of British politics. On balance, he decided that they did. Burke maintained that in cases of extreme emergency, and extreme emergency only, men are justified in deviating from fixed rules, provided that the deviation be limited to as small a compass and duration as possible. Comparing the Glorious Revolution to the Restoration in 1660, Burke maintained that, in both those cases, the English "regenerated the deficient part of the old constitution through the parts which were not impaired. They kept these old parts exactly as they were, that the part recovered might be suited to them."[98] As Burke saw it, a constitution is much like a living growth. When one part is lost, those remaining are preserved so that the missing element may be regenerated. In a sense, then, the purpose of the Revolution was restoration, not, to be sure, to a past form, but to a former function. Thus, Burke argued, the New Whigs are mistaken. The English Revolution offers no precedent for the doings in France. Quite the opposite: if anything, it actually demonstrates an aversion to radical change and a commitment to the principles of their ancient government.[99] All this, for Burke, proved two points. First, he argued that the topic of revolution does not lend itself easily to discussions of principle, for "the question of dethroning or . . . 'cashiering kings' will always be, as it has always been, an extraordinary question of state, and wholly out of the law—a question . . . of dispositions and of means and of probable consequences rather than of positive rights."[100] Second, Burke insisted that, as each revolution must be discussed in terms of necessity and practical circumstances, and not according to general rules, the English Revolution could not serve as precedent for the French or inspiration for their radical English defenders.

When, in the *Appeal,* Burke sought to prove his doctrinal consistency with the early Whigs, he turned, not to the Revolution, but to the period around 1710 and the trial of the Tory clergyman Dr. Sacheverall.[101] In many respects, this was a perfectly acceptable approach. Some of the leading Whig prosecutors of Sacheverall had been active in the Revolution, and the trial record was often used as a measure of Whig orthodoxy throughout the eighteenth century. What is more, Burke's analysis does accurately recreate much of the argument of the Whig prosecution. In fact, the Whig managers of the prosecution quite consciously downplayed their radical side. They did so, first, to retain power. This is the time of the Junto Whigs who governed in alliance with a number of other Whig factions and such independent allies as Godolphin and Marlborough. In attempting to consolidate their control of government and to solidify the new commercial order, the Junto could not afford to alienate the Queen or the more conservative members of their coalition. In addition, as a minority ruling party, they were concerned with holding off a resurgent Tory Party. Both of these factors led them to moderate their doctrine and to present themselves as a respectable and safe ruling group. Moreover, the Whig case against Sacheverall was conservative by nature, for they were arguing that his brand of Toryism was a threat to the stability of the post-revolutionary regime. That is, they were forced to claim that, by preaching absolute non-resistance, he was preaching sedition, for the present regime had been founded in resistance to the previous one. To support this rather deceptively simple position, the Whigs resorted to a wide variety of arguments. Nonetheless, in general, two points seem to characterize their treatment of the issues: first, most of the Whigs advanced only limited claims of a right to cashier governments; second, in their anxiety to touch all bases, the Whigs did eventually cover much of the ground of traditional Whig resistance theory.

For his part, Burke ignored most of the political background and maneuvering of the day. He simply assumed that the Whig speeches at Sacheverall's trial could be seen as an effort to put Whig principles on record, and he further took for granted that those principles had not changed since the days of the Revolution because "the ministers and managers for the Commons were persons who had, many of them, an active share in the Revolution."[102] According to Burke, the goal of the Whigs was to "preserve our whole inheritance in the Constitution, in all its members and all its relations, entire and unimpaired, from generation to generation."[103] Burke cited the arguments of no fewer than seven of the managers, and quoted the Declaration of the Prince of Orange for good measure. In his view, the essence of the case was, however, both quite simple and completely in keeping with Whig tradition: the managers denied that the Revolution either gave or reaffirmed any popular right to establish a new government, maintained that it created no essential change in the Constitution, and defended it primarily on the basis of its necessity. Indeed, Burke argued, the managers not only believed that the Revolution had made no essential change in the English Constitution, they further recognized that it could not have done so, for the leaders of the Revolution had possessed no such right. In fact, contrary to clear statements elsewhere in his writings, Burke, arguing from an ancient constitution perspective, treated the Revolution as an attempt to recover the original form of English government. Therefore, as he saw it, the trial managers did not see the crown as elective, but rather simply suggested that their predecessors had bypassed an unsatisfactory representative of the legitimate royal line, and resettled authority on one deemed more appropriate. Having done so, Burke said, the Revolution Whigs provided for the future by asserting that henceforth the succession was to be continued in the hereditary line of Protestant descendants of King James I.[104] Finally, he concluded, the Sacheverall Whigs' own actions were consistent with the principles of their ancestors. They had not sought to extend their own power or to abridge the rights of others; rather, they had acted only because they had been forced to do so by the excesses of their Tory opponents.

The third, and perhaps most important, stage of Burke's story of the history of eighteenth century Whiggism concerned two transmissions: from the Sacheverall Whigs to the Whig establishment under Walpole and from Walpole to Rockingham as the leader of the orthodox party. The first of these offered little difficulty. In the *Appeal,* Burke made the moves necessary to establish Walpole as the key actor in the mid-century Whig story. He first denied all claims that Walpole was unprincipled and corrupt, insisting instead that he had always been a solid party man.[105] In addition, by including Walpole among the managers of the Sacheverall trial he quoted, Burke presented him as a legitimate voice of the Revolutionary tradition.[106] Proving that Rockingham and his followers were the only legitimate descendants of Walpole, was more difficult. Here Burke relied on two factors. First, he made much of one of the most important characteristics of the Walpolean regime—its continuity in personnel. As Plumb notes, "most of the men whom Walpole had made stayed with him and stayed loyal; and these were the men who were to be called the Old Corps, the backbone of his party that was to prove unbreakable until its leaders grew too old to face a new king and a new generation in 1760."[107] When Walpole left office, it was only to be succeeded by his aides, the Pellhams. It was, therefore, crucial to Burke's case that Rockingham entered politics as a junior colleague of the last of the Pelham connection, the Duke of

Newcastle. Years later Burke wrote of the Rockingham Whigs as they had been in the 1760s, "they did not affect to be better Whigs than those who lived in the days in which principle was put to the test. Some of the Whigs of those days were then living. They were what the Whigs had been at the Revolution,—what they had been during the reign of Queen Anne,—what they had been at the accession of the present royal family."[108]

Second, in the *Thoughts on the Cause of the Present Discontents* and its companion piece, *Observations on a Late Publication Entitled "The Present State of the Nation,"* Burke formulated a new political mythology.[109] In those works, written during the Petitioning Movement, Burke claimed an exclusive mantle for the Rockingham Whigs as the true Whig party. He argued that a new Court Party had formed, largely under the influence of Lord Bute, and now sought to dominate politics from behind the scenes. The plan was, as Burke saw it, to separate the Court from the Ministry, to create a party in the Commons to support the Court against the Ministry, and to render government secure against popular control or responsibility.[110] Burke insisted that one of the prime tactics of the Bute alliance was the penetration and subversion of all existing political connections through a skillful use of corruption. Burke contended that the only answer to this new threat to the people's liberties lay with the people themselves. The voters should, he said, watch the conduct of their representatives closely and remove from office any who supported or compromised with the new cabal. Moreover, as only the Rockingham party was powerful enough, disciplined enough, and pure enough to resist the cabal, the people should accept their leadership and eschew both such politically independent, hence powerless, figures as William Pitt and the weak, therefore corruptible, non-Rockingham Whig connections.[111]

IV

Burke's version of Whig history is superficially plausible, but a close examination shows it to contain a number of difficulties. To begin with, he was not always consistent, and what he said in such major works of sustained political argument as the *Reflections* and the *Appeal* does not always square with what he says elsewhere. For instance, though those later works seek to hedge revolutionary theory with many conditions and limits, in the *Popery Tract* Burke explicitly argued for the right of a people to cashier a government for breaking a contract or, indeed, for losing the support of a majority of the population.[112] Similarly, throughout his other discussions of history, he repudiated the ancient constitutionalism which he praised in the *Reflections*. Nor can it be claimed that these differences follow from a change in opinion over time, for, as late as 1796, Burke could be found writing to Thomas Hussey about the limitations of the doctrine of passive obedience: "The Doctrine of Passive obedience, as a Doctrine, it is unquestionably right to teach; but to go beyond that, is a sort of deceit; and the people who are provoked by their Oppressors do not readily forgive their friends, if whilst the first persecutes and the others appear to deceive them."[113] Again, at the time of the American War, Burke advocated a more radical view of the Revolution, itself: "the Revolution is a departure from the ancient course of the descent of this monarchy. The people at that time reentered into their original rights; and it was not because a positive law authorized what was then done, but because the freedom and safety of the subject, the origin and cause of all laws, required a proceeding paramount and superior to them."[114] In one of his letters to Langrishe, Burke took yet another, less benign, view of the Settlement: "to insist on everything done in Ireland at the Revolution would be to insist on the severe and jealous policy of a conqueror, in the crude settlement of his new acquisitions, as a *permanent* rule for its future government."[115] In that letter Burke tried to save his claim to consistency by inventing a distinction between the principles of the Revolution and its acts—in this case for the purpose of defending religious toleration in Ireland—but this distinction is not much help. The simple truth is that Burke could not reconcile all of his various statements on history, for his position often varied with the political context of the particular controversy he was dealing with.

A second problem with Burke's view of Whig history is that his account of the Revolution conflicts with those put forward by some of the most important Whig participants. Burke could find supporters for his interpretation. As J. P. Kenyon argues, the official Whig line was that "James had abdicated by fleeing abroad, by destroying the writs for parliament . . . and by jettisoning the Great seal," and that Parliament, upon finding the crown vacant, had merely remedied the defect.[116] From this perspective, then, the Party position was quite conservative: they saw themselves as enforcing a contract, but a historical one rather than a rationalistic one, and their rebellion was an act of self-protection. It was, therefore, both an irregular necessity and no true precedent for future conduct.[117] However, not everybody saw it Burke's way. Locke may have been, as some modern scholars assert, too radical for the mass of Whigs, but he was there, he was read, cited, and respected, and he did defend revolution as a remedy for breach of contract. Moreover, if Locke was too radical, Sidney, whose popularity and influence is widely conceded, said much the same thing.[118] He, too, defended the right of the people to remove kings or change their government for any reason whatsoever.[119] Even so sober and representative a Whig as Atwood held that, "the most absolute of the English monarchs never believed that their children had a right to the Crown except the people consented that they should succeed."[120] Atwood was not completely clear but he appears to have thought that, while elections usually occur within the royal family, the people may even go outside the former king's family, if they wish, in electing a new king.[121] In applying his model specifically to James II, Atwood argued that his fleeing the kingdom violated the contract of government and would in itself, though there were other abuses as well, have justified the people in resuming their rights.[122] Thus, a major problem with Burke's interpretation is that it did not credit the diversity of Whig opinion at the time of the Revolution. He drew on only one strand of thought and that was the most conservative.

Burke's interpretation of the Revolution was too narrow in yet another respect. His Revolution Whigs seem to spring upon the stage fully grown, without origin or context. However, most modern scholars see the birth of the Whig party to lie, not at the Revolution, but at the Exclusion Crisis some eight or ten years earlier.[123] According to J. R. Jones, the Whigs first organized to oppose the succession of James II; that is, to "exclude" him from the line of descent. Therefore, "the first Whigs were, and had to be, a party, something more highly organized and disciplined than a mere alliance or coalition of small and autonomous groups. They possessed, and required, organization in both Parliament and country, effective discipline, and a wide popular appeal, stimulated and maintained by a large-scale propaganda machine. In Shaftesbury they had the leader with the necessary ability, determination, experience, and unscrupulousness to weld them together into a force strong enough to challenge the King, the Court, the Church, and a powerful section of the political nation."[124] By the very nature of their cause, the Whigs' ideology and leadership had both to be radical. It is thus not entirely surprising that Locke's *Second Treatise* was originally an Exclusion Tract.[125] Burke, however, does not even discuss the Exclusion Whigs or the controversy which brought them into existence. Much the same bias is evident in his treatment of the *Declaration of Rights.* Burke quoted from the final draft of the Declaration, and even cited the explanations of that work advanced by some of its more conservative authors, but he ignored the more radical original draft and the accounts of its proponents. As Lois G. Schwoerer has shown, the *Declaration* originated in the desire of radical Whigs to enforce a contractarian version of the Settlement, was watered down to attain the support of conservatives and William, and yet retained some elements of its original purpose even in its final form.[126] By concentrating his attention solely on the compromise wording of the official documents and on the formal explanations of them, Burke robbed them of much of their force and gave them a meaning that not all of their originators would have accepted.

It is no less obvious that Burke's analysis of the Sacheverall Trial and of the Whig doctrine which flowed from it was inadequate. Indeed, Burke's tactics here reinforced and accentuated the similar remodeling of party doctrine he accomplished in his account of the Revolution. Burke's principal error was that he simply did not do justice to the variety or the ambiguity of the Whig inheritance. Where, exactly, did he go wrong? To begin with, he was mistaken to assume that the arguments of the Revolutionary period were maintained intact at the Sacheverall Trial. Moreover, he took no account of the effect on the Sacheverall arguments caused by their presentation in the context of a trial, where the purpose was to achieve a conviction and not to simply present a theory. Nor did Burke consider the requirement that the Whigs felt of broadening their case to win a minimum amount of support from independents and even Tories. In fact, both parties to the Trial centered their cases on resricted versions of their positions. Sacheverall, himself, for example, retreated from the arguments of his sermons, for he argued at the trial that he had never meant to question Queen Anne's right to rule, and insisted that he truly recognized Parliament's right to fill a royal vacancy. Most importantly, Burke's claim that the Whigs were speaking for the historical record—though it contains a grain of truth—led him to misconstrue their ideas in yet another way. Burke insisted that "the Whig managers for the Commons meant to preserve the government on a firm foundation, by asserting the perpetual validity of the settlement then made, and its coercive power upon posterity."[127] This was to give the trial a prospective force which its managers did not intend. They were not so much trying to control future generations as to correct the understanding of their own. Finally, in attempting to vindicate his claims about the managers' intentions, Burke was driven to misstating their arguments. It is true that some of the managers took positions consistent with Burke's interpretation. They agreed that the Revolution created no real break in the continuity of English government. Still, other members of the prosecution would have disagreed. The Trial witnessed the presentation of arguments about violated contracts, the right of the people to remove governments, and, indeed, many of the variations on Whig theory that Burke denied legitimacy.

Finally, a word should be said about Burke's claim that the Rockingham Whigs were the sole legitimate heirs of Walpole. There can be little doubt that Burke's great essays of the late 1760s forged a new and vastly influential interpretation of events. Nor can it be denied that, in some Whig circles, that interpretation took on something of the character of a political religion. Still, a question remains whether Burke's new faith was the true faith. In one sense it was, for it correctly reflected Rockingham's own opinion. Rockingham undoubtedly considered himself the continuer of the politics of Walpole and the Pelhams. As Ross Hoffman argues, Rockingham saw the Whig Party as "a long-continuing connection of men who had a large sense of public responsibility, who had settled the constitution perfectly, secured the Hanoverian dynasty, and understood the politics of Europe: men sagacious and temperate, natural leaders of the public, the wisest possible counselors of the throne."[128] Furthermore, many of Rockingham's, and Burke's, most characteristic views grew, in fact, out of this vision: their reluctance to cooperate with the radicals, their opposition to parliamentary reform, and their almost fanatical dislike of George III, to mention just a few. But the issue is not so easily settled. It is, for instance, at least arguable that the new regime of the early 1760s broke up all traditional associations, and that what followed must be seen as a new political constellation.[129] Similarly, many modern scholars argue that the Rockingham Party did not take form until after both Newcastle's death and the end of the First Rockingham Administration. That administration, itself, they say, resembled the essentially non-party coalitions of the time much more than a modern disciplined party.[130] It was, says Paul Langford, "an incoherent and incohesive amalgam of various elements."[131] However, if the party formed only after the end of the administration, it could not have developed in concert with Newcastle or with other Old Whigs, and its claim to any kind of authentic discipleship must be viewed as weak. Similar doubts exist in the area of intellectual continuity.

Against Burke's claim of theoretical consistency must be put the fact that many of the Rockingham party's ideas and positions developed only later. In July of 1765, for example, Burke can be found urging an alliance with Lord Bute and other recent opponents.[132] This is conventional political reasoning and a long way from the *Thoughts*. Finally, as the Rockingham Whigs were not the Old Whigs, either organizationally or intellectually, it is also true that other groups and factions could plausibly call themselves Whig. Were Stanhope and Grenville, for instance, not Whigs? What of the more radical Whigs? Was not a single advocate of Lockean contract and the right of resistance, as espoused by Sidney and Atwood, by Lechmere and the Walpole of the Trial, to be found? In the light of Burke's *Correspondence*, there can now be little doubt that Burke and his associates believed their own myth, but there remain substantial reasons to think that the politics they derived from it were exclusive and ungenerous.[133]

4

BURKE ON THE FOUNDATIONS AND NATURE OF GOVERNMENT

Burke's turn to history had, of course, important consequences for his assessment of British political institutions. On the one hand, it led him to view British governmental forms as the products of historical evolution. As such, Burke was prepared to grant them a degree of legitimacy on the basis of prescription. In a speech on parliamentary reform, Burke defined prescription as a form of authority based on the fact that an institution "has existed time out of mind."[1] However, Burke admitted that, in certain circumstances, as, for example, in the case of a constitution imposed by force and sustained through terror, a claim based solely on prescription might carry only limited moral weight. Therefore, he maintained that prescription generally needs to be supplemented by a second form of legitimacy. He argued that, ideally, "it is accompanied with another ground of authority in the constitution of the human mind, presumption. It is a presumption in favor of any settled scheme of government against any untried project, that a nation has long existed and flourished under it."[2] The full test of legitimate government, then, is not simply long endurance, but long endurance accompanied by prosperity and happiness. As Burke noted in the *Reflections,* "old establishments are tried by their effects. If the people are happy, united, wealthy, and powerful, we presume the rest. We conclude that to be good from whence good is derived."[3] On the other hand, in Burke's opinion, England's constitutional structure functioned as a device for facilitating further progress through a systematic airing of popular grievances and demands, the institutional formulation of policies to relieve the pressures those demands created, and the legitimation of the policies by legal enactment and popular ratification. As he put it in the *Appeal,* in English government: "there is a perpetual treaty and compromise going on, sometimes openly, sometimes with less observation."[4] In short, England's limited monarchy created a structure of politics which embodied a political process which encouraged, and controlled, the kind of progressive reform Burke sought.

I

Burke's adoption of an evolutionary mode of thought, combined with his emphasis on the importance of particular circumstances in political matters, committed him to a substantial degree of relativism on questions of constitutional forms. He argued that, even where the starting points are similar, different political systems will develop in different ways and in different directions. Thus, what might be appropriate for one government could well be fatal for another. In noting the inaccuracy of all predictions about the course of the French Revolution, Burke wrote, "the world of contingency and political combination is much larger than we are apt to imagine. We never can say what may or may not happen, without a view to all the actual circumstances. Experience, upon other data than those, is of all things the most delusive. Prudence in new cases can do nothing on grounds of retrospect."[5] Nor were such thoughts limited to Burke's later years. Early in his career he had refused to speculate on the possibility of his son following in his Whig party footsteps: that, he said, "must depend upon the future State of things, and the Situation in which he is found relative to them . . . and the progressive Sagacity, that keeps company with times and occasions, and decides upon things in their existing position,is that alone which can give true propriety, grace and effect to a man's conduct. It is very hard to anticipate the occasion; and to live by a more general rule."[6] As John Morley noted long ago, Burke was undoubtedly much influenced by Montesquieu's dictum that governments must be adapted to the societies for which they are intended and that no single form is best for all times and places.[7]

Indeed, in an age where great stress was often placed on constitutuional devices, Burke's evolutionary presumptions led him to de-emphasize their importance. He told a French correspondent that he would not judge the French revolutionaries by their adoption of liberal Bills of Rights or republican forms, for, though "forms are not without their value . . . they hold a low place indeed in the scale of moral agency.[8] Not only is no one form suitable for all circumstances and environments, but a variety of forms might serve much the same purpose. Moreover, forms often tell us little about the effective politics of a nation. In his letter to the Sheriffs of Bristol, written during the American War, Burke denied the importance of abstract discussions of the nature of Parliamentary power: "the completeness of the legislative authority of Parliament *over this kingdom* is not questioned; and yet many things indubitably included in the abstract idea of that power, and which carry no absolute injustice in themselves, yet being contrary to the opinions and feelings of the people, can as little be exercised as if Parliament in that case had been possessed of no right at all."[9] It is a common mistake, according to Burke, to take the form for the reality. Radicals, for example, believe that the arbitrary imposition of republican forms will automatically improve the quality of their government. Indeed, even French aristocrats and government bureaucrats were deceived into believing that the pre-revolutionary weaknesses of their society could be cured by a mere change of forms.[10] And the conservative defenders of the Irish Protestant Ascendency are just as bad: "they must be singularly unfortunate who think to govern by dinners and bows, and who mistake the oil which facilitates the motion for the machine itself."[11] Burke was far more interested in the principles which the forms embodied and whether those principles were actually observed. The essential issue is not how government looks but what it does.

Nonetheless, Burke was adamant that a regular constitution was a necessary feature of all good government. Like David Hume, he saw government as a struggle between liberty and authority and felt that the primary virtue of a constitution was that it regulated that struggle through the rule of law. In explaining the guiding principle of his work on economical reform, Burke said, "government is made for the very purpose of opposing that reason to will and to caprice, in the reformers or in the reformed, in the governors or in the governed, in kings, in senates, or in people."[12] Burke's concern for the rule of law is at the center of his well-known distinction between natural liberty, which is the rule of appetite, and social liberty, which is regulated and therefore guaranteed liberty. As he told Depont, "the Liberty I mean is *social* freedom. It is that state of things in which Liberty is secured by the equality of Restraint; A Constitution of things in which the liberty of no one Man, and no body of Men and no Number of men can find Means to trespass on the liberty of any Person or any description of persons in the Society."[13] Burke's greatest expressions on the importance of the rule of law come, of course, from his writings on the French Revolution, as when, in the same letter, he promised Depont to sing the praises of the French Republic when "this real *practical* Liberty, with a Government powerful to Protect, impotent to invade it, be establish'd."[14] Still, the theme runs through all his works. It can be found in the defense of Wilkes in the 1760s, in his opposition to the Gordon rioters in the 1780s, when he hoped that Parliament would not entertain "the Idea of reviving departed penalties on Roman Catholicks to reward the rebellion and other atrocious Crimes of their adversaries," in his defense of lenient treatment for those same rioters, and in his writings on Ireland in the 1790s.[15] Even at the height of his campaign against France, he denounced a scheme by Pitt to advance money to the Emperor without the consent of Parliament, calling it legal and necessary but also unconstitutional: "that is, against the spirit, use, and fundamental duties of the House of Commons," and urged French Laurence to support the principle of the grant while opposing the mode of making it.[16]

In Burke's view, the primary value of modern constitutional government is that it provides a measure of stability in human affairs. On one side, it offers some area of liberty for all members of society. Burke painted the picture both positively and negatively. Ireland, for example, he believed showed what life would be like without just and restrained government: "Except in cases of direct War, when government abandons Law, it proclaims Anarchy."[17] Granted, he said, those who criticize such misgovernment will be called seditious, but that is of small moment when compared to the alternative of acquiescing in the scandal. It is generally best to support government, Burke agreed, "but whenever a hostile spirit on the part of Government is shewn the Question assumes another form.—This is no casual Errour, no lapse, no sudden surprise. Nor [is] it a question of civil or political Liberty. What contemptible stuff it is to say, that a Man who is lashed to Church against his conscience would not discover that the whip is painful, or that He had a conscience to be violated, unless I told him so."[18] On the positive side, Burke spoke of free societies in the most glowing terms. As he wrote to the Stewards of the Bell Club in Bristol: "In a free Country, every man thinks he has a concern in all public matters; that he has a right to form, and a right to deliver an opinion upon them. They sift, examine, and discuss them. They are curious, eager, attentive, and jealous; and by making such matters the daily subjects of their thoughts and discourses, vast numbers contract a very tolerable knowledge of them; and some a very considerable one. And this it is that fills free Countries with men of ability in all stations . . . In free Countries there is often found more real publick wisdom and sagacity in Shops and manufactories than in the Cabinets of Princes, in Countries, where none dares to have an opinion until he comes into them."[19] In short, though much can be said of Burke's opposition to and critique of natural freedom and claims of abstract rights, none of that should be allowed to blind one to the very high premium he put on an extensive measure of guaranteed liberty within society.

On the other side, constitutionalism preserves a necessary degree of social hierarchy among men. Burke believed that many of our moral duties are involuntary, given to us by our standing in society or by the very nature of things.[20] We enter into a given society, which has an established structure determined long before our birth, and we are obliged to accept the duties inherent in our place in that structure. Burke believed that a man comes into a community with the social status of his parents, and endowed with all the benefits and duties of their place, and "neither he, nor any man, or number of men, have a right . . . to free themselves from that primary engagement . . . The place of every man determines his duties."[21] For example, in one of his defenses of the French monarchy, Burke insisted that monarchy not only best reflected and preserved the natural social order but was also, in turn, sustained by it. Thus, he continued, monarchy need not be arbitrary, for it cannot "enjoy a moment's permanence or security upon any scheme of things which sets aside all the ancient corporate capacities and distinctions of the kingdom, and subverts the whole fabric of its ancient laws and usages, political, civil, and religious . . ."[22] Moreover, if part of the regular order falls, so, typically, does the rest. Burke told Fitzwilliam that his defense of hereditary monarchy during the Regency Crisis was predicated on his loyalty to the aristocracy: "I was convinced to a certainty, that whatever tended to unsettle the succession, and to disturb the recognized ranks and orders, and the fixed properties in the nation would be of all men the most fatal to your friends . . . whether you are considered as politicians; or as private men of weight in your Country."[23] Burke understood that his position could be misconstrued as an apology for aristocratic greed and social elitism, but he was unrepentant, for he believed that the same law which protected great property protected small as well. As Burke saw it, the alternative to a secure social hierarchy was not equality but anarchy.

Yet another consequence of Burke's historically-based approach to government was his hostility toward social contract and revolutionary theory. Burke did not deny that society originated in a social contract; however, he did suggest that time and circumstances have rendered that fact largely devoid of meaning. In the *Appeal,* Burke maintained, "though civil society might be at first a voluntary act, (which in many cases it undoubtedly was,) its continuance is under a permanent standing covenant, coexisting with the society; and it attaches upon every individual of that society, without any formal act of his own."[24] Again, in the *Reflections,* he argued, "at some time or other, to be sure, all the beginners of dynasties were chosen by those who called them to govern . . . But whatever Kings might have been here or elsewhere a thousand years ago, or in whatever manner the ruling dynasties of England or France may have begun, the king of England is, at this day, king by a fixed rule of succession according to the laws of his country."[25] Of much greater importance than abstract theories of contract, however, are two other points. First, Burke considered it vital that we recognize the logic of consent which lies beneath all governments. As he insisted in the *Popery Tract,* "in all forms of government the people is the true legislator; and whether the immediate and instrumental cause of the law be a single person or many, the remote and efficient cause is the consent of the people, either actual or implied; and such consent is absolutely essential to its validity."[26] Thus, if contract theory may be taken as a euphemism for government by consent, then Burke is clearly a contract theorist. Like Hume, he believed that the doctrine contains a profound truth within a shell of nonsense.[27] Second, Burke believed that governments are best judged by how well they perform, not by their origins.[28] Many governments, according to Burke, originated in conquest and settled into legality only over time. He saw no reason to reject such governments if they were now satisfactory. On the other hand, good title does not guarantee good rule. As Burke sarcastically noted in the *Reflections,* "But King James was a bad king with a good title, and not a usurper."[29] Origins count, and so does experience, but, for Burke, in judging governments, what counts most is current performance.

Burke could not ignore that social contract theory is often, perhaps usually, employed to endorse the right of the people to hold government to account, to resist abuses of power, and to justify revolution. As in the question of origins, Burke was ambiguous on the right of revolution. The abstract question is, he said, difficult: "but I am satisfied that no occasion can justify such a resumption, which would not equally authorize a dispensation with any other moral duty, perhaps with all of them together."[30] Burke was a prudent man and recognized that all government was impossible if men would fly to arms at every provocation. In particular, he was incensed by the French radicals' claim that government could be cashiered for "misconduct." In his view, that is far too vague a notion.[31] Burke's reservations about revolution were so strong, in part, because he broke with a major theme of such Whigs as John Locke who saw the dissolution of government as leaving an organized society ready to be given a new state. In Burke's view, the dissolution of government leads to anarchy and the destruction of all society: "when men, therefore, break up the original compact or agreement which gives its corporate form and capacity to a state, they are no longer a people . . . They are a number of vague, loose individuals, and nothing more. With them all is to begin again."[32] Nonetheless, Burke did, as we have seen, defend the Revolution of 1688. He maintained that extreme cases permit the violation of normal rules; that is, that the general rule that revolution is undesirable may be set aside in an emergency, and that the Revolution was such an extreme case.[33] Granted, Burke said, that some alteration of the normal line of succession was accomplished in 1688, but that was preferred by men who "did not wish, in effect, to recall King James or to deluge their country in blood and again to bring their religion, laws, and liberties into the peril they had just escaped . . ."[34] Moreover, it was of great importance to Burke that the Revolution had been as limited as possible. Only the slightest deviation in the royal succession was accompanied by no change in the Constitution. Finally, the Revolution was justified by its consequences. That England had been prosperous and stable since the Revolution, was, for Burke, good reason to maintain a continuity in her political forms.[35]

II

When one turns to Burke's discussion of the British political system, one immediately encounters a problem. Most eighteenth century political thinkers held that the Revolutionary Settlement had created, or rather reinvigorated, a mixed or balanced government.[36] In this consensus view, mixed government preserved the freedom of the subject by balancing elements of monarchy, aristocracy, and democracy against one another. In the mutual strivings for power among the elements of the balance, something close to a compromise acceptable to all three could be achieved, and, in addition, each element would be kept in its appropriate place by the counteraction of the other two. Burke at times accepted the rhetoric of mixed government, as in the *Appeal,* when he explained away a claimed inconsistency in his thought by insisting that one who defends a mixed government must defend each of its elements in its own terms. Thus, he continued: "he ought not to apprehend that his raising fences about popular privileges this day will infer that he ought on the next to concur with those who would pull down the throne; because on the next he defends the throne, it ought not to be supposed that he has abandoned the rights of the people."[37] Yet, when Burke was being most careful to state his position precisely, he took a different line. In a long passage in the *Appeal,* Burke argued that "the circumstances and habits of every country, which it is always perilous and productive of the greatest calamities to force, are to decide upon the form of its government," and those circumstances dictated that England should be a monarchy.[38] As he put it, in England and France, "everything republican which can be introduced with safety into either of them must be built upon a monarchy,—built upon a real, not a nominal monarchy, *as its essential basis;* that all such institutions, whether aristocratic or democratic, must originate from their crown, and in all of their proceedings must refer to it; that by the energy of that mainspring alone those republican parts must be set in action, and from thence must derive their whole legal effect . . ."[39] In short, when Burke was being careful about how he described the structure of English government, he almost always called it a limited monarchy. In his view, "monarchy" described its essential nature, while "limited" distinguished it, as a constitutional system with functioning checks and balances, from such absolutistic systems as France.

For Burke, then, the centerpiece of English government was the Crown. He believed that the king should be actively involved in government and the true head of any administration. In the *Reflections,* Burke explained that the English king "is a real King, and not an executive officer . . . The direct power of the king of England is considerable. His indirect, and far more certain power, is great indeed."[40] As this statement implies, Burke felt that the powers of the king were necessarily imprecise. Like virtually all eighteenth century political thinkers, Burke saw the king as having an important constitutional role as a formal sovereign and as a kind of general overseer of the political process. Burke also saw the king as one of the three necessary elements in all legislation, for law could not be made without his consent. In addition, as the head of the administration, the king was both the font from which all public officials derived their authority and the chief mover in foreign affairs. Moreover, Burke assigned an important function to the king in the selection and direction of the Prime Minister, Cabinet, and administrative personnel of the nation. Finally, Burke differed somewhat from many other Whig theorists, though less so from Whig politicians, in his willingness to grant that the monarch was the primary policy-maker in government and that administrations, including chief ministers, were his agents and responsible to him. In so doing, he understood that the logic of his position committed him to admit that the king was not, in fact, responsible to the will of Parliament or of the people. In the *Reflections,* he responded to Richard Price's claim that the English king was the servant rather than the ruler of his people: "Kings, in one sense, are undoubtedly the servants of the people because their power has no other rational end than that of the general advantage; but it is not true that they are, in the ordinary sense (by our constitution, at least), anything like servants; the essence of whose situation is to obey the commands of some other and to be removable at pleasure."[41] Therefore, Burke continued, making the link explicit, "as he is not to obey us, but as we are to obey the law in him, our constitution has made no sort of provision toward rendering him, as a servant, in any degree responsible."[42] Burke is not here thinking of kings as totally unbound by law; rather, he has in mind the theory of sovereignty, which holds that every state must possess some supreme law-making power which is not subject to any higher authority. In the passage following the one just cited, he goes on to compare the king to parliament: "in this he is not distinguished from the Commons and the Lords, who, in their several public capacities, can never be called to an account for their conduct . . ."[43] Within the sphere of his proper powers, Burke is saying, the king answers to no one. Still, Burke also held that he may not act outside that sphere.

Even in his most strongly oppositionist works, Burke was consistent in his support of limited monarchy.[44] In his "Thoughts on the Present Discontents," Burke claimed that a change had occurred in English politics since the time of the Stuarts and that, while that change had altered the nature of the king's role in government, it had left his power largely intact: "the power of the crown, almost dead and rotten as Prerogative, has grown up anew . . . under the name of influence."[45]. The key to this new system was the authority of the Crown to choose its own ministers and its ability to gain support for those ministers in Parliament. Such authority was neither immoral nor illegal in itself; indeed, Burke admitted, held within its proper limits, it provided energetic and responsible government. Thus, Burke was obliged to justify his frequent opposition to royal policy in particular matters by concluding that the king's authority was often abused, for "the discretionary power of the crown in the formulation of ministry, abused by bad or weak men, has given rise to a system, which, without directly violating the letter of any law operates against the spirit of the whole constitution."[46] What rendered the system unconstitutional in Burke's mind, it should be noted, was not the control of the administration by the Crown but the control of Parliament and the corruption of the people by the administration. To be sure, we are dealing in part with Burke's adoption of the traditional tactic of attributing, for political and constitutional reasons, to the king's ministers actions which were known to be the king's. At times in his private correspondence, Burke held the king directly responsible for misgovernment: "the whole depends on the King. As long as the King thinks proper to keep them [i.e., the ministers], though they will quarrel, they will remain: . . . though the Interest of his Kingdom would have have led him to a change long enough ago, yet the Interest of his System, which is far nearer and dearer to him, will . . . make him defer a change . . ."[47] Yet, the point remains valid. In his formal defenses of his opposition to government policy, Burke's proposed remedy was seldom a reduction in the power or influence of the king over the ministry.

Burke believed the aristocracy, as represented in the House of Lords, to be the second branch of the British constitution. In a general sense, it was, in Burke's mind, the coordinating body of the political system. By sharing naturally in the powers of the other branches, it could tie policy together and provide a measure of continuity and long-term responsibility. More specifically, Burke thought that the aristocracy contributed to politics in four ways. First, it represented the permanent long-standing property of the nation. Burke wrote to the Duke of Richmond, "you people of great families and hereditary trusts and fortunes are not like such as I am . . . we are but annual plants that perish with our season and leave no sort of traces behind us. You, if you are what you ought to be, are the great Oak that shade a country and perpetuate your benefits from generation to generation."[48] Again and again, he returned to the theme that only the aristocracy endured over generations and, therefore, only it could speak for the traditional values of English society. In a letter to William Weddell during the French Revolution, Burke insisted that only an aristocratic party "was attached to the antient [*sic*] tried usages of the Kingdom, a party therefore essentially constructed upon a Ground plot of stability and independence."[49] Secondly, the aristocracy served as a body of royal advisors. Indeed, one of the consistent themes of Burke's opposition to the ministerial policies of the late 1760s was his claim that the king was allowing policy to be usurped by a coterie of closet politicians rather than heeding the counsel of his proper advisors—men like Rockingham and the other Whig lords—who had governed the nation so well in the first half of the century.[50] Along with insuring good government, Burke believed that such deference on the part of the monarch would go a long way toward building support for his policies by incorporating the nation's natural elite into his rule. Third, the aristocracy, through the use of its influence on the electorate, could largely control the composition of the House of Commons. In thanking Lord Fitzwilliam for choosing French Laurence to replace Burke in Parliament, Burke wrote, "I was, and am, clearly and uniformly of opinion, that you never ought to recommend a Member for any place in which you have an influence, who will not take your general Line, both as to persons and things—and mark a decided attachment to yourself . . ."[51] Finally, Burke held the aristocracy responsible for providing much of the local government of the nation.

The question of the composition of the political aristocracy is not, for Burke, a simple one. It begins, of course, with the hereditary nobility and the greater gentry. Burke saw nothing wrong in sons inheriting their father's influence. He told the Duke of Portland: "I certainly never meant to exclude the younger Branches of illustrious families, which your Grace will know I always considered as the permanent substantial parts, the Bones and sinews of every free commonwealth, from popular Trust and favor."[52] However, it is also clear that Burke did not consider every member of a noble familty to be entitled to participate in government. In the same letter to Portland, he continued, "these things are only to be solicited under circumstances of prepossession, and not claimed, as it were, as a matter of right."[53] It appears, then, that MacCunn is correct in suggesting that Burke thought that the proper spokesmen for the aristocracy should come from a smaller group drawn out of the whole on the basis of their ability and experience.[54] To this base in the established hierarchy, Burke would have added a number of men drawn from the other orders of society. Burke suggested two main sources for such additions to the aristocracy: men who had created their own fortunes and professional public servants like himself. He was, Burke said, new to the political class but he strove to "illustrate himself and his family by the services he might have the fortune to render to the publick."[55] Such men, Burke believed, were "bound, with all the activity and energy of Minds, animated and awakened by great hopes and Views, to support those aristocratick principles, and the aristocratick Interests connected with them, as essential to the real Benefit of the Body of the people, to which all names of party, all Ranks and orders in the State, and even Government itself ought to be entirely subordinate."[56] Nor was this the full extent of the aristocratic part of society. Burke distinguished between the formal aristocracy and what he called the "aristocratic interest." While membership in the aristocracy proper should be restricted to men of proper heritage and special ability, Burke would include in the aristocratic interest all those who followed the lead of that class or who believed the success of society to somehow depend on them.

The word "natural" has many meanings, and it is important to distinguish in just what sense, if any, Burke's aristocracy can be called natural if we are to fully understand his position. To be sure, Burke did believe that some people were born with superior intelligence and ability to others and that all societies were composed of unequal ranks. In those terms, then, he held aristocracy to be natural. On the other hand, it was unnatural and conventional in at least two ways. First, aristocracy could be a matter of human contrivance. Just as the French were seeking to destroy it, so could it be created artificially in other contexts. When William Langrishe complained of social disorders in Ireland, Burke replied, "if the disorders you speak of be real and considerable, you ought to raise an aristocratic interest, that is, an interest of property and education, amongst them,—and to strengthen, by every prudent means, the authority and influence of men of that description."[57] Second, whatever the factors which create it or the inevitability of its existence, Burke felt that much of the value of an aristocracy was a result of its social and cultural advantages. One might well note that the characteristics he mentioned in the letter to Langrishe cited above, property and education, are matters of human invention. Both are established by social conventions and maintained by political institutions. When one turns to Burke's famous description of aristocracy in the *Appeal from the New to the Old Whigs,* it is obvious that "natural" aristocrats are, to a large degree, made not born: "to be bred in a place of estimation; . . . to be taught to respect one's self; to be habituated to the censorial inspection of the public eye; to look early to public opinion; . . . to have leisure to read, to reflect, to converse; to be enabled to draw the court and attention of the wise and learned, . . . to be habituated in armies to command and to obey; to be taught to despise danger in the pursuit of honor and duty; to be formed to the greatest degree of vigilance, foresight, and circumspection . . . to be led to a guarded and regulated conduct, . . . to be employed as an administrator of law and justice, . . . to be a professor of high science, or of liberal and ingenuous art; to be amongst rich traders . . . and to possess the virtues of diligence, order, constancy, and regularity, and to have cultivated an habitual regard to communetative justice: these are the circumstances of men that form what I should call a *natural* aristocracy, without which there is no nation."[58] While nature may provide the raw material, it takes education, training, and experience to make an aristocracy a useful social class.

Just as Burke recognized the partly conventional nature of the aristocracy, he also understood the disadvantages of allowing it a too predominant role in the state. There is no reason to doubt the essential truth of Burke's assertion in Parliament, though it is something of an overstatement, that "I hold their order in cold and decent respect. I hold them to be of an absolute necessity in the Constitution; but I think they are only good when kept within their proper bounds."[59] Burke believed that chief among the faults of many aristocrats was their inability to pursue a consistent plan of action. His correspondence is sprinkled with comments like this one: "as to any plan of Conduct in our Leaders there are not the faintest traces of it—nor does it seem to occur to them that any such thing is necessary. Accordingly every thing is left to accidents; . . ."[60] Furthermore, he suggested that when they did form a plan, it was all too often foolish or crazy. In a letter written during the French Revolution, Burke complained to Mrs. Crewe, "the world seems to me to reel and stagger. The Crimes of Democracy, and the madness and folly of Aristocracy alike frighten and confound me."[61] To make matters worse, the folly was frequently combined with arrogance. When the Duke of Bedford attacked Burke in the House of Lords, Burke made no concession to Bedford's nobility in his reply: "my merits, whatever they are, are original and personal: his are derivative"—they originated in Henry VIII's disspoilation of the Church and his funnelling of its wealth to his cronies—"the lion, having sucked the blood of his prey, threw the offal carcass to the jackal in waiting."[62] The virtues of the aristocracy are, then, limited and comparative. They are, nonetheless, very real. As Burke explained to Richmond, "comparing our proceedings with any abstract standard, we have been very faulty and imperfect; but if you try yourselves by comparison with any other existing body of men, I believe you will find a more decent regular consistent, and prudent series of proceedings among yourselves than among any of them or all of those put together."[63] Moreover, the faults of the aristocracy are the other side of their virtues. Their laziness and lack of enterprise follow from their "honest disinterested intentions, plentiful fortunes, assured rank, and quiet homes."[64] Thus, to eliminate the faults, one would have to destroy the virtues as well.

The Commons, and its representatives in The House of Commons, was, for Burke, a distinctly junior partner in British government. Burke was not a democrat; he did not think that the House of Commons existed to enact the people's will. Rather, he believed that the proper role of the Commons was to control the other branches of government in the people's interest by serving as a check on misgovernment. As Burke put it, the British Constitution "is formed, in a great measure, upon the principle of jealousy of the crown, . . . I go farther: it must keep alive some part of that fire of jealously eternally and chastely burning, or it cannot be the British Constitution."[65] Originally, according to Burke's interpretation of history, the Commons was not part of the Constitution. Over time the need for some link between the people and their government became obvious, and the House was created to fill that need: "it was hoped that, being of a middle nature between subject and government, they would feel with a more tender and a nearer interest everything that concerned the people than the other remoter and more permanent parts of legislature."[66] Generally speaking, Burke held that there were two ways in which the Commons could influence government: on the one hand, it could refuse its consent to legislation, thus, in effect, exercising a veto power.[67] On the other hand, it could insure that the conduct of administration was in the hands of a ministry acceptable to the people. For the House to play its role properly, it had to be independent of the Crown. Burke described the ideal Commons to a colleague in 1784, "an independent house of Commons; a house of Commons like the last, equally an Enemy to indefinite prerogative, and to wild unprincipled Liberty; an house of Commons fitted and disposed to support, the only plan of Government that deserves to be supported . . . a scheme of method and reason, and not of fancy and Caprice."[68] In addition, the Commons ought, in Burke's opinion, to be close to the people: "the virtue, spirit, and essence of a House of Commons consists in its being the express image of the feelings of the nation. It was not instituted to be a control *upon* the people, as of late it has been taught, by a doctrine of the most pernicious tendency. It was designed as a control *for* the people."[69] Burke always maintained that the Commons should, indeed, act in the interests of the people, rather than in behest of their fleeting will, and that it should not be subject to the passing whims of mere numbers. Nonetheless, he insisted that it is the people's institution and must never forget where its primary loyalty lies.

As Burke rejected a democratic interpretation of the House of Commons, he also denied a localistic or special interest interpretation of its role. He argued in one of his speeches at Bristol that, "Parliament is not a *congress* of ambassadors from different and hostile interests, which interests each must maintain, as an agent and advocate, against other agents and advocates; but Parliament is a *deliberate* assembly of *one* nation, with *one* interest, that of the whole—where not local purposes, not local prejudices, ought to guide, but the general good, resulting from the general reason of the whole."[70] Burke also accepted as a logical extension of his principle that, "if the local constituent should have an interest or should form a hasty opinion evidently opposed to the real good of the rest of the community, the member for that place ought to be as far as any other from any endeavor to give it effect."[71] Naturally, such views, when applied to the real world of politics, led Burke into conflict with his electors. As he wrote to Champion, "they judge of him solely by his merits as their special Agent . . . . [But as] almost all small services . . . depend so much on the pleasure of the Crown . . . the Members are . . . driven headlong into dependence, by those, whom the constitution and . . . the very nature of things had contrived to keep them independent of a Court influence."[72] In Burke's view, the House of Commons was to look after the interests of the Commons of England as a whole, and its members need not be, in fact should not be, tied too closely to any given district or interest group.

Burke argued that the major threat to the House of Commons performing its proper function was that it might become corrupted by the executive. Every age, he maintained, has its own particular form of corruption; that of his own was not royal absolutism exercised independently of Parliament, but rather the manipulation of Parliament by the crown and its ministries. Thus, he argued, "the control of Parliament upon the executory power is lost; because Parliament is made to partake in every considerable act of government."[73] Burke recognized that the executive had formidable means at hand to gain its ends. For example, it had large sums of money with which representatives could be seduced: "independence of mind will ever be more or less influenced by independence of fortune."[74] Nonetheless, if the executive should gain control of the Commons, the consequences would be severe. In Burke's view, the effective control of the people over government would be lost. Elections would become meaningless. Administration candidates would rarely lose, opposition victories would be set aside by the House itself, and victorious candidates would be bought off after the contests were over. This, Burke felt, was what gave the attempt of the House of Commons to invalidate the election of Wilkes its significance. Such an act, he argued, violated the most basic of all rights: "it is a right, the effect of which is to give to the people that man, and *that man only,* who, by their voices actually, not constructively given, they declare that they know, esteem, love, and trust."[75] If allowed to succeed, such subversion would institute a new form of tyranny: "government might then be carried on without any concurrence on the part of the people; without any attention to the dignity of the greater, or to the affections of the lower sorts."[76]

III

An analysis of Burke's views on the nature of the British constitution would be incomplete without some discussion of his defense of the established church. Such a discussion, however, is perilous indeed, for one must do justice to both sides of Burke's position. On one hand, he was a strong believer in the value of organized religion. For example, in his "Speech on a . . . Petition of the Unitarian Society," he argued, "in a Christian commonwealth the Church and the State are one and the same thing, being different integral parts of the same whole."[77] As such, Burke believed that political morality was necessarily linked to religious belief, and that belief could not, therefore, be left a matter of public indifference. Moreover, he always insisted that a state church could make a major contribution to the advancement of good manners and the civilization of men. Yet, on the other side, Burke was also a proponent of a relatively broad degree of religious toleration. What Burke said of the English reformers of the previous century was true of himself: "they think the dogmas of religion, though in different degrees, are all of moment, and that amongst them there is, as amongst all things of value, a just ground of preference. They favor, therefore, and they tolerate."[78] In discussing Burke's views on establishment, then, it is important to catch the balance in his thought correctly. One must recognize that religion was important to him and that he saw support for organized religion as following from that commitment, but one must also understand that Burke was prepared to see value in religions other than his own and to allow others to worship God in their own way. Thus, I cannot accept J. C. D. Clarke's characterization of Burke as an Anglican political thinker. Clarke maintains that Anglican political thought developed in opposition to the radical ideology of the left-wing Whigs and Dissenters. Its chief themes were an emphasis on the divine origins of political, specifically royal, authority, the importance of the royal prerogative, the nature of England as a church-state, and the necessity of religious unity.[79] Clarke holds that Burke began as a typical Whig, but evolved over time into Anglican-style conservatism.[80] In short, "Burke's achievement in his later works was to give eloquent but unoriginal expression to a theoretical position largely devised by Anglican churchmen."[81] In addition, Clarke does not see Burke as an advocate of broad toleration, for he concludes that Burke favored toleration only for Trinitarian Christians. In this and the next section, I will suggest that Clarke both underestimates Burke's originality and overestimates the importance of religious orthodoxy and unity in his thought. I believe that Burke was a sophisticated student of religion, that he had great respect for religious freedom and diversity, and that he defended an establishment largely because of the social, cultural, and political advantages it offered.

By the late eighteenth century, Whig writers had built a formidable case for a combination of religious establishment with toleration for a broad range of dissenters. The key to the Whig position was the argument that religion is both true and useful. Thus, along with its central contribution to the salvation of souls, they saw an established church as playing an important supplemental role as a device for maintaining social order, an important preserver of culture, an educator of the people, and a softener of manners. However, because most religions, and almost all Christian churches, performed at least some of these functions, the Whigs were prone to permit them all to practice, provided their doing so did not interfere with the maintenance of public order. Within the general framework of Whig thought, three distinct approaches developed. First, as perhaps best exemplified by William Warburton's *Alliance of Church and State,* many Whig writers employed a contract argument.[82] Rejecting the view that the Church is not a visible society,

Warburton saw church and state as "two Societies, made up of one and the same Number of Individuals, with each its distinct Personality and Will; each different from those of the other, and from those of the Individuals . . . each Society . . . hath its own proper Views and Interests . . . it pursues its proper Interests only . . ."[83] However, Warburton continued, the state perceives that the moral teachings of religion support its mission, and the church comes to see the benefit of state protection. Thus, they enter into an agreement in which the state pledges to defend the interests of the church, and the church promises to support, through its teachings, the authority of the state. As the church, lacking in physical power, is the weaker of the parties, it must give up more. The church, therefore, agrees to eschew politics, while the state is allowed a role in governing the church and in choosing its clergy. Warburton saw no difficulty in religious variety. In his opinion, the state merely enters into a contract or establishment with the largest church: "because the larger the Religious society is, where there is an Equality in other Points, the better enabled it will be to answer the Ends of an Alliance."[84] Yet, as all churches have some social value, the state should agree to toleration for the smaller churches on the condition that they accept a Test Act—that is, a law debarring dissenters from political office—to protect the established church from being governed by non-members.[85]

Warburton's emphasis on contractual legalism obscured the role of social utility in his thought; with a second group of writers, men like Paley, Priestly, and Tindal, it was at the forefront of the argument.[86] These writers represent a position which Lesie Stephen has called "theological utilitarianism;" that is, they argued that man naturally seeks his own happiness and that good and bad may be defined in terms of pleasure. However, God has made man so that his happiness is attained through service to the public good. In short, virtue is preferable to vice because God rewards it. As for institutional structures, all three writers agreed on a basically Erastian position. In their view, the state must have supreme secular authority, and any church exists at the pleasure of the state. Moreover, since even Scripture does not specify whether there should be a religious establishment, the state is free to act as it feels best. As Paley put it, "the authority therefore of a church establishment is founded in its utility; . . . the single end we ought to propose by them is, 'the preservation and communication of religious knowledge.' "[87] While the church, then, cannot claim any right to be protected, the theological utilitarians believed that the state would see reason to do so, for society benefits from the useful "scheme of instruction" provided by a church.[88] Further, once established, the church should be given extensive freedom and protected by a test act. Finally, as other churches also contribute to society's well-being, they should be extended toleration. Thus, the ideal situation is "a comprehensive national religion, guarded by a few articles of peace and conformity, together with a legal provision for the clergy of that religion; and with *complete* toleration for all dissenters from the established Church, without any other limitation or exception than what arises from the conjunction of dangerous political dispositions with certain religious tenets."[89] As all of these writers were quick to note, this ideal may be seen to correspond closely to the existing arrangement in England.

The third line of defense of the Whig position on establishment was grounded in historical precedent. During the Bangorian controversy, as part of their attack on Whig predominance in the Church, conservatives like Atterbury argued that the authority of Convocation over the Church was precisely analogous to that of Parliament over the state. In reply, William Wake employed historical evidence to show that the state in general and Parliament in particular had always exercised control over the Church.[90] What was especially effective about Wake's argument was his interpretation of history as an evolutionary process and his examination of evidence in its temporal context. By employing such an approach, Wake was able to demonstrate that Atterbury was confused on the evidence. Conyers Middleton made even more impressive use of history.[91] Middleton, a Church of England cleric, rejected the doctrine of the Bible as a product of literal inspiration, and insisted on treating Scriptures according to the same standards applied to secular historical evidence. As Stephen puts it, Middleton held that, "all that was required was to induce men to look upon the history of Moses as they looked upon the history of Marlborough" and all claims of miracles and prophecies would dissapear.[92] Still, according to the Whig historians, even if the Biblical accounts of miracles is not to be credited, religion has its uses. They fully admitted that society requires order and the maintenance of order requires religion. Thus, they asked: if we must have religion, and an establishment, why not keep the one we have?

Over the course of its development, Burke's own position showed signs of the influence of all three Whig approaches. Thus, Burke's earliest writing on the issue of establishment was an essentially Lockean defense of Irish Catholicism, the "Fragments of a Tract

Relative to the Laws Against Popery in Ireland," written in the mid-1760s but never published.[93] After a survey of the penal laws against Catholics, Burke proceeded to argue that political authority is always derived, either immediately or ultimately, from the consent of the people: "in all forms of government the people is the true legislator; and whether the immediate and instrumental cause of the law be a single person or many, the remote and efficient cause is the consent of the people, either actual or implied; and such consent is absolutely essential to its validity.[94] Surely, then, Burke continued, no one can seriously claim that the Irish Catholics, who compose about two-thirds of the total population of the country, would agree to laws which exclude them from all the rights of citizenship. To this rather uncharacteristic argument based on consent, Burke next added another novelty—a natural law argument. He contended that, even if the Irish would agree to such an absurd set of acts, natural law would render those laws void, for it specifies that no community may consent to any law which is prejudicial to its own interests.[95] If, Burke asked, we can prefer the interests of the few to those of the many, why not that of fewer still to them, and so on until we prefer one to all.[96] In regard to religious establishments in particular, the key to Burke's argument is his refusal to treat religion as any kind of a special case. By not specifying otherwise, indeed by not even mentioning the matter, he upheld the same principles of majority-rule and consent there as apply in the rest of the tract. In the remainder of the "Tract," Burke made two additional points. Since Catholicism is the traditionally established religion of Ireland, Burke believed that the Irish Catholics were punished "for acting upon a principle which of all others is perhaps the most necessary for preserving society."[97] Further, persecution simply does not work. As Burke ironically noted, after one hundred years of oppression, Ireland was more full of Catholics than ever.[98] However, the reader is left without a solution, for the work ends abruptly at this point. Aside from the fairly obvious implication that the penal laws ought to be repealed, Burke does not indicate what is to be done to reconcile Ireland's religious antagonisms.

To one familiar with Burke's later works, the "Tract" appears rather strange; especially in its almost deductive use of the contract and natural law arguments, it seems a long way from the historical and prudential cast of his more mature writings. Indeed, within a few years, we find him abandoning its analytical and Lockean format for other forms of argument in favor of the same conclusions. I believe that this is because he came to feel that contractualism led to certain undesirable consequences. To be sure, the argument form had its strengths: Burke accepted the principle of a religious establishment based on consent rather than some arbitrary conception of religious truth, and he always believed that the religious beliefs of non-majority groups should be tolerated and respected. Nor would it bother him that different creeds would be established in different places. Some thirty years later, he would write to William Smith, "my humble, but decided opinion is, that all the three religions, prevalent more or less in various parts of these Islands, ought all, in subordination to the legal establishments, as they stand in the various countries, be all countenanced, protected, and cherished."[99] As for the claim that the direct application of his argument to Ireland would benefit Catholicism at the expense of the Church of Ireland, Burke had a reply: "if on Account of such Sentiments, people call me a Roman Catholick, it will give me not the smallest degree of disturbance. They do me too much honour, who aggregate me as a Member of any one of those respectable Societies which compose the body of Christianity."[100]

In my view, what would give Burke second thoughts about his use of contract theory is its more directly political ramifications. In the "Appeal From the New Whigs to the Old" Burke offered his most extensive critique of contract theory. He argued that political authority does indeed rest on a kind of consent or contract but that, once that contract is established, it may not be altered by anything less than universal agreement. Such an act would imply the destruction of the society and the creation of a new one: "the Constitution of a country being once settled upon some compact, tacit or expressed, there is no power existing of force to alter it, without the breach of the covenant, or the consent of all the parties."[101] Even the vote of a majority cannot transcend the right of each person to incorporate himself into a society of his own choosing. As Burke put it, "the number engaged in crimes, instead of turning them into laudable acts, only augments the quantity and intensity of the guilt."[102] Burke here has broken with Locke. Where Locke separated the process of creating a state into two steps, a social contract followed by a political one, Burke has telescoped the process into a single stage. Thus, in his view, the abrogation of the political contract returns a people to anarchy and not to some pre-political, but still social, state.[103] From a pre-social state, the only path to majority-rule is through, first, an agreement to create a society and then a second agreement, also by unanimous consent, to be ruled by the majority. Majority-rule, then, is not the natural form of government, but can exist legitimately only where it has been directly agreed to.

Whatever the reasons, Burke's mature writings reflect a movement away from contractualism toward an eclectic mix of religious, historical, and socially utilitarian arguments for an established church. Even in so polemical a work as the *Reflections on the Revolution in France,* Burke's argument is subtle and nuanced rather than abstract and dogmatic. Let us, then, turn to the *Reflections* for what is probably the fullest statement in all of Burke's work.[104] The arguments offered there can be grouped into five categories. First, Burke suggests that the establishment of religion allows a people to recognize God in their corporate capacity. They may thus perform their national homage to the institutor and author and protector of civil society.[105] Second, Burke holds that an established church preserves a sense of continuity in society, for it reminds "the temporary possessors and life-renters . . . (that they) . . . should not think it among their rights to cut off the entail or commit waste on the inheritance by destroying at their pleasure the whole original fabric of their society, hazarding to leave to those who come after them a ruin instead of a habitation."[106] Third, especially in a political system in which the people exercise considerable power, an established church will "consecrate the commonwealth" by elevating the people's eyes from the concerns of the moment to those of higher purpose and dignity. The people, Burke says, "should not be suffered to imagine that their will, any more than that of Kings, is the standard of right and wrong."[107] Properly informed, the people will not appoint to office as if their were appointing to a position of self enrichment but as though they are filling a sacred function. Fourth, an established church both benefits and controls education, which is even now almost totally in the hands of the clergy. Finally, by providing the means necessary for doing their job out of public funds, an establishment frees the clergy from control by great patrons or narrow-minded politicians. As Burke put it, the English "tremble for their liberty, from the influence of a clergy dependent on the crown; they tremble for the public tranquility from the disorders of a factious clergy, if it were made to depend upon any other than the crown."[108]

As Burke made clear, his developed theory rests on an application of his doctrine of prescription to church affairs. He asked in the *Reflections,* "if by great permanent establishments all these objects of expense are better secured from the inconstant sport of personal caprice and personal extravagance are they worse than if the same tastes prevailed in scattered individuals."[109] The same theme runs through and unifies all of Burke's later writings on the value of church establishments. For example, in the "Speech on the Acts of Uniformity," Burke defended the established church, not on the grounds of absolute truth, but as an institution which had done good service over a long period of time.[110] Of the various writers on church-state relations we surveyed earlier, this brings Burke closest to the utilitarianism of Paley and his school and the historicism of Middleton. Yet, Burke's view seems deeper and more profound than either. This, I think, is due to his eclecticism. Of the mid-eighteenth century currents of establishment thought, only contractualism is missing from Burke's synthesis. By combining historical and social-utilitarian themes with an emphasis on the fundamentally spiritual nature of religion, Burke is able to ennoble the concept of establishment without losing sight of the need for religion to have worldly consequences.

IV

The second pillar of Burke's position on the political aspects of religion was his advocacy of religious toleration. As in the case of his discussion of governmental institutions, this was, in part, a response to what Burke perceived as the course of historical development. As he put it, "in proportion as mankind has become more enlightened, the idea of religious persecution, under any circumstances, has been almost universally exploded by all good and thinking men."[111] Writing to James Boswell during the anti-Catholic agitation in 1779, Burke deplored violence against Catholics, saying, "a religious war was not exactly the thing I expected in my time . . . the American rebellion is more to my Taste than that which you are cooking in the North. I think it behooves as well to resist an act of Taxation as an act of Toleration; and it would hurt me rather more to have the Excise in my own house, than the Mass in my Neighbours."[112] As far as Burke was concerned, wars of religion ought to be a thing of the past; all religions—especially all Christian religions—did too much good for one to quarrel with another. The different branches of Christianity should be seen, "rather as divisions, made for convenience and order, than Seperations [*sic*], from a diversity of Nature, or from irreconcilable contradiction in principle."[113] Moreover, unlike many religious liberals, Burke had no desire to stop with toleration among Christians. After expressing his support for the established Church in a letter to William Burgh, Burke continued, "I would give a full civil protection, in which I include an immunity, from all disturbance of their public religious worship, and a power of teaching in schools, as well as Temples, to Jews, Mahometans and even Pagans."[114] Indeed, on other occasions, he extended the same freedom to believers in purely rational or natural religion.[115]

To his argument from historical evolution, Burke joined one from principle. In the "Popery Tract," he asserted that all persecution is wrong, even that which is most plausible, the persecution of new and very small groups and he stuck to that position throughout his life.[116] Burke's reasons for supporting toleration were twofold. On the one hand, as we have seen, he felt great respect for all religions and was unwilling to see them as anything but equally acceptable alternative ways to worship God. On the other hand, Burke insisted on approaching the issue from a political perspective and judging policies according to their political consequences. As he wrote to an unknown correspondent: "I would turn my mind to what is more within its competence and has been more my study . . . I mean the moral, civil, and political good of the Countries we belong to."[117] Viewed from that perspective, Burke believed, two considerations stood out. First, when we enact laws against certain beliefs, we divide our community unnecessarily. As he said in the famous letter to Sir Hercules Langrishe, the penal laws in Ireland have "divided the nation into two distinct bodies, without common interest, sympathy or connection."[118] No wonder, then, that Irish Catholics do not support the Constitution: "until we give them some share in it, I do not know on what pretence we can examine into their opinions about a business in which they have no interest or concern."[119] Second, there is the issue of consistency. As a believer in political freedom, Burke noted, "I should think myself, irrational and inconsistent (to say no worse) if I refused to apply my Ideas of Civil to religious Liberty."[120] In rejecting the application of the theory of virtual representation to the situation of the Irish Catholics, Burke pointed out that inclusion into the community is the fundamental basis of all other rights.[121] Therefore, to deny that membership must also threaten those rights as well.

Burke's argument for toleration is dependent on an unstated assumption that religious dissent does not necessarily lead to political disloyalty. However, he also insisted that, when dangerous political consequences followed from some religious belief or practice, toleration should not be extended. The beliefs Burke denied toleration fall into two classes. First, Burke attacked "atheism," by which he apparently meant both atheism proper and some forms of Deism. Citing John Leland's ponderous tomes for support, Burke lashed out: "these are the wicked Dissenters you ought to fear; these are the people against whom you ought to aim the shaft of the law."[122] Unfortunately, he was not quite clear on why atheists should be disciplined. Burke understood that morality and religion could be separated, and he elsewhere urged that disbelievers and advocates of natural religion be left unmolested. It would seem that, over time, Burke came increasingly to think that attacks on religion—given its central importance to society—were also attacks on the very foundations of human existence and thus should be forbidden. Second, as a disciple of John Locke, Burke would permit state action when "the person dissenting does not dissent from the scruples of ill-informed conscience, but from a party ground of dissension, in order to raise a faction in the state."[123] For example, Burke would have no sympathy for one whose religious scruples led him to deny the validity of a constitutional monarch's crown and therefore into rebellion against the existing political system. Clearly, the judgment of likely political consequences of various religious beliefs is a difficult matter. It is perhaps the best indication of Burke's relative liberalism on the issue, that he saw so few exceptions to the principle of toleration.

In Burke's time, the two most important groups which were commonly cited as exceptions to toleration were the Catholics and the Protestant Dissenters. As for the Catholics, Burke was both clear and consistent throughout his career. He believed that Catholics, in England and in Ireland—where the problem was more serious but otherwise essentially similar—should be extended full political rights and have the freedom to publicly practice their religion. Burke wrote to John Curry that he regulated his conduct by an abhorrence "of all kinds of public injustice and oppression, the worst species of which are those which being converted into maxims of state, and blending themselves with law and jurisprudence corrupt the very foundations of all equity, and subvert all the purposes of Government."[124] In Ireland, the consequence of such policy was, in his view, to corrupt *both* classes: "the protestants are generally corrupt and Jobbish; as people long possessd (sic) of a monopoly are apt to be. The Catholicks are uncorrupted, at least as yet; but they are light, frivolous, and inconsistent . . . No great reliance is to be had on the friendship or the Enmity of either."[125] Yet, as evil as the law itself was, the attitudes of the dominant group and of its spokesmen were even worse. Indeed, "nothing is more discouraging to the loyalty of any description of men than to represent to them, that their humiliation and subjection make a principal part in the fundamental and invariable policy which regards the conjunction of these two Kingdoms.[126] If, on the other hand, the Catholics could be fully assimilated, England would be made "what we ought always to have been, one family, one body, one heart and soul, against the family-combination, and all other combinations of our enemies."[127]

Burke understood that if men like John Locke and his disciples, who were otherwise so tolerant, supported restrictions on Catholic political rights, then the problem was indeed serious, and more than statements about the nobility of inclusion was needed. Therefore, he also sought to reply to the arguments advanced against Catholic rights; that is, to the claims that Catholics were inherently disloyal. Burke began by constantly insisting that Catholics in both England and Ireland were, in fact, among the most reliable of subjects. In the 1770s, he contrasted the obedience of Ireland to the radicalness of America; in the 1780s, he compared the peacefulness of the English Catholics to the violence of the Gordon rioters; and, in the 1790s he matched the loyalty of the Irish Catholics to the pro-French sympathies of the Dissenters. As Burke saw it, the goals of the Catholics were perfectly in keeping with English traditions; all they wanted was a share in the constitution, and their methods—petition and supplication—were open and mild.[128] Moreover, even if they obtained their goals, their political power would not be great.[129] To those who feared the power of the Catholic clergy or that English and Irish Catholics would respond to attempts at political leadership by the Pope, Burke scoffed: "I believe there is no Penitent in Ireland who would not laugh his Priest to scorn, if sitting in the Confession Box, instead of interrogating him on the seven deadly sins, he was to say a word to him on this topic of the Election, or any other political topic whatsoever."[130] Why, then, the concern? Burke thought it a combination of bigotry and politics. As he said of Ireland, "these miserable Creatures, the Zealots of the ascendency, have been fed with this stuff as their Nurse's pap, and it is never to be got out of their habit."[131] On the political side, the exclusion of the Catholics profited their opponents: "wherever such Factions, predominate in such a manner, that they come to link . . . a pecuniary and personal Interest with the licentiousness of a party domination, nothing can secure those that are under it.[132] Finally, in both England and Ireland, but especially in Ireland, the bigotry of some and the interest of others was supported by the indifference of most. To some extent, Burke argued, the exclusion of Catholics continued simply because it was part of the existing system.

Burke's relationship with the Protestant Dissenters was somewhat more complex. Here Burke's enthusiasm for toleration came to be somewhat mitigated by the changing role of the Dissenters in eighteenth century English politics. Until late into the century, the Dissenters generally were content to follow the lead of the Whigs in most political matters, and in the specific area of church-state relations were willing to settle for toleration within the existing system. On this basis, Burke accepted the Dissenters as junior collegues in the reform coalition and consistently defended their interests. For instance, on the occasion of a petition by Methodists for relief, Burke defended establishment but argued that "I know nothing but the supposed necessity of persecution that can make an establishment disgusting. I would have toleration a part of establishment, as a principle favorable to Christianity, and as a part of Christianity."[133] He then proceeded to urge the repeal of the offending regulations even though they were rarely enforced: "a penal law not ordinarily put in execution seems to me to be a very absurd and a very dangerous thing . . . liberty under a connivance! Connivence is a relaxation from slavery, not a definition of liberty."[134] Even in rejecting, in his "Speech on the Acts of Uniformity," a request to substitute adherence to Scriptures instead of to the 39 Articles as a test for state support, Burke was careful to affirm his belief in toleration: "the matter, therefore, does not concern toleration, but establishment; and it is not the rights of private conscience that are in question, but the propriety of . . . a title to public emoluments . . ."[135] If the state is to establish a church, it must have the right to define what that church is to be, and this, to Burke's mind, is a different and quite separate issue from that of whether the state is to tolerate other churches as well.

However, increasingly in the second half of the century, the Dissenters began to reject the leadership of the old-line Whigs and to become more radical in their politics. Consequently, Burke's support for their cause lessened. Still, even here, he continued to advocate toleration as a rule, and to insist that the exception to that rule he began to make in regard to the Dissenters was solely a response to their mingling of politics with their religion. Thus, in July 1791, one finds him berating the Dissenters for their support of the French Revolution abroad and for their radical activity at home. Moreover, Burke abandoned the distinction he had previously been making between the machinations of the Dissenter leaders and the loyalty of the great majority of their rank and file by referring to "the Phalanx of Party which exists in the body of the dissenters, who are, at the very least, nine tenths of them entirely devoted . . . to the principles of the French Revolution."[136] Burke was even inclined to read the new Dissenter militancy into Fox's apostacy from the true Whig faith. Fox, he concluded, was forced into his support for the French radicals by the Dissenters, for "they knew Mr. Fox better than I did. The several shots they fired, to bring him to, produced their effect."[137] Thus, one should not be surprised by the almost unrelieved hostility of Burke's speech on the petition of the Unitarian Society.[138] He opened by insisting on the right of the state to act in matters of religion: "as religion is one of the bonds of society, he [the magistrate] ought not to suffer it to be made the pretext of destroying its peace, order, liberty, and its security."[139] And that, Burke claimed, is precisely the goal of the Unitarians, for, "this faction are not confined to a *theological* sect, but are also a *political* faction," and, "their designs they declare to be to destroy the Established Church . . . If they should find the State stick to the Church, the question is, whether they love the constitution in *State* so well as that they would not destroy . . . [it] . . . to destroy that of the Church. Most certainly they do not."[140] In short, before Burke would even consider the Unitarians' petition, he would have them disband and act as individuals content to enjoy their rights in peace.[141]

5

BURKE ON THE NATURE AND EXTENT OF STATE AUTHORITY

The widespread preoccupation of eighteenth century political writers with constitutional forms has misled scholars into failing to give a number of other matters the consideration they deserve.[1] One of these is the question of the nature and scope of state authority. Only within the last fifty years have scholars turned their attention to what eighteenth century English government actually did, and to the rationales or principles which were used to explain and justify its programs. Against an older view that governments of that time were largely paternalistic or mercantilistic, Sir Lewis Namier held that politics in Burke's day was best understood as a struggle for place, privilege, and reward conducted within a narrow political and institutional framework. As he saw it, politicians had little serious regard for issues, and employed ideas only as weapons against their enemies and screens for their own venality.[2] Namier's position soon came to constitute a new orthodoxy. Thus, in a recent text, Ian Christie writes, "government in the late eighteenth century dealt with only a very restricted range of activity: the administration of the revenue, diplomacy and defense, law and order, and the regulation of foreign trade. The machinery required was small, and the conduct of affairs was in the hands of a handful of ministers presiding over a group of departmental offices which were miniscule compared with the government establishments of the twentieth century."[3] As scholars reconsidered the role of eighteenth century government, so did they also review the administrative theory of the time. Increasingly, the absence of strong government came to be attributed to a combination of an awareness of the inherent limitations on and weakness of governmental structures, a lack of confidence in the possibility of meaningful social reform, and a rising tide of liberal laissez-faire economic theory.

The issue of the role of government is a vital concern for students of Burke's political thought. If Burke actually meant government to serve as a device for processing demand and carrying out reform, he should also have recognized that it required ample and broad authority to act, the power to accomplish its purposes, and freedom from excessive structural and ideological barriers. Burkean scholarship, however, has largely denied that he believed government to have such capacity. At first, the generally accepted interpretation of Burke as a conservative suggested that, though he saw government as paternalistic in many respects, he was opposed to any extensive program of governmental action. Alfred Cobban, for example, argued that Burke anticipated the major elements of the romantic critique of the political and economic thought of the Enlightenment, and thus shared its rejection of the latter's emphasis on progressive reform.[4] Following the lead of such economic historians and students of the history of political and social thought as W. L. Dunnes, Fredrich Hayek, Joseph Cropsey, and Donal Barrington, the conservative paternalist view of Burke came under attack just after World War II.[5] Some scholars noted that Burke maintained close relations with Adam Smith, that Smith was the father of political economy and an advocate of laissez-faire, and, therefore, inferred that Burke must have shared Smith's ideological positions on economic issues. Concurrently, Peter Stanlis and his disciples claimed that, as a natural law thinker, Burke believed that the laws of nature maintained the right to property and the necessity of free competitive markets.[6] On this basis, they held that Burke was a staunch opponent of all forms of state intervention in society, especially in the economy, whether those advocated by the French Revolutionaries in his own day or by Marxists in ours. Ironically, neither of these lines of interpretation challenged the claim that Burke preferred a relatively inactive government. Instead, in the words of one writer, the new orthodoxy on Burke was that: "most scholars have identified his economic theory as similar or identical with that of Adam Smith in *Wealth of Nations,* a free market, laissez-faire system of free trade and natural liberty in economic enterprise, a world removed from modern socialist and Marxist collectivist systems."[7] For these writers, only the form of Burke's argument required reassessment; his conclusions, they insisted, remained the same.

The case for Burke as a disciple of political economy has recently taken on increased sophistication. For example, Gertrude Himmelfarb has sought to clarify the relationship between Burke and Adam Smith.[8] She sees Smith as the founder of a new school of thought: "what Smith did—and this was his historic achievement—was to convert a minor heresy into a new and powerful orthodoxy."[9] According to Himmelfarb, in Smith's own formulation this new theory had mostly positive connotations, for it stressed the gradual improvement of society, recognized that the good of society must also be the good of the poor who formed its major part, and endorsed a number of important forms of public measures to aid the unfortunate. However, according to Himmelfarb, Smith's disciples turned his generous theory into a weapon to be used against the poor. Among these, she maintains, very nearly the worst was Edmund Burke.[10] Himmelfarb holds that in his "Thoughts and Details on Scarcity," Burke, though generally supporting Smith, made two crucial innovations. First, he proposed that labor be treated as a commodity to be bought or sold on the same basis as all other commodities. Labor was, therefore, not a fit subject for government regulation, but must be governed only by the marketplace. Indeed, even in those circumstances where the poor could not sell their labor for a living wage, they had no right to public support. Rather, they were a matter for charity instead. Second, Himmelfarb claims that, to reinforce his denial of a government interest in combating poverty, Burke made a sharp distinction between the "laboring people" and the "poor." In his view, she says, the poor were defined as only those who could not work under any conditions, and only they deserved even charity. Those who merely would not work, in Burke's system of classification the laboring people (no matter how poor in the conventional sense of the term), deserved no help whatsoever—not even the uncertain one of charity. In sum, Himmelfarb holds that Burke's form of laissez-faire was much more extreme than Smith's, and was, moreover, the primary source for the still harsher ideas of men like Malthus and the Poor Law reformers.

If Himmelfarb is right, a gap would seem to open up between Burke's social conservatism and his radical economics. A number of writers, C. B. Macpherson and Isaac Kramnick most prominent among them, have sought to close that gap. In his book on Burke, Macpherson tells us, his goal is to solve "the question of the coherence of his two seemingly opposite positions: the defender of a hierarchical establishment, and the market liberal."[11] According to Macpherson, Burke sought to achieve consistency by pouring the new wine of capitalism into the old bottle of natural law. He agrees with Stanlis that Burke ascribed to the view that the universe is bound together by a harmonious law much like that of the medieval

Christian natural law thinkers. However, Macpherson continues, "to rest the explanation there is to overlook the fact that Burke had put a quite different content into his natural law. It is a social and economic content, which can only have been derived from his reading of his own contemporary society."[12] Burke's genius, in Macpherson's interpretation, was to see that the emerging market society, with its advocacy of free trade abroad and laissez-faire capitalism at home, required both the same kind of internal order as traditional society and an ideological defense of that order. Thus, "Burke needed the natural and divine law because he had to show not only that the capitalist order was just but also that it was naturally acceptable to the working-class. The whole structure of society, Burke insisted, depended on their submissiveness."[13] In Macpherson's view, Burke could be both a defender of hierarchy and of capitalism because he recognized the extent to which capitalism had inserted itself into the traditional social order. Kramnick's contribution to the argument is to modify slightly Macpherson's view of the eighteenth century.[14] Kramnick, noting Burke's expressed defense of aristocratic government, argues that Burke's intention was to reconcile the two branches of the eighteenth century aristocracy, the capitalists and the traditional landed groups, by showing them that their interests were identical. J. G. A. Pocock has extended this part of the thesis even further, arguing that Burke's attack on the French Revolution was part and parcel of his defense of the new Whig and commercial order. In Pocock's opinion, it was not the traditional aristocratic order for which Burke cared, for that order had passed; rather, he sought to preserve commercial civilization against an alliance between radical republicans and manipulators of vaporous public credit.[15]

I believe that all of these explanations fail to adequately account for Burke's positions on a number of policy issues. In this chapter, I will argue that Burke is, in fact, best seen as a moderate in the debate about mercantilism and free trade. I believe that Burke's political and economic thought forms one consistent whole: a whole best explained by his well-known allegiance to the Rockingham Whigs' program of limited and carefully controlled reform. Consistent with the general Rockingham outlook, Burke usually favored free trade and a free economy, but he did so as a matter of utilitarian policy choice rather than abstract principle. When Burke saw an opportunity for useful reform, he did not permit abstract considerations about the teachings of some new economic science to deter him. Moreover, I will argue that, as Burke's well-documented relationship with Smith suggests, his Whig understanding of economic issues was supplemented by the ideas of the Scotch Enlightenment. What the Whig approach lacked was a sense of the goals which utilitarian and prudential rule-making should serve. In my view, Burke found these goals in his reading of the literature on civilization and commerce produced by Smith, Hume, and their associates. They convinced Burke that man has a moral nature which can be developed through association with other men in society, and that social and economic policies should be judged according to how much they contributed to such development. Finally, I will examine Burke's positions on a number of topics—imperial trade, administrative reform, poor relief, and regulation of the slave trade—to show that the theme of prudential reformism runs through his handling of specific issues as well.

I

There can be no doubt that Burke and Adam Smith were close friends or that Burke was familar with and influenced by Smith's writings. In fact, the first record of their acquaintance antedates Burke's entry into politics. Having secured Smith's address from David Hume, Burke wrote to Smith in praise of his *Theory of Moral Sentiments:* "I am not only pleased with the ingenuity of your theory; I am convinced of its solidity and Truth; and I do not know that it ever cost me less trouble to admit so many things to which I had been a stranger before . . . A theory like yours founded on the Nature of Man, which is always the same, will last, when those that are founded on his opinions, which are always changing, will and must be forgotten."[16] From that point on, the relationship continued until Burke's death. They read each other's works, wrote frequently, Smith, for example, congratulated Burke on his appointment as Paymaster General, and visited together. Indeed, when Burke, in the late 1780s sought a respite from the internal conflicts incident on the decline of the Whig party, he went to Scotland, where Smith served as his host in Edinburgh and tour guide at Loch Lomond.

What is open to question is the specific nature of Smith's influence on Burke. However, before turning to a more detailed consideration of that topic, two points should be made clear. First, it must be understood that, no matter what the issue in question, Burke always thought for himself. Moreover, this consideration is even more evident in regard to Burke's economics. In particular, he prided himself on his knowledge of economic theory. For instance, in his "Letter to a Noble Lord," Burke made a clear claim to independence in economic matters: "If I had not deemed it of some value, I should not have made political oeconomy an object of my humble studies, from my very early youth to near the end of my service in parliament . . . Great and learned men thought my studies were not wholly thrown away, and deigned to communicate with me now and then on some particulars of their immortal works."[17] Nor was this all, for Burke also claimed a talent for applied economics. Many years later, he explained his approach to administrative reform: "I proceeded upon principles of research to put me in possession of my matter, on principles of method to regulate it, and on principles in the human mind and in civil affairs to secure and perpetuate the operation."[18] Indeed, Burke was unwilling to be just a theorist; he had also to be politically active. Where the perfect was impossible, he would attempt the possible. Both at the time it was under debate and ever afterward, Burke held that one of the strongest features of his plan for economic reform was its practicality. In short, it would almost certainly be an error to assume that Burke's position on any issue was simply a derivative of Smith's. Second, one should be careful to note exactly what in Smith's thought attracted Burke's interest. Viewed in hindsight, it might well make sense to see Smith as the founder of classical economics, but that is not so obvious a judgment when one's attention is focused on the eighteenth century context of his work. From that vantage point, two other aspects of Smith's thought are probably more important. First, as Donald Winch points out, Smith was a rather sophisticated disciple of classical republicanism and, like his associate David Hume, a skeptical Whig.[19] Second, Smith, as a Scotch social scientist, was primarily concerned with the development of modern commercial civilization.[20] That is, he sought to explain the relationship between the growth of commerce and the growth of culture, and to build a science of man grounded on that explanation. Smith's *Wealth of Nations* was published only sixteen years after Burke's letter opening their friendship and is easily open to being interpreted as merely the applied side of his already developed moral theory.[21] In the light of his belief in the essential unity of morality and politics and his commitment to an active political career, Burke would have been far more likely to respond to this side of Smith's work than to the abstract theoretical pronouncements which later political economists found so compelling.

Smith's concern with practical politics and his interest in actual history gives his thought a flexibility not often appreciated.

Where Ricardo later saw fixed laws, Smith saw only prudential rules. Campbell, for instance, insists that Smith's thought is really a form of utilitarianism: "It is because men, by following their spontaneous moral sentiments, play their part in a system which is conductive to the happiness of mankind, that Smith recommends that these moral sentiments should continue to serve as guides for conduct. They find their justification in the fact that they are a means towards the production of general happiness."[22] Indeed, even Smith's advocacy of a free economy has a strongly prudential element. As Campbell puts it, "Smith is prepared to consider each case for government intervention in economic life on its own merits," for there can be no general rule on the subject.[23] In fact, the scope of governmental economic action permitted by Smith is quite broad. While he confined government to three areas, external defense, justice, and public works, as Winch suggests, "it can be shown that these categories, and the principles put forward by Smith to guide intervention within them, allowed wider scope for the state than the nineteenth century laissez-faire image suggests."[24] When in Book V of the *Wealth of Nations,* for example, Smith outlines the items the state can finance, one is impressed by the length of the list.[25] Along with the raising and supporting of professional armies and navies and the maintenance of a system of courts, the state can provide those things which are socially desirable but not capable of bringing a profit to individuals. Among these are roads, bridges, canals, harbors, a system of public education, forts to protect trade with barbarians, the collection of duties and customs, trading companies, joint stock companies, banks, insurance, water works, and so on. For example, Smith argues that public education is essential, even for the lower-classes, because every member of society should possess certain essential skills and as a brake on the force of religious enthusiasm.[26] Similarly, in the second chapter of Book V, Smith adds additional permissible state functions, among them banking, postal delivery, the lending out of national treasures, leasing of public lands, building public parks, and the taxing of land, houses, profits, various commodities and types of employment.[27] Again, in chapter 3, Smith, in spite of his well-known opposition to a large national debt, holds that the state may acquire one and build the institutions necessary to manage it.[28]

I know of no list of legitimate state functions composed by Burke comparable to Smith's. Still, when, in a letter on the opening phase of the French Revolution, he described his idea of a good practical government, he did so in characteristically generous terms. It is, he said, one in which "the grand secret had been found of reconciling a Government of real energy for all foreign and domestick Purposes, with the most perfect security to the Liberty and safety of individuals."[29] Further, it is clear that, for Burke, the discovery of such a balance was a matter of prudence and experience. In the *Appeal,* he attacked the dogmatic French radicals by denying that government is a matter of absolutes: "the lines of morality are not like the ideal lines of mathematics. They are broad and deep as well as long. . . . Prudence is not only the first in rank of the virtues political and moral, but she is the director, the regulator, the standard of them all."[30] Political genius, Burke often claimed, lies in the linking of principles to circumstances. In another context, he wrote, "I never ask what Government may do in *theory,* except *theory* be the *Object;* when one talks of *Practice* they must act according to circumstances."[31] Burke, of course, did not derive his emphasis on prudence from Smith. Rather, it was, for them, a common value of such importance as to give the rest of their thought a similar coloration. Smith and Burke both saw the choice of economic policies, not as an issue of potentially dangerous state interference with natural economic laws, but as a matter of difficult practical choices. In their opinion, those choices had to be made on the basis of essentially utilitarian considerations, and judged by their consequences for real human beings.

One of the major sources of misconceptions about both Smith's and Burke's positions on economics has been the assumption that, because they favored free trade, they desired an economy free in all respects. It is true that both Smith and Burke were advocates of free trade. However, for my purposes here, what is of interest is less their support for free trade than the nature of the arguments they used in its defense. In a long middle section of the *Wealth of Nations,* Smith considered the various systems of political economy.[32] His argument soon turned into an extended critique of mercantilism. Smith saw the mercantilist system as the result of a successful attempt by merchants to convince the politicians to do what is either unnecessary, because left to itself the economy would do it anyway, or foolish. Interestingly, his argument was based on prudential grounds, rather than on deductions from an abstract theoretical model. Smith proceeded by assessing the ability of the most common mercantile devices to promote a favorable balance of trade.[33] In general, he found that those devices did little or nothing to increase total national wealth, but served only to redistribute the wealth a nation already had. For instance, the corn laws, according to Smith, were a failure because they either prevented food from being delivered to market, by making it not worth the farmer's effort to sell, or they caused the food supply to be used up too quickly by creating a false sense of plenty. Ironically, he argued, in the latter case the laws led to the very famine they were intended to prevent.[34] Smith's test for sound legislation, then, was simple: economic policies are to be judged by their ability to contribute to increases in national wealth. He believed that, in general, governmental interference in the economy fails that test. It does not create or expand national wealth, and the benefits it establishes go to those who are already powerful and really don't need the advantage. Almost by default, then, Smith preferred free trade: it sometimes increases wealth, and, even when it does not, at least it does not distort the economy. From a policy perspective, he thought the conclusion clear: "the statesman, who should attempt to direct private people in what manner they ought to employ their capitals, would not only load himself with a most unnecessary attention, but assume an authority which could safely be trusted, not only to no single person, but to no council or senate whatever, and which would nowhere be so dangerous as in the hands of a man who had folly and presumption enough to fancy himself fit to exercise it."[35] It was not, for Smith, a matter of principle; he rejected state regulation of trade because it usually did not work.

Burke similarly favored free trade. As he wrote to Samuel Span of Bristol, "the World I apprehend is large enough for all, and we are not to conclude that what is gained to one part of it is lost of course to the other. The prosperity arising from an enlarged and liberal system improves all its objects: and the participation of a trade with flourishing Countries is much better than the monopoly of want and penury."[36] In another letter to Bristol, Burke repeated the argument that the prosperity of trading partners is interrelated. Therefore, he continued, aiding one also benefits the other. By the same token, to limit or reduce the trade of one partner harms the other as well. Thus, Burke insisted that Bristol was being shortsighted in trying to suppress Irish trade. He asked, "is Ireland united to the Crown of Great Britain for no other purpose than that we should counteract the bounty of Providence in her favor?"[37] However, like Smith, Burke based his position on prudence, not principle. He told Bristol, "it was, as a man attached to your interests, and zealous for the conservation of your power and dignity, that I acted . . ."[38] And again, "I do not pretend to be an antiquary, a lawyer, or qualified for the chair of professor in metaphysics. I never ventured to put your solid interests upon speculative grounds."[39]

For Burke, as for Smith, policies are to be judged according to their consequences. If those consequences are good, then the policies are defensible. Further, the question cannot be decided in advance. It is a matter of detail and calculation, and a proper subject for the politician rather than the theoretician.

If the basic principle of free trade is itself no more than a generalization of what is usually best on utilitarian grounds, then it would make sense to consider proposals for exceptions on the same terms. This is, in fact, precisely what both Smith and Burke did. Smith, for example, was often quite harsh in his assessment of the Empire, and especially of imperial policy toward the American colonies. At one point in *Wealth of Nations* he wrote, "a great empire has been established for the sole purpose of raising up a nation of customers who should be obliged to buy from the shops of our different producers, all the goods with which these could provide them."[40] Moreover, in the past, English policy had done little to increase the value of the colonies, for generally it has served only to depress the total wealth of the Empire, and to redistribute it somewhat from its natural course.[41] Nonetheless, Smith still concluded that, on balance, the Empire was a good thing, for it secured the benefits of trade within an enlarged sphere.[42] Nor did he believe that England should stop regulating American trade. Quite the contrary, Smith argued that the Navigation Acts, though not very favorable to commerce, were justified by their contribution to national defense. In his opinion, they were, in fact, "the wisest of all the commercial regulations of England."[43] Moreover, Smith went on to endorse the British efforts to make the Americans pay a fair share of the costs of Empire, even if that eventually led to American independence.[44] At the end of the section on colonies, Smith wrote, "if any of the provinces of the British empire cannot be made to contribute towards the support of the whole empire, it is surely time that Great Britain should free herself from the expence of defending those provinces in time of war, and of supporting any part of their civil or military establishments in time of peace, and endeavour to accommodate her future views and designs to the real mediocrity of her circumstances."[45] In sum, in Smith's view, even the imperatives of trade can be overcome by other considerations.

Burke's own critique of the Empire could well have come from Smith's book. This sentiment, from Burke's *Observations on a Late Publication on the Present State of the Nation,* might have been written by Smith: "do not the laws absolutely confine the colonies to buy from us, whether foreign nations sell cheaper or not? On what other idea are all our prohibitions, regulations, guards, penalties, and forfeitures, framed? To secure to us, not a commercial preference, which stands in need of no penalties to enforce it; it finds its own way; but to secure to us a trade, which is a creature of law and institution."[46] But Burke, no more than Smith, did not condemn completely the imperial system of the Navigation Acts. He granted that it was harsh and ungenerous: "Sir, that policy was, from the beginning, purely commercial; and the commercial system was wholly restrictive. It was the system of a monopoly."[47] However, the system had its advantages: the Americans were familiar with it, had, in spite of all its faults, prospered under it, and they possessed the image and substance of the British constitution.[48] Burke did not, therefore, favor ending the system of regulation, but preferred to rationalize it. Principally, he wanted the British to admit that the cost of the British colonial and mercantile system was sufficiently great for the Americans that it was equivalent to a considerable tax burden.[49] On the other hand, he hoped that the Americans would recognize that the value of the efficient flow of trade, the co-ordination of the governments of the several units of the Empire, and the provision for the defense of all overcame whatever British regulation cost them. In Burke's view, the Navigation Acts served purposes which went beyond the mere accumulation of wealth and which thereby legitimated them.

II

In the next two sections of this chapter, I turn to two of the central props of the case for Burke as a laissez-faire theorist: his discussion of poor relief in the *Thoughts and Details on Scarcity* and his advocacy of economic reform, a plan to streamline and improve the nation's administrative system. The *Thoughts and Details on Scarcity* was written in 1795 but not published until 1800, three years after Burke's death.[50] According to C. B. Macpherson, the work was provoked by the so-called Speenhamland system.[51] There, under the pressure of poor times and widespread unemployment, the Justices of the Peace had established a system of paying laborers a supplement to their wages based on family size and the cost of bread. When the Pitt Administration took up the issue of Poor Law reform, Macpherson contends, Burke became fearful that it would consider extending a similar plan to the nation at large. He therefore wrote the *Thoughts* in an effort to forestall such an attempt.

Burke was incensed, according to Macpherson, because he felt that the Speenhamland program was "an unnatural and impious interference with the laws of the market."[52] In Macpherson's interpretation, Burke believed that these laws required that labor be treated like any other commodity, and that it receive only that price which was determined by supply and demand. Macpherson argues that Burke, consistent with the emerging laissez-faire doctrine, held that for the state to attempt to maintain the price of labor at some other level would be both dangerous and ultimately unsuccessful. In thus placing the *Thoughts* in the context of Burke's political theory in general, Macpherson agrees with many of Burke's conservative admirers that he was a classical natural law thinker. However, Macpherson sees Burke as more than a mere advocate of natural law, for Burke insisted, he says, that laissez-faire was "a necessary part of the natural order of the universe. It was, even, divinely ordained, which set the seal on its being both necessary and equitable."[53] In a very important sense, then, Macpherson suggests, Burke merged traditionalism with liberalism by forcing a liberal free enterprise content into the form of Christian natural law.

That the *Thoughts* should be considered Burke's major work on economics is on the face of it a strange thing. To begin with, though written some time before his death, and in a period in which Burke seemed to be flying to pen at every provocation, the essay was never published by Burke. Further, it was, as Burke himself said, "hurriedly scribbled" in reply to some members of the House of Commons, who "seemed to think the general high prices of all articles of consumption a thing not easily accounted for."[54] There are two points here. First, the essay bears obvious marks of rapid composition and careless editing—hardly the sort of thing we would expect in an intended major work. Second, it deals, not with general economic theory or even with the poor law, but only with the very narrow matter of what can be done to help the poor through an economic crisis. Moreover, if Burke were primarily concerned with the Speenhamland plan, he had an odd way of showing it, for he scarcely talked about that at all. Indeed, Burke made the narrow focus of the essay clear throughout his argument, both by what he discussed and by what he did not discuss. For example, he considered the negative political and economic effects of public granaries, and whether the current profit margins of farmers and middlemen was exorbitant. However, Burke did not address such common themes at the time as the existing Poor Law, the subsistence theory of wages, or whether there was a need for greater discipline among the poor. Finally, to all appearances, Burke did not think much of the work, for he described it to Pitt this way: "it contained some Reflections and a good many small details. You will probably think the first not very well founded and the latter not a little tedious."[55] In the event, the work was forwarded to Pitt for his consideration with instructions to use it as he wished. We have no record of Pitt's reaction to the essay, though Burke later expressed doubt that it had been given much attention. In the end, the Administration did not propose a Speenhamland-based national system of poor relief.

When one turns to the text of the "Thoughts and Details," the expected theme does surface. Burke did, indeed, argue that government action to help the poor through the current economic crisis was both unnecessary and undesirable.[56] He held it unnecessary because he thought that the crisis was not that serious: "never, since I have known England, have I known more than a comparative scarcity. . . . Even now, I do not know of one man, woman, or child that has perished from famine: fewer, if any, I believe, than in years of plenty, when such a thing may happen by accident."[57] Burke thought poverty to be relative; he believed that the laboring people of the nation fared better in the bad years of his own time than they had in the good years of earlier periods.[58] He claimed that government action was unwise for several reasons. To begin with, Burke maintained that the poor were poor because they were numerous. Therefore, compared to the poor, "that class of dependent pensioners called the rich is so extremely small that, if all their throats were cut, and a distribution made of all they consume in a year, it would not give a bit of bread and cheese for one night's supper to those who labor, and in reality feed both the pensioners and themselves."[59] Moreover, such income redistribution would be unjust, according to Burke, for there exists an implied contract between the various economic classes of the nation which guarantees the farmer and the middleman their fair profit.[60] To violate that contract would be a kind of taxation on certain classes for the benefit of others. For Burke, the central point was, as Macpherson contends, that labor is a commodity, which like any other, must have its price set by the market. In short, says Burke, "the moment that government appears at market, all the principles of the market will be subverted."[61] That would be a particularly unfortunate development, Burke believed, because the laws of the market are not merely man-made, but reflect a higher law. Indeed, "we, the people, ought to be made sensible that it is not in breaking the laws of commerce, which are the laws of Nature, and consequently the laws of

God, that we are to place our hope of softening the Divine displeasure to remove any calamity under which we suffer or which hangs over us."[62]

As harsh as Burke's position appears thus far, there is yet worse to come, for he did not rest with the demonstration that in normal times, and by ordinary laws, governmental intervention in the economy on behalf of the poor is wrong. Burke proceeded to insist that such intervention is mistaken even in periods of true famine. As he put it, "the impossibility of the subsistence of a man who carries his labor to a market is totally beside the question, in this way of viewing it. The only question is, What is it worth to the buyer?"[63] Did Burke, then, think that nothing could be done to aid the poor? In fact, he suggested only two possible remedies. First, for the poor, themselves, the answer was, he said, patience: "patience, labor, sobriety, frugality, and religion should be recommended to them; all the rest is downright *fraud*."[64] Second, for the rest of society, Burke maintained that the obligations of charity come into play. In his opinion, "without all doubt, charity to the poor is a direct and obligatory duty upon all Christians . . ."[65] Still, even here, in Burke's opinion, the poor have no *right* to aid. Charity, it seems, is optional: "the manner, mode, time, choice of objects, and proportion are left to private discretion; and perhaps for that very reason it is performed with the greater satisfaction, because the discharge of it has more the appearance of freedom . . ."[66] The problem, for Burke, was not truly one of justice, as it might be for later generations. Rather, he saw it as a matter of scarcity. As there was not enough food to go around in bad times, and barely enough even in periods of prosperity, government mandated redistribution was no answer. It would not end starvation, but merely insure that others would die in place of those who now suffered. Charity, on the other hand, according to Burke, could do some, though not much, good. Those who did have ample resources would still survive, and the excess of their plenty could save at least some of the poor. Burke did not think himself callous. He regarded the fate of those who suffered as tragic, but he also considered it irremediable.

However, while the principal theme of the *Thoughts and Details* supports the laissez-faire interpretation of Burke's economics, some attention should be given to a number of subsidiary points as well. The most important of these is a contradiction between Burke's reliance on what he believed to be taught by the laws of nature and economics and his utilitarianism. Throughout the work, Burke frequently admitted the complexity of the issues he was dealing with, and to a consequent uncertainty about his answers. Burke, in short, was unsure of himself: at times he was dogmatic and inflexible, but at other times he was compassionate, prudential, and relativistic. For example, in speaking of the proper limits of state authority, he wrote, "nothing, certainly, can be laid down on the subject that will not admit of exceptions,—many permanent, some occasional."[67] In addition, it must also be remembered that Burke did not think that to say something is a matter for charity was an empty gesture. In a letter to William Windham, written in the same year as the essay but on a different topic, Burke held "charity has its own Justice, and its own Rules, as well as any other part of human intercourse; and if I give a Cottage to a poor man to live in, I have no more right to turn him out of it than if I had let it to him for Rent."[68] Burke considered the obligations of society to the poor at least as important as the poor's obligations to society.

Burke did not, then, want the poor to be abandoned. His argument was traditional, not laissez-faire. Burke spoke of the duties of the powerful rather than the rights of the rich or poor. In his opinion, the poor cannot demand care as a matter of right. Yet, in fact, so long as the question was not raised as one of right, Burke was willing to advocate government action to help the poor. For instance, during the crisis of 1795 he recommended that Parliament enact bounties to encourage the importation of corn, and he encouraged the Administration to send ships to both Africa and South America to purchase grains to ease the shortage.[69] Moreover, Burke lacked the moral censoriousness of many of the reformers of his day. Though some of his opinions seem harsh by our standards, he, nonetheless, felt a genuine sympathy for the poor. Perhaps the most revealing passage of the *Thoughts and Details* in this regard is his argument against prohibition: "under the pressure of the cares and sorrows of our mortal condition, men have at all time and in all countries called in some physical aid to their moral consolations—wine, beer, opium, brandy, or tobacco."[70] Burke at least never pretended that the life of the poor was anything but hard, and he did not seek to rationalize that hardness away.

It seems to me, then, that the claim that Burke was a political economist rest on a one-sided interpretation of the *Thoughts and Details*. Granted that some of the elements of such a position are present in that work, it is also true that there is much else as well. In fact, the work, as a whole, is much too ambiguous and confused to be interpreted quite so confidently, especially if one goes on to consider Burke's other writings on the same issues. At times Burke can sound like a case-hardened political economist. Yet, more often Burke expressed compassion and concern for the poor. Early in his career he wrote from England to an Irish associate, "I see that you have but one way of relieving the poor in Ireland. They call for bread, and you give them 'not a Stone,' but the Gallows."[71] To be properly understood, Burke's writings on economics must be placed in some kind of comparative perspective. It is a mistake to consider him in isolation. If, for example, he is studied in league with a proto-political economist like John Townsend and the more compassionate Adam Smith, much of interest emerges. Perhaps most important, all three writers can be seen to share a number of characteristics. They all, for example, opposed certain features of the existing poor law system. Townsend claimed, "there never was greater distress among the poor; there never was more money collected for their relief."[72] Similarly, Smith insisted that the Poor Laws actually harmed the poor by preventing their moving to areas where there was work.[73] Further, all three held that wages can only be determined by a free contract between employer and worker. Even Smith, the most compassionate of the group, believed that any government attempt to regulate supply and demand must fail, and that free trade in labor was the only possible policy.[74] The only difference between Smith and Townsend on the issue was that Townsend was even more empathetic: "the slave must be compelled to work; but the freeman should be left to his own judgment and discretion."[75] The truth is that a fairly broad consensus of opinion on economic matters existed among informed observers in Burke's time, and many of his opinions are, therefore, not distinctive.

It is not, then, on such points as the centrality of the market as a determiner of prices and a distributor of goods, or on the inevitability of poverty and hunger that Burke can be singled out from the common run of economic thinkers. Where the differences developed is on other issues, as Townsend veered off to one side of Burke and Smith to the other. On the social function of poverty, for instance, Townsend argued: "the wisest legislator will never be able to devise a more equitable, a more effectual, or in any way a more suitable punishment, than hunger is for a disobedient servant."[76] Townsend took this position because, in his view, the poor had to be kept in subordination. He believed that they could not be trusted to work willingly, for they were made of different stuff from the rest of society: "if a new and equal division of property were made in England, we cannot doubt that the same inequality which we now observe would soon take place again: the improvident, the lazy, and the vicious, would dissipate their substance; the prudent, the active, and the virtuous would again increase their wealth."[77] Smith, on the other hand, was much more generous. He argued that high wages are a sign of national prosperity and hence good: "no society can surely be flourishing and happy, of which the far greater part of the members are poor and miserable."[78] He also showed a greater scepticism about the rich, arguing that the master generally had an unequal advantage in the wage relationship, that employers could be counted on to act in their own selfish interest and contrary to that of the public, and even dared to suggest that profits are properly low in prosperous countries.[79] On all of these issues, Burke occupied a middle ground. He believed that rich and poor shared a common human nature, and saw poverty as an evil, not as a necessary incentive. On the other hand, he thought that little could be done for the poor, and, unlike Smith was not particularly optimistic about the future. Similarly, Burke was far less sceptical of the rich and powerful than was Smith, but considerably more so than Townsend. Generally, Burke lacked both Townsend's anger and hatred and Smith's generosity and concern. In short, it seems highly inappropriate, in light of his relative moderation when compared to men like Townsend and Smith for Burke to be characterized as a central figure in the development of the economic dogmas of the nineteenth century.

III

A second piece of evidence which is often cited in support of the interpretation of Burke as a political economist is his participation in the economic reform movement. Of his famous speech on economic reform, Isaac Kramnick writes, "it is as a cold-hearted, cost-accounting calculator, economist par excellence that Burke spoke to the Commons in his famous speech of 1780."[80] According to Kramnick, even Burke's use of language was "characterized by the same bourgeois cum sexual zeal he would attribute to Hastings and his cohorts," and, "the tone of the speech is obsessive in its efforts to eliminate waste in the King's household, and to replace it with public frugality."[81] Though somewhat more moderate in tone, C. B. Macpherson largely agrees with Kramnick. Admitting that the speech was less about political economy and reductions of the royal household than about the elimination of what Burke believed to be illegitimate royal influence in Parliament, he, nonetheless, believes that its economic content demonstrates that Burke's thought was totally permeated by capitalist values. He argues, "perhaps the most interesting general propositions are some, mentioned in passing as being self-evident, which reveal Burke's perception of the extent to which the market had become the determinant of all values, and his acceptance of an assumption which justified a policy of laissez-faire."[82] The arguments, then, differ, but, whether we view Burke as a sex-crazed castrator of royal power or an inadvertant spokesman for the emerging elite, the conclusions are the same. Kramnick and Macpherson, alike, agree that the speech on economical reform proves that Burke was a confirmed advocate of political economy.

However, I do not think that their arguments are convincing. It must first, as Macpherson acknowledges, be understood that the speech, in spite of its title, does not deal with economic theory. In the speech, itself, Burke made his reasons for introducing the legislation quite clear. First, Burke wished to respond to the public clamor for administrative reform: "it is necessary from the demands of the people, whose desires, when they do not militate with the stable and eternal rules of justice and reason (rules which are above us and above them), ought to be as a law to a House of Commons."[83] From this perspective, Burke primarily sought to make government more efficient and more effective. Second, he also wanted to reduce corruption by removing the possibility of governmental funds being misused to buy off Parliament or the voters. Thus, in later explaining the defeat of his plan, Burke told a correspondent: "the objects which I proposed, were *radical,* Systematick Oeconomy; a plan of *prevention;* the establishment of order and responsibility; the taking away corruption under the name of general and secret services; the permanent reduction of influence . . . and not the reduction of a few places and pensions."[84] In addition, aside from such elimination of offices or streamlining of procedures necessitated by the demands of efficiency, Burke did not seek to alter the scope of government or to change its basic functions. In particular, he showed no interest in defending natural property rights or even in making government as cheap as possible. As Burke wrote years later, "economy is a distributive virtue, and consists, not in saving, but in selection."[85] In fact, he maintained, "expense and great expense, may be an essential part in true economy."[86] Rather, Burke sought to give the public administration power and funds adequate to do its job, while, at the same time, insuring that the people would pay no more than a fair price for their services. In this sense, he insisted that his bywords were utility and, especially, justice. Indeed, in the seven rules that Burke claimed to have used as guides for drafting his proposals there is a good deal of discussion of order and honesty, but virtually nothing about cutting expense.[87]

If Burke's goal was to provide effective and orderly government at a reasonable price, and if the nature of his economic thought was essentially utilitarian and prudential, how did he plan to accomplish his purposes? I believe he had three devices in mind. First, to insure that government would be effective and intelligent, Burke proposed to attract men of talent. He, therefore, rejected a reform commonplace of the time by observing; "I do not think the great efficient offices of the state to be overpaid. The service of the public is a thing which cannot be put to auction and struck down to those who will agree to execute it the cheapest."[88] Burke believed that, in modern society, one cannot rely on virtue to staff the state; rather, "an honorable and fair profit is the best security against avarice and rapacity; as in all things else, a lawful and regulated enjoyment is the best security against debauchery and excess."[89] Burke's second device was to establish greater administrative rationality and order as a means of increasing government efficiency. For example, Burke noted that England was not properly a monarchy but a pentarchy, for the Crown's authority was divided into five separate and sovereign jurisdictions. To demonstrate the consequences of such duplication, Burke told the hilarious tale of Mr. John Probert, whose search for administrative wealth in Wales provoked a rebellion: "the rocks poured down their goatherds, and the deep caverns vomited out their miners. Everything above ground and everything under ground was in arms."[90] Yet, even here, Burke did not propose simply to abolish these jurisdictions. Instead, he would unite them to the Crown, simplify their procedures to make them efficient, sell off useless estates, replace the semi-feudal tenant-rights of those tenants who would remain with low rents, and compensate those who would lose offices under the reform.[91] The third of Burke's devices was, indeed, to economize where possible. This he planned to do, as he said, by principle: "to put affairs into that train which experience points out as the most effectual, from the nature of things and from the constitution of the human mind."[92] For instance, Burke suggested that the king's tables be contracted out by bid to professionals.[93] However, even here the purpose was not solely to save money. In the interest of economy, Burke intended to limit the Civil List according to the importance or justice of the demand and the inability of the claimants to enforce their requests, but he never considered wholesale reductions.[94] In short, Burke believed his economic reform plan to be sensible, moderate, balanced, and generous. He intended it for real application, and crafted it to win support, both within and outside Parliament. It was meant as the product of a principled, but worldly politician, and not of a fanatical dogmatist.

IV

Thus far my case for Burke as a moderate on economic policy has been essentially negative. What is now required is evidence that Burke advocated the expansion of governmental authority in some cases. I turn, therefore, to his proposal for a slave code to improve the position of slaves in the West Indies, and to prepare the way for the gradual emancipation of those slaves. Burke's interest in slavery developed early. In his *Account of the English Settlements in America,* he adopted the Scotch stages of civilization approach to the explanation of the nature of American Indian society. The Indians, he maintained, offer a model of what all societies, including the European, were like at their origins.[95] An important consequence of Burke's employment of this view of cultural history was that it committed him to a belief in a substantial measure of racial equality. Thus, in the second Volume of the *Account,* Burke held that the black slaves of the West Indies should be governed with regard to their common humanity: "I know that they are stubborn and intractable for the most part, and that they must be ruled with a rod of iron. I would have them ruled, but not crushed with it. I would have a humanity exercised which is consistent with steadiness."[96] Moreover, he proceeded to suggest that slaves are less productive workers than free men only because they do not profit from their work, and, therefore, take no interest in it. For that reason, he maintained, their productivity could be improved through better treatment, and this, in turn, could lead to a reduction in the importation of new slaves.[97] In fact, Burke argued, if free men labor better than slaves and the law of England is, after all, "favourable to liberty," why not free the slaves?[98] Burke proposed that, after a brief period of servitude to the owner of the mother, slaves born in the islands should be given a small plot of land in exchange for a rent. This would, he thought, spur the former slaves to greater effort, for "the necessity of paying the rent would keep them from idleness; and when men are once set to work through necessity, they will not stop there; but they will gradually strive for conveniencies, and some even for superfluities."[99] Eventually, he said, everyone would benefit: the mother country by increased trade, and the colony through the addition of a large number of useful new citizens.

Burke next turned to the issue of slavery about the year 1780. At that time, he drafted a "Negro Code" to regulate the slave trade until it could be completely abolished.[100] Three aspects of the Code are worthy of particular note. First, Burke's purpose was moral, not economic. His intention was to free men, not to create a free labor market. Second, the Code was to be only a temporary expedient, for his long-term interest was less to regulate slavery than to create the means of ending it. The preamble of the Code makes Burke's intention to abolish slavery clear: "whereas it is expedient, and conformable to the principles of true religion and morality, and to the rules of sound policy, to put an end to all traffic in the persons of men, and to the detention of their said persons in a state of slavery, as soon as the same may be effected without producing great inconveniences in the sudden change of practices of such long standing . . ."[101] Third, to prepare for that eventuality, Burke proposed to make extensive use of governmental power. The code provided for the inspection of ships involved in the slave trade. Burke sought to require that they be inspected and certified by governmental officials, be limited in the number of slaves they could transport according to their size, and forced to offer proper food, exercise, and medical treatment.[102] Similarly, the code would limit the slave trade to certain designated ports in Africa, and these, too, were to be inspected by government officials.[103] Burke insisted that churches, schools, and hospitals were to be built for the slaves, and they were to be taught trades. Moreover, no slave over the age of thirty-five, pregnant, able to read, feeble, or falling into any of several other humanitarian categories was to be sold, and, if sold in violation of the law, was to be returned to his or her home. In yet another set of regulations, Burke covered the actual shipping of slaves. He wanted slave traders to be licensed, slaves to be provided with musical instruments for entertainment, and negro foremen designated as protectors of the others.[104] Finally, Burke offered a series of rules to govern the treatment of the slaves once they arrived in the Indies.[105] Here he returned to an idea from the *Account,* that of giving the workers a regular day off each week, and added a great deal more: an Attorney General was to head a staff of inspectors to oversee the port, participants in the trade, and even the physical conditions of the slaves. Among other things, Burke instructed these supervisors to care for the religious needs of the slaves, register their births, school their children, encourage their marriages, keep their families together, and even encourage their eventual purchase of their own freedom.

Nothing came of the Code at the time it was drafted, but Burke frequently returned to it and, indeed, built on it. For example, he revived the code in 1792 when the House of Commons first accepted the principle of a gradual abolition of the slave trade. At that time, he sent a copy to Henry Dundas who, along with his membership in the Pitt administration, was a leader in the anti-slavery movement. Burke explained his reasoning: "if the African trade could be considered with regard to itself only, and as a single object, I should think the utter abolition to be, on the whole, more advisible than any scheme of regulation and reform. Rather than suffer it to continue as it is, I heartily wish it at an end."[106] However, he continued "at the time when I formed the plan . . . an abolition of the slave trade would have appeared a very chimerical project," for the House was not then prepared for it.[107] Therefore, Burke felt that the plan had to take the state of political opinion into consideration, and work to gradually discourage slavery and make it odious. Further, Burke feared that an immediate abolition of the trade would provoke the slave owners to clandestine means to continue the supply of slaves. Better, he said, to allow the trade openly at present, to regulate it, and then to gradually phase it out. However, once the preliminary goal of ending the slave trade was accomplished, largely, Burke said, by making a foreign supply of slaves unnecessary, the broader goal of ending slavery altogether could be broached. In Burke's view, this, itself, should be a two-stage process. In the first stage, both the planter and the slave had to be placed under stringent control, for "we must precede the donation of freedom by disposing the minds of the objects to a disposition to receive it without danger to themselves or to us."[108] In the case of the slave, this meant that, "the minds of men being crippled with that restraint can do nothing for themselves; everything must be done for them" and, therefore, "regulations must be multiplied."[109] In short, Burke believed that only when the slave and the slave holder had both been adequately prepared would the time be ripe to abolish slavery totally.

Two weeks after Burke sent his letter, Dundas introduced resolutions into the House which would have abolished the slave trade after a period of regulation. The House voted to end the trade in 1796, but the Lords refused to agree, and no plan was passed.

Burke's interest in slavery did not, however, end there. In April 1796, Philip Francis moved a bill to regulate and improve the conditions of slaves in the West Indies. Burke, now out of Parliament, wrote to William Windham asking him to make a copy of the Negro Code available to Francis. He expected a favorable reaction, he told Windham, for Francis "had but one notion; that indeed perfectly agreed with mine—which was to give property to the Negroes. But as this was without any scheme whatever to effectuate and support it, I referred him to the plan in your hands."[110] Burke thought that his plan might provide a frame for Francis' more limited proposal. Burke's Code continued to serve the anti-slavery movement. It was revived in 1802 by Canning in his effort to end slavery, and was considered as a framework for emancipation by William Wilberforce as late as 1822.[111] It seems likely that the persistence of Burke's Code was due to its comprehensiveness. As Burke, himself, suggested, it was relatively easy for the anti-slavery movement to decide what was to be done; the difficulty lay in deciding how to do it.[112] Burke thought that he had found a way, and that was the use of extensive amounts of state power. He did not shy away from such an alternative because he believed that where the purpose was just, the power must be sufficient. Burke always believed that the extent of political authority depends on the nature of the moral goal to be served. In the case of slavery, its abolition was a sufficiently important matter to justify very broad authority indeed.

V

During Burke's long political career he dealt with many other matters involving the use of state authority. A complete examination of all of these issues for a common theme on state intervention would, however, accomplish little, for it is clear that Burke simply refused to commit himself to some absolute standard of interventionalism or natural rights. Burke was, in fact, not an early laissez-faire liberal, a paternalist, or a mercantilist. If he must be labeled, it should be, as he himself would have it, a moderate Whig with grounding in the advanced currents of the Scottish Enlightenment. Like his friend and ally Adam Smith, Burke believed that all men possess a moral nature which both can and should be improved through association with other men in a society. In his view, the state, whatever its formal structure, has an obligation to promote the moral development of its members and is to be judged, in part at least, by how well it performs that function. Further, whether the state should intervene or play a role in any given area is to be determined, according to Burke, not by reference to abstract rights, which he is supposed to have attacked in politics but defended in economics, but by prudential considerations as to what policy might best serve that larger goal. Burke believed that questions of policy could only be answered through experience and practical reasoning. When viewed in this light, his economics was both sophisticated and consistent with his politics.

6

THE POLITICS OF TRUSTEESHIP

When viewed from the perspective of the development of the theory and practice of representative government, the cornerstone of Burke's political thought is his theory of trusteeship. For Burke, a common commitment to the principles of trusteeship should link together the aristocrats of good will, their associates among the professional politicians, and the articulate public in a reformist coalition. Burke saw the parliamentary representative, whether the hereditary member of the House of Lords or the elected member of the House of Commons, as, in some sense, an agent of the people. Burke believed, therefore, that the representative was to give his talent and experience to the service of his constituents. Their good was to be his only rule, and only they could judge whether he was doing his job effectively. Moreover, the people, alone, Burke felt, had the authority to remove a representative from office. Thus, a member of the House of Commons could, Burke argued, be properly removed for failing the popular trust. Still, Burke qualified his theory of agency in two important ways. First, he maintained that legislative trusteeship is largely defensive in nature. Burke insisted that the responsibility of the representative was less to enact the will of the people than it was to protect them against the misrule of others. Second, in his distrust of popular opinion, Burke diluted his demand for popular control of government with a strong dose of virtual representation. For example, he argued for a restricted electorate, holding that it was both unnecessary and undesirable for all of the people to have the vote. Unfortunately, the limitations Burke placed on popular government had the effect of reducing the value of the principle of trusteeship, itself. In particular, they weakened the theory at a number of critical points. In the form advocated by Burke, the theory of trusteeship lacked the means to enforce governmental accountability, was unable to provide for sufficent popular influence on government policy-making, and could not generate the community of interest and respect between the party leadership and the people that he, himself, thought was necessary for effective reform.

I

In spite of its central role in his thought, few of the commentators on Burke's theory of representation describe a position which is both plausibly his and also coherent and systematic. For example, in her *The Concept of Representation,* perhaps the fullest consideration of the topic, Hanna Pitkin discusses a consistent theory, but it is arguable whether it is Burke's theory.[1] In Pitkin's view, the key to Burke's theory of representation is the concept of objective interest. She claims that, "for Burke, political representation is the representation of interest, and interest has an objective, impersonal, unattached reality."[2] According to Pitkin, Burke believed that, in any situation, there is a single correct action to take, and that a knowledge of that action, and a will to take it, should emerge from any parliamentary discussion of the matter. Pitkin further holds that Burke maintained that the substance of what is objectively right is determined by the needs of the nation. That is, the representative is not to serve local people, but to promote national interests: "Burke conceives of broad, relatively fixed interests, few in number and clearly defined, of which any group or locality has just one."[3] On this view, she continues, it is not necessary that each district or group choose a member of Parliament; it is sufficient that their interest be represented, even if only by a representative chosen from some other geographical location. However, if this is so, one might ask why must any of the members of Parliament be elected? Pitkin offers several reasons. First, she suggests that Burke understood elections as merely "a means of finding the members of a natural aristocracy."[4] Second, Pitkin sees Burke as recognizing that even virtual representation must have some basis in the actual. She argues that, while he did not think it essential that every area which shares an interest be represented, he did acknowledge that some must be. Finally, Burke, in Pitkin's opinion, believed that there must be some bond of sympathy between the people and their rulers, and that such a bond can be maintained only if at least some of the rulers are directly elected.[5] Still, even in these cases of actual representation, Pitkin asserts that Burke encouraged the voters not to seek to control their representatives through instructions, and recommended that representatives be removed only for corruption or lack of ability.[6] In fact, Pitkin claims that Burke regarded representation as merely a special case of his general theory of government as trusteeship. Therefore, she thinks that for Burke to say that government is a trust was only to say that it must be conducted in the interest of the governed. It was not, however, to say that government must be popularly controlled. In fact, in Pitkin's view, Burke did not believe that government should be controlled by the people or accountable to them.

Pitkin's rich analysis contains much of interest, but I would like to concentrate on the ideas that Burke held a theory of objective interest and viewed policy-making as its implementation regardless of the popular will. It seems to me that the most superficial reading of Burke's major works makes clear that he did not believe in objective interest. He often discussed the issue, and the evidence of his position is both abundant and consistent. In his early writings, Burke associated the concept with Bolingbroke; later, he came to see it as a characteristic feature of the argument of the French revolutionaries and their English disciples. In either case, he denounced it in the strongest terms. In the "Thoughts on the Causes of the Present Discontents," for instance, Burke referred to the effort to judge real politics by some ideal of objective interest as "a scheme of perfection to be realized in a monarchy far beyond the visionary republic of Plato."[7] In his opinion, politics is not to be a matter of truth-enactment, for, "whether a *measure* of government be right or wrong, is *no matter of fact,* but a mere affair of opinion, on which men may, as they do, dispute and wrangle without end."[8] Burke repeated the sentiment in any number of later works. In the Appeal from the New to the Old Whigs," he attacked the tendency to abstract thinking of those who insist on doing what is "right:" "with them there is no compromise. All other governments are usurpations, which justify and even demand resistance."[9] Indeed, Burke continued, "no man who assumes their grounds can tolerate the British Constitution in Church or State."[10] Why not? Because, in Burke's view, the British Constitution embodies the principles of compromise and moderation. It forms a political system in which all parties must eschew absolutes and seek to resolve their differences peacefully through bargaining in Parliament. For Burke, therefore, the chief political virtue was not wisdom but prudence. As he put it in the *Reflections,* a good politician is one who "when the equipoise of the vessel in which he sails, may be endangered by overloading it upon one side, is desirous of carrying the small weight of his reason to that which may preserve its equipoise."[11] Moreover, Burke felt that, since he serves moderation and compromise, and not absolute truth, a good politician does not easily override the wishes of his constituents. He has no basis for doing so: without some objective standard, he would only be substituting his own arbitrary judgment for theirs. There are times when this may be necessary, but they are few, and should be approached with proper recognition of the people's ultimate right. Indeed, Burke made it clear that, in the final analysis, it is the will of the people which must prevail—no matter how mistaken the representative might believe it to be.[12]

Most of the more traditional approaches to Burke's theory of representation, such as those of O'Gorman and MacCunn, realize that Burke believed in conflict resolution through compromise. They, therefore, reject the thesis that Burke believed in some general good and all that it entails.[13] However, their treatment of the issue of accountability—that is, of the relationship between the representative and his district—is often inadequate. Many of them come near to denying that Burke held the representative accountable at all. O'Gorman, for example, writes, "Burke believed that government should exist for the good of the people but not that it should be controlled by the people."[14] MacCunn makes a more detailed statement of the same position: "by all means let electorates express their grievances, wants, and demands, both on their own account and on that of the larger British public behind them; by all means let them watch how their representatives vote, but let them never presume to dictate to the men of their choice how these things are to be dealt with and remedied."[15] In short, Burke is commonly seen as believing that representatives are to be chosen, but the choice is to be meaningless, for they are not to be judged. Once again, though from a rather different perspective, the question is why have elections at all? Are we really to believe that Burke thought representation through elections essential to free government, but that he also held that such representation should have no direct policy consequences? Like Pitkin, these commentators see elections as serving a variety of functions in Burke's theory. For instance, they agree that virtual representation requires, in his view, some basis in actual representation if it is to be effective. In addition, they usually admit that Burke would allow for the removal of an incompetent or corrupt representative. Still, a problem remains, for this position fails to account for the occasions when Burke maintained that electors should keep careful tabs on the policy stands taken by their representatives and vote accordingly. Thus, while these writers wish to avoid the suggestion that Burke saw the close control of the representative by the elector as a matter of normal politics, some of them argue that he considered interventions into the political process by the electorate to be permitted in certain special cases. Alternatively, others seek to resolve the dilemma by an appeal to tradition. Chapman, for example, writes, "the choice of the people at any discrete moment, Burke said, whenever it can come to act, is or ought to be irresistible, but he was confident that unless it were momentarily stirred up into a 'tumultuary and giddy choice,' it would act consistently with the choice of the people at other discrete moments, that is consistently with the choice of the nation, in the perfect freedom of duty."[16] Unfortunately, this saves Burke from inconsistency at the cost of making him a romantic believer in the wisdom of a timeless majority. The difficulty, therefore, remains; the commentators cannot explain why Burke considered meaningful representation vital or how he integrated it into his thought.

II

The place to begin an examination of Burke's theory of trusteeship and representation is with the four speeches he made during his two campaigns at Bristol. Of these, the first, upon his arrival at the polls in 1774, is of little interest here, and the fourth, which admitted the impossibility of winning the poll in 1780, is also, except for one point, of little significance. In the second speech, delivered after the election of 1774, Burke offered his most theoretical statement of the relationship between voters and representatives. The issue which concerned him most immediately was that of instructions. The other successful candidate had just endorsed the right of the electors to instruct representatives on how to vote in Parliament, but Burke sought to disagree. He acknowledged that a representative should be close to his constituents; their wishes must have great weight with him, and he should give his complete attention to their interests. Yet, Burke insisted that the means the representative is to employ in serving them is for him alone to determine. Government is not, in his view, a mere matter of deciding what the people want. It is not a question simply of will or inclination, but also of judgment. Therefore, Burke maintained, "your representative owes you, not his industry only, but his judgment; and he betrays, instead of serving you, if he sacrifices it to your opinion."[17] Burke argued that judgments may be mistaken, and those most prone to error are those which are most remote. The representative is the man on the scene; he is the political expert who can discuss and debate the issues with other experts in the legislature. In short, Burke asked, "what sort of reason is that in which the determination precedes the discussion, in which one set of men deliberate and another decide, and where those who form the conclusion are perhaps three hundred miles distant from those who hear the argument?"[18] Therefore, Burke concluded, a member of Parliament cannot content himself with simply following the dictates of his constituents. He must participate in debate and discussion, study issues carefully, and consider the interests of the entire country before he decides how to vote, for he represents the Commons of England and not merely his own district.

At first blush, the second Bristol speech seems to support the view that Burke held that representatives are not accountable to their districts. However, a study of the third speech considerably modifies that impression. The third speech opened Burke's campaign for reelection in 1780, and was, therefore, a detailed defense of his conduct in office. Indeed, while the speech included some discussion of the theory of representation, it was primarily a reply to four specific charges. The first of these was that Burke had neglected the affairs of the city. Burke admitted that he spent little time in Bristol, but he denied that he had not served the city well. In fact, he suggested, "I could hardly serve you as *I have done,* and court you too."[19] Burke also passed quickly over the second charge: that his stand in favor of abolishing imprisonment for debt conflicted with Bristol's interest. He pointed out that an imprisoned person cannot repay his debts, and suggested that debtors should be free so they can fulfill their obligations.[20] To the third charge—that he had supported Irish trade—Burke also pleaded guilty. However, he once again insisted that his judgment was superior to that of the the voters, maintaining that his support of Irish free trade would benefit Bristol in the long run. The choice was, he claimed, between liberalization and war. Burke asked the voters to look at America, where all concessions were refused; the result was that, "from war and blood we went to submission, and from submission plunged back again to war and blood, to desolate and be desolated, without measure, hope, or end."[21] Surely, he argued, England can learn from experience to avoid such foolishness. By far the largest section of the speech was taken up with the final issue, the question of Catholic emancipation.[22] Bristol was a zealously Protestant city, but Burke had voted to repeal a series of anti-Catholic acts. Yet again, his defense was simply that his votes had been correct. Burke asked: "what must be the sentiments of a man, who would wish to perpetuate domestic hostility, when the causes of dispute are at an end: and who, crying out for peace with one part of the nation on the most humiliating of terms, [i.e., with America] should deny it to those, who offer friendship without any terms at all."[23] In Burke's view, the basic value of religious toleration and considerations of practical political prudence combined to validate his stand.

Although the third Bristol speech was, for the most part, a detailed lawyer's brief, rather than an abstract exposition on representation, when assessed in conjunction with the other Bristol speeches it does provide a consistent theory of representation. The second speech and the opening passages of the third speech ask for the sympathetic understanding of the voters. Burke stressed the difficulty of the job of a representative, and he asked that the voters judge him on his overall record rather than on a few controversial actions: "most certainly it is our duty to examine; it is our interest too: but it must be with discretion; with an attention to all the circumstances, and to all the motives . . . look gentlemen, to the *whole tenor* of your member's conduct."[24] However, Burke also recognized an obligation to account for his actions, and he did, in fact, try to do so. Generally, his tactic was to claim that, where he and Bristol disagreed, the long view showed that he was right and they were wrong. In his defense of Irish trade, for example, he said, "instead of requiring it from me, as a point of duty, to kindle with your passions, had you all been as cool as I was, you would have been saved disgraces and distresses that are unutterable."[25] Further, because the representative is more informed than the voter, Burke argued that the voter ought not to seek to instruct him. Otherwise, "if we do not permit our members to act upon a *very* enlarged view of things, we shall at length infallibly degrade our national representation into a confused and scuffling bustle of local agency."[26] Still, Burke was also clear on another point: if the district and the representative disagreed persistently, the voters had a right to remove the representative. Burke said as much in the third speech, but it is the fourth and last speech which was most unequivocal. He said, "I received your trust in the face of day, and in the face of day I accept your dismission."[27] His consolation, Burke maintained, lay in the contemplation of his own integrity: "it is certainly not pleasing to be put out of the public service. But I wish to be a member of parliament, to have my share of doing good and resisting evil. It would therefore be absurd to renounce my objects, in order to obtain my seat."[28] Thus, while Burke advocated broad leeway for the representative, he never denied that, in the end, the judgment of the electors must prevail.

III

If one were to combine the arguments on representation presented in the various Bristol speeches, and to restate them more systematically and more completely, I think it would become clear that, for Burke, the relationship between a representative and his constituents is a kind of trusteeship. What this means is that, first, like a trustee in regard to a trustor, a representative must serve the interests of the voter. He is to act in what he believes to be the best interest of his client. The representative ought to consult with his electors, listen to their complaints and ideas, and be mindful of their needs. Of the voters, Burke said, "their wishes ought to have great weight with him; their opinions high respect; their business unremitted attention . . ."[29] Yet, in the end, while the voter is fully capable of feeling and expressing a need for action, he is not fully competent to decide what that action should be. Burke, therefore, believed it to be the duty of a representative to shape the vague feelings of a district into governmental policy.[30] Further, just as it is up to the representative to decide what the interests of his constituents are, Burke held that any action he undertakes should be consistent with his own record and philosophy. As Burke told the people of Bristol in explaining why he favored a liberalization of Irish trade: "if I had been capable of acting as an advocate in opposition to a plan so perfectly consonant to my known principles . . . I should only disgrace myself, without supporting, with the smallest degree of credit or effect, the cause you wished me to undertake. I should have lost the only thing which can make such abilities as mine of any use to the world now or hereafter: I mean that authority which is derived from an opinion that a member speaks the language of truth and sincerity, and that he is not ready to take up or lay down a great political system for the convenience of the hour . . ."[31] In addition, Burke claimed that when a representative acts in Parliament, he is to act for the good of the entire nation; where the interests of his district conflict with those of the nation, it is the latter which are to prevail: "if the local constituent should have an interest or should form a hasty opinion evidently opposed to the real good of the rest of the community, the member for that place ought to be as far as any other from any endeavor to give it effect."[32] This is so, not because there is a clash of abstract objective interests, or between general and particular wills, but simply because what benefits the country at large is preferable to what benefits a single district. Burke thought in terms of groups with interests, material and otherwise, not in terms of objective goods. In his view, politics is based on compromise and bargaining, rather than the search for some abstract right, and Parliament is an arena for debate and conciliation, not a Platonic Academy.

Burke's argument placed him at a considerable distance from those who favored instructions for representatives or saw the legislature as a mere reflector of public opinion. In Burke's view, "the people are the natural control on authority; but to exercise and to control together is contradictory and impossible."[33] Thus, the relationship between voter and representative is rather more complicated than first appears to be the case. Burke felt that the people are to express their grievances, but it is up to the representative to discover the actual remedies. He wrote, "the people are the masters. They have only to express their wants at large and in gross. We are the expert artists, we are the skillful workmen, to shape their desires into perfect form, and to fit the utensils to their use. They are the sufferers, they tell the symptoms of the complaint; but we know the exact seat of the disease, and how to apply the remedy according to the rules of art."[34] Just as a trust is administered in the interest of the trustor but without his direct supervision, so should the elector not generally interfere in the representative's handling of his affairs. Even in his relatively activistic moods, Burke urged a degree of caution. In the *Thoughts on the Present Discontents,* even as he told the electors to carefully scrutinize the conduct of their representatives and to enforce a rigid code of conduct on them, he also suggested that such close examination should be only a rare and temporary expedient: "this interposition is a most unpleasant remedy. But it is a legal remedy, it is intended on some occasion to be used; to be used then only, when it is evident that nothing else can hold the constitution to its true principles."[35] Moreover, as Burke grew older, his sympathy for popular control declined. After the election of 1784, he wrote to William Baker: "But at present the picture of the English Nation does not appear to me in a very favourable light . . . To be sure they do not intend, formally to deliver over themselves and their posterity to servitude . . . But they are so fond of aggrandizing the Crown . . . that they are totally indifferent to the consequences."[36] Burke always maintained that the people had the right to control their representatives, but he was still prepared to question the wisdom of their exercising that right for insufficent cause.

However, given that the representative ought to be allowed great freedom, given that he ought to be judged liberally, and given that he ought not to be removed for trivial disagreement, Burke admitted that he may yet be removed. At Bristol, Burke claimed to take a certain pride in being attacked, for, "the charges against me, are all of one kind, that I have pushed the principles of general justice and benevolence too far . . ."[37] Moreover, he promised that, if reelected, he would continue to act in the same manner.[38] Nonetheless, Burke acknowledged that it was up to the voters. He fully accepted that it was their right, indeed, their duty, to judge and remove him if they felt that he was not serving them adequately. In a letter to Champion, Burke both criticized and defended Bristol: "they judge of him solely by his merits as their special Agent. But it is not for us to complain of the character of our masters but to obey them . . ."[39] The issues discussed at Bristol were among the most important concerns of Burke's career—American policy, the government of Ireland, and Catholic rights—and he felt strongly that Bristol was not simply mistaken but positively unjust in its positions. But, when the time came, he made his case, accepted the judgment of the people, and retired in good grace. In other of his works, Burke went even further. In the "Thoughts on the Cause of the Present Discontents," he urged the voters to keep very close tabs on their representatives. He suggested that the struggle between the administration and its opponents was so important that "the electors ought to esteem it no less culpable in their member to give a single vote in Parliament to such an administration, than to take an office under it; to endure it, than to act in it."[40] Burke believed that such control was made both possible and necessary by the virtues of freedom. He maintained that in a free country every man has a concern in all public matters and a right to form deliver an opinion upon them.[41] Burke had no intention of dispensing with those virtues. His distaste for instructions to the representative before he acts ought not to obscure Burke's very real commitment to his accountability after he acts. He never doubted the representative's obligation to explain himself, and he defended the right of the voters to consider and reject that explanation and the representative with it.

Viewed against the background of the politics of the late eighteenth century, the interpretation of Burke's theory of representation as a form of trusteeship must however be qualified. It must be understood that Burke did not think that the representative's role was exclusively, or even principally, legislative in nature. In his time, the role of Parliament as a legislature was just becoming paramount, and representatives were often seen in lights other than as lawmakers. According to Burke, one of the most important of these functions was as part of a system of checks on the power of the Crown. He believed that an important part of his responsibility as a member of the House of Commons was to oppose any improper actions by the administration. In fact, Burke was so convinced of the importance of this role that he argued that it would be a step toward tyranny for Parliament to ever become an active force in government. For example, among the complaints Burke levelled against the court cabal in the "Thoughts on the Cause of the Present Discontents" is that, "the control of Parliament upon the executory power is lost; because Parliament is made to partake in every considerable act of government."[42] Another important function of a representative was to promote the interests of his district by lobbying governmental officials for a share of the multitude of perquisites and benefits which were so much a feature of the politics of his day. In this Burke was diligent but, as an opposition leader, poorly placed to serve his constituents. He was, therefore, relatively unsuccessful. He complained to Champion of the awkwardness of his situation: "almost all small services . . . depend so much on the pleasure of the Crown . . . the members are driven headlong into dependence."[43] Thus, an important reason why Burke thought it unnecessary for voters to have the authority to instruct representatives was that so much of what the representative did was outside the sphere of legislation. To a significant degree, his job was not primarily to initiate or enact programs, but, rather, to respond to actions taken by the administration and to win favors for his district. In short, the members of Parliament did not rule; they defended the people against royal misrule. For this reason, if one is to describe Burke's position on representation as a form of trusteeship, one ought also to recognize that the trusteeship was essentially defensive in nature.

IV

The speeches at Bristol were not, however, Burke's final word on the concepts of trusteeship and representation. They set themes to which he frequently returned. In particular, when, in the 1780s, Burke sought to formulate a remedy for the misgovernment of India by representatives of the British East India Company, he found it necessary to revise and supplement his theory. This was so for several reasons. First, the issue of accountability caused Burke difficulties. Since Burke was unwilling to admit the Indians to a controlling role in their government, it was unclear just how the East India Company and its administrators could be held responsible. Second, Burke's efforts to bring justice to India revealed an important tension in his thought. Burke was a fervent believer in political stability and the security of property, but he was also a strong advocate of individual rights. In Indian affairs, these two positions came into conflict. In defending the rights of the people of India, Burke was obliged to question the constitution of India and to suggest limiting the property rights of Englishmen. In response to a call to respect the chartered rights of the East India Company, Burke replied, "no charter should protect . . . mismanagement from correction, and such public grievances from redress," for charters are mere matters of convention and use, and "are kept, when their purposes are maintained: they are violated, when the privilege is supported against its end and its objects."[44] Third, the application of the theory of trusteeship to Indian affairs raised an important issue which Burke had not had to deal with at Bristol. India was a largely alien society and culture, and had virtually no experience of constitutional government, representation, or individual rights. How, then, could Indian affairs be judged by the standards of European political morality ?

Burke's problem was that, in his consideration of Indian politics, he reached the limits of his prudential approach to political reform. What was required was some universal, absolute, and objective moral standard. In search of such a set of principles, Burke turned to natural law. This was an awkward tactic, but a necessary one. It was awkward because, as I argued in chapter 2, while Burke never denied the existence of natural law, he only rarely appealed to it directly.[45] As he saw it, the major weakness of natural law lay in its application. For natural law to be of practical value, it must be recognized and enforced by government, and Burke perfectly understood that much could be lost in that process: "these metaphysic rights entering into common life, like rays of light which pierce into a dense medium, are by the laws of nature refracted from their straight line. Indeed, in the gross and complicated mass of human passions and concerns the primitive rights of men undergo such a variety of refractions and reflections that it becomes absurd to talk of them as if they continued in the simplicity of their original direction."[46] In light of this difficulty, Burke generally preferred to avoid debate about abstract rules and to remain on the level of existing constitutions, laws, and issues. However, in the case of India, his turn to historical experience for standards of morality would not work, for it could be maintained that European traditions and practices were normative only for Europeans. In short, the example of India made clear to Burke that some transcultural principles were necessary if British imperial government were to be called to account. As he searched for a means of replying to the arguments of Warren Hastings and his allies, a reassertion of natural law seemed to afford the best means of holding them responsible for their conduct in India, even if their actions were arguably acceptable by Indian standards. By adopting natural law, Burke could reply to Hastings' claim that the normal government of India was despotic, simply by saying, "But if it has no written law, it neither does nor can cancel the primeval, indefeasible, unalterable law of Nature and of nations;" moreover, "judges are guided and governed by the eternal laws of justice, to which we are all subject. We may bite our chains, if we will, but we shall be made to know ourselves, and be taught that man is born to be governed by law; and he that will substitute *will* in the place of it is an enemy to God."[47]

So fortified, Burke's fully developed answer to the problem of good government in India followed three lines of argument. First, Burke did not completely forget his ordinary practice of judging acts by their consequences when he considered Indian matters. He maintained that misgovernment will lead to rebellion and a loss of power. When a commonwealth becomes too perverted from the purpose for which it was created, he predicted, "neither God nor man will long endure it: nor will it long endure itself."[48] To justify arbitrary government by the claim that despotism incites restlessness in the people, which can only be controlled by further despotism, is to start on a downward spiral that will end only in civil war and a scorched earth. Rather, Burke concluded, such considerations call for policies the very opposite of those employed by Hastings.[49] Second, he insisted that Indian morality, as well as English, condemned Hastings and his like. In his speech opening the impeachment of Hastings, Burke asserted that, "it is not in this instance only that I must do justice to the East. I assert that their morality is equal to ours, in whatever regards the duties of governors, fathers, and superiors; and I challenge the world to show in any modern European book more true morality and wisdom than is to be found in the writings of Asiatic men in high trust, and who have been counsellors to princes."[50] Finally, Burke employed natural law. In the speech just cited, Burke denied the legitimacy of what he called Hastings' "geographical morality."[51] In contrast, he said of the prosecutors, "we think it necessary, in justification of ourselves, to declare that the laws of morality are the same everywhere, and that there is no action which would pass for an act of extortion, of peculation, of bribery, and of oppression in England, that is not an act of extortion, of peculation, of bribery, and oppression in Europe, Asia, Africa, and all the world over."[52]

Burke chose two devices for enforcing this enlarged moral understanding in India: first, in the East India Bill, named for Fox but probably drafted by Burke, himself, he offered institutional reform for India government. Second, the impeachment proceedings against Hastings were intended to hold the chief malefactor responsible for his share in the crimes, and, therefore, to demonstrate that Indian officials both could and would be disciplined. In drafting the East India Bill, Burke faced a serious dilemma: how to assert governmental control over the East India Company without at the same time giving the King and future administrations a major new source of corruption. Burke's answer was to transfer administration of Indian affairs to a seven member board appointed by Parliament. This, he contended, would free the Company to return to purely commercial matters. In addition, he also proposed a number of reforms in India to both protect the natives against misgovernment and to render the Company's officers in India more responsible to those in England. As Cannon notes, his intention was clear: "Burke did not mean it to lay the foundations for a great and vigorous expansion of British power, but to ensure that those territories already in British hands were governed with some regard to the interests of the native population."[53] Nonetheless, the East India Bill provoked a storm of criticism which continues to this day. Burke's contemporaries were most offended by what they perceived as the bill's violation of chartered rights and by its transferral of power to a parliamentary appointed commission. This, they argued, would give the administration, at that time the Fox-North Coalition, a virtually unbeatable store of patronage. Modern critics generally attack the Bill on other grounds.[54] They see it as impractical, naive, and administratively unworkable. Ehrman, for example, argues that the fixed seven year length of the board's terms of office would bring it into conflict with any new administration chosen after its selection, that the political-commercial distinction on which it was based was unworkable, and that it failed to deal with questions raised by the Crown's rights in India.[55]

Nonetheless, Burke thought the Bill defensible. Moreover, the basis of his defense was a restatement and adaptation of his theory of trusteeship within the context of the imperial system. To begin with, he insisted that power could not be left with the officials of the Company, for they had "made a common cause and identified themselves with the destroyers of India."[56] Nor could the Crown be trusted. In line with long-standing arguments of the Rockingham Whigs, Burke maintained: "let it once get into the ordinary course of administration, and to me all hopes of reformation are gone."[57] On the other hand, he felt that there was strong logic and ample experience behind the establishment of a commission appointed by parliament.[58] At first, Burke argued that his intention, to be confirmed by subsequent legislation, was that the commission would not be political. Rather, it was to work much like a court.[59] In fact, Burke held, the claims that the commission would become a device of party were themselves party-inspired. The commission would be composed of nonpartisans and Parliament, as its superior, could insure that its conduct would be unimpeachable. However, on further consideration, Burke continued, a party connection might well be a good thing, for it would provide a means of enforcing the trust-like nature of imperial government. While the people of India could not vote for their rulers, those of England could. Therefore, if the commission became a factor in English politics, and if its control passed from one party to another with the rise and fall of governments, its conduct could be scrutinized and regulated by the voters. In a case of Indian misgovernment, the party in power would have to answer for the conduct of the board, and the electors could enforce responsibility when they voted for members of Parliament.[60] As for the argument from chartered rights, Burke explained that he did not act from any principled antagonism to charters. In his view, only great abuses by the company of its authority would justify altering its charter. However, he thought that such abuses had occurred: "there is not a single prince, state, or potentate, with whom they have come into contact that they have not sold; not a single treaty they have not broken, and not a single prince or state who trusted in the Company and was not ruined."[61] Parliament had granted the company's charter. Surely, Burke argued, in such desperate circumstances, it could also modify that charter.

Though it took up an enormous portion of his time and attention for a number of years, the logic of Burke's effort to impeach Warren Hastings can be quickly recounted, for it is little more than an application of his case for trusteeship. In Burke's opinion, Hastings, as an official of the East India Company, was accountable to the Company. In turn, the Company had authority in India as a trustee both of the Mogul Empire and of the British Government. Therefore, in the face of misconduct by Hastings, and the failure of the Company to act to correct his abuses, the obligation for redress defaulted to the British Parliament. As Burke saw it, the stakes were very high, for it was only through impeachment that, "magistracy, which tries and controls all other things, is itself tried and controlled. Other constitutions are satisfied with making good subjects; this is a security for good governors."[62] Burke knew English history well, and, therefore, knew that impeachment was a process prone to abuses, particularly when mere political disputes were elevated into claims of crimes or even treason. Thus, he admitted that impeachment ought to be a last resort. However, in his eyes, every other means of enforcing responsibility had been tried and found wanting. In addition, the accusations against Hastings involved "substantial crimes, . . . they are no errors or mistakes, such as wise and good men might possibility fall into, which may even produce very pernicious effects without being in fact great offenses."[63] Finally, Hastings' offenses were exacerbated in several ways: they were systematic and, therefore, revealed a positive plan to subvert proper governmental forms and practices; he was the head of the conspiracy and not a minor figure; the evidence was shockingly clear; and, lastly, he showed no sign of remorse but, rather, set up his conduct as a model to others.

V

Burke's attempt to extend the idea of trusteeship to Indian affairs was only partially successful. On the one hand, his addition of a natural law dimension and his authorship of the East India Bill gave his theory a normative grounding and a practical thrust which it had previously lacked. Yet, on the other hand, that extension also served to compound and magnify a number of difficulties which were already causing him serious concern. Thus, to maintain that trusteeship played a central role in Burke's thought, and to note that he made frequent use of it, is not to suggest that it was unproblematic. In fact, I believe that Burke's theory of representation was flawed in several important respects, and that many of these flaws flowed directly from his conception of trust. For example, since Burke saw trust as pervasive in nearly all human relationships, his application of the concept to any given set of circumstances was necessarily inexact. Consider his basic analogy of the Indians as beneficiaries and the East India Company as trustee. In law there are many such relationships. Just which one did Burke have in mind as a basis for comparison? Similarly, if the Company were to be treated as the trustee, then what was the role of the British Parliament to be? Was it the political equivalent of the Chancellor in Equity? But that was a job for a lawyer, and Parliament, as the Hastings trial demonstrated, was not well suited to be a court. I would, however, prefer to concentrate attention here on three issues. The first is the question of executive accountability. I believe that Burke failed to reconcile his assertion that Parliament has a right to oversee the conduct of administration with his acceptance of a right in the king to choose his own ministers. Second, Burke, in my view, failed to develop a coherent view of popular control of government. Burke offered a very impressive critique of majority rule, but this critique also undercut his own claim that representation serves as a control on government in the name of the people. Finally, I think that Burke's treatment of the nature of representation, that is his theory of virtual representation, raises but does not resolve fundamental questions about the conditions under which it would be possible to say that a representative reflects the will of his constituents.

The question of accountability, of to whom Ministers are responsible, was raised most graphically for Burke by the events surrounding the fall of the Fox-North Coalition government in 1784. The Coalition had arisen out of the contest for power following the death of Lord Rockinham and the collapse of the successor Shelburne government. Combining the forces loyal to North with the Rockingham Whigs, now under Portland, the Coalition was the only force in Parliament capable of governing but, nonetheless, it had won the hatred of the king for its stand on the American war. When Fox, the party's leader in the Commons, introduced his India Bill transferring control of India from the East India Company to a commission appointed by Parliament, the opposition sought to defeat the Bill in the House of Lords. After negotiating a secret agreement with Pitt, the king, violating the norm that the monarch should not seek to influence votes in Parliament, made his personal opposition to the Bill public.[64] Consequently, the Bill was lost, the king dismissed the ministry, and Pitt was named to form a new government. Pitt struggled at first, losing a series of votes in the Commons, but also gaining support. Once he decided the time was ripe, Pitt called for a dissolution of Parliament. In the ensuing elections, the public gave Pitt, and the king, a solid victory.

The rout of the Coalition embittered Burke until the end of his life. In his view, the king and Pitt had violated the most basic norms of the constitution, and the people had endorsed their crime. Indeed, as one scholar points out, it is hard to defend the victors: "no constitutional defense of the king's action is possible, nor was any attempted at the time by his supporters: they either dismissed the allegations as false, or engaged in a different controversy over the right of peers to advise their sovereign."[65] In June 1784, Burke put his position on record in his reply to the Speech from the Throne, which had defended the king and chided the previous parliament for not supporting him. Burke began with an assertion that the king's actions were an assault on the traditional rights of Parliament. It was well-established, he claimed, that no man should be called to account for his vote in Parliament.[66] If, he continued, improper bills are introduced into the House, there exist valid checks for defeating them, "but whatever, by the manifestation of the royal displeasure, tends to intimidate individual members from proposing, or this House from receiving, debating, and passing bills, tends to prevent even the beginning of every reformation in the state, and utterly destroys the deliberative capacity of Parliament."[67] Moreover, the charge that the East India Bill threatened chartered rights was, according to Burke, utterly fallacious; indeed, he pointed out, in the past it had usually been the executive, not the legislative, branch which threatened charters. However, when it came time to move from denunciation to reform, from criticism of the king and Pitt to suggestions for avoiding such debacles in the future, Burke had little to offer. His problem was that, though he believed that, "it is a crooked and desperate design, leading to mischief, the extent of which no human wisdom can forsee, to attempt to form a prerogative party in the nation," Burke accepted the authority of the king to appoint ministers and to dissolve Parliament.[68] All that he could suggest was that the king should solicit the Common's advice before acting, should consider it carefully upon receiving it, and should ignore it only infrequently.[69] Clearly, in light of Burke's own preamble, this was inadequate. The king had already done what Burke said ought not to be done; to now counsel him not to repeat the imposition, which from his standpoint had been highly effective, was ludicrous. What Burke required were sanctions which could be employed by Parliament to vindicate its right. Unfortunately, he had already denied it those which were the most effective possible: control over the appointment and continuation of ministers and protection against arbitrary dissolutions. Nor is his reason far to seek. Burke was unwilling to embrace greater popular influence over Parliament as a weapon against royal misgovernment. In the same speech, just a few pages later, he denounced the king for calling elections on the grounds that frequent appeals to the people would make the Commons subject to the mob in the streets.[70]

This brings me to the second area of concern in Burke's theory of representation: the issue of popular control of government. Especially in some of his early works, Burke's language in defense of the people was often quite strong, and even as late as the mid-1780s, he justified economical reform by maintaining: "it is necessary from the demands of the people, whose desires, when they do not militate with the stable and eternal rules of justice and reason (rules which are above us and above them), ought to be as a law to a House of Commons."[71] On the other hand, it is clear that Burke accepted extensive limitations on the right to vote and refused to extend his endorsement of popular control to include anything like majority rule. One such limitation, for instance, was his willingness to permit Peers to control elections to the Commons.[72] Burke also accepted other limitations on popular participation, such as property and gender requirements for voting, and a malapportioned, even in terms of eighteenth century politics, electoral system. In fact, a sizable section of the "Appeal" consisted of a detailed, and theoretically impressive, critique of majority rule.[73] To begin with, Burke argued that, in those cases where moral issues are involved, the will of the majority cannot be substituted for what is right, for truth is truth without regard to the counting of votes.[74] Burke further developed his case through an analogy to the government of a corporation. He maintained that, if government is truly based on contract, there could be majority rule within the political system only if all the parties to the original contract agreed, but, he continued, given the general incapacity of the masses, who would be so foolish as to agree to such a principle? Moreover, Burke argued that, if, as would be likely, the original contract did not call for majority rule, it could not be created through legislation, for the constitution of a country can be changed only with the consent of all the parties.[75] What is more, if the contract is breached, society is not, Burke insisted, returned to a Lockean pre-governmental state of nature, which is unformed but still social; rather, society simply ceases to exist, and anarchy ensues.[76] Finally, Burke applied his abstract argument to the empirical data of English history, denying that the country was ever, even originally, governed by the majority principle, that the Revolution of 1688 had incorporated it into the system, or that it was even practically possible.

How, then, could Burke reconcile his support for popular control with his opposition to majority rule? An interesting solution to this dilemma is advanced by Harvey Mansfield, Jr., who asserts that Burke saw the political party, united on first principles, as a moderate and controlled response to the twin dangers of the unreliable statesmanship of a politician like Bolingbroke and an equally frightening majoritarian democracy.[77] Mansfield's argument is ingenious, but, unfortunately, it does not quite work. Its strength is that it provides a plausible account of the "Thoughts on the Causes of the Present Discontents." In that work, written in the early 1770s, Burke did indeed recommend party government as the answer to the machinations of the court.[78] The weakness of the argument, however, is that it fails to recognize that Burke thought of the politics of that period as exceptional. Thus, the "Thoughts" represented the highwater mark of his enthusiasm for the people. For that reason, Mansfield's suggestion does not account for those of Burke's later stands which were much less popular in tone. One might, for example, wonder why, if Burke meant to substitute loyalty to party for loyalty to a district, he said nothing about party at Bristol. There, Burke gave many reasons why he should not be expected to follow the popular will of Bristol, but none of them had anything to do with party. Similarly, in the 1790s, Burke was willing to split the Whig Party over the French Revolution, and was scathing in his criticism of both the Foxite Whigs and Pitt's administration. Burke was, to be sure, a party man, but, as these examples make clear, there were limits to his loyalty. Those limits, moreover, often came into play on the most vital issues. While Burke, at least, gave lip service to the ideal of party unity on major matters, combined with openness at the margins, it was precisely on the points of greatest importance that he was, in fact, most likely to break with party discipline. This is, perhaps, the mark of a moral man, but it is not necessarily that of a good party member.

It seems to me that Burke's answer to the problem of establishing popular government without endorsing majority rule lies in his definition of the "people." Mansfield writes about the role of the people in Burke's thought as though Burke saw them as an undifferentiated mass of equal or nearly equal individuals. But this is not always the case, for Burke often treated the people as a corporate body.[79] On these occasions, Burke acted as though the voice of the people, as MacCunn argues, is ". . . the voice not of the majority but of the organized people—the people in his own sense of the term, as shifted by the 'discipline of nature,' not only . . . into many ranks, classes, and interests, but into many grades of political capacity and incapacity."[80] Moreover, as Burke believed that society was one large corporate whole, so did he conceive of the various groups within it as smaller corporate entities. Since individuals vary widely in their places and talents, they ought also, in Burke's view, to differ in their right to participate in politics and in the extent of their control over the groups to which they belong, including over society at large. Thus, even early in his career, Burke opposed broadening the suffrage. In the "Observations on a Late Publication Entitled 'The Present State of the Nation,' " for instance, he rejected an increase in the number of voters: "I believe that most sober thinkers on this subject are rather of opinion, that our fault is on the other side; and that it would be more in the spirit of our constitution, and more agreeable to the pattern of our best laws, by lessening the number, to add to the weight and independence of our votes."[81] Burke believed that most people are incapable of choosing laws or policies for themselves; to give them the vote would be to expose them to the corrupting designs and finances of the ruling ministry. He felt that a better alternative was to restrict the vote to the leaders of society, allowing them to speak for the rest. Popular control and stability would be maintained, and little would be lost, for the natural ties of interest and affection in a hierarchical social order would insure that the leaders would look after the others. In this way, what was important about the principle of representation would be preserved—that the people be linked to their leaders and, through these leaders, retain control of the government—but the dangers inherent in majority rule would be avoided.

The third point of concern in Burke's theory of representation is his support for virtual representation. The concept of virtual representation is based on the belief that a commonality of interest between a district and a member of the legislature, a commonality frequently based on the member's election by a similar district elsewhere, rather than the actual choice of the representative by the district, can be sufficient to insure adequate popular influence in government. Thus, according to the theory, a member of Parliament who shared the interests of a district, and acted in its behalf could be said to represent it, even if he never set foot in it, and was not elected by it. The American Revolution and the parliamentary reform movement made virtual representation a central issue, for, in both cases, conservatives attempted to deflect attacks on the English political system which argued that it excluded relevant groups from participation in political affairs by arguing that such groups were, in fact, virtually represented in the House of Commons. For instance, Martin Howard, Jr. defended parliamentary taxation of the American colonies by noting that, "it is the opinion of the House of Commons, and may be considered as a law of parliament, that they are the representatives of every British subject, wheresoever he be."[82] Burke not only accepted virtual representation but often praised it highly. He wrote, "such a representation I think to be in many cases even better than the actual. It possesses most of its advantages and is free from many of its inconveniences . . . the peole may err in their choice; but common interest and common sentiment are rarely mistaken."[83] In the "Thoughts," Burke even extended virtual representation to include the king and the House of Lords.[84] The difficulty that virtual representation presents for the student of Burke's thought is that he appears to extend it too far; at times, it seems to replace actual representation entirely. One wonders, if a community of interest, and not actual choice, is all that is required, why should any one be allowed to vote? At an extreme, we are left with John Dickinson's concern: "is it possible to form an idea of a slavery more complete, more miserable, more disgraceful, than that of a people, where justice is administered, government exercised, and a standing army maintained, at the expense of the people, and yet without the least dependence upon them?"[85]

Burke replied to such questions by qualifying his defense of virtual representation in two ways. First, he maintained that virtual representation must have some basis in direct representation. Burke insisted, in arguing against the exclusion of Catholics from the franchise, that: "the member must have some relation to the constituent. As things stand, the Catholic, as a Catholic, and belonging to a description, has no *virtual* relation to the representative—but the *contrary* . . . Gratitude may not always have a very lasting power; but the frequent recurrence of an application for favors will revive and refresh it, and will necessarily produce some degree of mutual attention. It will produce, at least, acquaintance."[86] If there is no grounding in direct representation, Burke contended, member and elector become unfamiliar, understanding and sympathy between them are lost, and the loyalty necessary for virtual representation to make sense is destroyed. Second, there are, for

Burke, conditions under which even a combination of virtual and actual representation will not do. Where there is no true community of interest, virtual representation cannot serve as a substitute for direct representation. In discussing the issue of American taxation, Burke argued that the distance between the colonies and England, and the differences in their circumstances, made actual representation impossible, and any claim of virtual representation absurd.[87] To those who would extend the practice of virtual representation to America, Burke replied: "so, then, because some towns in England are not represented, America is to have no representatives at all."[88] While his conclusion that America should be left largely self-governing might be interpreted to mean merely that virtual and actual representation must be combined, I think Burke intended it to go beyond that. I believe that Burke meant that, to be truly a part of any community, a group must have meaningful direct representation. That is, it must have, not just *some* direct representation, but *substantial* direct representation: representation which has a chance to make a difference in Parliament. In the case of America, and in the cases of Ireland and the English Catholics, these conditions were not met. Burke thus proposed that these groups either be granted self-government or incorporated into the larger community complete with parliamentary representation.

One of the principal dangers of a theory of representation which treats it as a form of trusteeship is, then, that the concept of trust may become so attenuated that it loses most of its force. This, I believe, is the lesson of Burke's attempt to apply the theory to the government of India. Burke always insisted that effective representation requires some bond of affection between the trustor and the trustee, but no such bond existed between the East India Company and the people of India. Moreover, if the Company could not be relied upon to restrain its agents, the English Parliament and people, even more remote from Indian society and customs, could hardly be expected to do so. Thus, while the limitations of trusteeship are visible in other areas of Burke's thought, it is in regard to the non-European parts of the Empire that the theory completely breaks down. In the cases of such essentially European societies as Ireland and the American Colonies, Burke was able to stress the ties between the dependent society and England. In regard to Ireland, for example, Burke emphasized two points: that Ireland, had a degree of self-government through its own separate legislature, and that its self-rule was combined with the presence of men with Irish interests and backgrounds in the English Parliament.[89] It is, he said, "highly for the advantage of Ireland, that this Parliament, which, whether right or wrong, whether we will or not, will make some laws to bind Ireland, should always have in it some persons who by connection, by property, or by early prepossessions and affections, are attached to the welfare of that country.[90] In speaking of America and Ireland, Burke argued for the extension of common rights: "you cannot," he told the king, "have different rights and a different security in different parts of your dominions."[91] Yet, that is exactly what he proposed for India. None of the links Burke felt necessary for good government held in India, but he still sought to preserve British authority there. In Burke's own terms, that could not be done, for, without some substantial tie of affection or interest, any attempt by the English to govern India was destined to collapse in misunderstanding and rancor.

7

POLITICAL PARTIES AND THEIR USES

By the time Burke entered politics, the theory of party was considerably advanced. There were still those, even among active politicians, who denigrated party, and called for a suspension of all party ties.[1] Among more perceptive observers, however, party was no longer viewed as a temporary expedient to be adopted in exceptional circumstances but was accepted as a regular instrument of both government and opposition in all situations. In his *Essays,* David Hume, for example, argued that the point had been reached where "to abolish all distinctions of party may not be practical, perhaps not desirable in a free government."[2] Thus, in turning to Burke's discussion of political parties, the first question to consider is why, if parties had already won broad acceptance, did he find it necessary to devote so much effort to explaining and justifying them? In my opinion, the significance of Burke's writings on party lies in his view of party as the concrete embodiment of his theory of trusteeship. Burke believed that a properly formed and led party could serve as the basis of a coalition of good men united behind sound policies. In his view, such a combination would not merely provide a temporary expedient for resisting evil but would also act as a positive force for good. Burke held that party, then, could advance reform by removing some of the prime causes of and opportunities for corruption. He also held that it could, in an even more direct way, enable the aristocracy and its supporters to form themselves into the aristocratic interest and to become effective in politics. In this chapter, I will suggest that Burke's contribution to the theory of party was threefold. First, while not the first thinker to endorse party, he was one of the first to defend it as a permanent and necessary feature of representative government. Second, Burke perceived more clearly that most the consequences of the acceptance of party. Finally, through his association with the Rockingham Whigs, Burke played an important role in a number of attempts to link the theory and practice of party.

That Burke renewed the defense of party at the time and in the form that he did was a response, I think, to three factors. First, by the mid-1760s, a political vacuum had been created by the gradual decline of the Walpolean system of politics. Most students of eighteenth century politics agree that the fall of Walpole initiated a period of disintegration in the Whig party as it broke up into a number of small groups organized around various leaders. At the same time, Walpole's proscription of the Tories also broke down. This was, in part, the result of a decline in the importance of party labels, for men of generally Tory leanings had long since learned to call themselves Whigs as a means of gaining entrance into politics, and, after years in office, the Whig alliance had ceased to stand for anything very specific. Moreover, many of the Whig groups were willing to co-operate with the Tories as they maneuvered for power. Further, the new king, George III, encouraged the growth of Toryism as a means of reducing his dependence on the Whigs. When one places these political developments in the context of eighteenth century government, that is, of administrations which existed "not in order to legislate but in order to govern: to maintain order, to wage war and, above all, to conduct foreign affairs," one can see the central importance of holding office and of controlling the House of Commons.[3] Ironically, at the very time that writers like DeLolme were extolling British government for its balance and separation of powers, the chief political need was, in truth, more effective coordination.[4] A consideration of the party composition of a typical House of Commons will clarify matters. A December 1766, estimate divided the House into ten political groups: Rockingham's Whigs with 122 supporters, the king's friends with 100, Bute with 71, Chatham with 56, the Tories with 47, Bute Tories with 36, Bedford 35, Grenville 18, Doubtful 54, Absentees 16.[5] The total is 555, and the majority 228. Parliamentary experience suggested that generally some 200 to 220 votes would be needed to carry the House, though near the end of a session as few as 100 votes, or even less, might be sufficient. Since the king's friends usually voted with any administration, a politician would probably be able to govern with about 120 votes from other sources. A glance at the numbers shows that only Rockingham had any hope of forming such an administration, but practical considerations probably made it equally impossible for him. In short, with large umbrella parties on the decline, the need for coalition building made small parties, that is, blocs of unified and controlled votes, of greater importance than ever.

A second factor which contributed to the renewed interest in parties was the royal activism of George III after 1763. Both of the earlier Georges were, in a general sense, Court Whigs. They had been willing to work within the framework of the Walpolean Whig monopoly. George III, however, was strongly opposed to parties of any sort, and combined an intention to be more active in politics with a desire to free himself from the Whig leadership. It now seems clear that he was not out to subvert the constitution or to implement Bolingbroke's "Patriot King" ideal.[6] We need not postulate, as G. H. Guttridge does, a "New Toryism" to understand how George became an effective politician.[7] He simply used the parliamentary system to his own advantage. Given the resources of the crown and the tendency of many members of Parliament to support their monarch whatever the case, the king found ready support in Parliament. Moreover, as the common opinion of the time was that ministers were controlled by the Commons but chosen by and responsible to the crown, that support was magnified by his ability both to dismiss a popular administration and to keep an unpopular one in office. Burke caught something of this relationship in a letter to Lord Rockingham in which he explained the continuation of a weak and divided ministry, "the whole depends on the King. As long as the King thinks proper to keep them, though they will quarrel, they will remain . . ."[8] Yet, George III found that his attempts to conduct a non-partisan administration had, from his perpecitve, a negative side as well, for they alienated the traditional Whig leaders, who had learned politics under Walpole and the Pelhams. Seeing themselves cut off from power, those leaders combined to try to force their way back into office. Paradoxically, then, the king's campaign against parties promoted their resurgence.

Third, Burke defended parties because the greater involvement of the monarch in politics after 1763 appeared to him to be part of a conspiracy against liberty, and the reassertion of party seemed a sensible and necessary response. The classic expression of this view was, of course, Burke's "Thoughts on the Cause of the Present Discontents."[9] There Burke gave expression to the Rockingham Whig myth, for it was indeed a myth, of a secret government in which the king, in league with secret advisors, usually Lord Bute among others, excluded the Rockingham group from power, subverted whatever administration was in place, and directed affairs from behind the scenes.[10] Interestingly, others beside the Rockingham Whigs believed in a conspiracy. In a letter to Rockingham, Burke reported speaking to Temple of the "Court System and their Scheme of having dependent administrators" in terms which indicate that Temple concurred.[11] Similarly, the *Letters of Junius*, representing a relatively independent Whig position, are full of references to a ministerial plot against traditional English rights.[12] Further to the left, the language was often even stronger. Richard Price, in arguing against the American War, asked: "would it not be a fatal preparation for subduing yourselfs? Would not the disposal of *American* places, and the distribution of an *American* revenue, render that influence of the crown irresistible, which has already stabbed your liberties?"[13] The conspiracy myth even played a central role in the arguments of American radicals as they sought to justify their resistance to English authority. Whether true or not, there is no reason to doubt the sincerity of those who employed it. In a letter intended only for Rockingham, Burke wrote, "I do not say this from the least glimmering of hope . . . but solely, that in the Triumph of this mischievous System . . . nobody may be able to justly reproach your Lordship or your friends with having omitted any one justifiable or rational attempt to destroy it."[14] The myth was not a mere slogan, cynically put out for public consumption by a group of political insiders who really knew better. It was part of a creed which united the Rockingham Whigs for nearly thirty years. It animated their passions, governed their political strategy, and found expression in their public writings and their private correspondence.

I

Were the Rockingham Whigs a political party? The answer depends, in part, on the time period in question, for the group did not spring up all at once fully formed; it developed, rather, in a series of steps. Many of the central figures began their political careers as followers of the Duke of Newcastle in the early 1760s. As self-styled heirs of the political tradition of Walpole, they thought of themselves as part of "a long-continuing connection of men who had a large sense of public responsibility, who had settled the constitution perfectly, secured the Hanoverian dynasty, and understood the politics of Europe: men sagacious and temperate, natural leaders of the public, the wisest possible counselors of the throne."[15] Their pro-administration bias soon received a shock, for, in a dispute with the king over the broadening of the administration, Newcastle resigned from government, and, after a brief hesitation, urged his friends to join him in opposition. This proposal split Newcastle's allies—only about half actually went into opposition with him—but most of those who did urged both systematic and organized opposition to Bute's administration. These hardliners found a leader in Rockingham, who gradually eclipsed Newcastle as the head of the connection. By 1765, they were back in government as the first Rockingham administration. They did not yet, however, think of themselves as a party, and their administration was a traditional alliance of diverse elements. In a letter to Charles O'Hara, Burke revealed just how amorphous their idea of administration was: they could, he said, remain in office for a long time if they only acted wisely, which means "taking in Lord Bute, or at least not quarrelling with him, and enlarging their Bottom by taking in the Tories, and all the men of Business of the house of commons not listed against them."[16] Caught between Bute and Pitt, the Rockingham Administration fell quickly. Once again, the failure of the connection to govern effectively led to a reconsideration of the importance of organization. Moreover, though now out of office and reduced in size, the Rockingham Whigs were "no longer a sprawling confederation of groups of every description," but had become a relatively cohesive combination of old-line Court Whigs, aristocratic Whig family connections, and former Country Tories.[17] They were unified by their common loyalty to Rockingham, a vague attitude of fidelity to the revolutionary creed of Walpole, and their desire to defend the middle ground between the proto-conservatism of the king and his allies and the radicalism of the urban reformers.

In the eighteenth century, the label "party" was employed indiscriminately to describe all sorts of political groups. Typically, it meant nothing more than a loose and temporary parliamentary alliance formed in support of some leader.[18] Such groups generally had no organization to speak of, no support in the country at large, and little, if any, conception of a program to enact if they should achieve office. Indeed, the hope or expectation of office was often their only point of mutual concern. Most twentieth century scholars have, quite correctly in my view, refused to extend the designation "party" to these associations. However, it seems clear that the Rockingham Whigs were something more than a typical parliamentary group. When Burke, in the *Thoughts on the Present Discontents,* defined party as "a body of men united for promoting by their joint endeavors the national interest upon some particular principle in which they are all agreed," he seems to have had something rather different in mind.[19] Modern students of party, in fact, when they define their subject, appear to be rather close to Burke. Karl Lowenstein, for example, offers this definition: a party is a ". . . combination of persons holding similar ideological beliefs and possessing, for their realization, a permanent organization."[20] While modern definitions vary, most stress four elements: a permanent organization, a common ideology or philosophy, a willingness to compete in electoral or legislative politics, and a desire for office. The Rockingham Whigs endured for about thirty years, including a period after Rockingham's death under different leaders. They shared a common philosophy of moderate Whiggism, which was best expressed in Burke's writings, but which was also enunciated elsewhere by others. They organized and competed both in Parliament, as exemplified by their adoption of devices like the legislative caucus, and in the nation at large, as witnessed by the electoral activities of William Adams. Finally, they entered government two or perhaps three times: with Rockingham at the end of the American Revolution, under Fox and Portland in a coalition with North after the fall of Shelburne, and—provided one is willing to consider the group loyal to Portland and Fitzwilliam to still be the Rockingham Whigs—in support of Pitt in the early 1790s. To be sure, the Rockingham Whigs did not possess any of these characteristics to the degree that modern parties do, but, in my opinion, they were close enough to be considered a different subspecies of the same thing.

I call the Rockingham Whigs a different subspecies because certain characteristics of their party distinguish them from more modern political parties. To begin with, as Burke always emphasized, the party was exclusive. It was unabashedly aristocratic. One of the clearest expressions of his position came in a letter to Fitzwilliam in 1791: "that party had always had, from fools and knaves, the reproach, from honest and wise men, the estimation, of being an aristocratick party. Such I always understood it to be, in the true sense of the word; that is to say, a party grave and moral, equally removed from popular giddiness and profligacy on the one hand, and from servile Court compliances on the other."[21] Most of the time, Burke felt that the party's aristocratic leadership was a great strength, but, on occasion, he admitted that it had its disadvantages: "on paper we are the strongest of all, but we never can appear with true numbers. Our people act from principle, and, of course, very irregularly, and many of them very feebly . . ."[22] According to Burke, the landed class was given to pleasure and indolence; it seldom applied itself to politics, and, when it did, it often did so erratically. Secondly, The Whigs, though a party of principle, often had difficulty explaining just what that principle was. Burke's most detailed discussion of party philosophy probably occurred in the *Appeal From the New to the Old Whigs.*[23] There, he made clear that, at least as he saw it, the party was loyal to the tradition of the revolution, comitted to some degree of reform while opposing radicalism, and espoused a politics of moderation.[24] However, beyond this he did not go, and—given the party's notorious divisions on such vital issues as parliamentary reform and the French Revolution—it is questionable just how far he could have gone and remained a spokesman for the party as a whole. Third, in part as one of the consequences of the aristocratic bias of the party, there were periods when its link to the people was visibly weak. At times, Burke could argue for a proposal by saying, "it is necessary from the demands of the people, whose desires, when they do not militate with the stable and eternal rules of justice and reason (rules which are above us and above them), ought to be as a law to a House of Commons."[25] Yet, on other occasions, he denied that he ever courted public favor, and it appears as though he then thought of his party as little more than a handful of aristocrats and their dependents in Parliament.[26] Finally, it seems doubtful that the Rockingham Whigs ever seriously considered the possibility of true party government. While they often talked of going into government in concert, they lacked the strength to staff an administration on their own. Their more plausible goal was a coalition in which they had "the great strongholds of government in well-united hands, in order to secure the predominance of right and uniform principles; of having the capital offices of deliberation and execution of those who can deliberate with mutual confidence, and who will execute what is resolved with firmness and fidelity."[27] As we have seen, on their own, the Rockingham Whigs commanded barely half of the votes needed to control the Commons; they were quite aware that the rest would have to come from outside their own ranks.

II

Burke's defense of party rests on three interlocking arguments. Like David Hume and the Walpoleans before him, Burke saw party as an integral feature of popular government. At the outset of his "Observations on a Late Publication Entitled 'The Present State of the Nation,' " Burke argued that "party divisions, whether on the whole operating for good or evil, are things inseparable from free government."[28] Thus, in a sense, party is neither good nor bad as such. In a letter to William Baker, he wrote, "let those who are ashamed of the persons or the designs of their party, shuffle away their connections with it, and while they cabal in private, disavow one another in publick. The connection and friendship of good men is their glory. It is a thing which bad men cannot long mimick; no wonder they should look upon it with malignity and envy."[29] This sensitivity to circumstance has led some commentators to consider Burke a reluctant advocate of party, to insist that he thought party to be merely a necessary evil. Harvey Mansfield Jr. claims that Burke saw party as a form of public conspiracy, at best an unfortunate but necessary expedient.[30] Frank O'Gorman agrees, and insists that Burke meant party to be used for "annihilating conflict" and then cast aside.[31] This, it seems to me, is a misreading of Burke. As a careful examination of the *Thoughts on the Present Discontents* makes clear, it is the intervention of the people, not the use of party, which is to be limited to times of crisis. Burke wrote, "I see no other way for the preservation of a decent attention to public interest in the representatives, *but the interposition of the body of the people itself,* whenever it shall appear . . . that these representatives are going to overleap the fences of the law, and to introduce an arbitrary power."[32] What many scholars have missed is that Burke viewed party as morally neutral. In his opinion, parties may, and often do, serve evil men and ends, but that is only one possibility. They are also capable of much good. According to Burke, the greatest patriots in the greatest commonwealths have endorsed parties, and England, herself, was governed by party in one of her most illustrious periods.[33]

Burke's second line of defense for parties was a consideration of the positive benefits parties can offer. These, he said, center on the desire of those who engage in politics to see their views prevail. As Burke put it, "I find it impossible to conceive, that any one believes in his own politics, or thinks them to be of any weight, who refuses to adopt the means of having them reduced into practice."[34] Burke began by examining the advantages which accompany parties whether they share in office or not. First, he maintained that party can link the people to their government, and, therefore, insure a measure of popular understanding and control of administration.[35] In addition, Burke suggested that, in times of uncertainty and confusion, party provides a guide to action. He argued that one of the characteristics of politics is that it is often unclear what is right and, in fact, there are numerous occasions when the question is not really one of right but of convenience. At such times, the prudent man needs guidance as he seeks to discover what is useful to the commonwealth. Party, if properly constituted and motivated, can provide a means of judging the flow of interest and benefit.[36] Burke further saw party as a boon to the weak, for, "in a connection, the most inconsiderable man, by adding to the weight of the whole, has his value and his use; out of it, the greatest talents are wholly unserviceable to the public."[37] Burke also offered a reverse corruption thesis: if corruption spreads by contact, so might virtue. In a party, then, "virtue will catch as well as vice."[38] A party can expose evil, communicate the alarm to its members, and organize them to defend their interests and that of the nation. Burke claimed that, "whilst men are linked together, they easily and speedily communicate the alarm of an evil design. They are enabled to fathom it with common counsel, and to oppose it with united strength."[39] Lastly, according to Burke, when in government, party can, if in the proper hands, control corruption and give strength to policymaking. Often, he said, the problem is that government is weak and indecisive, not that it is too strong. In such cases, "what we want is to establish more fully an opinion of uniformity, and consistency of character, in the leading men of the state," and party can provide the missing sense of purpose and direction.[40] It is worth noting that Burke's conception of the use of party was strongly instrumental. That is, he concentrated on the value of party as a means to some goal: in this case, of course, the goal of reform. Given a plan, Burke argued, party is an effective means of enacting it.

Only in Burke's third line of defense, an argument that the particular circumstances of late eighteenth century English politics require the formation of party, can one find any indication that he did not think of party as a permanent feature of political life. However, even here, I think, the evidence indicates that Burke thought of the politics of the 1760s and 1770s as an instance of a general problem—the rooting out of corruption—rather than as a unique situation. The problem, as he viewed it, was a renewed threat to the people's liberty. "Few," Burke said, "are the partisans of departed tyranny."[41] Each age, he continued, has its own forms, and the form of tyranny in his time was a new style of executive abuse under the guise of constitutionalism: "the power of the crown, almost dead and rotten as prerogative, has grown up anew . . . under the name of influence."[42] Interestingly, Burke believed himself to be dealing with a system of government, and a party system at that. In his view, its essential feature was the separation of formal authority in a ministry, chosen as in the past, from real authority, which would be vested in a "secret cabinet." He believed that the secret cabinet actually governed, but was screened from observation by the powerless formal cabinet. Moreover, since Parliament's constitutional authority to block administrative action was unchanged, Burke argued that the practitioners of secret government found it necessary both to organize a parliamentary party to support the crown and to destroy the traditional Whig party which might oppose it. The former purpose, he thought, could be accomplished easily enough by the manipulation of rewards and punishment and by the use of a rhetoric of "king's friends" to hoodwink the gullible. However, Burke insisted that the destruction of the opposition would be more difficult. Still, he noted that there were means to hand. The tried and true methods of divide and conquer could be employed. Opponents of the new system could be harassed, as was Wilkes, and even destroyed. Those who were unaware could be brought—temporarily—into government. After a time, the bulk of the dupes would be cast out and the most corruptible added to the ruling coalition. The result, Burke maintained, was ironic, for the satellite "party goes out much thinner than it came in; and is only reduced in strength by its temporary possession of power."[43] Finally, Burke said, to further obscure responsibility, the leaders behind the new system work through proxies to attain their ends, especially when they wish to attack their enemies.

Burke rejected the most commonly recommended remedies for this form of corruption: shorter parliaments, increasing the number of voters, eliminating placemen, and extending the vote to America. None of these would improve the situation, he thought, and each had liabilities of its own. For example, he argued that adding voters would only increase the general level of political incompetence. Burke claimed that, "most sober thinkers on this subject are rather of opinion, that our fault is on the other side; and that it would be more in the spirit of our constitution, and more agreeable to the pattern of our best laws, by lessening the number, to add to the weight and independency of our votes."[44] For Burke, the simple truth was that the House of Commons could never control the administration unless it was controlled by its constituents.[45] But Parliament had, in his opinion, become subservient to the will of the court, and its elections were carefully regulated to prevent any change. What he believed was required, therefore, was for the people to reaffirm their power over the Commons. The people should seek a return to the times when "every sort of government [had] its administration correspondent to its legislature," and the legislature corresponded to the will of the nation.[46] The solution was thus in the people, for "until a confidence in government is re-established, the people ought to be excited to a more strict and detailed attention to the conduct of their representatives. Standards for judging more systematically upon their conduct ought to be settled in the meetings of counties and corporations. Frequent and correct lists of the voters in all important questions ought to be provided."[47] Still, Burke was no democrat. He believed that the people, left to themselves, were prone to violence and extremism. Thus, Burke felt that party should play another role as well. It must also serve to control and domesticate the people even as it works for reform. According to Burke, the people must have organization and leadership, for, "when bad men combine, the good must associate; else they will fall, one by one, an unpitied sacrifice in a contemptible struggle."[48] Moreover, he left no doubt that he felt that this leadership could only come from a party, one formed "to oppose a ministry dangerous from its very constitution, as well as its measures," and, of course, that the very prototype of such a party was the Rockingham Whigs, men who "nothing but the strongest and most uncorrupt sense of their duty to the public could have prevailed . . . to undertake the king's business at such a time."[49]

A final consideration is in order. Along with his praise for party, Burke also presented a harsh and unsympathetic picture of those who do not work in party. In part, his position was made clear in his explanation of his rejection of the politics of the elder Pitt. Pitt was something of an anachronism. A believer in the ancient constitution, he espoused limited government, individual rights, and was violently anti-party.[50] At first, Burke was somewhat attracted to Pitt, but he ultimately remained loyal to Rockingham. In a letter to a friend, Burke explained his choice: "opposition never was to me a desirable thing . . . but then the walk is certain; there are no contradictions to reconcile; no cross points of honour or interest to adjust; all is clear and open and the wear and tear of mind, which is saved by keeping aloof from crooked politicks, is a consideration absolutely inestimable."[51] In the "Thoughts on the Present Discontents," Burke urged his readers not to fall for the cant of the non-party politicians. When they say, "not men but measures," he argued, they intend to excuse their own lack of principle, for, "would it not be an extraordinary cast upon the die, that a man's connections should degenerate into faction, precisely at the critical moment when they lose their power, or he accepts a place?"[52] In the "Observations," he denounced the administrations formed by such men. They speak of an administration of ability and virtue, he said, but that "conveys no definite idea at all; nor does it apply specifically to our grand national distemper. All parties pretend to these qualities."[53] If, Burke continued, in such an administration, each man remains loyal to his previous associates, the administration will be ineffective. On the other hand, if the various individuals do not remain loyal to their old friends, how can we expect them to honor any promise or commitment they might now make. The antiparty politician, no matter how honest, will, in Burke's opinion, gradually lose his purity and become a mere time server. He asked: when these politicians maintain that all politics is corrupt, do they not condemn themselves? Burke argued that such a charge not only condemns all human nature, it denies the possibility of any meaningful reform, for, "if all men who act in a public situation are equally selfish, corrupt, and venal, what reason can be given for desiring any sort of change, which, beside the evils which must attend all changes, can be productive of no possible advantages?"[54] Burke was never one to deny the evil or unpleasantness in politics, but, as he said at Bristol, he entered politics to have his share of doing good.[55] That good, Burke believed, could only be accomplished in combination with others.

III

It is widely acknowledged that Burke made a major contribution to the eighteenth century discussion of the nature and significance of political parties, and, therefore, played an important role in their acceptance as a vital feature of representative government. What is perhaps less generally appreciated is that, as a leading "man of business" for the Rockingham Whigs, and as an astute analyst of the politics of his time, he also wrote extensively on the question of party tactics. Since the parties of Burke's day were almost exclusively parliamentary, with little or no base in the country at large, the obvious place to begin an analysis of this aspect of his thought is with the techniques the Rockingham Whigs employed in the Legislature itself. Their ideal, of course, was party government in which all of the administrative positions were in the hands of members of the same party, and that party had a majority of the seats in both houses of Parliament. However, I have already suggested that no eighteenth century party came near realizing that ideal, for no party controlled enough seats and, moreover, the political conventions of the time militated against any attempt by a single party to exercise decisive control of policy-making. Thus, Burke admitted that even a Rockingham administration must include other political factions: "no system of that kind can be formed, which will not leave room fully sufficient for healing coalitions . . ."[56] For this reason, throughout his long association with Rockingham and his successors, Burke was a strong advocate of coalition with other groups. As late as the 1790s, Burke was a prime mover in the decision of Portland and Fitzwilliam to accept the split between the Old and New Whigs as final and enter the Pitt administration. He explained to Fitzwilliam: "I, therefore, instead of blaming Ministry or opposition, set myself to think in what manner they might in future cooperate to the correction of former errours and to the recovery of our former place in Europe."[57] In fact, almost up to his own death, long after he had retired from Parliament and while he was beset with painful illnesses, Burke continued to plan and calculate the potential advantages of various alliances. One of his last letters to his protégé, French Laurence, was taken up with a long examination of the comparative merits of Laurence throwing his support to Pitt or Fox.[58] Indeed, even then he was somewhat less concerned about the demise of the Whig party as he had known it than with the possibility of creating a new third force bound to neither of the great parliamentary leaders.

Still, over time Burke became increasingly disenchanted with coalition government. The simple truth is that most of the Rockingham experiments with coalition government ended badly. The Rockingham administration of the late 1760s was very brief, and its major accomplishment—the passage of the Declaratory Act—was widely regarded as one of the principal causes of the American Revolution. Similarly, the Rockingham-Shelburne Ministry ended the American War, but, after the death of Rockingham, broke up in a bitter feud between Fox and Shelburne. Indeed, only the Fox-North coalition did not collapse through internal contradictions. However, even it failed as the aggressive attacks of the king's allies and Pitt's war of attrition wore it down. Moreover, the alliance with Pitt in the early 1790s was wracked by dissension and mistrust, split the Whig party over Irish politics, and led to the conversion of Portland and several other leading Whigs to Pitt's new style conservatism. It is not surprising, then, that Burke came to see the basic weakness of coalitions as the lack of trust and cooperation which frequently characterized relations between the component parties. In speaking of the misunderstanding between Pitt and the Whigs, he wrote: "it is plain that Mr. P. is made to think, that his new Colleagues instead of coming in for his support have coalited with him for the purpose of [hindering] and controlling his power if not of tripping up his Heels."[59] The results of such misunderstandings were often devastating. At a minimum, they could destroy an administration or reduce a party's strength, and they might even destroy the party. In another of the letters written after his retirement from active politics, Burke reflected on the decline and fall of the Whig party. He concluded, "undoubtedly the manner in which the D: of Portland conducted the late Coalition (between the Whigs and Pitt in 1794) was the cause of the utter dissipation of the Party . . ."[60] Yet, it is important to note that Burke's lament was couched in terms of coalition and not of party. He did not become disillusioned with parties in the 1790s, so much as with the Whig party, in particular, and with coalitions of parties in general.

Eighteenth century administrations were not generally expected to have a legislative program; they existed primarily to maintain order, to encourage trade, to tax, and to conduct foreign affairs. As Pares puts it, "I know of no deliberate attempts to make acceptance of office conditional upon stipulations as to policy earlier than the beginning of George III's reign."[61] As policy-making was considered the preserve of the monarch, the traditional view was that ministers were responsible only to the King. A minister was to offer advice to the crown as to what was in the king's interest, and he was to seek to carry out the king's will, whatever it might be. It was broadly conceded that parliament could attempt to influence and even direct an administration, harass it when it did not pursue policies acceptable to parliament, and might even seek to force it from office. However, an administration was not necessarily expected to resign in the face of a hostile majority in parliament, so long as it maintained the support of the king, and, if a government fell, parliament had no right to choose its successor. How, then, could a party, even one in government, force a recalcitrant king to accept their views on policy? One technique, which the Rockingham Whigs attempted on three occasions, was the mass resignation. The theory was that the party would demonstrate to the king that his government could not continue without its support. Once out of government, the party would then obstruct policy in the Parliament. This, in turn, would prove the unpopularity of the royal program, and force the king to recall it to office. A typical example of the tactic occurred at the end of the American War. In July 1783, Burke advised Fox that cooperation with Shelburne was impossible and urged resignation: "if that be the case, the only question upon your staying in will be, whether office be or be not the best post to occupy in the war that *must* be between you."[62] Unfortunately, the ploy almost never worked. The key to success, Burke noted, was party unity: "if your friends will not act with you all plans are vain."[63] Yet, most mass resignations were carried out only halfheartedly. In fact, the Whig leaders usually tried to hedge their bets by urging some of their supporters to remain in government after they left themselves. Moreover, in every case, some members of the administration rejected their own party and refused to leave office. Given the paramount importance of office in the period, it is easy to understand why. Indeed, the resignations usually freed the king of unwanted allies, and, as he seldom had much difficulty in replacing the departed ministers, they often left him stronger than he was before the crisis.

Once out of office, the party had a number of options. The most common opposition tactic—the harassment of administration on all issues—the Rockingham Whigs eschewed as irresponsible and factious. Rather, they preferred an approach which was rather unusual in the eighteenth century: a selective opposition to government policy on the basis of a principled set of programs of their own. While we can see in such a choice an important step toward the modern idea of responsible representative government, this tactic had serious liabilities in their time. In some circles, opposition was legitimated only by its lack of principle and discrimination. To oppose everything meant that no particular point had to be taken too seriously. On the other hand, principled opposition was believed disloyal, for opposition was easily confused with treason. Moreover, with the general ambivalence on the nature of ministerial responsibility, the lack of clear ties to a popular electorate, and the absence of large parties which might actually carry out their programs after overturning and replacing a prior administration, the likelihood of a successful policy-based opposition was quite remote. Nonetheless, the Rockingham Whigs attempted it a number of times, and even, on occasion, attained results. Burke explained the logic of principled opposition in a letter to Rockingham early in the American war: "for if no other persons, and no other regular system, are held out to the people at large, as objects of their confidence in time of distress, they must of necessity resort to the ministry."[64] Similarly, Burke's "Letter to the Sheriffs of Bristol, On the Affairs of America," was a masterful statement of policy-based opposition.[65] Burke linked the American policy of the North administration to the conventional Rockingham rhetoric of secret government, and, therefore, portrayed the government's program as a threat, not only to America but to England as well, that could only be met by united popular support for the Rockingham party.

Since the idea of ministerial responsibility was unclear and such devices as votes of confidence largely unknown, the question of how an unsuccessful or unpopular minister was to be removed from office was a most difficult one. One possibility, long sanctioned by tradition, was impeachment. Impeachment had, of course, been fairly common in the preceding century, and, as in the Sacheverall Affair, it remained part of the inventory of possible weapons well into the eighteenth century. Indeed, in an aside in the *Thoughts,* Burke lamented its passing.[66] I have already discussed, in the previous chapter, the most famous case of impeachment in Burke's career, that of Warren Hastings for his supposed maladministration of India. The Hastings case was not a party issue, for Burke drew support from a variety of groups in the House of Commons. In the end, even Pitt and a number of his supporters voted with Burke. Nonetheless, Burke saw Hastings' impeachment trial as a precedent for resisting the use of corruption to control the House. He made the point clear to Dundas: "a body of men, united in a close connexion of common guilt and common apprehension of danger in the moment, with a strong and just confidence of future power if they escape it, and possessed of a measure of wealth and influence which perhaps you yourself have not calculated at any thing like its just magnitude, is not forming, but actually formed in this Country. This faction is at present ranged under Hastings as an Indian leader; and it will have very soon, if it has not already, an English Leader of considerable enterprise and no contemptible influence."[67] Modern scholars consider Burke's charge overblown, but, from his perspective, the issue was a vital one. He believed that public officials must be held responsible for their actions. Yet, he could not see how that was to be done. Impeachment was not, for Burke, a matter to be lightly entered into. It was always unwieldy and, in certain circumstances, it could be unjustifiably harsh. If parties somehow came to be tied up in it, it could poison the atmosphere and make the forbearance and comity essential to free government impossible to sustain. Yet, in the absence of other, more effective, remedies, Burke felt that impeachment could be a very regretable necessity.

The final parliamentary tactic, secession, was perhaps also the most extreme and the most dangerous. Burke believed that secession should be considered only in regard to such matters of surpassing importance as American policy. The central characteristic of these issues was that the Rockingham Whigs not only could not persuade or defeat the administration but were also unwilling to accept the legitimacy of its policy. As Burke put it in his *Letter to the Sheriffs of Bristol,* secession was a last recourse when "I cannot conscientiously support what is against my opinion, nor prudently contend with what I know is irresistible."[68] In the case of America, Burke felt that the colonies were bound to be defeated with consequences serious for both their own political systems and that of England. Therefore, he argued that the Whigs should issue a public statement decrying administration policy and absolving themselves of any responsibility for the consequences. They should then absent themselves from Parliament, and return only when government underwent some change of heart or when some other issue of equally great significance arose. However, secession was prone to serious difficulties. First, it ran much the same risks as mass resignations, though at a different level. If a party seceded from parliament, it only made it easier for the administration to carry its proposals, and usually denied the party's position the defense and publicity it required. Moreover, all the attempted secessions of the Rockinghams floundered on the rocks of non-cooperation. Of that of 1777, Hoffman notes, "so ill-executed was this policy that not even all of Rockingham's friends fell in with it."[69] Finally, with the public mood inflamed by heated controversy, the tactic could be hazardous. In weighing the advantages and disadvantages of the 1777 secession, Burke cautioned Rockingham that it might lead to trials for treason: "you are then, not to consider what they may legally and justly do, but what a Parliament, omnipotent in power, inflamed with party rage, and personal resentment, operating under the implicit military obedience of Court discipline, is capable of."[70] Yet, in spite of dangers and the Whigs' bad experiences with the device, Burke maintained his enthusiasm. As late as 1789, he proposed an informal secession as a way out of the party's difficulties over the Regency Crisis.

The logic of the Rockingham Whigs' position led them to extend their political activity beyond Parliament, itself. As Burke consistently acknowledged, for the House of Commons to serve as a trustee for the people's interests, it had to be kept free of control by Court or Ministerial influence. Since this, in turn, required that the members of parliament be properly elected and carefully reviewed by the electors, it was necessary for advocates of reform to go behind parliament to the people at large. In Burke's view, if the secret link between court influence and parliamentary authority could be broken, and that between parliament and the people restored, the party, as leader of the popular cause, would be in a position to block any attempt by the crown to subvert the constitution and could force its way into power. In its early years, the party generally limited itself to searching for candidates who would support it in parliament and to trying to match those candidates with patrons who controlled various electoral districts. Given the nature of the unreformed electoral system this approach made sense. With only a small fraction of England's adult males enfranchised, and in a system with badly skewed electoral districts, any attempt to run a slate of candidates committed to a common program in a bid for popular support would have failed badly. Still, elections did mean something, and appeals for votes did have relevance in at least some districts. Thus, through the 1770s and 1780s, the Whigs' electoral tactics gradually became more sophisticated. Burke was a strong advocate of such endeavors; his own campaigns at Bristol were part of the program, and he was an active party manager in its efforts elsewhere as well. Indeed, Burke's letter to the Duke of Portland describing the 1780 election at Bristol is a classic exposition of electioneering tactics.[71] Its understanding of the niceties of urban campaigning would do a modern ward heeler proud. However, the Rockingham Whigs soon learned that popular appeals could be double-edged. In 1784, after being dismissed by the king and replaced by Pitt, they appealed to the people. But the people ratified the king's victory. Burke was bitter: "the people did not like our work; and they joined the Court to pull it down. The demolition is very complete. Others may be more sanguine; but for me to look forward to the Event of another twenty years toil—it is quite ridiculous."[72] Still, Burke and the Whig party persisted. Just two years later we find him apologizing to Gilbert Elliot for being late in replying to a letter. His explanation was that his time had been swallowed up by an election in Westminster.[73] In 1790, six years after the collapse of the Coalition, the Whigs set a new standard. That year, the highly contested election, Donald Ginther reports, "was far more elaborately organized by the parliamentary opposition than had been any previous election of the century." [74]

IV

One issue remains. Thus far, I have discussed how Burke saw representation within the existing political system, but another matter of vital importance was the question of parliamentary reform. This issue was doubly crucial for Burke. First, as an important example of the complex political dynamics which can develop when his views on trusteeship and representation, political parties, and reform come together, Burke's stand on parliamentary reform reveals many of the weaknesses of those theories. In fact, I would argue that the inability of the Rockingham Whigs to realize Burke's ideal of an effective reform coalition, was, from a mechanical standpoint, a consequence of their failure to become a party adequate to the task Burke set. Thus, it seems to me that there are two central areas where the limitations of Burke's theory of trusteeship are most clearly revealed: in his response to the domestic movement for parliamentary reform, where the Rockingham Whigs failed to create a sufficient link between the people and their representatives, and in imperial affairs, where Burke was unable to establish devices or procedures for controlling colonial authorities. Second, parliamentary reform was so important an issue for Burke because it was an issue which would just not go away. From his entrance into politics in the early 1760s until his death in 1797, Burke was never long without being forced to face proposals to restructure English politics by changing either the composition of parliament or its mode of election. In the early years of his political career, he was confronted by the movement in support of John Wilkes and the Middlesex electors in their campaign to place Wilkes in the House of Commons against the opposition of both the House, itself, and the king. Then, in the late 1770s, as the American War dragged on and domestic problems increased, a new movement took up where the earlier one had left off. With the tentative and partial help of the Whigs, the reformers launched a petitioning movement which seemed, at first, to offer great promise. However, the conservative Whigs distrusted the radicals. While the Whigs were prepared to refine the existing system, through what they called "economical reform," they were unwilling to substantially restructure the system of representation. With the movement thus split, the reform forces were defeated in Parliament in April 1785. Yet, the story did not end there, for, by 1790, a new wave of parliamentary reform agitation was underway.

I begin, then, with the Wilkes Affair, for Burke's handling of the issues raised by that conflict was mirrored in his reaction to the later debates on parliamentary reform. Burke's attitude was complex. He, and the Rockingham party generally, sought to use the reform movement, but they wished to contain it as well. Wilkes was not close to the Rockingham Whigs, and the Whigs rather disapproved of him for both moral and political reasons. Nonetheless, they felt that the cause of free elections was sufficiently important that they supported him in the parliamentary debates on whether he should be seated. The standard Whig case was that Wilkes' libel case had already been decided elsewhere, that parliament had no right to set aside the choice of the people, and that expulsion required a law passed by both Houses and could not be had by the resolution of a single house. Moreover, they held that the expulsion was not really based on the stated reasons. As Burke argued, "resistance to power has shut the door of the House of Commons to one man; obsequiousness and servility, to none."[75] On the other hand, the Rockingham Whigs opposed the demands for structural reform. Denying that parliament was ever intended to be a fully representative body, Burke insisted that any attempt to make it one was unwise. Shorter parliaments, he claimed, would only increase the corruption for "I should be fearful of committing, every three years, the independent gentlemen of the country into a contest with the treasury."[76] Place bills, that is, proposals to eliminate those who held some other governmental post from sitting in parliament, would also backfire: they would force legitimate interests to seek influence through illegitimate means, and, moreover, deny parliament the advantage of sound military and professional opinion.[77] Nor did Burke believe that increasing the number of voters would help. Indeed, as I have suggested, he thought that the opposite might be true.[78] Finally, in a passage of considerable comic inventiveness in the *Observations on a Late Publication on the Present State of the Nation,* Burke mocked as utterly impractical any attempt to extend representation to include Americans in the Commons.[79]

As they supported Wilkes in parliament, the Rockingham Whigs also joined the First Petitioning Movement of 1769–70. This was an attempt by the combined forces of Rockingham, Pitt, and the Wilkites to gather signatures for a petition to the King requesting the dissolution of parliament. At first, Rockingham and some of the more conservative Whig leaders were reluctant to support the drive because they feared the radicalism of some of its advocates, and because they thought it inconsistent to petition the king for redress of grievances which flowed from his own actions. On the other hand, Burke was a strong supporter of the movement from the beginning. He was always more aware than Rockingham of the value of allies from outside the existing system, and also more sympathetic to the urban reformers. As he put it, "if we mean to get *redress,* we must strengthen the hands of the minority within Doors by the accession of the publick opinion; strongly declared to the Court, which is the Source of the whole mischief."[80] Moreover, he recognized petitioning as a time-honored and essentially conservative mode of reform.[81] Finally, Burke stressed the importance of controlling the radicals.[82] In the end, Rockingham came around, and the party played a major role in both drafting—Burke, himself, wrote several—and circulating the petitions. Indeed, in the eyes of many scholars, the territorial connections of the Whigs and their influence at the county level of politics in various parts of the country were instrumental in securing the signatures of something like one-quarter of the voting population of England.[83] Yet, it would be difficult to consider the campaign a success. It did not lead to the reform of Parliament, and its internal conflicts between the Rockingham Whigs and their more radical allies both reduced its effectiveness and created a well of suspicion which made future attempts at collaboration more difficult.

The same ambivalence about appeals for popular support runs through Burke's attitude toward the reform agitation of the late 1770s and early 1780s. This movement began as a rather diffuse protest against high taxes, government corruption, and the war in America.[84] The Rockingham Whigs, in league with the radicals led by Christopher Wyvill, sought to build on the protests and to turn them into a concerted campaign against the crown and Lord North's administration. Thus, they once again launched a petition movement, this time concentrating their fire at the county level. As an indication of the extent of the Whig involvement in the movement, N. C. Phillips estimates that they directly inspired twelve of the twenty-seven county petitions, and he suggests that their influence was absent in only two.[85] At first, the radicals and the Whigs achieved a considerable measure of agreement, but over time they split on the question of parliamentary reform. The radicals sought to include it in the petitions, while the Whigs wished to limit them to demands for an end to corruption and a purifying of the existing system. As O'Gorman puts it, the Whig objective "was not to make Parliament more efficient or more representative. It was to restore the checks and balances in the constitution and the proper separation between the executive and the legislature."[86] The final break between the two parties came in the spring of 1780, when the radical defeated efforts by the Whigs to limit the London petition to a call for economical reform, to strike all mention of parliamentary reform, and to take control of the Yorkshire meeting.[87] With these defeats Rockingham, who had always been uneasy about popular movements, lost most of his enthusiasm for cooperation with the radicals, and the Whigs reverted to more traditional political tactics.

What unity was achieved by the county movement was grounded on economical rather than parliamentary reform. Economical reform was a plan to oppose misgovernment by destroying the corruption on which it depended. The Rockingham Whigs proposed that a systematic review of all offices of state be undertaken, that those positions which were used merely to reward an administration's followers be eliminated, that those offices which were necessary be streamlined and rationalized, that the levels of taxation and expenditure sufficient to manage public business be determined, and that all waste and fraud in government be put to an end. Both reform groups agreed on economical reform as a minimum program; however, the Whigs saw it as all that was required, while the radicals regarded it as a useful basis for further action. Veitch notes: "Burke and his friends . . . were on the whole well satisfied to have restricted illegitimate influence and to have stopped up the channels of direct corruption; advanced reformers remained, on the contrary, unsatisfied, and accepted economical reform as no more than a preliminary, though it might be a necessary preliminary, to more drastic measures of constitutional reconstruction."[88] At first, prospects seemed bright: the House of Commons, on April 6, 1780, passed Dunning's famous motion declaring that the influence of the crown was increasing and ought to be reduced. But this was the high water mark. When asked shortly thereafter to put teeth into its stand, the House demurred, and economical reform was defeated. It might be thought that his support of economical reform represented an advance over the pious cries for elector vigilance which characterized Burke's earlier opposition to structural reform, and to represent a movement toward accepting parliamentary reform. For example, he wrote to the Chairman of the Buckinghamshire Meeting: "I will not deny that our constitution may have faults; and that those faults, when found, ought to be corrected," and continued "I most heartily wish that the deliberate sense of the Kingdom on this great subject should be known. When it is known it *must* be prevalent."[89] Yet, even in this letter Burke remained cautious: "on the whole that constitution has been our own pride, and an object of admiration to all other nations. It is not everything which appears at first view to be faulty in such a complicated plan that is determined to be so in reality."[90] Further, Burke continued to express reservations on grounds of practicality and possible corruption. In his "Speech on a Bill for Shortening the Duration of Parliaments" he said "I do not seriously think that this Constitution, even to the wrecks of it, could survive fire triennial elections."[91] Moreover, new themes began to creep into his argument. For instance, Burke now began to join Rockingham in questioning the intentions of the reformers. He asked if the advocates of parliamentary reform really meant to preserve the system by broadening it. Rather, Burke suspected that, "the great object of most of these reformers is, to prepare the destruction of the Constitution, by disgracing and discrediting the House of Commons."[92] Probably the best indication of the growing gulf between Burke and the radicals may be their different assessments of the election of 1784. Burke felt that it was a tragedy in which the people had turned on their best friends—the Whigs—while the radicals treated it as a a clear victory which had returned a Prime Minister, William Pitt, pledged to parliamentary reform and given him increased support in the House.

With the political crises of the 1790s, one sees a further hardening of Burke's position on parliamentary reform. Though the new movement for reform grew out of such previous efforts as the two petitioning movements, and even employed some of the same methods, Burke argued that conditions and times had changed. In his opinion, what had been acceptable in the past was no longer. As he told John Noble, "if ever there was a time, peculiarly unfavourable, to any alteration, in anything which touches Church or State, it is this Moment."[93] According to Burke, the reformers had learned to speak a new language of abstract rights and he did not approve of it.[94] Burke left no doubt what he felt the source of this new extremism to be. Similar tactics, he thought, were written large in the example set by the revolutionaries in France.[95] As the changed circumstances of the 1790s had produced new demands, Burke now believed that a new response was in order. Insofar as it applied to the issue of parliamentary reform, this response contained three elements: first, Burke urged all parties to suspend normal politics and to join in a common resistance to French imperialism; second, he supported the move of the Portland Whigs toward a coalition with Pitt's administration; and, third, he argued that all discussion of parliamentary reform should be put aside until the crisis passed.[96] Burke was fully in accord with public opinion on the issue. With the Proclamation against Sedition of May 21, 1792, the Pitt administration turned forceably against the radicals, a wave of repression ensued, and further demands for reform were met by arrests and trials for sedition.

Still, to simply say that Burke became even more vehement in his opposition to parliamentary reform in the 1790s is to tell only part of the story. It is an important part of the story, for the ramifications of Burke's rejection of reform extended to other areas as well. For example, he now opposed parliamentary reform in Ireland because of its possible effect in England: "tho' the grounds are a little different yet the principle is so much the same, that it would be impossible long to resist an alteration of the same kind on this side of the Water; and I never have doubted, since I came to the Years of discretion, nor ever can doubt, that such changes in this Kingdom would be preliminary steps to our utter ruin . . ."[97] However, Burke admitted that, in light of the specific context of Irish politics, with its exclusion of the Irish Catholics from virtually all power, he was obliged to offer the Irish reformers a substitute for what he would deny. Thus, characteristically, Burke proposed to improve the Irish political system by broadening it to include the Catholics. As he saw matters, the exclusion of Catholics from the Irish suffrage "seems to be only to mark jealousy and suspicion, and not to provide security in any way."[98] Similarly, in a well-known letter to Langrishe, Burke argued that the incorporation of the Catholics would ease their grievances, could be accomplished by degrees, and would derail the question of parliamentary reform.[99] Moreover, Burke maintained that, if some substitute for parliamentary reform was not introduced in Ireland, all bets would be off. What, he asked, if the question were one of equal representation for all or no representation whatsoever?[100] I do not know if, on this issue, the road to Ireland ran both ways for Burke. It is unclear whether similar considerations informed Burke's attitude toward parliamentary reform in England, for he obviously thought that a much more open and laudable system already. And that, in my view, precisely demonstrates his dilemma. Though Burke never completely shut the door on parliamentary reform, he also never found a specific reform plan he could endorse. Adamantly in favor of government responsible to the people, he was yet unwilling to accept the one device which could make that responsibility effective: a popularly controlled parliament which, in turn, controlled the administration of the country's business. Burke's theory of trusteeship did not, necessarily, entail universal suffrage or mass democracy, but it did require that the electorate, however determined, be able to enforce its will.

8

THE DECLINE AND FALL OF THE THEORY OF SOVEREIGNTY

From the 1770s on, a series of controversies served to test the practical effectiveness of Burke's approach to politics. I have already argued that his theory of representation, centered as it was on the concept of trusteeship, proved to be seriously flawed when he attempted to apply it to domestic reform. In this chapter, I will argue that the same weakness marred Burke's stand on a major issue of imperial policy: the government of the American Colonies. Viewed from one perspective, Burke's involvement in the opposition to government policy during the American crisis constitutes one of his major successes. Indeed, if the key to Burkean reform was the union of party and public behind a viable reform program, then American politics probably provided the high water mark of his long political career. Under the pressure of events, the Rockingham Whigs formulated, in the Declaratory Act and the repeal of the Townshend program, a distinctive approach to imperial matters. Based on that approach, the first Rockingham administration devised a plan for significant imperial reform, conducted an impressive campaign to win public support, and enacted their plan into policy. In addition, they made adjustments in their program over time, persevered even while out of office, and, finally, returned to power. When their second term in power came too late for their revised program to be carried out, the Rockingham Whigs accepted the implications of their own line of thought and moved on to grant American independence. In all of this Burke played a central role. His defense of the first Rockingham administration helped develop and rationalize the Rockingham view of late-eighteenth century politics, and his two great speeches on American affairs both offered a characteristic critique of imperial policy and outlined a novel reformulation of the structure of the Empire. Moreover, he was among the first of the Rockingham Party to recognize the inevitability of American independence, and to advocate separation on terms of mutual benefit. However, when the Rockingham Whigs came to power near the end of the American war, they were unable to broaden their support beyond the anti-war movement or, indeed, to even hold that alliance together. The reasons for their failure are both complex and disputable. Certainly, the death of Rockingham, the personal animosity between Fox and Shelburne, the opposition of the king, and the nature of the old electoral system are all important considerations. Yet, I would argue that the character of the Rockingham Whigs and their approach to politics were also vital factors. As in the case of parliamentary reform, Burke and his allies proposed to act for, but not with, the people. This stand alienated them from the people, but did not reconcile them to the king. Thus, the king was able to prevent the Rockingham Whigs from achieving success within the established political system, while their own aristocratic bias rendered them both unwilling and unable to go outside it.

I

The Stamp Tax crisis marked several beginnings. It was the occasion of Burke's introduction into English politics, the start of his long association with Rockingham, and the founding event of the Rockingham Whigs. In addition, as Oliver M. Dickerson points out, it also saw the introduction of the "American issue" into British politics.[1] The crisis thus provided the context for Burke's first consideration of colonial matters. It arose out of the government's chronic need for revenue and a desire to rationalize the empire which emerged after the war with France. In particular, on the American continent, the old colonial system seemed clearly inadequate to govern the American colonies, integrate Canada into the Empire, supervise the development of the western lands, and, at the same time, provide protection against the Indians and other potential enemies. The new situation raised many issues, and, even where agreement existed on ends, there was little consensus on policies to achieve those ends. For example, both American and British politicians recognized that an army would have to be maintained in America, but they did not agree on how to pay for it. It seemed only fair to the British that the Americans pay a share of the costs of defending their own borders, but the Americans were reluctant to finance imperial programs which seemed to serve only English interests. The Prime Minister at the time, George Grenville, mindful of the dangers of laying further burdens on his English constituents and aware of the unpopularity of the American position in England, fell back on an old device: he proposed to extend the Stamp Tax, which already existed in England, to America.[2] Grenville was a skillful politician and a cautious one. He took care to accommodate American opinion as far as possible, even agreeing to postpone the tax for a year, and he so carefully gauged Parliamentary opinion, that the bill imposing the tax passed without serious opposition. As the foremost British student of the Stamp Tax puts it, "the Parliamentary opposition would have been powerless to prevent the passage of the Grenville ministry's American legislation in 1764 and 1765 even if it had shown any serious inclination to do so."[3]

The Grenville administration, however, was short-lived. George III bitterly resented Grenville's attempts to dominate him, and the King maneuvered to replace Grenville with a more amenable minister. After considerable confusion and a number of false starts, the King settled on Lord Rockingham. At first, the Rockingham administration did not have an American policy to speak of. When signs of unrest appeared in the Colonies, its initial inclination, reflecting the thinking of the Duke of Cumberland, its de facto head, appears to have been to employ a policy of strict enforcement and repression of dissent.[4] Cumberland's sudden death, in the fall of 1765, ended the movement in that direction and gave Rockingham a breathing space to reconsider. Thomas suggests, "the significance of Cumberland's death for American policy can be seen in retrospect as ending the possibility that the administration might seek to apply the Stamp Tax by force."[5] As Rockingham thought the issue through, he became convinced that force would not succeed in governing America, and accepted the argument being made by various English commercial and manufacturing interests that only a repeal of the Tax could end the crisis and save imperial trade. This analysis effectively reduced his policy choices to two: suspension or repeal of the Stamp Tax. Though suspension was popular in some circles, and with the King, Rockingham quickly rejected it as inadequate, for, if the act were suspended for a definite period the question would simply revive at the end of that time and, if it were suspended indefinitely, pressure in England to enforce the act and in America to repeal it would continue the crisis. Having decided on repeal, Rockingham turned to a consideration of what form it would take, and, perhaps of equal importance, how it could be sold to his own associates, the King, and a majority of Parliament. Finally, Rockingham decided to cloak his policy in strong language.[6] Shortly after Christmas 1765, he arrived at a plan of joining repeal to an act maintaining Parliament's right to tax the colonies and denouncing the resistance of the Americans as illegal.

Thus was born the Declaratory Act: it was modeled on the Dependency of Ireland Act of 1719 and viewed by Rockingham as a mere political necessity. Years later, writing to a close associate, Burke admitted that the Act was never intended as a principled theory of the Empire, but was a practical attempt to meet the colonial demands, while at the same time preserving as much of England's authority over America as possible.[7] Yet, in spite of its origin in expediency and practical politics, the Act was to serve for a long time as the intellectual cornerstone of the Rockingham Whigs' approach to American affairs. That the Act attained such significance was largely due to Burke's subsequent attempt to formulate an intellectually coherent approach to American politics. The development of Burke's thought during the Stamp Tax crisis seems to have mirrored that of the Rockingham party in general with two exceptions: he appears to have made a decision on the issue prior to most of his allies, and he never seriously entertained the possibility of upholding the Stamp Tax by force. In a letter dated December 31, 1765, Burke told Charles O'Hara that, "since this monarchy, a more material point never came under the consideration of Parliament."[8] He continued on to assert that, in his view, "the Liberties, (or what shadows of Liberty there are) of Ireland have been saved in America," and confided that he had already decided to vote for repeal regardless of what position the party took.[9] A later letter to William Dowdeswell gives us an indication of Burke's reasoning: he suggested that Dowdeswell, in the debates in Parliament, refrain from going into detail on the Tax, and instead simply damn it as a revenue (presumably a reference to the American position that Parliament had no right to tax America for purposes of raising a revenue), and further maintain that it would take an army to enforce the Act.[10] For his part, Burke said little during the debate on repeal about enforcing the Declaratory Act. Indeed, something of his thinking on the matter was revealed by his comparison of the Parliamentary right to tax America to "such dormant parts of the constitution as the royal veto on legislation, which had lapsed since Queen Anne's reign."[11] Like Rockingham, Burke apparently had no intention of actually testing their administration's assertion of parliamentary sovereignty.

It seems likely that if the Rockingham administration had continued, American affairs would have been allowed to cool down for a period before any further efforts at imperial reform were made. However, the administration proved to be indecisive and unstable, and, therefore, short-lived. It was followed by a government headed by William Pitt the Elder, but divided by a number of policy differences. The American situation was problematical: the Americans expected much from Pitt, but he had always defended the right of Parliament to lay taxes on the "external" commerce of the colonies, and he had also threatened to support the use of force if conciliation failed to produce peace and submission in America. At first, his administration seemed uncertain. Shelburne produced a plan for the development of the American interior which would have both avoided increased taxation, relying instead on a requisition system, and also given the Americans substantial control over Indian and intercolonial affairs.[12] Yet, at the same time, Townshend pushed through the Cabinet a proposal to tax the colonies in a manner which, though external, was undoubtedly for the purpose of raising revenue. In the end, the choice between these two approaches to American affairs was probably determined by events outside the scope of American politics. The government's financial crisis continued, and Pitt's first option for raising revenue, a deal which would have extended the charter of the East India Company in return for a share of its income, floundered on the rocks of parliamentary opposition and the financial weakness of the Company.[13] With the failure of this plan, Pitt had little alternative but to seek an American revenue.

Pitt's policy was popular in England. In fact, from this time on, the harsh American policies of all administrations almost always had the support of Parliament and the public. Thomas quite correctly notes, "decisions and debates on America were concerned with the nature, extent, and timing of punitive and coercive measures, not with the principle of the assertion of British authority."[14] In response, Burke adopted a two-tiered approach. First, he was obliged to defend the Rockingham administration's opposition to the use of force against the Americans and its record as a genuine reformist body. Thus, in late 1769, Burke published the "Observations on a Late Publication Entitled 'The Present State of the Nation.' "[15] In that work, Burke argued that the Townshend taxes represented a return to the program of the Grenville Administration: a "disorderly despotism" at home combined with a lack of spirit abroad.[16] On American affairs, Burke offered an argument which moved by a kind of reverse logic. Rather than rejecting attempts to tax America in principle, he began with practicalities.

The Americans, he asserted, "must be governed in a manner agreeable to their temper and disposition; and men of free character and spirit must be ruled with, at least, some condescension to this spirit and this character."[17] Now, Burke continued, one of the characteristics of free governments is that their citizens, acting through their representatives, have the right to consent to taxes. But Burke believed that such participation was impossible in the case of the Americans. In a long passage of high comedy, he went on to ridicule the proposal that American representatives serve in the British Parliament: laudable as the idea might be in theory it is, he said, absolutely impractical.[18] For Burke, the only reasonable conclusion was that England should not tax America: not, indeed, as a matter of law or right but, as the Rockingham administration had recognized, as a matter of expediency.[19] What, then, about an American revenue? It must, Burke said, be seen for the illusion it is: America will never produce money to balance the English budget. Does this mean that the Americans are to forever live off the wealth of the Empire? Burke denied that America benefited unfairly. He argued, "we ought rather to infer from our having laid the colonies under many restraints, that it is reasonable to compensate them by every indulgence that can by any means be reconciled to our interest."[20] Burke argued that America already paid its share of imperial expenses in the income it lost because it was unable to trade freely with the rest of the world.

Second, Burke maintained that the tactics of the administrations which followed the Rockingham government were mistaken, and that their reliance on force would only compound the crisis. Among the events leading to the American conflict, two stand out as helping to define the development of Burke's thought: his appointment as agent for the New York Legislature and the passage of the Boston Port Bills. Burke approached his job as New York agent with the same trustee theory of representation he espoused at Bristol. In an early letter to James DeLancey, the head of the New York legislative committee with which he corresponded, Burke insisted on the right to serve New York as he saw best. If, he said, the Legislature was unhappy with his position, "I shall wish them to employ a person more pleasing to them, and more capable of rendering them the Service that is acceptable to them."[21] In fact, Burke did pursue New York's interests in the manner he thought most fitting and not necessarily as they directed. For instance, in another letter, dated the same day as his acknowledgment of his appointment, he refused, on the grounds that it was inconsistent with his stand on the Wilkes case, to support a New York request that he seek legislation to bar judges from sitting in the Legislature.[22] Burke wrote two kinds of letters to New York: formal letters, which contained only reports of actions and unemotional analyses of events, to the Committee, and informal letters of detailed analysis and opinion to DeLancey to be forwarded to the Committee or not at the latter's discretion. Of the formal letters, Burke quite correctly said that he reported matters "not as I saw them, but as the leaders in them represented their own measures."[23] His letters of opinion, on the other hand, stressed the determination of the English government, the unity of public opinion behind the government, and the inability of his own party and especially of himself to influence the administration. They reveal, in short, a deep and growing pessimism about any change in British policy.

In the words of a noted British authority on the American Revolution, "the Boston Tea Party raised, for what proved to be the last and most crucial time, the problems of imperial authority, which had troubled Britain's relations with the American colonists since the end of the Seven Years War. It proved to be the conclusive challenge because the home Government chose to make it so."[24] Burke also saw the Tea Party, and the consequent British reprisals, as a turning point in the struggle. In his letters to New York, he carefully reported on the English side of developments. His goal, he said, was to "discern . . . the temper of Parliament and of the Nation . . . which I thought it my Duty to lay before you without heightenings or without palliation."[25] This temper, according to Burke, "both within doors and without, at present sets strongly against America."[26] The Administration was intent on disciplining the colonies, and both Parliament and the people were likely to support them in any strong action they might take. Writing again a month later, Burke repeated his warning and added his own opinion: "I am full of trouble on Account of the late most unfortunate Transactions. My advice has little weight any where. My Wishes are, and my Endeavours ever have been, and ever shall be equally for the Good and the Freedom (without which hardly any good can be) of the whole."[27] In another letter to John Noble, Burke said of the Boston Port Bill,"a more complete Scheme of senseless Tyranny never was devised by the pride and folly of man."[28] In Burke's view, the Tea Party demonstrated the growing, and understandable, desperation of the American colonists. Further, the British reaction, which he considered both extreme and poorly informed, confirmed his opinion that little sympathy for America or understanding of the issues existed in England. Moreover, it was becoming increasingly obvious to Burke that the logic employed by the Rockingham administration, with its policy of repeal of the Stamp Tax combined with passage of the Declaratory Act, was now of little use. It pointed in both directions. On the one hand, it called for a recognition of American circumstances, but, on the other, it demanded a reassertion of British authority.

II

By the spring of 1774, Burke was aware that American affairs were headed toward a turning point. Yet, few other writers or politicians in England were much concerned by colonial issues, and even Burke saw any crisis as still some time off.[29] In a letter to Rockingham, he wrote, "the American and foreign affairs will not come to any Crisis, sufficient to rouse the publick from its present stupefaction, during the course of the next Session. I have my doubts whether, those, at least of America, will do it for some years to come."[30] Burke believed that the American problem was serious, but he felt that the internal divisions of the Americans, the transitoriness of public opinion in a republic—as each of the American colonies was—and the general inertia of English opinion would combine to prevent a confrontation from developing. Thus, when on the occasion of the debate about the repeal of the Tea Tax, Burke rose to deliver the first of his great American speeches, the "Speech on American Taxation," on April 19, 1774, his intention was not so much to offer specific ideas for averting an immediate conflict, and even less to present proposals for a new colonial system, as to warn the English of the dangerous nature of the road they had embarked upon.[31]

In the speech on American taxation, Burke considered three topics: the historical development of the colonial system, the nature of the system as it then existed, and the need for compromise with the Americans if it were to continue. He began his history with the Navigation Acts. Prior to 1764, he argued, the imperial system was harsh and ungenerous to the Americans, but it also afforded them some benefits: being basically a commercial system, it protected and encouraged certain of their industries, and it did not tax them for revenue. Therefore, the Americans accepted their lot. They became used to the imperial regulations, they prospered under them, and they enjoyed a measure of self-government. Burke explained his point: America "had the image of the British Constitution. She had the substance. She was taxed by her own representatives. She chose most of her own magistrates. She paid them all. She had in effect the sole disposal of her own internal government."[32] However, with the Grenville administration, Burke argued, things changed. For the first time, an attempt was made to tax America for revenue; moreover, "had this plan been pursued, it was evident that the provincial assemblies, in which the Americans felt all their portion of importance, and beheld their sole image of freedom, were *ipso facto* annihilated."[33] Fortunately, according to Burke, danger was avoided when the first Rockingham administration repealed the Stamp Tax and passed the Declaratory Act. In his view, both these actions were essential, for they combined to join together two vital principles: "they took *no* middle lines. They differed fundamentally from the schemes of both parties; but they preserved the objects of both. They preserved the authority of Great Britain; they preserved the equity of Great Britain."[34] Burke maintained that the settlement effected by the Rockingham administration would have held America in peace forever, if it had not been breached by later governments. Of these, of course, he saw the Chatham Administration as the worst offender. Chatham, himself, Burke maintained, was not at fault, save in so far as he defaulted control of American policy to Charles Townshend. For Burke, Townshend's error was that he sought to please everybody: "to please universally was the object of his life; but to tax and to please, no more than to love and to be wise, is not given to men."[35] In short, Townshend taxed America to please England, but then retreated from the taxes to please America. The result, Burke felt, was predictable: confusion, conflict, and alienation.

In Burke's opinion, what was required was a new approach to imperial matters. He hoped that a timely reform of imperial organization, and the adoption of a more generous attitude toward the Americans, would stave off yet another round of conflict. Basic to such a new approach, Burke argued, was a valid and consistent theoretical understanding of the issues involved.[36] Burke maintained that, within the Empire, the Parliament of Great Britain had a dual role: it was, at the same time, both the local legislature of England and the supervising legislature of the Empire as a whole.[37] As he saw it, in the first capacity, the English Parliament should not attempt to intervene in the affairs of the other local legislatures of the Empire. So long, he said, as they were equal to the "common ends of their institution," they should be left free to govern their own societies as they saw fit. However, in its imperial role, the English Parliament might occasionally have to act against the will of some local legislature, for, "it is necessary to coerce the negligent, to restrain the violent, and to aid the weak and deficient, by the overruling plenitude of her power."[38] Unfortunately, Burke was quite vague on how to distinguish between Parliament's two functions. Moreover, the only specific issue he mentioned, the refusal of a local legislature to meet its share of imperial expenses, was not an example likely to promote American confidence in his theory. Still, Burke was, at least, clear that intervention by the British Parliament was to be rare. He said, "but then this ought to be no ordinary power, nor even used in the first instance. This is what I meant, when I have said at various times, that I consider the power of taxing in Parliament as an instrument of empire, and not as a means of supply."[39] It appears that Burke thought that the guiding principle should be that Parliament could control and regulate to insure the smooth functioning of the Empire, but was not to substitute its judgment for that of the people on the scene in regard to something that concerned only a single colony. For example, Burke held that each of the local legislatures should be free to decide how to finance its share of imperial expenses. Only when one of those bodies defaulted on its obligation to contribute, did he think there were grounds for coercive parliamentary action.

It seems to me that Burke's concept of the Empire was, like that of many of the American critics of Parliament, essentially a federal one. Where he differed from men like John Dickinson was in his greater recognition that, in the event of protracted and serious disagreement, the will of the superior authority must prevail. However, Burke was unwilling to permit matters to ever reach such a degree of impasse. Both the opening and concluding passages of the "Speech on American Taxation" implored Parliament to seek compromise with the Americans. England, Burke said, should not quibble over legalities. For example, in urging a return to the principle of commercial regulation as the basis for taxation as opposed to taxation for revenue, he suggested, "the distinction, which is as nothing with regard to right, is of most weighty consideration in practice."[40] To the claim that a repeal of the Tea Tax would be an insult to the dignity of England, he responded, "but what dignity is derived from the perseverance in absurdity is more than ever I could discern."[41] Burke mocked, ridiculed, begged, and pleaded, all intended to get Parliament to give up what he considered its silly pretenses and distinctions. Do not, he stressed, push these distinctions and fine points, for, "when you drive him hard, the boar will surely turn on the hunters. If that sovereignty and their freedom cannot be reconciled, which will they take? They will cast your sovereignty in your face. Nobody will be argued into slavery."[42] Burke understood that a right to rule which is defended but never exercised may well be an absurdity, but he also knew that Parliament could not reassure America by claiming an authority which was both constitutional and arbitrary. Whatever the legal niceties, Americans saw such an authority as little more than naked power, and considered its exercise to be tyranny.

In the months following the speech on American taxation, English politics came increasingly to focus on colonial policy. By the beginning of 1775, American affairs had become the center of the opposition's attack on the conduct of the administration. As debate intensified, Burke continued to rethink his position. Writing to a friend in early March, he explained his attitude toward North's government: "I have been a strenuous advocate for the superiority of this Country—but I confess I grow less zealous when I see the use which is made of it. I love firm government; but I hate the tyranny which comes to the aid of a weak one."[43] Burke was not concerned only with the politics of the issue; he wanted to make a clear moral statement. As his brother reported to Richard Champion, "America was not on his mind only as a politician, it hung on his conscience as a being accountable for his actions and his conduct."[44] Thus, when Burke began his second great American speech, the "Speech on Moving Resolutions for Conciliation with America," he was intent on getting to the heart of the matter. That heart was, in his view, no longer the Declaratory Act.[45] Indeed, Burke disposed of the Act in two short sentences. "I am not determining a point of law; I am restoring tranquillity," he argued; therefore, "it is not what a lawyer tells me I *may* do, but what humanity, reason, and justice tell me I ought to do."[46] If, he continued, the Americans have violated the Declaratory Act, or some other law passed in its shadow, so be it; there is nothing to be done about it. Burke asserted, "I do not know the method of drawing up an indictment against a whole people . . . I am not ripe to pass sentence on the gravest public bodies, intrusted with magistracies of great authority and dignity, and charged with the safety of their fellow-citizens, upon the very same title that I am."[47] In the current situation, he held, force will not work: it is temporary, uncertain, beyond English experience, and destructive of that which it would seek to preserve.[48] Burke suggested that those who advocated coercion note how far it had driven the Americans already. As England tried to dissolve their various colonial governments, they formed a national government, "sufficient for its purposes, without the bustle of a revolution, or the troublesome formality of an election;" moreover, "the new institution is infinitely better obeyed than the ancient government ever was in its most fortunate periods."[49] Surely, Burke argued, if this is the result of force, it is time to try something else.

Since Burke believed that America could only be governed according to the nature of its people, and not by some abstract theoretical model of imperial authority, the largest section of the speech was a detailed examination of American character. As he put it, "the question is not, whether their spirit deserves praise or blame,—(but) what, in the name of God, shall we do with it?"[50] In America, Burke claimed, three circumstances have combined to produce a completely new society.[51] The first two of these, he said, the size of the population and the extent of its commerce and wealth were well understood and obvious, but the third, the freedom-loving spirit of the Americans, was not. In fact, Burke argued, "this fierce spirit of liberty is stronger in the English colonies, probably, than in any other people of the earth . . ."[52] Nor did he consider this character the result of chance; in good Scottish Enlightenment style, Burke held that it was a consequence of the colonists' descent from English stock, their popular governments, their heritage of religious dissent, their possession of slaves, and their education in the law.[53] In Burke's view, in dealing with the Americans, therefore, England had only three choices: she could try to change their spirit, to punish it, or to work in conformity with it.[54] Burke rejected the first two alternatives with ease: England had already tried to punish America and failed, and the American spirit could not be changed at will. In considering the factor of education, he observed, "you cannot persuade them to burn their bodies of curious science, to banish their lawyers from their courts of law, or to quench the light of their assemblies by refusing to choose those persons who are best read in their privileges."[55] Thus, he felt that only the third choice remained. Governing America in conformity with the character of its people required, Burke argued, two things. First, there must be no more conflict: "the proposition is peace. Not peace through the medium of war; not peace to be hunted through the labyrinth of intricate and endless negociations; not peace to arise out of universal discord . . . not peace to depend on the juridical determination of perplexing questions, or the precise marking of the shadowy boundaries of a complex government. It is simple peace, sought in its natural course and in its ordinary haunts."[56] Burke maintained that only when coercion had ceased, could a new start be made.

Burke did not, however, believe that quiet, or even the repeal of a few offending laws, would be enough to end the dispute.[57] Thus, the second requirement was the meaningful incorporation of the colonies into the constitution.[58] Burke rejected two of the more common proposals for effecting such an incorporation. He thought American representation in Parliament impossible, and he felt that applying the theory of virtual representation to America unreasonable. Rather, he proposed to remodel American government on the examples of Wales, Ireland, Chester, and Durham.[59] In each of those cases, Burke noted, English constitutional rights and practices were extended, but its revenue-producing taxes were not. Burke, therefore, advanced a series of nine resolutions, which would repeal the revenue taxes in force in America, remove all the penal legislation passed to assert English authority there, and give the Americans the authority to govern and tax themselves through their own legislatures. Burke's own summary of his plan is probably the best: "my resolutions, therefore, mean to establish the equity and justice of a taxation of America by *grant,* and not by imposition; to mark the *legal competency* of the colony assemblies for the support of their government in peace, and for public aids in time of war, to acknowledge that this legal competency has had *a dutiful and beneficial exercise,* and that experience has shown *the benefit of their grants,* and the futility of Parliamentary taxation, as a method of supply."[60] Burke admitted that his plan would not produce an American revenue, but he insisted that it would bring peace. To those who thought that the plan would undermine the Empire, he could only reply: "the very idea of subordination of parts excludes this notion of simple and undivided unity. England is the head; but she is not the head and the members too."[61] In short, Burke hoped that, where force did not serve, generosity might work. In his words: "my hold of the colonies is in the close affection which grows from common names, from kindred blood, from similar privileges, and equal protection. These are ties which, though light as air, are as strong as links of iron."[62]

From his own day to the present, Burke's American speeches have undergone extensive criticism from both right and left. In one way or another, most of the objections to his position are based on the claim that his support for the Declaratory Act and his desire for conciliation with America were mutually inconsistent. Put somewhat differently, it is generally asserted that the Declaratory Act was an insurmountable barrier to settling the crisis along the lines Burke proposed. O'Gorman writes, "the difficulty with the American policy of the Rockinghams was that they stood by the Declaratory Act and continued to advocate conciliation. They did not realize that to stand by the Declaratory Act made conciliation impossible."[63] O'Gorman's argument has an undeniable plausibility. While the Declaratory Act began as a political expedient, intended by Rockingham only to gain support among his Cabinet colleagues and in Parliament for his policy of repealing the Stamp Tax, it did take on a life of its own. Under the pressure of criticism from their parliamentary opponents and adverse public opinion, the Rockingham Whigs elevated the Declaratory Act into a matter of principle. Burke, himself, contributed strongly to this development. In the "Observations on a Late Publication on the Present State of the Nation," he referred to the passage of the Act in these terms: "for they resolved, as a preliminary to that repeal, to assert in the fullest and least equivocal terms the unlimited legislative right of this county over its colonies . . ."[64] Moreover, Burke was slow to back away from the Declaratory Act. This was partly, as I have suggested, in response to domestic political considerations, but it was also due to a misunderstanding of the American position. Burke once remarked that he did not advocate repeal of the Declaratory Act because the Americans did not ask for it and did not appear to object to the Act.[65] However, Edmund Morgan has shown that the Americans did reject the principle stated in the Act, but were misled by its language.[66] They distinguished between a parliamentary right to legislate, which they accepted, and a right to tax, which they rejected, but they did not understand that Parliament's assertion of a right to legislate for the colonies included a claim to the right to tax. In short, Burke's defense of the Declaratory Act was unfortunate, for, by 1774, that defense deprived his thought on America of some of the flexibility which had been so prominent a characteristic of his position during the Stamp Tax controversy.

However, those interpretations of Burke which see his stand on the Declaratory Act as unchanging after 1767 or 1768 are simply mistaken. By the time of the first American speech, he was clearly retreating from the Act, and, by the second speech, he had, albeit without saying so, just about given it up. This silent repudiation of the Declaratory Act had important consequences, for it freed Burke for a greater sympathy for American claims to self-government. One might simply compare the discussion of the Declaratory Act in the "Observations" to this passage from a letter to Charles O'Hara, written in July 1775: "How could you imagine that I had in my thoughts any thing of the Theoretical separation of a power of Taxing from Legislation? I have no opinion about it. These things depend on conventions real or understood, upon practice, accident, the humour or Genius of those who Govern or are governed, and may be, as they are, modified to infinity. No bounds ever were set to the Parliamentary power over the Colonies . . . but the reason and nature of things, and the growth of the Colonies ought to have taught Parliament to have set bounds to the exercise of its own power. I never ask what Government may do in *Theory,* except *Theory* be the *Object;* When one talks of *Practice* they must act according to circumstances."[67] Burke's de-emphasis of the Declaratory Act did not solve all of his problems. Indeed, he continued to be troubled by the question of what practical authority England was to retain over the colonies. However, after March 1775, at least the Act itself was no longer, for Burke, an obstacle to peace in America.

III

To best understand Burke's thought and the various commentaries on it, it should be viewed within a framework of other analyses of and proposed solutions for the American crisis. John Derry's comment is a good place to begin: "the heart of the conflict was not a struggle between two different traditions of political behaviours, or two wholly different concepts of constitutional practice, but rather a disagreement within a common political tradition, a dispute about the meaning of a common political heritage, a controversy in which confusion became all the more bitter because the combatants shared certain assumptions."[68] The political tradition in question was one of constitutional government, and it included such elements as mixed and balanced government, representative institutions, and support for certain basic individual political rights. The discussion was narrowed to the confines of a single tradition in another, less obvious, sense. Virtually none of the major thinkers or politicians actually saw the American problem in terms set by the standard theories of colonial affairs. That is to say, the discussion rarely appealed to the traditional mercantilist position that England was a society possessing colonies which were not part of its political system and which could be exploited at will. Rather, even on the administration side of the debate, most writers agreed that England and America formed a single political community and that their residents shared a common body of law and rights. Whatever questioning there was of the single community premise came primarily from those radicals who held that America must become independent precisely because it could not be included in the English political system.

It is convenient to divide the commentators on the American problem into four groups. The first is composed of those who took what was clearly the majority position—support for the English policy of coercion—and thus might be called the orthodox school. For the most part, the defense of established policy was conducted in terms of the traditional theory of sovereignty. As one proponent put it, the starting position was that, "there must be in every state a supreme legislative authority, universal in its extent, over every member."[69] This was not necessarily an argument for absolutism, but rather an assertion that some final authority must exist to declare what the law in fact is. In England, it was commonly said, this authority was Parliament, perhaps better understood as the king in Parliament. Implied in this view, though not often expressly stated, was the further assumption that the American colonies were part of the English political system and thus bound by acts of Parliament. Joseph Galloway, an American writer, said it well: "whatever British subject, or foreigner, has . . . become an occupant of the English territories in the colonies, he is truly a member of the British state, and subject to the laws of its supreme authority."[70] As a member of the British state, Galloway continued, he is also entitled to all the rights of Englishmen, including those to a voice in the legislature and to consent to taxes, either directly or through his representative. The central weakness of the orthodox argument was, of course, that no American, as such, actually had a parliamentary vote. To cover this obvious gap between the theory and political reality, the orthodox thinkers invoked virtual representation. This held that, "it is the opinion of the house of commons, and may be considered as a law of parliament, that they are the representatives of every British subject, wheresoever he be . . ."[71] According to the theory of virtual representation, then, a member of the House of Commons, for example, while chosen by the voters of his own electoral district, represents the entire Commons of the Empire. The appeal to virtual representation did not satisfy the American critics of Parliament. Indeed, it only inflamed the situation, for, from the American standpoint, it added insult to injury. It told the Americans that the abuses they perceived would not only not be corrected, but that they existed for the Americans own good and had been enacted with their consent. Thus, in applying the theory to America, some of the more moderate members of the school, like Thomas Hutcheson, recognized its inadequacy, and, therefore, suggested that, since such practicalities as the long distances involved prevented the Americans from having any actual representation, this "necessary abridgement of what are commonly called English liberties" ought to be balanced by a corresponding immunity from certain taxes.[72] Only Joseph Galloway, however, with his proposal for an American Congress, which would be supreme over the colonies but subordinate to the English Parliament, to my knowledge, sought to provide an institutional mechanism to compensate for the denial of American participation in Parliament.[73]

By insisting that England and America formed a single political community but denying the Americans effective participation in that community, the orthodox view could be seen as hypocritical. Moreover, the Americans refused to believe that their interests were safe in English hands when the English claimed that Parliament could do with America as it willed. In the context of such distrust, the policy of coercion was a grave mistake, for it confirmed American fears, unified them against England, and eventually forced them to fight. Still, it would probably be wise to heed Bernard Donoughue's warning: "it does not follow that because the coercive measures failed, others more conciliatory would have succeeded."[74] It may well be that, by 1775, no approach could have won sufficient support in both England and America to end the crisis. Donoughue's point is especially well-taken in regard to the consideration of the second group of thinkers, for the failure of the orthodox school has often been taken, mistakenly, I believe, as a negative proof of the validity of the stand taken by the British moderates. Where the orthodox thinkers either denied a breech in the Anglo-American community or attributed it to the machinations of evil doers, the moderates recognized that it existed and was based on real differences of interest. They, therefore, sought some means of reconciling those differences. Apart from the Rockingham Whigs, William Pitt and his followers were probably the most important of the English moderates. Pitt approached the struggle through the concept of an ancient fundamental constitution which established broad governmental powers, but, more importantly, also prescribed a body of basic individual rights which government could not violate.[75] Among these was the right to consent to taxation. Therefore, for Pitt, "no tax for the purpose of raising revenue was to be levied on the Americans without their consent, expressed through their colonial assemblies."[76] However, in his view, the parliamentary regulation of trade was another matter; as it was not a taking of property in the same sense, it was permissible. As Edmund Morgan notes, Pitt's distinction was the actual source of the internal/external debate.[77] Pitt's plan for ending the conflict, presented to Parliament on February 1, 1775, thus called for voluntary requisitions from America to pay a share of imperial expenses, recognition of the American Congress as a legitimate American legislature, and American acceptance of Parliament's right to govern America in all matters whatsoever.[78] For my purposes, Pitt's difference with Burke comes to this: Pitt believed that the Declaratory Act was unconstitutional, for it upheld the power to tax the colonies, but also held that Burke was wrong to question English authority in other areas. Pitt's plan has appealed to scholars, who have seen it as an anticipation of the twentieth century Commonwealth, but it was totally unacceptable to the English Parliament, where the House of Lords defeated it by 68 to 18.[79] It is equally unlikely that Pitt's approach would have satisfied the Americans. His position closely resembled John Dickinson's scheme, which, though it had attracted considerable support in the late 1760s, was considerably behind colonial opinion by 1775.[80]

To Burke's political left, the third group, the English radicals, represented a small segment of the population but a significant body of opinion. While their views were quite diverse, the radicals agreed, for the most part, on four points. First, they rejected the theory of sovereignty as a starting point. For example, in the parliamentary debate of October 1775, former Governor Johnstone referred to the theory as "unintelligible jargon."[81] Against the rationalistic assertion that two distinct authorities could not exist in the same community, the radicals pointed to the numerous real-world cases of divided power and suggested that, far from unusual, it was the hallmark of all truly free governments. Second, the radicals saw a link between reform in England and the redressing of American complaints. In their opinion, the same flaws in the political system had produced both sets of evils. The majority of English subjects and all Americans suffered from a common exclusion from power, and, because of that exclusion, both were at the mercy of others. Thus, many would have agreed with Richard Price that the threatened extinction of liberty in America would be only the first step: "would it not be a fatal preparation for subduing yourselfs? Would not the disposal of *American* places, and the distribution of an *American* revenue, render that influence of the crown irresistible, which has already stabbed your liberties."[82] Third, as the problem was the same, so was the remedy: the antidote to exclusion was participation. The radicals believed that each individual has a right to self-government, and is, therefore, properly bound to society only by his own consent. Moreover, as they believed that the right to self-government carries over into society, they held that each individual has a right to participate in the government of his society. Further, the radicals held that what is true of individuals is also true of communities. As one put it, civil liberty is "the power of a *civil society* or *state* to govern itself by its own discretion, or by laws of its own making, without being subject to the impositions of *any* power of appointing and directing . . . over which they have no control."[83] Fourth, in applying their ideas to imperial government, the radicals generally advocated some form of federalism: either a system of divided sovereignty like that proposed by John Dickinson and William Pitt or a super-legislature which would include representative from both America and England. Some radicals, Richard Price among them, also questioned the policy of coercion on prudential grounds. Price maintained that it was doubtful if England could win an American war, that a war would significantly increase the national debt, and that victory in America would leave the colonies so damaged as to be of little value to England.[84] The radical argument has found more favor with modern scholars than it did in its own day. Perhaps the best evaluation of its practicality is Robert Toohey's suggestion that a reformed parliament would probably have been even less sympathetic to the American cause that the historical one.[85]

The fourth group is composed of those who favored American independence. Not all of these writers did so out of sympathy for the Americans. An interesting variation on the independence argument was offered by Josiah Tucker, a frequent and unconventional writer on economic and political topics. Tucker considered himself a moderate Whig, but he is best known as a critic of John Locke. Tucker argued that, "Mr. Locke and his followers have extended the privilege of voting, or of giving *actual* consent, in all the affairs of government and legislation, beyond what was ever dreamt of before in this, or in any other civilized country."[86] Applying his critique of consent theory to a consideration of the state of the American colonies, Tucker accepted the principal assumption of the orthodox thinkers. In his view, the doctrine of sovereignty required that, "there can be no medium between legal subjection to the supreme legislature on the one hand, and an absolute separation from it on the other."[87] However, at this point Tucker departed from the usual line of argument to draw his own unique conclusion. He maintained that colonies are more trouble than they are worth: they are a drain on wealth, of limited benefit to trade, and prone to be rebellious.[88] Therefore, it follows, Tucker insisted, that the colonies ought to be set free. Further, Tucker held that, once independent, the Americans would be unable to unite into a single country, and would likely war among themselves or be threatened with conquest by some other European power. In either case, he expected the Americans to petition for the return of British rule, and, moreover, to accept it on British terms. In the unlikely event that the Americans did succeed in forming a country, Tucker argued, their manufactures would be unable to compete with England's, and they would be obliged to resume trade with England: "for trade is not carried on for the sake of friendship, but of interest."[89] In a sense, Tucker was arguing a paradox: if England waged war for the colonies, they would be lost, but, if she set them free, they would eventually recognize their own limitations and return to the fold.

Adam Smith was, at points, close to Burke but, as he had no need to square his opinions with the requirements of practical politics, he was able to consider alternatives which Burke was most reluctant to face. As a result, Smith's comments on America contain more intelligence in less compass than any other body of work I am familiar with. Unfortunately, there is no reason to think that his ideas had any influence on English opinion. On most political issues, Smith advanced a highly sophisticated moderate Whiggism, but his study of the role of commerce in modern civilization led him to criticize the existing colonial system.[90] In the *Wealth of Nations,* Smith argued that the American colonies were of great potential benefit to England, but that the government's strict regulation of American trade only reduced their value. In his opinion, the colonial system, as codified in the Navigation Acts, tended to depress trade and to redistribute it into narrow and unnatural channels.[91] Indeed, Smith claimed that one of the primary reasons why the English colonies had prospered more than those of other nations was not that English regulation worked well but that it was relatively ineffective and had thus done little harm.[92] Since trade is good and free trade even better, the gradual relaxation of regulation, according to Smith, was called for, and it would probably be a good thing if it eventually ended altogether.[93] Of course, Smith admitted that would mean American independence, but political independence, he felt, would have little effect on economic co-operation. As matters stood, Smith believed that the colonies would never produce enough revenue to cover England's expense in ruling them. He argued that the colonial assemblies would never vote money to support a system of requisitions, and the Americans would not permit Parliament to tax them without their own consent, for, if they did, "the importance of those assemblies would from that moment be at an end, and with it, that of all the leading men of British America."[94] As for coercion, Smith thought that it probably would not work and that, since America would one day become an extensive empire in its own right, "one of the greatest and most formidable that ever was in the world," the alienation of the Americans was not a matter to be lightly chanced.[95] In short, as Smith saw it, England had two choices. First, it could free the colonies. Nothing bad would come of that, for the American trade, which was all that was of value in the connection anyway, would remain and grow. Second, England could admit American representatives to Parliament in proportion to the taxes paid by the colonies, repeal the regulations which discriminated between the colonies and the mother country, and tax and govern the two halves of the Empire as one. Finally, none of this was for Smith a matter of principle. He cheerfully admitted that he saw nothing immoral or unconstitutional in England taxing America.[96] He merely thought it exceedingly stupid.

Most of the supporters of American independence were, of course, Americans. Interestingly, they are worth considering separately, for their ideas were somewhat different from those of their British allies. As John Derry has pointed out, "the ultimate irony was that virtually no English defender of the American cause fully shared the American point of view."[97] In part, this is because there was no single American point of view. However, it was also because, except for such mavericks as Tucker and Smith, almost all English writers, even those who claimed to be for American independence, actually espoused some form of Anglo-American association dominated by England. Often all they meant by "independence" was a degree of American self-government within a generally federal system. By 1775, a number of articulate Americans, on the other hand, favored complete separation, and a consideration of their arguments reveals a considerable gap between them and even the most sympathetic English commentator. As early as March 1766, Richard Bland, in his "An Inquiry into the Rights of the British Colonies," advanced the Lockean argument that the Americans, in sailing to the colonies, had left England's authority behind, and were, therefore, free to contract with one another, and with the English king, to establish new governments.[98] Thus, according to Bland, each colony formed "a distinct State, independent, as to their *internal* Government, of the original kingdom, but united with her, as to their *external* Polity . . ."[99] Bland proceeded to argue that English attempts to tax the colonies were a violation of their fundamental charter rights and, as such, illegal. However, Bland did not specify a remedy for these abuses. That was left to later writers, like Thomas Jefferson, who made Bland's argument the basis of their own. In his "A Summary View of the Rights of British America," Jefferson repeated Bland's claim that the colonies were independent political societies and could not be bound by the English Parliament.[100] Granted, he said, that some Acts of Parliament are unjust, but, "the true ground on which we declare these acts void is, that the British parliament has no right to excerise authority over us."[101] But Jefferson went further yet, for, in the Declaclaration of Independence, he held that America not only ought to be independent but already was. Indeed, Jefferson announced, America had been independent of the English Parliament since the 1620s.[102] The only tie left to be severed in 1775–76, in his opinion, was the one with the king, and that tie had been shattered by King George's violations of his compact with the Americans.

IV

As the colonial crisis deepened, Burke grasped at straws. When the New York Legislature voted conciliatory resolutions, he wrote, "I congratulate you on the success of your Endeavours and hope they will have the desired effect in leading to that reconciliation for which they were so honestly intended and so earnestly pursued. I wish that we on our side had been as earnest to meet you with conciliatory Measures."[103] Finally, however, the news of Lexington reached England, and Burke fully understood that war was now inevitable. One of his first reactions was to lash out, to place the blame. He spared no one. The Americans had trusted Pitt, who "refused to put himself into a responsible Situation to serve; and when he came into power himself, if he did [not] actually produce at least made one of the administration who laid the Tax which is the fatal Cause of all this mischief; and indeed never did them a single service, that I can recollect, in the whole Course of his Life."[104] According to Burke, the king and his ministers were perfectly happy with the conflict, and the people were only too willing to support them. Indeed, even the merchants, who would suffer most from the end of the American trade, were on the Ministry's side. Further, Parliament, itself, was "thoroughly dipped; and there will be no way of getting out, but by disgracing England or enslaving America."[105] Burke saw no prospect that ordinary political measures would save the situation; he even suggested that Rockingham should lead his party in a formal secession from Parliament as a protest against the war.[106]

However, in November 1775, Burke made one last proposal to compose the imperial disagreement. The basis of his plan was a paradox: he counseled that Parliament use its legislative supremacy to enact American immunity from English taxation.[107] In Burke's view, there would, therefore, be no need to repeal the Declaratory Act, for that Act, itself, would sustain American freedom from arbitrary government. Each colony would then be permitted to govern itself through its own Assembly, and an American legislature could be created to coordinate inter-colonial affairs. The English Parliament would retain its power to regulate imperial commerce and to supervise the empire generally, but any revenue raised through such regulation would be remitted to the colonies. The sleight of hand involved here was, of course, obvious: Burke was really proposing a solution analogous to the repeal of the Stamp Tax. The Americans would gain a victory on the substantive issues under debate, while the English would save face by preserving their formal sovereignty over the colonies. Yet that sovereignty, in turn, would never again be used. Parliament, in short, would act to deny its ability to act. Clever as it was, the plan was totally impractical: neither party found it acceptable, and, even if they had, the sovereignty which Parliament had put down would have remained to be taken up again at some time in the future. The problem with such fantastic ideas is that they can work only if everyone shares the fantasy. Unfortunately, the popular fantasy in England at the time was of another sort, as the peace proposal offered to the Americans by the administration show. This plan, the Howe Peace Commission Plan, was nothing more than an offer to consider grievances after an American surrender and acknowledgement of English sovereignty over America.[108]

Once Burke recognized that conciliation was impossible, he began a process of reconsideration which ultimately ended in the acceptance of American independence. The first step came in January

1777. In a long letter to Rockingham, Burke proposed a new three-part plan of action.[109] First, since at this point he thought it probable that the Americans would lose the war, he suggested that they be encouraged to accept peace on the basis of his own earlier conciliatory proposals. Second, for their part, the Whigs would promise to act as intermediaries between the government and the Americans. Third, Burke argued that, to demonstrate their sincerity and to free themselves for their role as mediators, Rockingham and his associates should secede from Parliament and have nothing to do with the further prosecution of the war. In a sense, Burke's suggestion called for the Rockingham party to assume a leadership role in the crisis consistent with its own self-image as a reforming elite. As he saw it, from a vantage point of practical neutrality, the party could work to secure a peaceful and orderly American return to the Empire and, thereby, avoid further bloodshed or permanent damage to British constitutional liberties. In pursuit of this strategy, Burke authored memorials to be sent to the colonists and to the king. The "Address to the British Colonists in North America," is unproblematical. It was meant only to assure the Americans that they still had friends in England, and that, if they gave it a chance, they would find that the English constitutional system was always open to reform.[110] However, the "Address to the King" is much more interesting.[111] Burke began with a repetition of points he had made previously. He first asserted that the problem was a result of Parliament's claim that it had a right to tax the colonies without their consent, and, as was common in his previous treatments of the controversy, he noted that the colonists denied that right. He further maintained that, whether the Americans were correct or not, their opinions had to be taken into account.[112] But, then, for the first time, he went on to affirm that, as a matter of fact, the American interpretation was correct.[113] Thus, he insisted, to punish them for saying what was true, made no sense: "we could not conceive, when disorders had arisen from the complaint of one violated right, that to violate every other was the proper means of quieting an exasperated people."[114] In fact, Burke held, to deny the American argument would require the rejection of the very principle of popular consent upon which the authority of both king and Parliament rested, and that, he asserted, would in turn subvert the rights of Englishmen: "you cannot have different rights and a different security in different parts of your dominions . . ."[115] In view of such violations of basic liberties, Burke said, the Whigs would leave Parliament in protest: "we cannot permit ourselves to countenance, by the appearance of a silent assent, proceedings fatal to the liberty and unity of the empire . . ."[116] They would return, he announced, only when they could be of use in ending the struggle through a return to the proper maxims of government.

The "Letter to the Sheriffs of Bristol, On the Affairs of America," which was both a defense of the Parliamentary secession and a formal repudiation of the Declaratory Act, marks a further step toward Burke's acceptance of American independence.[117] Dated April 3, 1777, the "Letter" was occasioned by the passage of two bills through Parliament: the first suspended, under certain conditions, the writ of Habeas Corpus in America, and the second provided for letters of marque to be used against American shipping. Burke opened the letter with an attack on the bills. He saw them as invasions of basic English liberties, which, moreover, established different legal standards in different parts of the Empire. As he put it, "there is no equality among us; we are not fellow-citizens, if the mariner who lands on the quay does not rest on as firm legal grounds as the merchant who sits in his country-house. Other laws may injure the community; this dissolves it."[118] Turning from the bills to the conflict underlying their passage, Burke admitted that he had, at first, defended complete English authority in America: "if any gentlemen were about to see how one power could be given up [merely on abstract reasoning] without giving up the rest, I can only say that they saw farther than I could."[119] However, he continued, he now realized that such power can be preserved only if it is used with extreme caution and accepted as legitimate by the people over whom it is exercised.[120] Even in England, itself, Burke argued, "the completeness of the legislative authority of Parliament *over this kingdom* is not questioned; and yet many things indubitably included in the abstract idea of that power, and which carry no absolute injustice in themselves, yet being contrary to the opinions and feelings of the people, can as little be exercised as if Parliament in that case had been possessed of no right at all."[120] In the light of these considerations, Burke continued, he had been forced to reconsider his stand on American politics, and to see that, in view of the changed circumstances, especially the new American attitudes toward British authority, since the Rockingham administration had passed the Declaratory Act, a new approach was necessary. In his opinion, the key to that new approach was that Parliament must give up its claim to authority to tax America.[122] Burke denied that the surrender of complete sovereignty would lead to American independence, but, if it did, he thought that, "independency without war was preferable to independency with it."[123] Would not, he asked, an independent America friendly to England be better than one occupied by force?

For Burke, the final step came with the news of the Battle of Saratoga. That loss affected English opinion in two ways: first, as Rockingham's comment to Burke, "My dear Burke, my heart is at ease," indicates, it was now clear that England would not win the war; and, second, when the Franco-American alliance was announced a few months later, the American war had to be assessed within the wider framework of a potential Anglo-French conflict.[124] The administration, itself, was shaken. It, therefore, resorted to a defensive war in America in which its strategy was one of holding what territory it could while it launched new efforts to negotiate peace with the Americans. The Carlisle Commission was authorized to offer guarantees that England would not suspend colonial governments, that colonial administrations would be staffed by Americans, and that the American Congress could continue to operate as a permanent institution at a level between the colonial legislatures and the British Parliament.[125] Even American independence was not to be rejected out of hand. As might be expected, Burke went further: he now saw the war as lost, and began to openly advocate American independence. In April 1778, he reported to Champion that he had supported a motion in Parliament to authorize the peace commissioners to recognize American independence.[126] Thus, even before the beginning of the second Rockingham Administration, Burke was ready for peace: "when the natural Bonds of dominion are so broken, it is better, I am sure, to look for a friendship that will hold, than an Authority that will not."[127] He repeated those hopes in a letter to his old American correspondent, Henry Laurens: "the reign of violence and trick, I hope, is over. Fair dealing and moderation, on both sides, may bring all right, and fix things upon a new foundation, which, by being laid in the nature of things, as they now stand, may promise permanence to the superstructure."[128] Perhaps, Burke said, the two halves of the English nation could find a community in their separate political identities which they had been unable to achieve within the same institutional system.[129]

V

Two major misconceptions must be dispelled if an accurate understanding of Burke's position on American affairs is to be achieved. First, contrary to the claims of many of the students of his thought, Burke did have a coherent view of the Empire. As the "Speech on American Taxation" makes clear, that view was essentially federalist.[130] For Burke, the authority of the British Parliament was both imperial and local. It governed the island of Great Britain as the representative institution of England, Scotland, and Wales, while it ruled the Empire as a superintending authority over a diverse set of local governments. As for the particular case of America, Burke held that each of the various American assemblies was competent for the internal government of its own colony. The federalistic nature of Burke's imperial thought was obscured by the fact that he was more candid about the need to preserve some measure of final central authority in the English Parliament and placed more emphasis on the obligation of the supervising authority to act with restraint than did most federal thinkers. Moreover, of the two poles of his imperial thought, parliamentary supremacy and conciliation between England and the colonies, I would argue that it is accommodation which predominated in practice. Burke put matters in what he believed to be the proper perspective when, in the "Address to the King," he said, "to leave any real freedom to Parliament, freedom must be left to the colonies."[131] Burke's emphasis on conciliation was based on a number of considerations. Perhaps the most important was his remarkable ability to put himself in the Americans' position. As he wrote to the king, "we should think ourselves unjustifiable, as good citizens, and not influenced by the true spirit of Englishmen, if, with any effectual means of prevention in our hands, we were to submit to taxes to which we did not consent, either directly, or by a representation of the people . . ."[132] Burke believed that it came down to a simple question: if the English would not consent to taxation without representation, why should the Americans? Yet, although the question seems obvious, it took an uncommon intelligence to ask it.

A second misconception is that Burke's rigid adherence to the Declaratory Act prevented him from achieving either consistency or, more importantly, a solution to the American controversy. I would instead draw attention to how far Burke moved on the issues over time. It is also worth noting that, throughout the controversy, Burke was always ahead of ministerial and public opinion. Burke's flexibility can, I think, be attributed to two considerations. First, he was always very much aware of the uniqueness of the problem. In the "Observations," he wrote, "the object is wholly new in the world. It is singular; it is grown up to this magnitude and importance within the memory of man; nothing in history is parallel to it. All the reasonings about it, that are likely to be at all solid, must be drawn from its actual circumstances."[133] Second, Burke saw the American conflict in historical or developmental terms. Thus, he explained his reversal on the Declaratory Act by citing changed circumstances: "when the dispute had gone to these last extremities . . . the concessions which had satisfied in the beginning could satisfy no longer; because the violation of tacit faith required explicit security."[134] Similiarly, Burke offered the Americans hope for redress by pointing to the experience of the past: "this constitution has therefore admitted innumerable improvements, either for the correction of the original scheme, or for removing corruptions, or for bringing its principles better to suit those changes which have successively happened in the circumstances of the nation or in the manners of the people."[135] Burke believed that little in politics need be accepted as final or unalterable; if the English and the Americans would only commit themselves to living together, they could find a way to do so.

There is, of course, some truth to the claim that Burke had no viable solution to the American controversy, for no one involved in the matter was able to find a formula which satisfied everybody. Still, I think his critics confuse the issue by focusing on questions of governmental structure. Burke saw the struggle, rather, in terms of citizenship. In denying that his party had encouraged the American Revolution, Burke once wrote: "*General* rebellions and revolts of a whole people never were *encouraged,* now or at any time. They are always *provoked.*"[136] I believe that a strong case could be made that, from Burke's perspective, the real cause of the American Revolution was England's unwillingness to consider an Empire with a number of centers of authority, but with a single form of citizenship. In opposing a plan to tax absentee Irish landlords, Burke asked, "is not such an Irish tax as is now proposed a virtual declaration that England is a foreign country and a renunciation on your part of the principle of *Common naturalization,* which runs through this whole empire?"[137] Further, unlike many other writers on imperial themes, Burke insisted that this citizenship must be based on a body of common rights extending equally to all parts of the empire.[138] To the argument that the lack of a vote for some Englishmen provided precedent for English taxation of America even though there was no American representation in the English Parliament, Burke replied with comtempt: "so, then, because some towns in England are not represented, America is to have no representatives at all."[139] Thus, as in so many other cases, those of the Irish, the Dissenters, and the

English Roman Catholics come readily to mind, Burke's proposed answer to American grievances was to effectively incorporate them into the British political system. If Englishmen had a right to consent to taxation, Burke did not see how that right could be denied in America. In his view, if British liberty was made real in the colonies, the Americans would no longer desire independence, for, "slavery they can have anywhere. It is a weed that grows in every soil. They may have it from Spain, they may have it from Prussia. But, until you become lost to all feeling of your true interest and your natural dignity, freedom they can have from none but you."[140] In short, Burke did not see the problem as one of structure, but as one of building a sense of membership in a common enterprise.

In my view, then, there is an important sense in which Burke's stand on the American crisis may be judged a success. Early in the conflict he formulated an understanding of the Empire which was comprehensive and consistent, well ahead of administration policy and public opinion, and responsive to American concerns as well. As a member of the Rockingham administration, he worked effectively to implement that plan. When his approach encountered difficulties, he made corrections to respond to the new circumstances. When it finally became clear that no reform could satisfy all of the parties, he was among the first to accept the necessity of American independence. Simply put, on America Burke and his allies provided the kind of leadership his theory of trusteeship called for. Yet, at a deeper level, the very success of the Rockingham Whigs was a portent of difficulties to come, for that success hid an internal contradiction in their thought. Ironically, Burke's proposed solution to the American crisis rested on a repudiation of his own theory of trusteeship and virtual representation. Burke was quick to recognize the ultimate absurdity of the orthodox argument that the Americans were included in the British political system, even though they did not elect members of Parliament, and that Parliament, therefore, had the right to legislate for America. He fully understood that such a slender link between the colonies and England was too weak to hold the Empire together. In the next two chapters, we will examine cases where Burke was not so perceptive, and, consequently, where the results were not so happy. In the matter of the French Revolution, Burke relied on his theory of trusteeship to provide a basis for an argument that reform from above was a meaningful alternative to revolution from below. Ultimately, the theory held. Burke and his allies were able to sway both public and elite opinion, and to keep trusteeship working. However, the cost was very high, for Burke's ideological crusade against the radicals split the reform party and helped delay extensive political reform for many years. Even worse, in Irish politics, Burke failed to rally opinion behind a moderate reform proposal. The Pitt Administration refused to consider any attempt to court the Catholic population, and, therefore, found itself supporting a reactionary Irish Ascendency. As a result, the failure of trusteeship based reform led to reaction, and reaction led to rebellion.

9

THE FRENCH REVOLUTION AND THE CRISIS OF EUROPEAN CIVILIZATION

The discussion and analysis of Burke's position on the French Revolution is a central test for most studies of his thought. This is so not because of any intrinsic difficulty in the topic but because one's handling of the French Revolution reveals how effectively one's approach covers the entire reach of Burke's thought. Michael Freeman's *Edmund Burke and the Critique of Political Radicalism* is a good example.[1] Freeman opens with a claim that a "perennial issues" approach to political theory is valid. Thus, he believes that what Burke said about the radicalism of the 1790s is useful to us because we face similar issues today. As he puts it, "the main thesis of the present book is that Edmund Burke, in the face of a particular revolution which he detested and feared, proposed a general conservative theory of revolution and of political radicalism in order to combat and refute the general radical ideas he believed the revolutionaries to hold."[2] Freeman sees the foundation of Burke's theory to lie in Christian metaphysics, specifically in his adherence to traditional natural law, and argues that for Burke the chief error of the radicals was to challenge the morality inherent in the "nature of things."[3] After discussing Burke's views on revolution in general, Freeman turns to the French Revolution as a particular case. Unfortunately, what he unwittingly demonstrates is that Burke has no theory of revolution in general. Indeed, Freeman's own treatment of Burke's presumed general theory is so contaminated with arguments drawn from the French example that the two categories—general and French—collapse into one.[4] By the end of the book, Burke emerges as the one thing he always refused to be: the author of a universally applicable political theory. Ironically, Freeman is joined in his preoccupation with the counterrevolutionary Burke by some recent radical critics. C. B. Macpherson, for instance, sees the

French Revolution as forcing a major reorientation on Burke.[5] Although he notes many of the more reformist themes in Burke's early writings, Macpherson insists that Burke reversed himself in the 1790s. Thus, he argues, "the impression of Burke as the arch-conservative seemed indelibly fixed: his crusade against the French Revolution had eclipsed all his other works" and goes on to interpret Burke as an apologist for early Capitalism.[6]

That the conservative and radical strategies for interpreting Burke lead to such similar conclusions ought to be a sign that they, in fact, rest on common assumptions. For example, Freeman and Macpherson both assume that the Revolution dwarfed Burke's other concerns. Yet, that was not the case. In the early days of the Revolution, Burke was probably more interested in the Regency Crisis, and, indeed, while the split in the Whig Party during the crisis did not precisely prefigure the later split over the Revolution, it certainly prepared the ground for that break.[7] Later, as the Revolution became more of an issue in English politics, Burke's interest was divided between it and the Hastings Impeachment. Finally, in his last years, after leaving Parliament, Burke's *Correspondence* shows as much concern with the deteriorating state of Irish affairs as with the French Revolution. During the so-called Treason Trials of the mid-1790s, Burke's letters seldom mention the trials but are full of pained discussions of Ireland. Nor were these various concerns separate isolated issues for Burke. He constantly sought to find common denominators. In a draft of a letter to Loughborough in 1796, Burke linked Hastings and France thusly: "Our Government and our Laws are beset by two different Enemies, which are sapping its foundations, Indianism, and Jacobinism. In some Cases they act separately, in some they act in conjunction. But of this I am sure; that the first is the worst by far, and the hardest to deal with; and for this amongst other reasons, that it weakens, discredits, and ruins that force, which ought to be employd (sic) with the greatest Credit and Energy against the other; and that it furnishes Jacobinism with its strongest arms against all *formal* Governments."[8] Here we have it all: Burke combining India and France in a letter about Ireland—a letter in which he suggests that domestic reform is a prerequisite to a successful campaign against radicalism.

Thus, for the student of Burke's thought, the principal difficulty presented by the French Revolution is that it reveals elements of both continuity and change in his position. Burke saw the Revolution as a unique and novel event. In the *Reflections,* he wrote, "it appears to me as if I were in a great crisis, not of the affairs of

France alone, but of all Europe, perhaps of more than Europe. All circumstances taken together, the French Revolution is the most astonishing that has hitherto happened in the world."[9] And in the *Thoughts on French Affairs,* he noted, "one must not judge of the state of France by what has been observed elsewhere. It does not in the least resemble any other country. Analogical reasoning from history or from recent experience in other places is wholly delusive."[10] At the same time, Burke approached the Revolution through the framework provided by his previous experience. In his eyes, the Revolution was the occasion of yet another opportunity for, and challenge to, Whiggish reform. As he watched the Revolution unfold, Burke became increasingly convinced that it was the perfectly predictable result of the French monarchy's failure to achieve timely and moderate reform. It grew, in a sense, out of a failure of trusteeship. This was the point of Burke's contrast in the *Reflections* of the English Revolution of 1688 with the French Revolution. In the first case, he argued, the political elite had responded to a threat quickly and effectively, and, therefore, had avoided disaster. In the latter case, no reform had been forthcoming, and the nation was destroyed accordingly. Burke's conclusion from this analysis was also familiar: that reform was the only true alternative to Revolution. The French Revolution, then, in my opinion, caused no change in Burke's fundamental orientation: he continued to promote progress, and, therefore, still defined himself as a reform politician, and he remained true to his Whig creed of aristocratic government. However, the Revolution did lead Burke to introduce new themes into his argument. What is new is, in part, a sense of a changed situation: Burke now believed that reform must be achieved in a revolutionary context. He no longer saw himself as debating the peaceful and rational improvement of the British system, but as involved in a multi-dimensional conflict to restore a stable regime in France, to purge Europe of radicalism, and to defend the advanced English constitution against those fanatics who would destroy it. As Burke's assessment of the political circumstances of France emphasized what was novel, so, he believed, should the response be based on a new strategy and employ new tactics. Therefore, in recognition of the ideological nature of the conflict, he waged a campaign to discredit radicalism at home, and he promoted a joint European crusade against the revolutionary government of France. In short, to understand Burke, I believe that one must see the Revolution as he saw it. While he believed that a new threat required new forms of countervailing action, he also maintained that his new approach was in support of values which were both tested by time and progressive in their own right.

I

I begin with Burke's analysis of the causes and course of the French Revolution. Burke's understanding of the Revolution developed slowly. At first, his comments were ambiguous and noncommittal. For instance, in a letter to Charlemont dated August 9, 1789, he wrote, "the spirit it is impossible not to admire; but the old Parisian ferocity has broken out in a shocking manner . . . But if it should be character rather than accident, then that people are not fit for Liberty, and must have a Strong hand like that of their former master to coerce them."[11] Even such a landmark event as the Fall of the Bastille on July 14, 1789, was met only by a mild statement of surprise accompanied by an expression of concern for the future. As late as November 1789, after the Declaration of the Rights of Man and the October unrest, Burke was still reluctant to condemn the French reformers: he told Depont, "but it would ill become Me to be too ready in forming a positive opinion upon matters transacted in a Country, with the correct, political Map of which I must be very imperfectly acquainted. Things indeed have already happen'd so much beyond the scope of all speculation, that persons of infinitely more sagacity than I am ought to be ashamed of anything like confidence in their reasoning upon the operation of any principle or the effect of any measure."[12] Gradually, however, Burke began to formulate a position. I think that the development of his thought can be divided into five distinct stages: (1) an initial period of inattention and uncertainty combined with rather wary statements of disapproval on specific points; (2) sometime in the fall of 1789 this disapproval hardened into open opposition, but Burke continued to be courteous in his style and was nervous about the issue of his own consistency; (3) by the time of the publication of the *Reflections* in November of 1790, Burke's tentative concern had hardened into certainty, and he was becoming increasingly intolerant in his claim to be the voice of true Whiggism; (4) after the French Declaration of War in February 1793, Burke resigned from the Whig Club, thus breaking openly with his party, and became an outspoken advocate of a European crusade against Jacobinism; and (5) finally, by the fall of 1795, Burke recognized that the Revolution might succeed, and feared that the war against Jacobinism had a good chance of failure. Meanwhile, becoming concerned about the potential absolutism he perceived among the refugees, he declared a mere return to an unreformed Ancien Regime unacceptable. At the time of his death in July 1797, Burke was pessimistic about the future; still opposed to the Revolution, he, nonetheless, had become increasingly alienated from its opponents. Moreover, Irish politics had largely superseded the Revolution as his major concern.

The centerpiece of Burke's anti-Revolutionary rhetoric actually developed slowly, and did not appear in his discussions of French politics until rather late. That centerpiece was the claim that the Revolution had so far followed, and was likely to continue to follow, an inevitable course of ever increasing violence and chaos. At the height of his anti-Revolutionary zeal, for example, Burke wrote to one correspondent, "Nothing has happen'd but what was the Natural and inevitable effect of that fatal Constitution, and its absurd and wicked principles. Nothing has been the effect of accident; Every successive Event was the direct result of that which preceded it; and the whole, the Effect of the false Bases on which that constitution was originally laid."[13] Similarly, he argued that the proposals of the English radicals, whatever their intent, could only lead to the same kind of disaster which had engulfed France: "their Revolution too will run exactly the same course, as it is founded on the same principles which that of their Brethren in France; it will be pursued in the same manner and all its proceedings will be executed by the same necessities."[14] As James T. Boulton has pointed out, there is here an intimate relationship between Burke's politics and his literary techniques.[15] His message was simple—like causes produce like results—but its presentation was not. Burke's argument was the very traditional claim that there exists a cosmic and divine natural order, which creates binding moral obligations on man. In the past, he continued, the English succeeded by adhering to that order, but the French are destined to fail because they violate it. However, the techniques Burke used to deliver that message were complex indeed. Especially in the *Reflections,* but throughout his writings on the Revolution, Burke used a wealth of images of order, drawn from the Bible, from nature, and from analogy to the the family, and of disorder, like drunkenness and sickness, to reinforce his point. One simply cannot, Burke maintained, have radical reform without its being accompanied by anarchy, and that anarchy will necessarily be followed by tyranny and international conflict.

This concern with what one might call the pathology of the Revolution led Burke to focus a great deal of attention on its causes. He believed it obvious that, if unrest and radical reform inevitably lead to revolution, the best way to avoid revolution is not to permit unrest and radical reform to begin. Thus, Burke's analysis of the Revolution begins with his description of France prior to the agitation for reform. In his view, France was an important and stable part of the commonwealth of Europe. All of Europe, Burke declared, was "virtually one great state, having the same basis of general law, with some diversity of provincial customs and local establishments."[16] The same religion, with minor variations, prevailed in all states, and each drew its politics and its economy from the same Germanic or Gothic customs. While the individual nations varied in their political institutions, none was a despotism and all, even the republics, were imbued with the principles of mixed monarchy. Moreover, all Europe shared a common culture based on the same traditional moral values: "this mixed system of opinion and sentiment had its origin in the ancient chivalry; and the principle, though varied in its appearance by the varying state of human affairs, subsisted and influenced through a long succession of generations even to the time we live in."[17] However, like all great human attainments, the civilization of Europe was a fragile thing, requiring great respect and care, for, "if it should ever be totally extinguished, the loss I fear will be great."[18] For this reason, along with its obvious rhetorical purpose, the paean to Marie-Antoinette in the *Reflections* played an important symbolic role in Burke's argument, for, "the Queen symbolizes all that is finest in a whole civilization, and with her perish the benefits which society derived from that civilization: dignified obedience, exalted freedom, the unifying and ennobling power of human emotions."[19] Finally, Burke argued that France, like all of Europe, was improving before the Revolution. The French king was well-meaning and concerned, if indeed a bit inept, and the governmental bureaucracy was both public-spirited and progressive.

How, then, could such a noble and beneficial system fail? Burke's many explanations can, I think, be grouped under two heads. First, he maintained that the old order had long been under attack by a revolutionary party. Burke usually stigmatized these revolutionaries with the label of "Jacobin," a term he seldom bothered to define. As he put it, "Jacobinism is the Vice of men of Parts; and in this age it is the Chanel [*sic*] in which all discontents will run."[20] That is, Burke saw the Jacobins as drawn from those elements of the middle and upper classes who believe that they had a natural right to power and privilege because of their intellectual or political merits. "Talents," Burke said, "naturally gravitate to Jacobinism," for "whatever tends to persuade the people that the *few,* called by whatever name you please, religious or political, are of opinion that their interest is not compatible with that of the *many,* is a great point gained to Jacobinism."[21] Such men come, according to Burke, in two varieties—the philosophers and the politicians.[22] The first group was composed of all those who attack religion and conventional morality, including, of course, those Burke listed as the "literary cabal" in the *Reflections.* In his words,"these atheistical fathers have a bigotry of their own, and they have learned to talk against monks with the spirit of a monk."[23] Among the philosophers, then, were writers like Collins, Toland, Tindal, and Bolingbroke. The second group, the politicians, were those who, without any real concern with the issues of religion and morality, realized that the philosophers had provided a means of weakening their enemies, and, therefore, employed those tools to further their own bid for power. As Burke saw it, "they do not commit crimes for their designs; but they form designs that they may commit crimes."[24] They sought to gain power, and to strengthen the state, so that they might give their desires free reign. According to Burke, their hero was Rousseau. He was "their canon of holy writ; in his life he is their canon of Polycletus; he is their standard figure of perfection."[25] What they admired most was his extremism and his hypocrisy: "he melts with tenderness for those only who touch him by the remotest relation . . . and sends his children to the hospital of foundlings."[26] In sum, Burke believed that, armed with the ideas of the philosophers, the politicians took dead aim at the French Crown and aristocracy. They did not miss their target, and the Revolution was their prize.

Second, Burke believed that the radicals had considerable help in undermining the pre-revolutionary French state from the government itself. In his view, the leaders of France encouraged revolution by repeatedly failing to make necessary reforms. Years earlier, in discussing the American Revolution, Burke had suggested a general rule: "we deplored, as your Majesty has done in your speech from the throne, the disorders which prevail in your empire; but we are convinced that the disorders of the people, in the present time and the present place, are owing to the usual and natural cause of such disorder . . . the misconduct of government . . ."[27] He saw no reason to alter his position in the 1790s. Indeed, in both the *Reflections* and the *Appeal,* Burke admitted that, in an extreme case, misgovernment might even justify revolution. In the *Reflections,* he suggested that, during the English Revolution, "aided with the powers derived from force and opportunity, the nation was . . . in some sense, free to take what course it pleased for filling the throne . . ."[28] However, Burke also insisted that such an extreme course was not often justified: before the people ought to resume power, he wrote, ". . . no occasion can justify such a resumption, which would not equally authorize a dispensation with any other moral duty, perhaps with all of them together."[29] Far better, then, he concluded, was reform: "I would not exclude alteration neither, but even when I changed it should be to preserve. I should be led to my remedy by a great grievance. In what I did, I should follow the example of our ancestors. I would make the reparation as nearly as possible in the style of the building."[30] Burke recognized that reform might be slow, but it was sure, and, moreover, it left room for further adjustment. In a letter to the King of Poland, Burke praised a series of Polish reforms both for what had been done and what had been left undone: "there is Room for a long succession of acts of Politick beneficence. Nothing is forced, or crude, or before its time. The circumstances which make the improvement gradual, will make it more sure, and will not make it the less rapid."[31] Burke was, in short, quite consistent on the issue of reform and revolution. From the 1760s to the 1790s, he always held that extreme oppression justified rebellion, but he also insisted that gradual and limited reform was better than either.

Unfortunately, in Burke's view, the French monarchy had made a botch of reform. Even in the *Reflections,* he conceded the need existed: "your government in France, though usually, and I think justly, reputed the best of the unqualified or ill-qualified monarchies, was still full of abuses . . ."[32] In his private letters, he was even more emphatic. Burke told one correspondent, "if any one means that system of Court Intrigue miscalled a Government as it stood, at Versailles before the present confusions as the thing to be established, that I believe will be found absolutely impossible . . . If it were even possible to lay things down exactly as they stood, before the series of experimental politicks began, I am quite sure that they could not long continue in that situation."[33] Many modern scholars place a significant share of the blame for the failure of reform in France on the vacillating policies of the king.[34] They argue that prerevolutionary France was less a true community or nation than a collection of various ranks, classes, and regions, each with its own highly structured body of rights and privileges. Thus, effective action was difficult, and, with so many focal points for resistance, change easy to block. Therefore, they argue that the only possible means of reform was a vigorous Crown. As J. M. Roberts puts it, the only sound tactic for the monarchy would have been "To capture the allegiance of reforming opinion, and mobilize it in the shape of a strong Third Estate which could over-ride the other two in support of a coherent strategy of reform."[35] A number of Burke's French contemporaries, including Voltaire, perceived this and supported a series of reform-minded royal ministers.[36] Burke understood it as well, but he also realized that Louis XVI was just not up to the task. Of Louis, Burke said, "His conduct in its principles was not unwise; but, like most other of his well-meant designs, it failed in his hands . . . The failure, perhaps, in part, was owing to his suffering his system to be vitiated and disturbed by those intrigues which it is, humanly speaking, impossible wholly to prevent in courts . . ."[37] In private, Burke even acknowledged that the Queen was among the worst offenders: "that most unfortunate woman is not to be cured of the spirit of Court Intrigue even by a prison."[38] In fact, on occasion, he admitted that, if it came to a choice between the revolutionary government and the Ancien Regime, he would be hard put to decide.[39]

For Burke, the combination of the abstract and detached radicalism of the reformers and the indecisive and venial corruption of the Crown was a recipe for civic collapse. Ignoring the lessons of experience and prudence, the French "chose to act as if you had never been molded into civil society and had everything to begin anew. You began ill, because you began by despising everything that belonged to you. You set up your trade without a capital."[40] The result, he thought, was both forseeable and ironic: "they have found their punishment in their success: laws overturned; tribunals subverted; industry without vigor; commerce expiring; the revenues unpaid, yet the people impoverished; a church pillaged, and a state not relieved; civil and military anarchy made the constitution of the kingdom; everything human and divine sacrificed to the idol of public credit, and national bankruptcy the consequence; . . ."[41] From foolishness, according to Burke, the Revolution had proceeded to the destruction of all social bonds and anarchy. Once freed from the discipline, and protection, of the laws, the people became the dupes of impostors and charlatans. They ran wild in their delusions: "but the deluded people of France are like other madmen, who, to a miracle, bear hunger, and thirst, and cold, and confinement, and the claims and lash of their keeper, whilst all the while they support themselves by the imagination that they are generals of armies, prophets, kings, and emperors."[42] The would-be animal tamers have become the animals, and the animals now direct the show. The National Assembly, Burke claimed, no longer governs, for it is controlled by the Paris mob, and, "under the terror of the bayonet and the lamppost and the torch to their houses, they are obliged to adopt all the crude and desperate measures suggested by clubs composed by a monstrous medley of all conditions, tongues, and nations."[43] Yet, Burke did not think that this was the end of the matter, for he predicted that anarchy could not long endure. It, in turn, could only lead to a seizure of power by some conspiratorial elite. Of the French people, Burke noted, "by their violent haste and their defiance of the process of nature, they are delivered over blindly to every projector and adventurer, to every alchemist and empiric."[44] Eventually one or a group of these adventurers will seize control of the state and use its power to discipline the mobs and restore order.

Still, the story would not be over, for despotism has a logic of its own. Burke asserted: "The design is wicked, immoral, impious, oppressive: but it is spirited and daring; it is systematic; it is simple in its principle; it has unity and consistency in perfection. In that country, entirely to cut off a branch of commerce, to extinguish a manufacture, to destroy the circulation of money, to violate credit, to suspend the course of agriculture, even to burn a city or to lay waste a province of their own, does not cost them a moment's anxiety . . . The state is all in all."[45] Nor did he consider such a state to be unstable. While many leading English politicians supported the Revolution on the presumption that it would weaken France, Burke maintained, "it is not to be imagined, because a political system is, under certain aspects, very unwise in its contrivance, and very mischievous in its effects, that it therefore can have no long duration. Its very defects may tend to its stability, because they are agreeable to its nature."[46] Burke saw several forces as working to unify and strengthen France: the economic policy of the confiscation of property and the issuing of paper currency, the supremacy of Paris, the Army, and, most of all, a systematic policy of repression at home and expansion abroad. Indeed, he argued that there was a close connection between the internal and external sides of the Revolution. In Burke's opinion, the Revolution had to be exported or die on the vine. As he put it, "it is not an enemy of accident that we have to deal with. Enmity to us, and to all civilized nations, is wrought into the stamina of its Constitution."[47] By its very nature, he suggested, the French Revolution must be at war with all of civilized Europe, for, while Europe exists unreformed, the Revolution can never be secure, and, so long as France remains revolutionary, Europe is in danger. Yet, Burke saw the imperialism of the Revolution as a mixed benefit for its leaders. Eventually, he insisted, the militarization of the Revolution would be its downfall. Sooner or later, the government would become incapable of controlling or disciplining the army. When that occurred, "in the weakness of one kind of authority, and in the fluctuation of all, the officers of an army will remain for some time mutinous and full of faction until some popular general, who understands the art of conciliating the soldiery, and who possesses the true spirit of command, shall draw the eyes of all men upon him. Armies will obey him on his personal account . . . But the moment in which that event shall happen, the person who really commands the army is your master . . ."[48] Only then, Burke concluded will the Revolution be over.

One final point concerning Burke's analysis of the pathology of the French Revolution remains to be considered. That is the question of whether Burke should be seen as some kind of genius of the Counterrevolution. Did he see further into the dynamics of the Revolution than other men? Some of Burke's protagonists seem to think so. Freeman, for example, claims that "Burke identified the classic conditions for revolution: a weak, highly centralized state presiding over a society divided between a decadent ruling class and an aspirant powerful new class. The chief cause of the French Revolution was not the conspiracy of intellectuals, but the policy of the French monarchy."[49] Freeman further believes that Burke correctly determined the necessary course of all revolutions.[50] Similarly, J. M. Robert's description of the Terror invokes memories of Burke: "much of the Terror was mindless. It was not an ordered movement, sweeping France irresistibly towards a clear goal of political and social reform . . . If it had a pervasive principle, it was one more often implicit than explicit and it lay in the fact that what all those involved in it were trying to do—save France—required the biggest attempt yet seen to nationalize the life of a whole State, to regulate it in all its aspects from a central source of impulse."[51] Burke's insistence on a link between French internal politics and the war holds up quite well under the test of modern scholarship.[52]

Yet, one wonders. Burke's view of the Revolution developed slowly and was never so clearcut as his defenders seem to think. Moreover, upon examination, much of what he said simply mirrors the classical sources on revolution. In the *Republic,* Plato held that despotism arisies out of anarchy, noted the relationship between tyranny and foreign wars, and referred to its militarization of the state.[53] Similarly, Aristotle suggested that, "in democracies changes are chiefly due to the wanton licence of demagogues," that democracies are generally followed by oligarchies, that oligarchies often fall because of the abuse of the masses or dissension among oligarchs, and that military leaders often seize control of declining oligarchies.[54] Burke had other sources at hand as well. I would think, for example, that he could find inspiration in the writings on Oliver Cromwell. Cromwell's position as Lord Protector was, after all, Janus-faced: on the one hand, it looked back to the classical world, but, on the other, it evoked the more modern concept of the military as the "protector of the constitution." Indeed, Burke had only to look to David Hume's *Histories.* After the death of the king, Hume wrote, "the bands of society were everywhere loosened; and the irregular passions of men were encouraged by speculative principles still more unsocial and irregular."[55] Only Cromwell's personal strength and the discipline of the army kept things going, Hume argued, for, "illegal violence, with whatever pretences it may be covered, and whatever object it may pursue, must inevitably and at last end in the arbitrary and despotic government of a single person."[56] I do not mean to suggest that Burke grounded his account of the Revolution directly on Hume or on anyone else. I merely wish to maintain that, along with an impressive elment of originality and a considerable talent for vivid expression, Burke drew on a traditional model of revolution which fit French circumstances rather well.

II

Burke's analysis of the causes and probable course of the French Revolution led him to see it as posing a multi-dimensional threat to European security. In his view, the Revolution, because of its ideological and imperialistic aspects, could not be contained within France, and would, by its very nature, spread until it was confronted by superior moral and political power. Thus, I believe that students of Burke's thought commit a serious error when they neglect one or another of the several facets of the crisis Burke felt was facing the international community of his day. Such a narrow focus seriously underestimates the magnitude of Burke's fears, and, moreover, distorts our understanding of his thought by making various aspects of his proposals for fighting the Revolution appear irrational or excessive. Before proceeding to consider Burke's strategy and tactics for opposing the Revolution, I will, therefore, first consider his interpretation of the threat it represented in more detail. First, Burke held that the Revolution promised to destroy the old order within France, and, with its elimination, remove one of the great centers of European civilization. He believed that it was not only an assault on the government of France, but an attack on the very culture of the most advanced section of the world. Second, Burke claimed that once France fell to the radicals, the remainder of Europe would be exposed to the danger of attack from that nation, and, consequently, the commonwealth of Europe would be exposed to the threat of a kind of civil war. In more modern terms, Burke believed that a revolutionary government in France would become both militaristic and expansionistic. Finally, Burke also feared that revolutionary France would become a threat by example. In part, Burke was concerned that France would export revolutionary propaganda which would undermine the intellectual foundations of European government. However, his anxiety went further, for he also argued that the mere existence of France's radical government would serve as an inspiration to radicals elsewhere. Here, Burke saw the danger as twofold. On the one hand, successful revolutions in other countries would lead to further rupture of the European community. On the other hand, unsuccessful revolutions would precipitate reaction which, in turn, would endanger freedom and block reform.

I will begin with France, itself. As we have seen, Burke was a firm believer in both the unity and the progressiveness of the European community: "the states of the Christian world have grown up to their present magnitude in a great length of time and by a great variety of accidents. They have been improved to what we see them with greater or less degrees of felicity and skill . . . The objects which they embrace are of the greatest possible variety, and have become in a manner infinite . . . Every state has pursued not only every sort of social advantage, but it has cultivated the welfare of every individual."[57] Such traditionalism was not entirely, or even largely, a conservative doctrine, for at its core, as J. G. A. Pocock has pointed out, was the belief that commerce and progress "can flourish only under the protection of manners, and that manners require the pre-eminence of religion and nobility, the natural protectors of society. To overthrow religion and nobility, therefore, is to destroy the possibility of commerce itself."[58] In Burke's view, the French Revolution threatened to do just that: "there is the hand of God in this business, and there is an end of the system of Europe, taking in laws, manners, religion and politics, in which I delighted so much."[59] When Burke, in the *Reflections,* deplored the end of the age of chivalry, and claimed as a result, "that of sophisters, economists, and calculators has succeeded, and the glory of Europe is extinguished forever," he meant to be taken literally.[60] Burke believed that a successful revolution in France would, by destroying what was perhaps the most shining example of Enlightenment culture, signal the advent of a new age. The hard-won achievements of time, he insisted, would be destroyed and replaced by the false idols of a temporary aberration. As he insisted that a queen was more than a woman, and a woman was more than an animal, so he believed that a society was more than a collection of self-interested calculators. Burke believed that the French materialists would reduce man to a machine. He was equally sure that they were wrong to do so. Indeed, the very attempt, would, itself, he thought, destroy much of what he valued.

Moreover, from the very beginning, Burke insisted that the French radicals had something more in mind than just the conquest of power in France. They sought, he noted, not to limit the French state, but to capture and strengthen it. They attacked monarchy for it weakness, not its excessive and arbitrary power, and they advocated a republic because, like Machiavelli, Harrington, and Montesquieu, they believed that it was more suitable for expansion.[61] In short, Burke said, "those who acted in the Revolution *as statesmen* had the exterior aggrandizement of France as their ultimate end in the most minute part of the internal changes that were made."[62] Viewed in this light, Burke held that the Revolution displayed a character totally new in the world; it took on the aura of a kind of secular holy war: "*a Revolution of doctrine and theoretic dogma.*"[63] He maintained that, like the Reformation, the Revolution could leave no part of the world unchanged and had to become imperialistic by its very nature. The French, Burke continued, "made a schism with the whole universe, and that schism extended to almost everything, great and small."[64] In the realm of politics, "this violent breach of the community of Europe we must conclude to have been made (even if they had not expressly declared it over and over again) either to force mankind into an adoption of their system or to live in perpetual enmity with a community the most potent we have ever known."[65] What was worse, according to Burke, like many of the other mutations of nature, the new French form of government possessed an amazing strength: "were France but half of what it is in population, in compactness, in applicability of its force, situated as it is, and being what it is, it would be too strong for most of the states of Europe, constituted as they are, and proceeding as they proceed."[66] In sum, Burke concluded, the Revolution must be destroyed or it will destroy everything in its path: "From all this what is my inference? It is, that this new system of robbery in France cannot be rendered safe by any art; that it *must* be destroyed, or that it will destroy all Europe . . ."[67] Like a cancer, the Revolution, Burke said, must be annihilated before it kills its host.

Finally, as the English Revolution inspired the American, and the American inspired the French, so Burke feared that the French Revolution would encourage reformers in other nations to imitate its example. Burke recognized the irony of France's support for the American Revolution for Louis XVI: where he "meant to found but one republic, he set up two; when he meant to take away half the crown of his neighbor, he lost the whole of his own."[68] With such an example in mind, he asked, can the leaders of Europe really believe that a martial republic can be established in their own vicinity without posing a threat to them? This was, he thought, especially so, for the spirit of proselytism attended the fanaticism of the French: "they have societies to cabal and correspond at home and abroad for the propagation of their tenets."[69] Indeed, the entire first half of Burke's "Thoughts on French Affairs," more than thirty pages, was given over to a survey of the progress of revolutionary ideas throughout the countries of Europe.[70] For example, Burke argued, "that this doctrine has made an amazing progress in Germany there cannot be a shadow of doubt."[71] He, therefore, predicted that there would soon be a German revolution even greater than the one in France. For Burke, the problem, was that everywhere he looked there was a French party, often led by the French ambassador, seeking converts. In England, for instance, he noted the Constitutional and Revolutionary Societies: "the National Assembly of France has given importance to these gentlemen by adopting them; and they return the favor by acting as a committee in England for extending the principles of the National Assembly."[72] According to Burke, when the principles and politics of the French Revolution are extended to other nations, their constitutions will be unable to cope. They are not made for such conflict. Burke maintained that, even with all its history of tyranny and rebellion, England "has never been debauched from its domestic relations. To this time it has been English liberty, and English liberty only."[73] To be sure, Burke felt that, "we cannot be too liberal in our general wishes for the happiness of our kind. But in all questions on the mode of procuring it for any particular community, we ought to be fearful of admitting those who have no interest in it, or who have, perhaps, an interest against it, into the consultation."[74] In the past, Burke insisted, all the parties to a given English conflict could, at least, be assumed to want the best for their country, even if they might have defined that best in different ways. With the advent of the French Revolution, however, he feared that there would always be a substantial pro-French party, intent on the realization of its alien creed regardless of the consequences.

As the preceding example indicates, Burke was particularly apprehensive about the effects of the French Revolution on England. His uneasiness was, in part, a product of natural prudence and caution. As he pointed out in the *Reflections,* "when our neighbor's house is on fire, it cannot be amiss for the engines to play a little on our own."[75] But it was also based on his judgment that England was particularly vulnerable to some of the propaganda coming out of France. Burke always insisted that the mass of English citizens, of all ranks and callings, were steadfast in their loyalty to the English Constitution. In the "Letters on a Regicide Peace," he claimed that, "the people have nowhere and in no way expressed their wish of throwing themselves and their sovereign at the feet of a wicked and ravenous foe . . ."[76] Rather, what Burke was afraid of was the fellow-travelling minority, both within and without Parliament. These, he admitted, were not, strictly speaking, Jacobins themselves, but they were, nonetheless, not to be trusted, for they could already be found attacking the government, "in the same modes, and on the very same grounds, and nearly in the same terms, with the Directory."[77] Modern scholars agree that there was cosiderable correspondence between the French Revolutionaries and the English reformers, and some see a revolutionary potential in English politics. E. P. Thompson, for instance, supports Burke's analysis, arguing that the politics of the 1790s "was not an agitation about France, although French events both inspired and bedevilled it. It was an English agitation, of impressive dimensions, for an English democracy."[78] Most writers, however, do not go so far.[79] They maintain that the English reformers, contrary to Burke's assessment, were moderate until near the end of the century. Veitch's comments on the Society for Constitutional Information is typical: "nothing could well be more harmless than the vague and high-flown sentiments exchanged during the period of French constitutionalism."[80] Burke, it seems, exaggerated.

At the center of Burke's concern stood the Protestant Dissenters. Early in his political career, Burke had been allied with the

Dissenters, especially in the movements for broader religious toleration. For example, in 1773 he had vigorously supported a Methodist petition for toleration.[81] Gradually, however, his support diminished as he became increasingly convinced that the Dissenters were overly political and radical to boot. Thus, in May of 1789, Burke could be found agonizing over his vote on a relief bill, and attributing his reluctance to support relief to the enthusiasm among Dissenters for Pitt's constitutional coup of 1784. His indecision soon turned to opposition. The turning point seems to have come in early March 1790. About that time, the Dissenters made three moves: they adopted a strategy of provocation against their opponents; they attempted to pressure Parliament by exacting electoral pledges from candidates; and they openly committed to French revolutionary principles.[82] Burke was furious. In response to a Unitarian petition, he exclaimed: "let them disband as a faction, and let them act as individuals, and when I see them with no other views than to enjoy their own conscience in peace, I, for one, shall most cheerfully vote for their relief."[83] "Rather," he argued, "George the Third, or George the Fourth, than Dr. Priestly, or Dr. Keppis . . ."[84] For a religious group to act as a political faction was offensive enough to Burke, but he also objected to the mode of argument the Dissenter employed. In a letter to John Noble, he complained that their arguments smacked of the natural law and abstract rights rhetoric of the French. He was offended, he said, by "the eager manner in which several dissenting Teachers shewed themselves disposed to connect themselves in Sentiment and by imitation (and perhaps by something more) with what was done and is doing in France . . ."[85] Similarly, over a year and a half later, Burke wrote to Henry Dundas that he was not much concerned with the scattered pro-French individuals, but that he greatly feared the "Phalanx of Party" which the Dissenters had become.[86] I have argued that Burke was, in many respects, a disciple of John Locke. Like Locke, one of the few justifications he accepted for discrimination against a religious group was the political consequences of that group's ideas and actions.

Burke did not believe that the Dissenters, taken alone, constituted a serious threat to the English political system. However, he was convinced that they had like-minded allies among certain other groups and parties. In his "Thoughts on French Affairs," Burke maintained that, while the Dissenters constituted the core of the pro-French party, they were joined by "all who are Dissenters in character, temper, and disposition, though not belonging to any of their congregations: that is, all the restless people who resemble them, of all ranks and parties,—Whigs, and even Tories; the whole race of half-bred speculators; all the Atheists, Deists, and Socinians; all those who hate the clergy and envy the nobility; a good many among the moneyed people; the East Indians almost to a man. . . ."[87] He even asserted that the sickness had spread even to his own party and among his own friends. In a letter to William Weddell, he described the Dissenters' seduction of Charles James Fox: "in their unprecedented compliment to Mr. Fox 'for Governing his conduct by the true principles of the Revolution,' they plainly alluded to a transaction not quite an hundred years old."[88] Yet more surprising, according to Burke, the radicals had made extensive inroads among the aristocracy itself. In his reply to the Duke of Bedford's criticism of his pension, Burke was quick to note the irony of Bedford's support of French ideas. The radicals, Burke said, "are the Duke of Bedford's natural hunters; and he is their natural game."[89] Still, Burke acknowledged that, in spite of their difference in objective interests, the support of a man like Bedford could be of great advantage to the radicals: "there is scope for seven philosophers to proceed in their analytical experiments upon Harrington's seven different forms of republics, in the acres of this one Duke."[90] Burke doubted that Bedford's lack of class interest would save him. He believed that, in the end, the radicals would turn on their sponsors, for, no matter what they were given, they would always "want new lands for new trials."[91] As sound as the English public might presently be, the example of men like Bedford demonstrated for Burke that no one was completely safe until the Revolution and its doctrine were both obliterated.

III

In considering Burke's strategy for opposing the French Revolution and its creed, several general points should be kept in mind. First, Burke was by no means a mere reactionary. He knew full well that the clock could not be turned back, and he would not have it so even if it could. The New Whigs, Burke insisted, were the extremists, not he, for, "they build their politics, not on convenience, but on truth . . . With them there is no compromise."[92] He, on the other hand, was, in his own eyes, a moderate: "the opinions maintained in that book never can lead to an extreme, because their foundation is laid in an opposition to extremes."[93] Second, though a reformer,

Burke was also yet a gradualist. As he put it, "the burden of proof lies heavily on those who tear to pieces the whole frame and contexture of their country, that they could find no other way of settling a government fit to obtain its rational ends, except that which they have pursue by means unfavorable to all the present happiness of millions of people . . .[94] Third, Burke always insisted that his response to the Revolution was consistent with his earlier stands on other issues. In the letter on his pension, he made a typical argument: citing his proposals for economic reform in the 1780–82 period as an example, he maintained that he had always been a practical-minded reformer.[95] The specific references changed, one time it was a comparison of his reactions to the American and French Revolutions and another it was his speech at the polls at Bristol, but Burke's theme never changed. He constantly claimed that not all change is reform—"the former alters the substance of the objects themselves, and gets rid of all their essential good as well as all the accidental evil annexed to them . . . Reform is . . . a direct application of a remedy to the grievance complained of . . . It stops there; and if it fails, the substance . . . is but where it was"—and that he favored only true reform and not mere change.[96] Fourth, Burke's tone and style were rarely hysterical or violent. Most often, he assumed the role of a man of affairs: he was knowledgeable, prudent, worldy and moderate. The "Fourth Letter on a Regicide Peace" is a good case in point. While it is often denounced by critics as excessively emotional, a close examination shows the letter to be a tightly controlled and very systematic work. Though over one hundred pages in length, it is a point-by-point refutation of the arguments which were being made by Burke's opponents in favor of the treaty at issue. Where there are flights of imagination and rhetoric, and there are several, they always serve some quite specific political purpose.[97]

Finally, while his analysis of French events was pretty well fixed by the time of the publication of the *Reflections,* Burke's strategy of opposition was quite complex and sophisticated, and, therefore, revealed itself fully only over time. At first, Burke claimed to have no solution to the crisis. He concluded the 1791 "Thoughts on French Affairs," on an open note: "the evil is stated, in my opinion, as it exists. The Remedy must be where power, wisdom, and information, I hope, are more united with good intentions than they can be with me."[98] Within a year, with the publication of the "Heads for Consideration on the Present State of Affairs," Burke offered a more detailed analysis, but one that was marred by a central inconsistency. In that work he tried to combine a balance of power argument with an insistence that the French Revolution presented a totally new threat to European civilization.[99] This ambiguity in approach, in turn, led Burke into confusion in his policy recommendations. In the balance of power portions of the tract, he held that France should be weakened but not totally defeated, but, in other sections, he treated the French ideology as an evil which must be exterminated. This was, then, one of the oddest of all Burke's works on the Revolution. His critique of government policy was powerful, but the remedy proposed did not seem adequate to the evil decried. As England was drawn into the War and the debate became more heated, Burke dropped the balance of power line and advanced to a more militant position. In his view, the central issue had become whether the War could be fought in the traditional way or whether a new, more rigorous, effort was necessary.[100] Some (Charles Fox, for example) even believed that trade with France could be continued as the war went on. Burke, for his part, was sure that a new form of warfare was required. He wrote, "you may as well think of opposing one of these old fortresses to the mass of artillery brought by a French irruption into the field as to think of resisting by your old laws and your old forms the new destruction which the corps of Jacobin engineers of today prepare for all such forms and all such laws."[101] At this point, Burke had finally reached his fully articulated position: the French Revolution, he maintained, was a new and monstrous phenomenon which was so antagonistic to civilization that only total warfare to the death could exist between them.

The first step, Burke believed, was to promote an accurate understanding of the political situation. He argued that each allied state must be brought to recognize the unique nature of the challenge, encouraged to form the will to resist, and mobilized to deny the enemy a cheap victory. The truth is, he said: "we are in a war of a *peculiar* nature. It is not with an ordinary community . . . We are at war with a system which by its essence is inimical to all other governments, and which makes peace or war as peace and war may best contribute to their subversion. It is with an *armed doctrine* that we are at war. It has, by its essence, a faction of opinion and of interest and of enthusiasm in every country."[102] Properly speaking, then, Burke maintained, France is not a state, but an organized faction within the community of Europe, and the French War is a form of civil war: "it is a war between the partisans of the ancient civil, moral, and political order of Europe against a sect of fanatical and ambitious atheists which means to change them all."[103] With its partisans in every state, one of the chief dangers of the French ideology is that it is ideally situated for subversion. To be sure, the French have arms aplenty, but their best weapon lies in the sapping of the strength of their opponents before the actual fighting begins. The example of the Ancien Regime of France was instructive for Burke: "if armies and fortresses were a defense against Jacobinism, Louis the Sixteenth would this day reign a powerful monarch over an happy people."[104] Even in England, he believed, the problem was acute, for, "public prosecutions are become little better than schools for treason,—of no use but to improve the dexterity of criminals in the mystery of evasion."[105] With subversion so rampant, the temptation to surrender could be overwhelming. Still, Burke held that the temptation must be resisted, for the struggle was not lost: "this seems the temper of the day. At first the French force was too much despised. Now it is too much dreaded."[106] As the defenders of traditional Europe ought not to resign the struggle prematurely, neither should they compromise. The French system is a cancer which constantly attempts to expand; a temporary peace only permits it to advance by some other means. The fight must be to the end: ". . . more safety was to be found in the most arduous war than in the friendship of that kind of being."[107] In short, according to Burke, if peace is made with France, the revolutionaries will not keep it. The only security lies in unity and unrelenting struggle.

As the campaign against international radicalism progressed, Burke made clear that he did not think that a purely defensive alliance against French militarism could be successful. Rather, he demanded that the war be carried into France, itself, by a European community-based invasion. As early as January of 1791, he wrote to a friend: "I cannot persuade myself that any thing whatsoever can be effected without a great force from Abroad. The predominant Faction is the strongest as I conceive, without comparison."[108] When the Revolution spread beyond the borders of France, Burke also expanded his rationale, for, where he had previously justified his call for invasion in terms of internal French politics, he now did so on the basis of the French threat to the rest of Europe. In the "Heads for Consideration of French Affairs," he argued that an offensive alliance was preferable to a defensive one because offensive alliances are held together by their common efforts while defensive alliances fall apart while awaiting action. In addition, he continued, "this evil in the heart of Europe must be extirpated from that centre, or no part of the circumference can be free from the mischief which radiates from it, and which will spread, circle beyond circle, in spite of all the little defensive precautions which can be employed against it."[109] How was such an invasion to be justified? Burke's explanations varied, but generally he relied on two arguments. First, he asserted that there is a natural right to intervene where one perceives injustice. To a French correspondent, he wrote, "that fury which arises in the minds of men on being stripped of their goods, and turned out of their houses by acts of power, and our sympathy with them under Such wrongs, are feelings implanted in us by our creator . . . They arise out of instinctive principles of self-defense and are executive powers under the legislation of nature, enforcing its first law."[110] Second, Burke appealed to international law. He maintained that, "the government of that kingdom is fundamentally monarchical. The public law of Europe has never recognized in it any other form of government. The potentates of Europe have, by that law, a right, an interest, and a duty to know with what government they are to treat, and what they are to admit into the federative society."[111] According to Burke, then, the community of Europe had a right to decide who was the legal government of France. Furthermore, in the event of a civil war within the boundaries of one of its member states, he felt that the community had an additional right to intervene in support of that party which it had determined to be the legitimate government.[112] Indeed, as an interesting corollary of this argument, Burke held that the proposed invasion of France should be conducted in league with representatives of the traditional French regime.

Once a successful invasion of France was accomplished, Burke saw yet one more task for the allied powers to perform: they would then have to establish some sort of interim government. This, Burke believed, would necessarily have to be a dictatorship of some form, for it must have power "equal at least in vigor, vigilance, promptitude, and decision, to a military government . . . no slow-paced . . . lawyer-like system, still less that of a showy, superficial, trifling, intriguing court . . ."[113] For Burke, the role of this temporary government would be to protect the counter-revolution, and to restore the real French nation. Indeed, in his opinion, "the truth is, that France is out of itself,—the moral France is separated from the geographical. The master of the house is expelled, and the robbers are in possession"[114] Since, in Burke's view, the true corporate people of France were in exile in "Flanders and Germany, in Switzerland, Spain, Italy, and England," they must be returned to their homes before a proper government could be reconstructed.[115] Only when this reverse migration was completed, would it be safe to restore the monarchy. It, in turn, should then "assist the dignity, the religion, and the property of France to repossess themselves of the means of their natural influence."[116] Finally, once reconstituted, the French elite could act to purify the remainder of society: "this will be compassed, when every gentleman, everywhere being restored to his landed estate, each on his patrimonial ground, may join the clergy in reanimating the loyalty, fidelity, and religion of the the people . . . that they may arm the honest and well-affected, and disarm and disable the factious and ill-disposed."[117] Thus, Burke held that the French should be left to themselves to punish the defeated revolutionaries.[118] In this regard, though he disclaimed any right to speak, Burke recommended against a general indemnity, but also counseled moderation: no one should be punished on a broad charge of rebellion, or for anything done in the field of battle, and punishment should be reserved for those who engaged in what would be considered criminal conduct by ordinary society.[119]

IV

It is not easy to assess the impact of Burke's writings on the debate about the French Revolution. To begin with, it should be understood that Burke's works, especially the *Reflections,* were widely read and much discussed in political circles.[120] In general, as Fennessy points out, their reception was mixed: while a number of Burke's friends and associates were fast to praise his efforts, criticism came just as quickly from other circles.[121] To cite just one example of the former, Sir Gilbert Elliot wrote to Burke, "your book contains the fundamental Elements of *all* Political knowledge, and lays clearly open to us the just foundations of *all* Social wisdom."[122] Similarly, in spite of the delicacy of their positions within the party, both Earl Fitzwilliam and the Duke of Portand recommended the *Reflections* as containing the essence of true Whiggism.[123] On the other side of the ledger must be set the enormous number of critical replies to Burke. Writers like Thomas Paine, James Mackintosh, and Mary Wollstonecraft all rushed into print in an attempts to refute him. Boulton makes a useful suggestion, which I will follow, that Burke's critics may be divided into four categories.[124] First, there were the spokesmen for the "popular" party. Largely allied with various political societies, these writers appealed to working-class radicals. Led by Thomas Paine, they attacked Burke as the advocate of privilege, oligarchy, and class repression. Second, the Dissenters agreed with the popular writers in their support for the rights of the people to make, reform, and cashier their governments, but gave their theories a special twist by their stress on religion and liberty of conscience. Third, Burke was opposed by a number of advanced Whigs. Men like his friend, Philip Francis, and James Mackintosh shared many of Burke's views, for they were linked to the aristocracy, but they also favored parliamentary and other reforms. Finally, Boulton recognizes a composite group of "others." That is, he holds that many of the critics are quite difficult to categorize, for they accepted much of Burke's argument but disagreed with him on details. Often they sided with Burke on the theoretical principles involved, but objected to the violence of his rhetoric or felt that the Revolution was justified by the oppressiveness of the Old Regime.

As the participants in the debate differed, so did the audiences they sought to reach. Boulton maintains that Burke aimed his argument at the last two groups listed above: the moderate to radical Whigs and a more general readership which was educated, undecided, and open-minded. Burke's arguments were selected to appeal to those groups, and, consequently, he was much less concerned about how they affected other readers: "he wished to expound a theory of society and government, but he was also determined to persuade a body of readers to adopt it . . . We must regard Burke as at once a thinker and a rhetorician."[125] For this reason, it is probably a mistake to compare Burke directly to Thomas Paine or to emphasize their mutual antagonism too strongly. Burke, indeed, felt nothing but contempt for Paine as a thinker. He wrote to a friend: "he is utterly incapable of comprehending his subject. He has not even a moderate portion of learning of any kind. He has learned the instrumental part of literature, a style, and a method of disposing his ideas, without having ever made a previous preparation of Study or thinking—for the use of it."[126] However, the modern reader ought not to repeat Burke's mistake. Paine was neither a poor writer nor a trivial thinker: he was, in fact, a master of style and a impressive thinker, but his style and thought were aimed at an audience different from Burke's. As Olivia Smith notes, Paine's work was part of a long-term radical effort to create "an informal printed language capable of expressing political ideas . . . an intellectual vernacular language."[127] Viewed from this perspective, perhaps Paine's greatest accomplishment was that, "the publication of *Rights of Man* demonstrated that a language could be neither vulgar nor refined, neither primitive nor civilized," but simply an effective means of communication and an encouragement to the lower classes to think about and participate in politics. Thus, Paine's simple style served to convince his lower class readers of his good faith and honesty, and the genuineness of his anger.[128] Similarly, it was also a means of making an implicit argument that politics can be understood by and affects everyone. Further, the energy of his language marked him as a man of solid robust common sense.[129] On the other hand, Paine's criticism of Burke's elaborate language and style made the point that elitist government depends on deceit and pomp and show—as did his frequent allusions to the theater.[130] To criticize Paine, as Fennessy does, for failing to understand Burke or for not considering the possibility of gradual reforms, is to miss the point.[131] Paine could offer a formidable intellectual challenge to Burke without meeting him point by point. In a sense, simply by writing, Paine carried his principal point.

Burke's chosen targets were men like Richard Sheridan, James Mackintosh, or Charles James Fox, himself. Generally speaking, these "new Whigs" did not defend Paine, for they were as uncomfortable with his radicalism and audience of lower-middle and working-class readers as was Burke. Rather, they appealed to Burke's own audience by adopting the tone and pose of rational defenders of the French Revolution who, though in agreement with Burke on many of his principles, were both somewhat more open to reform and shocked by his angry rhetoric. To refute Burke, the New Whigs would commonly offer their own reading of the intentions of the revolutionaries. Mackintosh, for example, argued that the French were merely seeking a form of constitutional liberty similar to that which the English already possessed.[132] In fact, they saw the French Revolution as an attempt to copy the English Revolution of 1688–90; that is, as an attempt to place limits on an exceedingly arbitrary monarchy, and to reform a long outmoded system of justice and administration. However, the New Whigs differed from Burke in their view of the Glorious Revolution in at least two respects. First, unlike Burke, they did not see it as a final settlement of the basic form of government. As Richard Price put it, "though the Revolution was a great work, it was by no means a perfect work; and that all was not then gained which was necessary to put the kingdom in the secure and complete possession of the blessings of liberty . . ."[133] Second, they emphasized the break in continuity of government at the time of the English Revolution. As small as it was, this break, they argued, affirmed the right of all men to make and cashier governments as they wished. On this interpretation, the French reformers were merely exercising the common human right to hold government accountable. The New Whigs were also considerably more optimistic than Burke about the extent of progress in political knowledge. According to Mackintosh, the French reformers were essentially moderates who wished to apply the new Enlightenment science of politics to a difficult situation: "a degree of certainty, perhaps nearly equal to that which such topics will admit, had been attained. The National Assembly were therefore not called on to make discoveries . . . They were fortunate enough to live in a period when it was only necessary to affix the stamp of laws to what had been prepared by the research of philosophy."[134] In such heady times, when, "men should learn to tolerate nothing ancient that reason does not respect, and to shrink from no novelty to which reason may conduct," Mackintosh felt that it ought not to be surprising if the French, on occasion, went too far.[135] Yet, he believed that such excesses were only transitory, and would be corrected over time. Honest men might deplore them, but would also understand that they were aberrations.

The nature and extent of the differences between Burke and his fellow Whigs is perhaps best revealed by an exchange of letters between him and Philip Francis in 1790. After reviewing an advance copy of the *Reflections,* Francis, a long-time friend and ally, especially in Indian affairs, wrote to Burke urging him to withhold publication.[136] Francis objected to Burke's work on three grounds: (1) he thought it unworthy of Burke to get into a mud-slinging debate with people of the quality of Richard Price; (2) he felt the essay was poorly structured and reasoned; and (3) he believed that Burke's harsh tone was unsuited to the importance of the occasion.[137] For instance, Francis criticized Burke's defense of the French Queen: "are you such a determined champion of Beauty as to draw your Sword in defense of any jade upon Earth provided she be handsome?"[138] Francis was primarily concerned about Burke's own reputation. He feared that, in opposing the Revolution, Burke would discredit himself among English moderates, split the forces of reform, and, therefore, do the progressive wing of political society great harm. Thus, he warned Burke, "the mischief you are going to do yourself is, to my apprehension, palpable."[139] In reply, Burke admitted the controversial nature of his work, but insisted that he would go ahead anyway: "I mean to set in a full View the dangers from their wicked principles and their black hearts . . . If any one be the better for the example made of them, and for this exposition, well and good."[140] Burke was stung by Francis' criticism, but he went to some lengths to avoid a break, even denying that he made it a practice to throw away friends who were critical. Nonetheless, he was intent on making it clear that the issues raised by the Revolution were simply too important for him to back down.

In early November of 1790, after the publication of the *Reflections,* Francis again undertook to discuss the Revolution with Burke.[141] This time, however, he went into more substantive detail. After again criticizing the style of the work and expressing his concern about its effect on Burke's reputation, he went to what he considered the heart of the matter. Francis claimed to agree with virtually everything Burke said about English politics, but he questioned the relevance of English examples to France. How, he asked, can you demand that the French follow the English model of constitutional reform, when they do not even have a constitution? Since the time of Lewis XI, Francis asserted, "there has been no power in France but that of a Despot, bad enough while it was exercised by a single vigorous hand, but infinitely worse, when it fell into weakness or minority, or when it was counteracted by the factions of the Nobility."[142] The truth is, he continued, that the Crown, Aristocracy, and even the Church, have joined together to exploit and oppress the people: "I mean the millions, who asked for nothing but protection against intolerable Oppression, both by the King and their Nobility; who, before they complained or resisted, had endured every thing, that could be endured."[143] Having no constitution to reform, the French could not act as the English had: "if they had no model in their own Country, they must, of necessity, begin anew."[144] Without examples to guide them, they have inevitably fallen into "errors." Francis did not try to excuse these: "with all mannner of reason and justice in the assumption of their power, they may possibly have exhibited a total want of wisdom in the exercise of it."[145] All he contended for, he said, was a tolerant understanding of the difficulty of the French circumstances and a sympathetic expectation of improvement in the future.

To this rather restrained criticism, Burke replied with considerable venom.[146] Still, he made two points which, between them, I think, reveal both the narrowness and the importance of his differences with the Whig left. First, Burke was insistent that he did not differ from Francis on the need for reform, but only on its pace. Burke asked, "when and where, my dear Sir, did you find me the advocate for any tyranny either ancient, or modern, either at home or abroad? When did you find me totally unmoved at the distress of hundreds and thousands of my equals, and only touched with the suffering of guilty greatness? I find this distincition neither in my sympathies, nor in my morals . . ."[147] Thus, Burke repeated a point he had often made: the issue was not to compare the new government to the old, for he had no intention of defending the Old Regime, but to compare what the revolutionaries had created to what they might have had. Second, Burke refused to accept the protestations of the good will of the French radicals. Francis, he said, put the case as if the radicals were led by "a set of wise and excellent patriots, proceeding with vigour indeed; but with all the attention to order and justice, which that vigour admitted: but that they are disgraced by the disorders of an ungovernable Mob. This, if you please, you may suppose, but I suppose no such thing."[148] Burke, rather, believed that the leaders of the Revolution had instigated the disorders of the mob. The difference between the potential of the Revolution and its actual accomplishments was, therefore, in his view and, contrary to what he saw as Francis' naive assertion, a result, not of errors or unplanned excesses, but of rational calculations and true intentions.

The similarity of their basic assumptions and principles helps explain something that might be otherwise unaccountable: that many of the New Whigs continued to work with Burke on other issues, were courteous and deferential even when expressing their dissent, and eventually moved to something like his position. For example, less than a month after the exchange described above, Burke wrote to Francis as though there had been no argument, and he worked congenially with both Francis and Fox on the Hastings impeachment for several months thereafter.[149] Similarly, even as as he attacked Burke's account of French politics, Mackintosh expressed considerable admiration for his ability as a thinker.[150] Moreover, over time, as the Revolution became increasingly extreme, Mackintosh became more critical of it. Finally, in December 1796, he wrote to Burke, saying that, "I can with truth affirm that I subscribe to your general principles," and, after admitting some unspecified disillusionment with politics, asked for a meeting.[151] Burke was somewhat dubious: he had once told French Laurence that, "I have not read, or even seen Mackintosh;—But Richard tells me, that it is Paine at bottom . . ."[152] Nonetheless, he replied the next day with an invitation for Mackintosh to come to Beaconsfield to see him. Burke was more hopeful than optimistic. As he wrote to French Laurence of Mackintosh's conversion, "I suspect by his Letter that it does not extend beyond the interior politicks of this Island, but that, with regard to France and many other Countries he remains as frank a Jacobin as ever. This conversion is none at all, but we must nurse up these nothings and think these negative advantages as we can have them."[153] In the event, Burke was mistaken. Mackintosh came, they got on well together, and his conversion proved more substantial than Burke expected.

Mackintosh's experience was not uncommon, for other English radicals also turned against the Revolution. William Cobbett, for instance, in 1798, referred to it in these terms: "the whole history of the French Revolution presents us with nothing but a regular progress in robbery and murder."[154] John Thelwell, who had been tried for sedition in the early years, was proclaiming by 1795 that, "faction after faction has triumphed in the blood of its predecessors . . . and during the space of six successive years they have been cutting each others' throats, upon personel disputes, and questions of ambitious ascendancy, till the public mind appears to have grown sick and weary of the contest . . ."[155] Of course, not all of the New Whigs became Burkeans; many remained true to their earlier support of the French radicals, and some of the converts continued to differ with him on other issues. However, that so many did is indicative of the degree to which most Whigs approached the Revolution from within a common framework and of Burke's skill at articulating and applying that perspective. I have suggested that the major differences between Burke and the Whig left on the Revolution were on the issues of the extent to which the French protestations of good will should be taken seriously and on the question of the pace or speed of reform. In work after work, Burke argued that the revolutionaries were insincere, power-hungry vandals, and that they did not mean to reform the state so much as to seize it and use it for their own evil purposes. At first, many of his colleagues were more willing than he to trust the French and to accept them as what they claimed to be. Gradually, however, experience undermined their confidence, and the French Declaration of War against England was the final straw for many. Once their faith in the French was destroyed, they no longer had any major differences with Burke. Unlike later generations, they knew him to be a reformer of long standing, and, where they disagreed on details or tempo, they had to admit that he, at least, had the advantage of having been right on France.

V

Burke's fight for the support of English public opinion was won at an enormous cost, for it led, finally, to the destruction of the Whig party and the end of all hope for aristocratic-sponsored moderate reform. At the outbreak of the Revolution, Burke faced a fluid situation. The French Revolution appeared quite popular in England. Though their reasons varied from honest sympathy with what they believed to be a misgoverned people to the real-politic consideration that internal conflict would weaken a dangerous rival, many of the politically active English supported the French reformers. Yet, there was also evidence that their support did not go very deep. In fact, by the time of the flight of the French royal family to Varennes in June 1791, the honeymoon was over and English opinion was beginning to turn. Emsley, for example, estimates that as many as two-thirds of the opposition Whigs, including their leader, the Duke of Portland and, of course, Burke, backed Pitt's early moves to strengthen England for a potential war with France.[156] In such a context, Burke say that there was both a need and an opportunity to rally support for his cause. Moreover, Burke was already unhappy with the party. In his view, it had blundered in the Regency Crisis, made a botch of its stand on parliamentary reform, and given aid and comfort to the radicals among the Dissenters. O'Gorman puts it well, "Burke's party enthusiasm was rapidly declining. He was, by this time, confining his political attention to the impeachment of Warren Hastings and took little interest in purely party matters."[157] Therefore, it should not be surprising that a move to divide the party, and to salvage the better part seemed logical to him. Burke later explained his thinking: "it was indeed . . . necessary, to separate those, who cultivate a rational and sober Liberty upon the plan of our existing constitution, from those, who think they have no Liberty, if it does not comprehend a right in them of making to themselves new constitutions at their pleasure;"[158] He decided, then, to first attempt to win the Party over to the anti-French side, but, that effort failing, to force a confrontion on the Revolution.

If, as Burke frequently estimated, some four-fifths of the nation was sound on France, it ought to have been relatively easy, once the radicals were uncovered and denounced, to build a broadly-based national anti-Jacobin coalition. During much of 1792, Burke devoted himself to the effort. He understood full well that the leaders of the Whig Party were becoming increasingly concerned about France and about growing radicalism, but were also, as yet, unwilling to risk the unity of the party. As Burke put it, "the Association for Parliamentary reform . . . gave a very great and serious alarm not most or first to the Ministers . . . but to the older and weighty part of the opposition—who saw upon that occasion the necessity of strengthening the hands of government."[159] Therefore, the obvious move was to attempt to take the party as a whole into the government. At first, both Pitt and the Whigs seemed amenable: "a Sort of Negotiation between Lord Loughborough and Dundas was commenced with the approbation of the Duke of Portland—for a comprehension of Parties, and putting the administration on a broader and, as they think, a safer bottom."[160] The sticking point, as Burke soon realized, was Fox.[161] Pitt would not accept him as a member of the government, and Portland would not abandon him. It appears that Pitt believed that if he could force Portland to break with Fox, the Whig party would be split and rendered virtually harmless. However, Portland suspected Pitt's motives and was not yet ready to sacrifice Fox for principle and office. After lengthy discussions in November 1792, Burke reported to Fitzwilliam that most of the party leaders supported a suspension of opposition, but that a minority had objected, and in the end nothing had been decided.[162] Burke was forced to admit the failure of his plan: "I believe, that no greater differences in political system ever did exist among the most nominal descriptions of men, than prevail at this hour between the two divisions of those who affect to be considered as of the same party."[163] Perhaps, he concluded, as "party ought to be made for politicks: not politicks for Party purposes," thought should be given to making themselves "rather a small well ordered Phalanx, than an apparently great, but confused, and radically discordant Corps."[164] His meaning was clear: effective anti-revolutionary action required discipline, and those who would not accept it should be expelled.

As it became obvious that his attempt to create a great coalition was failing, Burke sought to provoke a rupture. As early as September 1789, he had criticized Fox in a letter to Windham, and in the debates on the Army estimates in February 1790, Burke publicly quarrelled with him over France. After a public disagreement on the Quebec Bill in April 1791, the split was probably irremediable, and the publication of the *Appeal* in November 1791, simply recognized the obvious. In a significant passage in that work, Burke said of his opponents within the party: "they must have been animated with a very warm zeal against those opinions, [in the *Reflections*] because they were under no *necessity* of acting as they did, from any just cause of apprehension that the errors of this writer should be taken for theirs. They might disapprove; it was not necessary they should *disavow* him"[165] Throughout 1792 the split became increasingly bitter, and parliamentary debates in December revealed its full extent. In early 1793, Burke's friend Loughborough, acting on his advice, joined the government and, after war was declared on February 9, the more conservative Whigs began to leave the party, creating a "third Party" in an attempt to force Portland's hand. This was a slow process and one marked by considerable backing and filing. As one scholar puts it, "there was less a sudden breakdown in Whig unity, than a slow disintegration by unchecked attrition . . . The right wing deserted, not as an affronted bloc, but in a trickle of harassed and nervous individuals."[166] Burke began to step up the pressure. In March 1793, he resigned, in concert with several allies, from the Whig Club, and shortly thereafter he wrote the "Observations on the Conduct of the Minority." Fox, for his part, was convinced by the treason trials of late 1793 that Pitt was preparing a frontal attack on traditional English liberties, and thus became a increasingly strident critic of government policy. Finally, with Portland's outright commitment to the war effort in January 1794, came the final break. Burke's pounding and their own concern had overcame Portland's and Fitzwilliam's emotional and organizational ties to Fox.

Burke's comments on the split have served to confuse matters and to detract from our understanding of just how hard he worked to cause it. For instance, in the "Observations on the Conduct of the Minority, Particularly in the Last Session of Parliament," he presented what must be one of the most vicious indictments ever written by one party member against his own associates.[167] In fifty-three numbered paragraphs, Burke accused Fox, among other things, of treating with foreign powers, of defending France, of acting without concert with the party leadership, of opposing the prosecution of traitors, of opposing the war and attacking England's allies, of organizing the people against the war, of preaching dangerous and absurd political doctrines, of seeking to discredit Parliament, of attacking the role of Peers in the constitution, and of promoting Jacobinism. Finally, after all this, Burke concluded by suggesting that his old enemy, Pitt, was a better minister than his party colleague, Fox, could be, for "Mr. Pitt may be the worst of men, and Mr. Fox may be the best; but, at present, the former is in the interest of his country, and of the order of things long established in Europe: Mr. Fox is not."[168] Nor were Burke's activities limited to those public occasions where he could not do otherwise. In addition to the public struggle, he waged a steady backstage campaign. His letters of the time abound with attacks on his opponents within the Party. Even his long letter to Earl Fitzwilliam, explaining his break with the party and announcing his intention of resigning from Parliament, was full of self-justifying rhetoric. After describing one of Fox's attacks on him in the House, Burke concluded: "it was an exhibition absolutely new, to see a man who had sat twenty six Years in Parliament, not to have one friend in the House."[169] In fact, Burke's account does not square with his own admission that he provoked the exchange or with the harsh language of his publications.[170] Some time later, after retiring from politics, Burke was more candid. In a letter to French Laurence discussing his resignation from the Whig Club, he wrote: "I do not retract any one of the sentiments contain'd in that Memorial . . . It is written in a tone of indignation against the resolutions of the Whig Club, which were directly pointed against myself and others, who in consequence seceded from that Club; which is the last act of my life, that I shall under any circumstances repent."[171] In short, Burke had no regrets.

Breaking the party, and winning over Portland and Fitzwiliam in the process, was only part of the battle for Burke. He also wanted to enlist the former members of its conservative wing into the Pitt administration. Initially, Burke tried to steer a middle course. He urged the Portland Whigs to retain their independent identity and to continue to criticize Pitt in detail while supporting him on the general issues of the conflict. Of Pitt, he told Laurence years later, "I have no partiality at all to him or to his measures against which latter nothing but the accelerated motion of my illness could have hindered me from publishing my Opinion before this time. . ."[172] All that Burke claimed was that Fox was worse, for he was both a French dupe and a radical in domestic affairs.[173] Similarly, he did not, at first, propose to give up his self-definition as a moderate reformer: "I would persuade a resistance both to the corruption and to the reformation that prevails . . . I would not wish to excite, or even to tolerate, that kind of evil spirit which evokes the powers of hell to rectify the disorders of the earth."[174] As an example of what he had in mind, Burke proposed that a loan which Pitt's government had tendered to the Emperor without consultation with Parliament be supported as to substance but opposed as to method.[175] However, as talks of a more formal coalition progressed, Burke eventually supported a full union, though as much for reasons of Irish politics as French.[176] Finally, in July 1794, a number of Whig leaders, including both Portland and Fitzwilliam, took office under Pitt. After the coalition was formed, Burke's major concern was to encourage it to fight the war vigorously. He pursued two lines of argument. First, he tried to prove that the public was behind the war. The government, he complained, would not allowed a fair test of opinion; if they would only look, they would discover that, even if one-fifth of the people were Jacobins, the rest, "the majority, the other four-fifths, is perfectly sound, and of the best possible disposition to religion, to government, to the true and undivided interest of their country."[177] Second, he attempted to spur the administration to take the battle to France. This was not an easy task. As Burke reported to Windham, two discussions with Dundas accomplished nothing.[178] The problem, he believed, was that Pitt was not fully committed. At times, he complained, it seemed as if "Pitt and Fox are not contending for the Government of an independent Country, but who should be the Viceroy's deputy under a French Lord Paramount. Fox offering to yield his Country bound hand and foot, without a Struggle, Pitt mingling something of the Bully with his submission."[179]

Things had not, then, gone as Burke wished. Almost the first act of the coalition was to repudiate Fitzwilliam's attempt to reform Irish government and to remove him from office.[180] In domestic matters, the Pitt administration increasingly substituted repression for reform. Burke was quick to support the government's prosecution of English and Scotch radical leaders, and he vigorously supported the Treasonable Practices and Seditious Meetings Bills when they were introduced in Parliament.[181] Still, Burke was critical of anything which seemed to smack of vigilantism. In response to the violence of the anti-Dissenter Birmingham Riots of 1791, he wrote: "no Government, indeed no honest man will tolerate the excesses of the populace, which though to a degree provoked by the petulance of these people, were truly horrid."[182] Where had things gone wrong? For his part, Burke felt that the party had missed its opportunity: "I was in serious hope that the party which was at last rallied under its proper standards . . . might, either in Ministry or out of Ministry, as the publick necessities required, become some sort of Asylum for principles moral and political, and might control that disposition to factious servitude, which could see nothing, in the constitution or the country, but the power of one or two individuals."[183] However, according to Burke, Portland had allowed Pitt to use the Irish crisis to destroy the party and to send Fitzwilliam into a sort of political exile. Now, with no responsible and organized force on the right to counter Fox on the left, Pitt could trim as he pleased. Absolving himself of any serious responsibility for the situation, Burke claimed that his intention had been to form the conservative Whigs into what he called a third force.[184] In his view, that force would oppose the French Revolution and radicalism at home, but would also promote reform in Ireland, in India, and in a number of areas of English politics. Only after the battle was over did Burke fully understand the implications of what he had accomplished. Having helped to destroy the Whig party, he now saw what it had offered and, therefore, wanted to rebuild it. But that was not possible, and Burke was at a loss as to what to do. Increasingly, he was reduced to decrying the political trends of the time and voicing irrelevant and unrealistic proposals. As late as May 1797, only two months before his death, one of his last letters still called for a union of parties, including the supporters of both Pitt and Fox, in an ideological crusade against France.[185]

10

IRELAND, INDIA, AND THE DELUGE

In this chapter, I will argue that Irish politics, especially in the 1790s, demonstrated some of the unfortunate results of Burke's effort to split the Whig party and the consequent failure of his approach to political reform. For Burke, the themes of Irish politics interwove in curious ways with those of his reflections on France. In one sense, they liberated Burke from some of the restraints imposed on his reformism by the French revolution, for while the Revolution accelerated and hardened Burke's opposition to reform in England, it seems to have had the opposite effect on his stand on Irish politics. From the early 1770s to the mid-1790s, Burke consistently argued a reformist position in regard to Ireland. He insisted that Ireland's problems originated in Ireland and not in England, and maintained that the primary issue was the exclusion of the Catholic majority from participation in politics and from the full benefits of the constitution. Burke believed that the solution was the incorporation, over time, of the native Irish into the political community of the nation and of the British Empire. A central part of this solution was the extension of the vote, and Burke found himself advocating reforms in Ireland which he rejected in England. With the coming of the French Revolution and the increased repression in Ireland, Burke began to intensify his rhetoric in the mid-1790s. All of his writings of this period reveal a sense that he was in a race against time: he believed that Ireland must be reformed before repression led to the radicalization of the Irish masses and civil war. On the other hand, in Burke's perception of a link between failed reform and revolution, his thought on Ireland represented a confirmation of his thinking on France. As Ireland moved toward the Uprising of 1798, and England failed to control the spread of Jacobinism, Burke increasingly despaired. Unable to raise the support necessary to force Irish reform, Burke was defeated by the reactionary Protestant Ascendancy and by the British Administration's desire for stability at all costs. His defeat led him to assume an attitude of deep pessimism, a pessimism which was confirmed during his lifetime by the vigorous suppression of Irish political and religious dissent and by the Revolution of 1798 after his death.

I

For most of the Irish writers of Burke's time, especially those who spoke for the Protestant minority, the primary political concerns were the relationship between England and Ireland and the authority of the English Parliament to legislate for Ireland.[1] Even William Molyneaux, whose *The Case of Ireland* was perhaps the most influential of the Irish Whig tracts, seldom permitted his argument for reform of the imperial system to assume an internal dimension. Indeed, many of the Whigs, notably William King, in *De Origine Mali,* combined a case for Irish self-government with support for an internally repressive political system.[2] Burke, however, did not share their narrow focus. He was very much aware that Irish government corresponded very poorly to traditional Whig models. The Revolutionary Settlement of 1690 had, he recognized, taken different forms in England and Ireland: whereas in England it had insured something close to constitutional and representative government, in Ireland it had established the dominance of a relatively small Church of Ireland minority over a somewhat larger number of dissenters and a very much larger number of Catholics. The Irish political system soon came to rest on two principles: first, the total exclusion of the Roman Catholics and the near total exclusion of the Dissenters from participation in the political and social community, and second, an Irish Administration maintained by a process of bargaining and patronage between the Irish Protestants in power and the English government. Edith M. Johnston explains the logic well: "The Irish ascendancy could not maintain their position without the political and military shadow in the background; England, on the other hand, was faced with Ireland's strategic position and needed the tranquility of the neighboring kingdom."[3] At first, because the Irish executive was based in England, as few Lord-Lieutenants were willing to actually reside in Ireland for any length of time, the English found it difficult to manage the Irish Parliament, especially the Irish House of Commons. From the mid-1730s down to the late-1760s, therefore, England governed through a series of "undertakers:" Irish politicians who promised to manage Irish affairs in return for favors granted by the English administration. In the late 1760s, the English administration decided that the demands of the present Undertakers were excessive and determined to break their power. Thus, the Lord-Lieutenant, George Townshend, took up residence in Ireland and, after a bitter struggle, gained full control of Irish politics. Henceforth, the Lord-Lieutenant, himself, was the most important Undertaker, but the internal logic of the governing process remained substantially the same. Though later modified somewhat by the introduction of Irish Legislative Independence, in 1782, and by the growth of a professional civil service around the Lord-Lieutenant's office, this system continued in force throughout Burke's political career.[4]

The most complete statement of Burke's understanding of the nature of Irish politics can be found in his *Fragment of a Tract Relative to the Laws Against Popery in Ireland,* an unfinished work written sometime between 1761 and 1765.[5] Though the *Tract* remained unpublished during his lifetime, Burke often used it as a reference or even loaned it to associates in search of a quick introduction to Irish affairs. In the *Tract,* Burke denied that Ireland's difficulties were due to any of the most commonly cited causes, such as the harshness of nature, the religion of the poor, or even British trade policy. Rather, he suggested that all of Ireland's debilities might be traced to the penal laws enacted to control the Catholic population.[6] In his opinion, "we found the people heretics and idolaters; we have, by way of improving their condition, rendered them slaves and beggars: they remain in all the misfortune of their old errors, and all the superadded misery of their recent punishment."[7] According to Burke, the penal system removed all possibility of the Catholics improving themselves, for it closed most trades to them and denied them entrance to the professions. After noting that Catholics were not allowed to own the land they worked, for example, he insisted, "confine a man to momentary possession, and you at once cut off that laudable avarice which every wise state has cherished as one of the first principles of its greatness."[8] When such a system is applied to two-thirds of the people of a nation, Burke continued, one can hardly be surprised that it does not prosper. Worse yet, in a section entitled "possession," Burke pointed out that the beliefs which were punished in the 1760s had once been maintained by the law. While Burke considered all religious persecution to be wrong, he felt that this form was the most absurd: "you punish them for . . . adherence to the establishments of their forefathers.[9]

For Burke, the ultimate irony was that, "Ireland, after almost a century of persecution, is at this hour full of penalties and full of Papists.[10] He argued, then, that the penal laws were a failure in their own terms; not only did they render Ireland poor, but they also failed to reduce the number of Catholics.

Though Burke's analysis in the *Tract* was pointed enough, aside from the implied suggestion that the penal laws be repealed, he advanced no specific reforms. This is in part, perhaps, due to the unfinished nature of the work. It may be that Burke intended to offer specific ideas in some later section. However, it seems to me more likely that Burke was unwilling to deal with the implications of some of the arguments he employed. Along with the claim that the penal laws should be judged by their consequences, Burke, in the opening pages, went further. He also maintained that they were not, in fact, valid laws for two reasons. First, Burke held that a law is void unless it has been consented to by the community or its representatives: "in all forms of government the people is the true legislator; and whether the immediate and the instrumental cause of the law be a single person or many, the remote and efficient cause is the consent of the people, either actual or implied; and such consent is absolutely essential to its validity."[11] No one, Burke continued, can honestly believe that the people of Ireland have consented to a legal system so prejudicial to their interests.[12] Second, even if the entire community had expressly consented to the penal laws, they would still be invalid, for natural law holds that a community cannot enact a law harmful to itself. Citing Cicero, Suarez, and the *Digest,* Burke claimed that such a law "would be made against the principle of a superior law, which it is not in the power of any community, or of the whole race, to alter—I mean the will of Him who gave us our nature, and in giving impressed an invariable law upon it."[13] The difficulty is that these arguments proved too radical for Burke's taste. They appear, in fact, to have been drawn from Locke's *Letter on Toleration,* where they meshed quite comfortably with a natural law framework.[14] However, in Locke's hands, natural law provided a basis for resistance to authority and a right of revolution. When applied to English politics, such doctrines led to conclusions which made most eighteenth century Whigs uneasy. In an Irish context, their implications were truly unnerving: the end of English authority and the establishment of Catholic rule. Therefore, even apart from any principled objections he might have had to doctrines of active consent and majority-rule, Burke had good reason to rethink his position.[15]

Within a few years, Burke was ready with a revised stance. His new view, which I would describe as aggressive gradualism, remained his basic approach to Irish affairs for the rest of his life. A letter to Charles Fox, written in 1777, indicates that Burke remained critical of Irish government: "the resident lieutenancy may have made some change, and given a strength to government, which formerly, I know, it had not; still, however, I am of opinion, the former state, though in other hands perhaps, and in another manner, still continues."[16] What did change, however, is that his critique was, first, placed in a theoretical context which emphasized moderation and prudence and then joined to a list of recommended reforms. Thus, Burke's mature position on Irish affairs can be summarized in the following seven points: (1) political forms must be adapted to circumstances and times. In discussing the Irish Relief Bill of 1778, Burke wrote, "I should neither use, nor did I think applicable, any arguments drawn from the analogy of what was done in other parts of the British dominions . . . These things were governed, as all things of that nature are governed, not by general maxims, but by their own local and percular circumstances;"[17] (2) the time is appropriate for reform in Ireland, for this is an age of toleration and England's difficult international position obliges her to be conciliatory; (3) England is not responsible for Ireland's suffering. England is, in fact, indifferent to Irish concerns. The source of Ireland's troubles lies in Ireland, itself. As late as February 1797, Burke told a correspondent in Ireland, "if nothing can be done on your side of the Water, I promise nothing will be done here;"[18] (4) the central issue of Irish politics was the exclusion of the Irish Catholics from the Irish political system, but that issue was political and social and not truly religious. In a letter to William Smith, Burke denied "that either Zeal for the Tenets of Faith, or the smallest degree of Charity or justice, have much influenced the Gentlemen, who, under pretext of Zeal, have resisted the enfranchisement of their Country;"[19] (5) since the problem was exclusion, the solution was incorporation. The Catholics must be drawn into the political life of the nation; (6) this incorporation was to be accomplished by the extension of the franchise, and the removal of Catholic legal disabilities, especially in the areas of property-holding, education, and economic activity; (7) finally, progress toward Catholic emancipation was dependent on the goodwill of both the Irish Protestants and the English. As Burke wrote to John Curry, "to the great liberality and enlarged sentiments of those who are the furthest in the world from you in religious tenets . . . it is that you owe the whole or very near the whole of what has been done both here and in Ireland."[20] For Burke, this dependency made Irish politics very difficult and very complex. To attain the support of the Protestants and the English, the Catholics and their allies had to be strong enough to force reform, and yet moderate enough not to frighten their opponents into a policy of repression.

The high point for Burkean reform in Ireland probably was the passage of the Catholic Relief Bill of 1782. The Bill repealed or modified the penal laws on a variety of topics, including land-holding, education, and the Catholic clergy, but also codified the remaining disabilities into a rigid system. In a long public letter to Viscount Kenmare, written less than two years after the anti-Catholic Gordon Riots and after he had lost his seat at Bristol in part for his efforts in behalf of Ireland, Burke nonetheless denounced the Bill for not going far enough.[21] As he put it, "to look at the Bill in the abstract, it is neither more nor less than a renewed act of universal, unmitigated, indispensable, exceptionless, disqualification. One would imagine, that a Bill inflicting such a multitude of incapacities, had followed on the heels of a conquest made by a very fierce Enemy under the impression of recent animosity and resentment."[22] According to Burke, the Bill, in fact, denied Catholics so much that it amounted to an almost total segregation from society. They were denied participation in the offices of state, their church was treated as a dangerous alien body, and, most importantly, they were refused the franchise: "The taking away of a vote is the taking away the Shield which the subject has, not only against the oppressions of power, but of that worst of all oppressions, the persecution of private Society, and private manners. No candidate for parliamentary influence is obliged to the least attention towards them, either in Cities or Countries . . ."[23] Still, Burke argued that the enactment of the Bill was a good thing, for "the act, as far as it goes, is good undoubtedly. It amounts I think very nearly to a toleration with respect to religious Ceremonies."[24] Moreover, as a step forward, the act prepared the way for further reforms: "whether this scheme of indulgence, grounded at once on contempt and jealousy, has a tendency gradually to produce *something better* and more liberal, I cannot tell . . . If *this should be the case,* it was right in you to accept it such as it is."[25] Viewed as a whole, Burke's message seems relatively clear: the reformers should accept even limited progress when it was offered, but they should also keep constant pressure on until they achieved all their goals.

II

It is widely agreed that the French Revolution led Burke to become the leading English spokesman for social stability and political order in his day. Interestingly, there was no similar movement in his views on Irish issues. In his analysis of Irish government and events, as well as in his proposals for action, Burke still sounded the same reformist themes. For instance, he continued to hold that England had no interest in Ireland's problems: "they seem governed by the Counter-representations they receive from the Castle. The only impression they seem to have received is that of Terrour and perplexity. They find themselves well, and would be glad to remain in quiet, though three millions or three hundred millions, pass the nights with very little rest."[26] Thus, in Burke's opinion, the root of the problem remained the penal laws, which "divided the nation into two distinct bodies without common interest, sympathy or connection. One of these bodies was to posses *all* the franchises, *all* the property, *all* the education: the other was to be composed of drawers of water and cutters of turf for them."[27] Moreover, Burke still believed that this division into classes was based, as in the past, more on economics and race than on religion. And, again as before, Burke believed the only remedy to be gradual reform, aggressively pursued by the Irish Catholics and their allies, for "if they are frightened—and by their fright induced to dissolve their union, or to abate one of their efforts, or abandon any *one* of their Claims, it is all over with them."[28] Further, Burke maintained a similar position on issues other than the extension of the franchise. For example, when the English government offered to substitute financial support for the Catholic clergy as an alternative to Catholic eligibility for Parliament, Burke cautioned the Catholics to refuse: "I would much rather trust to God's good Providence, and the contributions of your own people . . . than to put into the hands of your known, avowed, and implacable Enemies . . . the very foundations of your morals and your religion."[29] With the money, he suspected, would come control, and the Catholics could hardly want control of their church put into the hands of the Ascendency.

But this is not to say that nothing had changed in Burke's stand on Ireland; his writings of the early and mid-1790s show a new stridency and anger in their rhetoric and a new sense of desperate urgency in their exhortations to reform. Note, for example, the reference to his Irish opponents in this letter to his son: "these miserable Creatures, the Zealots of the ascendency, have been fed with this stuff as their Nurse's pap, and it is never to be got out of their habit. Their low and senseless Malice makes them utterly incapable of forming a right judgment on any thing."[30] Burke was losing his sense of moderation. He no longer had the confidence in the gradual conversion of English and Irish Protestant opinion which he had once felt. He previously was sure of victory because he believed that his opponents represented no more than the rear guard of bigotry in a world steadily becoming more tolerant. However, the increased reification of his thinking, represented by his frequent use of words like "Castle" for Irish administration and "ascendancy" for Church of Ireland Protestants, reveals a new assessment of the staying power of his enemies and a consequent upgrading of the difficulty of the task before him.[31] At the same time, the need for reform had, in Burke's opinion, become even more acute. Just as he feared the extension of French Jacobin ideas to England, Burke also feared their spread to Ireland, where they might find an even more receptive audience among the Irish discontented. As he wrote to Hussey, "You and I hate Jacobinism as we hate the Gates of Hell—Why? Because it is a System of oppression. What can make us in love with oppression because the Syllables Jacobin are not put before the *ism*. When the very same things are done under the *ism* preceded by any other Name in the Directory of Ireland."[32] Burke believed that Jacobinism threatened religion, property, and traditional establishments, while the Ascendency's policies attacked the Catholics' religion, denied them the ownerships of property, and sought to destroy their way of life.[33] How, then, he asked, can one blame the Catholics for seeing that the only point of difference between the two tyrannies was that under Jacobinism their freedom would at least be equal to that of everyone else?

Burke's discussion of the Catholic Relief Bill of 1793, which gave Catholics the right to vote for members of Parliament but not to sit themselves, is a good example of his blending of old substance and new urgency. First, he stressed the timeliness of the move. In the age of the French Revolution, it would, he said, remove an embarrassing inconsistency: "if the question was to be put to you and me—*Universal* popular representation, or *none at all for us and ours*—we should find ourselves in a very awkward position."[34] Second, Burke stressed that the reformers' goal was limited, for all the Catholics desired was to be included in the existing political system, and that was no terrible request: "I have always considered the British Constitution not to be a thing in itself so vicious as that none but men of deranged understanding and turbulent tempers could desire a share in it . . ."[35] Further, Burke maintained that the bill did no more for the Catholics than the English Parliament had already given the Ascendency by accepting its declaration of legislative independence in 1782.[36] Third, Burke believed that the concession was safe. In his opinion, the bill's central point, a distinction between voting and governing, provided a reasonable basis for compromise. Burke held that, on the one hand, the right to vote was essential, for it was largely protective. It permitted voters to guard themselves against misrule by others. On the other hand, he believed that the right to sit in Parliament was of little importance, for few Catholics could meet the property qualifications, and Catholic voters would always be able to find Protestant candidates willing to serve their interests.[37] Finally, Burke argued that the danger of not passing the bill was extreme. He insisted that, if the franchise were not extended to Catholics, they would be left without redress because "the people of that description have no hold on the gentlemen who aspire to be popular representatives. The candidates neither love nor respect them, individually or collectively."[38]

The Catholic Relief Bill of 1793 came to mark a crucial turning point in the history of Irish reform.[39] It both failed to satisfy the Catholics and alienated the leaders of the Protestant Ascendency as well. The bill had originated in an attempt by Pitt to conciliate the Catholics, but strong opposition from the Irish administration and within his own government forced him to accept debilitating amendments. In addition, the extension of the franchise proved less valuable than first believed, for though it gave the Catholics the county franchise and that of the Parliamentary Boroughs if "otherwise qualified," the counties actually elected few of the members of the Irish Parliament, and the Ascendency quickly developed extralegal means of insuring that Catholics did not become otherwise qualified.[40] As Burke put it, "such a grudging and discontent was expressed as must justly have alarmed . . . the whole of the Catholick body—and I remember but one period in my whole life (I mean the savage period between 1761 and 1767), in which they have been more harshly and contumeliously treated . . ."[41] Forced to chose between the Ascendency and the reformers, the English administration came down firmly on the side of the Irish establishment. As early as May 1792, Henry Dundas refused to meet with Burke's son, the representative of the Irish Catholics, because it was, he said, the ministers' "firm determination . . . not to hold communications with any descriptions of Roman Catholics of Ireland except though the Government of Ireland."[42] Burke lamented: "my sanguine hopes are blasted, and I must consign my feelings on that terrible disappointment to the same patience in which I have been obliged to bury the vexation I suffered on the defeat of the other great, just, and honourable causes in which I have had some share . . ."[43]

III

Yet, events offered one last chance for reform in Ireland. As the campaign against the French Revolution dragged on, and the Whig tendency to schism manifested itself, Pitt and some of the leaders of the conservative Whigs returned to the idea of a coalition. After extensive negotiations, an agreement was reached and a coalition formed in July 1794. Pitt was quite generous with his new allies. As O'Gorman puts it, "a real party coalition had been achieved . . . George III chafed at giving the Whigs so many honors and favours—a sure indication that the coalition was as fair and as generous to the Portland Whigs as the circumstances of the time permitted."[44] Among the offices given to the Whigs were most of those responsible for Irish affairs, including the appointment of Earl Fitzwilliam to the Lord-Lieutenancy. This was in recognition both of the Whigs' close ties to Ireland and of Fitzwilliam's own reluctance to join with Pitt. Unfortunately, Pitt's concession was probably a mistake, for it raised expectations of Whiggish reform in Ireland which he had no intention of honoring. In the words of one student, "the homogeneous nature of the offices given to the Portland Whigs raised the old question of government by departments and encouraged the Irish opposition to believe that Ireland was to be the sole preserve of their English allies."[45] When Fitzwilliam began to fulfill his promise to the Irish Whigs that he would reform Irish government, the coalition nearly collapsed, and a special meeting between Pitt and the Whigs was held to iron out their differences. As they discovered that their agreement was understood differently by themselves and Fitzwilliam, the English Cabinet, its Whigs included, decided to recall Fitzwilliam. The reform episode was over before it had properly begun, but its consequences were great: the alienation of the Irish reformers, the destruction of the Portland Whigs as an independent force, and the conversion of Fitzwilliam into an independent critic of the administration.

Burke was deeply involved in every phase of the Fitzwilliam affair. He labored long and hard to create the coalition and he urged

Fitzwilliam to accept the Irish appointment. He wrote: "you are in the right to undertake Ireland; and yet I feel an anxious awe about it . . . You certainly go to a Farm terribly havocked by the last Tenants."[46] As Fitzwilliam prepared to leave for Ireland, Burke advised him on the leading issues of Irish politics.[47] Not surprisingly, the themes Burke sounded were much the same as he had urged earlier. The key, he held, was reform combined with moderation. Thus, Fitzwilliam should not attempt too much. For example, Burke suggested that Fitzwilliam avoid endorsing any move for a union of England and Ireland; such an idea was too radical to gain acceptance. Moreover, it would, in fact, accomplish little, for, as Burke so often said, Ireland's problems were internal. On the other hand, some issues were too trivial for Fitzwilliam to get distracted by. The eligibility of Catholics to serve in Parliament was a case in point. While the debate generates a good deal of heat, Burke noted, "yet, such is the State of Election Interests, and of all Interests in Ireland, that, if *three* Catholick Members were chosen, out of the three hundred, it is as many as could be rationally calculated."[48] According to Burke, Fitzwilliam should instead concentrate on doing real, if limited, good. That is, he should act according to Burke's standard of aggressive gradualism by promoting the alteration of "the immense Code of penal Statutes striking at their [i.e., the Catholics] property . . ."[49] The right to vote, Burke explained, was "[of] far greater moment than the eligibility to Parliament, and yet it is inconceivable, how little Benefit they have derived from it, or are likely to do for a long series of years to come" due to the hostility of the Protestants.[50] Further, Burke took what steps he could to ease Fitzwilliam's way. At one point, he wrote to Fitzwilliam describing a meeting between himself, the Irish leader Grattan, and a representative of Pitt.[51] Burke and Grattan had, he said, stressed that Fitzwilliam had no intention of governing Ireland independently of the English Cabinet, and that, though he would indeed push for reform, he would do so only in close consultation with Pitt. As a result, Burke reported, "we are both of opinion, that never man was more in earnest to settle this unhappy dispute with honor to you and the Duke of Portland than the Chancellour; and he certainly has considerable Talents for a Business of this nature."[52]

Thus, the failure of the Fitzwilliam mission was a bitter blow to Burke. At first, he did not know who to blame: "I do not care who is justified or who is blamed. The whole System and its whole Spirit, will stand condemned by every man, who does not think one or two Jobbs and Jobbers of more importance than the very Being of

Mankind."[53] Later, however, Burke rejected the position of Grattan and Fitzwilliam, who blamed Pitt; rather, he saw Pitt as misled more than sinister.[54] Instead, Burke believed that greater responsibility lay with the Irish administration, which had deceived Pitt into thinking that a struggle over places and power in Ireland was actually an assault on his position of authority in England: "it is plain that Mr. P. is made to think, that his new Colleagues instead of coming in for his support have coalited with him for the purpose of (hindering) and controlling his power if not of tripping up his Heels."[55] According to Burke, the consequences would be devastating, for the return to power of the Irish Junto would demonstrate that "the Rats are not tolerated, because it is hard to keep rats out of Ships, but the Ship is kept up for the Benefit of the Rats."[56] Indeed, he noted, "there has been some talk of sending Troops to Ireland. They would rather risque a thousand Civil Wars than the lowest of their Jobbers—or any part of their wild resentments."[57] As Burke saw it, then, the likely consequence of the frustration of reform would be repression and insurrection alternating in a spiral of violence.

Burke's stand on the Fitzwilliam affair has been subjected to extensive criticism.[58] He was, I believe, guilty of two revealing errors. First, given his lack of optimism and his intimate knowledge of the fragile nature of the Coalition, he should not have believed that Fitzwilliam could achieve extensive reform in Ireland. A marriage of convenience in England for pursuit of a war in France was, in reality, unlikely to work for good in Ireland. Burke should have understood that, in the conditions which prevailed in Europe at that time, an English administration was virtually certain to choose stability over reform in Ireland. Second, in the light of the lack of support in the English Cabinet, Burke should not have encouraged Fitzwilliam to attempt so much in so short a time. As a key figure in the talks prior to Fitzwilliam's going to Ireland, Burke knew what had been agreed to, and, while the precise details of the compromise have been debated ever since, it seems evident that it did not involve administrative support for immediate wholesale changes in the Irish government.[59] Burke's letter to Fitzwilliam concerning his meeting with Pitt's representative shows that he was aware of the limited nature of the Earl's mandate, as does a later one to Mrs. Crewe in which he described the agreement as a compromise and admitted that "things are not undoubtedly settled as I could wish them."[60] Burke errors on the possibility of reform and its correct pace reveal, once again, the inadequacy of his theoretical approach. Burke's theory of political office as a trust conceives of reform as a combination of popular support from below and practical action from above. However, neither of these ingredients were present in Ireland. As the Catholics were, in spite of their new possession of the franchise, effectively excluded from political power, they could not enact reform. The Protestants, for the most part, benefited from the exclusion of the Catholics and, therefore, did not desire reform. Finally, neither the Irish nor the English political leaderships, with a few exceptions like Earl Fitzwilliam, was willing to force reform over the opposition of the Ascendency. In short, the Irish political system could not accommodate gradualistic reforms of the sort Burke advocated.

IV

After the recall of Lord Fitzwilliam, the Irish problem became even more acute. With the repeal of most of the penal statutes, the Ascendency turned to direct social, economic, and coercive means of controlling the Catholic majority. Of this new approach, Burke wrote, "the only remaining grievance which the Catholicks suffer from the *Law* consists in certain incapacities relative to *Franchises.* The ill will of the governing Powers is their great Grievance who do not suffer them to have the Benefits of those capacities to which they are restored, nominally, by the law."[61] Thus, "they are treated like Enemies, and as long as they are under any incapacities their persecutors are furnished with a legal pretense of scouring them upon all occasions and they never fail to make use of it."[62] The consequences must, Burke thought, be disastrous. The Catholics would become radicalized, join in league with the dissenters, and "use the only means that is left for their protection."[63] The Catholic resistance would, he predicted, in a spiral of increasing violence, lead to British intervention in the form of martial law and military government. In Burke's words, "God forbid, that on a worthy occasion authority should want the means of force, or the disposition to use it. But where a prudent and enlarged policy does not precede it, and attend it too, where the hearts of the better sort of people do not go with the hands of the soldiery, you may call your constitution what you will, in effect it will consist of three parts, (orders, if you please,)—cavalry, infantry, and artillery,—and of nothing else or better."[64] Indeed, Burke believed the situation to be so near the breaking point that he urged the Catholic clergy to avoid overstating the duty of passive obedience so as not to lose credit with their congregations.[65]

In a long letter to French Laurence, written in May 1797, Burke reviewed the situation by imagining the likely consequences of a proposal for full Catholic emancipation.[66] He believed that emancipation would not pacify the Catholics unless it were accompanied by the removal of the "present Junto:" "It is impossible to persuade the people that as long as they (the Junto) govern, they will not have both the power and inclination, totally to frustrate the effect of this new arrangement as they have done that of all the former."[67] Moreover, the sheer logical inconsistency of maintaining in power a faction which derived its authority from its opposition to Catholic claims, while accepting the validity of those claims, would deprive governmental policy of all coherence.[68] But, if the Junto were dismissed, a Protestant reaction would follow, complete with a high potential for violence. In addition, the removal of the Junto would necessarily be followed by the accession to power of the Irish opposition, which, to retain credit with its supporters, must attempt parliamentary reform. If reform carried in Ireland, it would lead to similar action in England, and "such changes in this Kingdom would be preliminary steps to our utter ruin."[69] Moreover, Burke argued that such reform in Ireland would require a change in English administrations. In his opinion, the most plausible alternative to Pitt was a Foxite government in which Fitzwilliam was given responsibility for Irish affairs. However, this arrangement would be defective: Burke doubted that a Fox government would, in fact, give Fitzwilliam much support on Ireland; he was very concerned about Fox's softness on French matters; and a Fox administration would probably be hamstrung by the powerful opposition which Pitt could raise in Parliament. Burke concluded, "I see no ray of hope, but in some sort of Coalition between the heads of the factions who now distract us, formed upon a sense of the public danger," but as "their Animosity toward each other grows with the danger," that hope seemed remote indeed.[70]

Burke's desperation led him to consider what he had previously considered unthinkable. In the last few months of his life he began to reconsider co-operation with Fox on a limited number of issues, including Ireland, and, perhaps, even an eventual return to the Whig opposition. Two facts seem to have stimulated this move. First, the continued deterioration of the government of Ireland into a crude military despotism deeply disturbed Burke. In November 1796, he wrote to Laurence, "in Ireland it is plain they have thrown off all sorts of Political management and even the decorous appearance of it."[71] Second, there was the example of Fitzwilliam, who, in the aftermath of his alienation from his former allies among the conservative Whigs, was considering a rapprochement with Fox. Burke's first extensive consideration of the matter came in a letter, dated September 2, 1796, expressing gratitude for Fitzwilliam's decision to bring French Laurence into Parliament.[72] In the letter, Burke once again denounced both Pitt and Fox, and maintained a slight personal preference for Pitt. However, after considering at great length Fitzwilliam's proposal to support Fox, he pointedly refused to argue against it.[73] Still, Fitzwilliam's intention clearly shook Burke, for in December 1796, he returned to the issue of Irish parliamentary reform. Thus, he wrote, "as to the part Grattan and Ponsonby take about a reform, I am perfectly sensible of the mischief that must arise from the success of the Scheme, or even the struggle: But what can be done?"[74] After a period of equivocation, Burke finally endorsed Fitzwilliam's planned move in a letter to Laurence on June 1, 1797.[75] After noting Fitzwilliam's preference for Fox over Pitt and asserting that the stand of the Foxite Whigs on parliamentary reform bothered him still, Burke reported that Fitzwilliam would recommend an attachment with Fox, and continued: "if I am asked what I would myself advise in such a case, I should certainly advise the same . . ."[76] He would, however, Burke said, make his support contingent on two points: he would insist that the particular scheme of parliamentary reform be "practicable," and he would require that Grattan withdraw his proposal to tax the absentee Irish landlords.[77] Burke did not live to see the effects of his counsel: he died the following month, and, though Fitzwilliam increasingly co-operated with the Foxite forces, he did not formally rejoin the Whigs until after the Union of 1801.

V

Since my interpretation of Burke as an impatient reformer on Irish questions conflicts with established views, it would perhaps be appropriate to review three of the principal counter-arguments. First, a number of scholars argue that Burke's consistent opposition to both Irish legislative independence and Union with England demonstrate that he was an English imperialist.[78] Burke was indeed consistent on the issues. Late in his life, he told Lord Fitzwilliam, "I never liked—that total independence of Ireland which, without, in my opinion, adding any security to its liberty, took it out of the common constitutional protection of the Empire."[79] Burke believed that Ireland could not be completely independent of England, for he felt that the needs of commerce and defense would always link the two countries. Thus, in his mind, the question was not one of whether England and Ireland were to be related, but rather one of what the precise terms of the relationship were to be. In that regard, Burke believed that his theory of the empire offered a means of making the tie between England and Ireland a productive one. In his letter to Charles Bingham, Burke explained how: he argued that the imperial English legislature should allow the Irish extensive self-government, but, by maintaining a British veto on Irish legislation, should also provide a degree of protection for the Irish Catholics and Dissenters.[80] For Burke, the veto was of even greater importance after the declaration of Irish legislative independence in 1782, for it then became "little less than a breach of Order, even to mention Ireland in the House of Commons of Great Britain. If the people of Ireland were to be flayed alive by the predominant faction it would be the most critical of all attempts so much as to discuss the Subject in any public Assembly upon this side of the water."[81] On the other hand, in an Ireland firmly incorporated into the Empire and with Catholic emancipation enacted, the Irish Catholics would be doubly protected: first, by their own representatives in an Irish Parliament, and, second, by the English veto over the acts of the Protestant Ascendency.[82] Burke's position on a Union was equally clear. He always left the door open, explaining that the final decision must depend on the details of a particular plan, but he always expressed doubts. Burke felt that a Union was a dangerous gamble, for he thought that the English were not yet ready to accept the Irish on a basis of equality and that, until they were, Ireland would suffer too much from English prejudices to make a Union practicable.[83] It is worth noting that, in both instances, legislative independence and union, Burke's opposition was based on a concern for Irish, especially Irish Catholic, interests, and a belief that each would, in its own way, increase the power of the Ascendency.

A second issue is raised by Thomas Mahoney, who sees Burke's opposition to Pitt's proposals for free trade between England and Ireland as both the great mistake of his Irish career and a serious blot on his record as a reformer.[84] Mahoney argues that Pitt's plan would eventually have broken the Protestant Ascendency by raising up a middle-class commercial interest, which would have included Catholics, and by creating more and better jobs for the masses. However, as Beckett shows, it is highly doubtful that Burke's position should be considered an error.[85] The Irish opponents of the Free Trade Bill raised three objections. First, they pointed out that free trade did not, in fact, mean free trade. They argued that the Bill actually codified British commercial advantage. The Irish critics believed that the plan would fail to benefit Ireland, as similar plans in the past had also failed, for it would deny protection to infant Irish manufacturers against the competition of more mature British rivals. Moreover, they maintained that, during its movement through the English legislative process, the bill had been so amended as to lose all value to the Irish. Second, they held that the bill would have brought Ireland further under English political dominance. The bill required what would have become, in wartime, an essentially open-ended Irish contribution to English imperial revenue, and, after revisions in the English Parliament, also stipulated that the Irish Parliament enact, without modification, all measures passed by the English Parliament concerning "navigation, colonial trade, and certain branches of foreign trade."[86] Third, the critics claimed that it was extremely doubtful that the bill would have delivered the promised economic benefits. They saw no reason to think that the Ascendency would have been less zealous in controlling trade and manufacturing than it was in controlling everything else. They believed it far more probable that the Catholics would have been excluded from any benefits created by free trade. In addition, it should be understood that, along with this compelling economic case, Burke was required to consider the politics of the issue. Since the measure was universally unpopular in Ireland, and especially so among his Irish allies, Burke's position seems both reasonable and prudent.

The third argument is the broadest. Where the first two question Burke's reform credentials on specific issues, it holds that Burke was never a reformer at all. Rather, it insists that he was primarily interested in defending the existing Irish social structure and the place of the aristocracy within that structure. As one advocate puts it, "Burke, therefore, opposed the persecution of the Catholics because the stability of Irish society was at stake, and with it, the security of the empire. His hatred of persecution did not arise from a purely philosophical scruple but from the harsh realities of politics . . ."[87] A variation on the argument maintains that Burke preferred gradual to rapid reform because he felt that the extreme complexity of Irish affairs militated against drastic measures.[88] Supporters of this interpretation commonly cite three pieces of evidence. First, they note that in the *Letter to Langrishe,* Burke wrote, "if the disorder you speak of (Catholic Jacobinism) be real and considerable, you ought to raise an aristocratic interest, that is, an interest of property and education . . ."[89] The quote is indeed accurate, but its value is somewhat questionable, for its context is a denial by Burke that the disorder existed. In fact, his point was to show the inconsistency of a common Ascendency argument. The second bit of evidence is Burke's long-standing opposition to a tax on the Irish absentee landlords. However, Burke defended his position with a statement of his theory of imperial citizenship, and not with a defense of aristocracy. In his view, a tax on absentees would be unfair and discriminatory, for it would leave other forms of property and other parts of the Empire untouched. The most compelling point is the third: Burke's close ties to the Whig leadership, both in Ireland and England, and the admittedly aristocratic bias of that leadership.[90] Yet, whenever Burke perceived a split in the Irish Catholic reform ranks between the aristocrats and the middle-classes, he made clear that his sympathies were with the latter. For instance, in a long letter to his son, he wrote, "the Strength of the Catholicks is not in their dozen or Score of old Gentlemen. Weak indeed they would be if this were the Case. Their force consists in two things: their numbers and their growing property, which grows with the growth of the country itself . . ."[91] In sum, on the question of whether Burke preferred stability or movement, gradualism or immediate reform, the evidence is overwhelming. Burke played a continuing role in Irish politics for over thirty years, and, during that time, he never ceased to press for the broadest possible reform.

VI

No matter where Burke looked after the collapse of Earl Fitzwilliam's Lord Lieutenancy and the subsequent defeat of the Catholic Relief Bill of 1795 prospects were bleak. In Ireland, itself, Burke saw the threat as twofold: on the one hand, goaded by the repressive actions of the Irish government and Protestant majority, the Catholics seemed to be moving toward increased violence and rebellion. On the other hand, Burke was certain that the British response to Irish disorder would be to create a virtual military dictatorship. In England, matters seemed equally uncertain. In Burke's eyes, the widespread domestic unrest was a sure sign that the doctrines of the French Revolution were making headway. Moreover, the Pitt administration appeared to Burke to be unwilling to take the strong, indeed unprecedented, measures he thought necessary to provide civil order and a unified national opposition to France. Burke's sense of failure and melancholy is caught well by a passage near the end of the *Appeal:* "if a new order is coming on, and all the political opinions must pass away as dreams, which our ancestors have worshipped as revelations . . . he would rather be the last . . . of that race of men than the first and greatest of those who have coined to themselves Whig principles from a French die, unknown to the impress of our fathers in the Constitution."[92] In my opinion, Burke's late consideration of an alliance with Fox is more of a sign of his desperation and his lack of alternatives than a considered tactic. I believe another anecdote to be more indicative of Burke's opinion of Fox and his supporters at this time. When Fox, knowing that Burke was on his deathbed, asked for a last meeting, he was denied with a curt note from Burke's wife, saying in part, "Mr. Burke is convinced that the principles which he has endeavoured to maintain are necessary to the welfare and dignity of his country, and that these principles can be enforced only by the general persuasion of his sincerity."[93] Burke, then, showed no sign of a change in principles, and without such a change, any reconciliation with Fox was unlikely.

Burke, of course, had an explanation for the failure of his approach to reform. That explanation centered on two related points: the machinations of politicians and the infidelity of the people. Burke never forgave either George III or William Pitt for the role each played in the collapse of the Fox-North Coalition in 1784. In his opinion, they had conspired together to defeat both the Whigs and the constitution. Even after the lapse of years and under the threat of the French Revolution, Burke had nothing very good to say about Pitt. He told Fitzwilliam: "if I were myself in the vigour of my Life, . . . you ought not to bring me into Parliament with an Obligation to Mr. Pitt hanging about my Neck. It would never indeed induce me to go along with him in the Paths, in which, unguided by all moral and all political principle, he has lately walked . . ."[94] For Burke, the effects of treachery were reinforced by the blundering of the Duke of Portland upon the formation of his alliance with Pitt in the early 1790s. Burke had urged the Whigs to maintain a degree of distance from Pitt even as they supported him. However, the party, Burke felt, had missed its opportunity, "I was in serious hope that the party which was at last rallied under its proper standards . . . might, either in Ministry or out of Ministry, as the publick necessities required, become some sort of asylum for principles moral and political, and might control that disposition to factious servitude, which could see nothing, in the constitution or the country, but the power of one or two individuals."[95] But Portland had allowed Pitt to use the Irish crisis to destroy the party and to send Fitzwilliam into a form of political exile. As a result, the Old Whigs had ceased to exist as a political force. Burke told Fitzwilliam, "they are so many individuals, not a jot more separated from your Lordship, than they are from one another."[96] As for the people, they were simply too foolish, too easily led, and too vulnerable to electoral corruption to be relied on. Indeed, in 1784 they had ratified Pitt's chicanery: "I am persuaded they saw and comprehended sufficiently and even more distinctly than probably ever the people was able to perceive any one point of great political controversy. So that it was with their Eyes broad open that they Majority of the Nation has perpetrated this self felonious act."[97] Reform, for Burke, was always dependent on a tenuous confidence between the reform party and the people. As he saw it, that confidence could not survive the strain created by political maneuverings within the political elite and the passions of the people.

Thus, as I indicated in chapter six, I believe that an analysis of the deficiencies of Burke's approach to reform must begin with his theory of trusteeship. The example of India is instructive. Burke saw the British East India Company as merely a trustee for the English Parliament and people on the one side and the Great Mogul on the other. As he viewed matters, if, at any time, it abused its authority, it could, and indeed should, be called to account by the Parliament and people. Yet, it did not seem to have bothered Burke that the Indians had no say in their own government. This gap in his position was probably a consequence both of India's underdevelopment and of his theory of trusteeship. The simple truth is that Burke did not place a premium on the right to participate in government. Rather, he was generally content to defend effective government, provided that government was both honest and responsible to some form of popular authority. Thus, the theory of trusteeship had two sides. On the one hand, in the case of India, Burke felt that the Indians had a right to be governed well, and he was prepared to hold the Company accountable for any breach of that responsibility. As he put it, "all political power which is set over men, and . . . all privilege claimed or exercised in exclusion of them, being wholly artificial, and for so much a derogation from the natural equality of mankind at large, ought to be some way or other exercised ultimately for their benefit."[98] However, on the other hand, the theory of trusteeship could be used to deny the right of the Indians, and, in fact, the people in any system, to dictate the details of policy or even to play a role in government. Speaking of the English people some years earlier, Burke told Parliament: "our duty . . . is to give them information, and not to receive it from them: we are not to go to school to them, to learn the principles of law and government."[99] He continued, "as to the details of particular measures, or of general schemes of policy, they have neither enough of speculation in the closet nor of experience in business to decide upon it."[100] Just as Burke never questioned England's right to occupy India or the right of the East India Company to exercise government authority over the Indians, he never sought to broaden the role of the Indian people.

The contradiction inherent in the theory of trusteeship extends beyond Burke's Indian thought, for there is a similar confusion in his theory of the constitution. Burke believed that in normal circumstances the government would run smoothly, with the king conducting policy, but also attending to the advice of the House of Lords and heeding, at least, the negative wishes of his people as represented in the House of Commons. Yet, on those occasions when such unity was lacking, Burke was torn by an inability to choose between accepting the right of the king to rule and a commitment to something close to parliamentary sovereignty. During the constitutional crisis caused by the fall of the Fox-North coalition, the new parliament was met by a speech from the Throne which defended the king's and Pitt's actions and attacked the previous parliament for not supporting the king and his ministers. In response, Burke authored the Whig's official reply, "A Representation to his Majesty.[101] He argued that "thinking men will scarcely regard the *penal* dissolution of a Parliament as a very trifling concern," and held that charging the House of Commons with being too independent is almost to praise it.[102] Parliament must be free to debate and consider the good of the nation, Burke continued, and even the ministers of the Crown should be free to vote as they think best.[103] Burke claimed that there were ample means to block any improper legislation, "but whatever, by the manifestation of the royal displeasure, tends to intimidate individuals from proposing, or this House from receiving, debating, and passing bills, tends to prevent even the beginning of every reformation in the state, and utterly destroys the deliberative capacity of Parliament."[104]

Yet, even here, Burke's argument lost much of its effectiveness through the concessions he made to royal authority. Throughout the "Representation," Burke accepted, consistent with the position I have outlined, the Crown as the active executive power in the state and viewed the House of Commons as the people's check on government.[105] He even denied that the Constitution was based on a balance, asserting that each branch had certain powers to exercise, and that, when those powers were used properly, a balance would follow. But what, one asks, if they are not used properly? Burke believed that the ministers were responsible only to the king, and he held that they could not be removed by the Commons. Thus, though Burke maintained that the king should adhere to the advice of the Commons, for "it is a crooked and desperate design, leading to mischief, the extent of which no human wisdom can forsee, to attempt to form a prerogative party in the nation . . . ," he did not hold that the king was obliged to follow their wishes.[106] Indeed, Burke admitted that, if the king chose, he could even dissolve Parliament and seek to replace it with one more sympathetic to his views. Burke, in short, had no effective answer to maladministration, if that maladministration were supported by the king. As the Commons could not, in his opinion, remove the king's ministers, the opposition there, no matter how powerful, would be condemned to a struggle which it could not win. If the king lacked the votes he needed to prevail, he could simply retain his unpopular ministers, continue the struggle, and force a stalemate. At that point, as in 1784, the opposition would be confronted with a choice among a collapse of effective political authority, surrender, or an appeal to the restricted electorate of the day, where the resources of the administration would be brought into play against them.

The reason for Burke's indecisiveness in the face of what he believed to be royal misrule is not difficult to find. Like most thinkers of his time, he accepted the doctrine of sovereignty; that is, he believed that final political authority had to be vested somewhere. The advocates of mixed government could place sovereignty in Parliament, defined as the King-in-Parliament. However, that option was not available to Burke, for he insisted that sovereignty lay with the king. At times, under the pressure of particular controversies, Burke moved beyond his claim that Parliament was merely a check on royal power, and he then came close to holding that an administration was responsible to Parliament. For example, early in his career, in the "Observations" and the "Thought on the Present Discontents," Burke went as far as to defend party government. In those works, he urged the creation of a uniform administration as an antidote against the machinations of the Crown.[107] But parliamentary supremacy and party government, as Burke realized, can lead on to popular sovereignty. They are only a short way from arguments that the party in Parliament should represent the party out of Parliament and that both ought to represent the people at large. There were times when Burke came close to accepting this. Even during the French Revolution, he often appealed to popular opinion. Before making peace, he urged the administration, consult the people. Let them be fully informed: "they who have not the whole cause before them, call them politicians, call them people, call them what you will, are no judges. The difficulties of the case, as well as its fair side, ought to be presented," and then, if the verdict is to trust France, "the ministers stand acquitted before God and man for whatever may come."[108] Generally, however, Burke would not go so far. In 1784, for instance, he blamed the popular endorsement of the king's victory on their ignorance and stupidity.[109] Two years later, in a letter seeking to dissuade a young friend from engaging in politics, Burke noted, "I make a very great scruple of encouraging any one to engage with our party . . . It is not wise, nor honest, nor manly to engage others in a party whose very principle casts its roots [in] despair."[110] Burke understood that the people were often the only true alternative to the king, but he believed that they were too foolish and too corruptible to be an acceptable choice. He felt that the danger of popular tyranny was too great to be chanced. Burke believed it better to leave things where they were and to risk misgovernment of another, more limited, sort. The Whig dilemma of 1784 mirrored a similar tension at the heart of Burke's thought.

NOTES

Chapter One

1. Leslie Stephen, *History of English Thought in the Eighteenth Century,* 2 Vol., G. P. Putnam's Sons, New York, 1927, see especially Vol. II, pp. 219–251. John Morley, *Edmund Burke,* Harper and Brothers, New York, 1879.

2. Russell Kirk, *The Conservative Mind,* Gateway Editions, South Bend, Indiana, 1978, Peter J. Stanlis, *Edmund Burke and the Natural Law,* University of Michigan Press, Ann Arbor, 1958, and Francis Canavan, *Edmund Burke: Prescription and Providence,* Carolina Academic Press, Durham, North Carolina, 1987 are three representative examples of a general school. To varying degrees, most of these interpretations are grounded in Leo Strauss' distinction between natural law and natural right. See Leo Strauss, *Natural Right and History,* University of Chicago Press, Chicago, 1953.

3. Stanlis, p. 83.

4. Kirk, p. 44.

5. Burleigh Wilkins, *The Problem of Burke's Political Philosophy,* Oxford University Press, Oxford, 1967 and Michael Freeman, *Edmund Burke and the Critique of Political Radicalism,* The University of Chicago Press, Chicago, 1980.

6. C. B. Macpherson, *Burke,* Hill and Wang, New York, 1980 and Issac Kramnick, "The Left and Edmund Burke," *Political Theory,* Vol. 11, No. 2, May 1983, pp. 189–214. Also see, Issac Kramnick, *The Rage of Edmund Burke,* Basic Books, Inc., New York, 1977.

7. Alfred Cobban, *Edmund Burke and the Revolt Against the Eighteenth Century,* macMillan Co., New York, 1929.

8. Frank O'Gorman, *Edmund Burke His Political Philosophy,* Indiana University Press, Bloomington, 1973.

9. John MacCunn, *The Political Philosophy of Burke,* Russell & Russell, Inc., New York, 1965.

10. John D. Fair and John A. Hutcheson Jr., "British Conservatism in the Twentieth Century: An Emerging Ideological Tradition," *Albion,* Vol. 19, No. 4 (winter 1987), pp. 549–578.

11. Irving Babbitt, *Democracy and Leadership,* Liberty Classics, Indianapolis, 1979.

12. Anthony Quinton, *The Politics of Imperfection,* Faber and Faber, Boston, 1978.

13. Robert Blake, *The Conservative Party From Peel to Thatcher,* Methuen, London, 1985.

14. Quinton, p. 10 ff.

15. Fair and Hutcheson, p. 549.

16. For Collingwood on "present history," see R. G. Collingwood, *Essays in the Philosophy of History,* McGraw-Hill Book Company, New York, 1965, pp. 34–56. Also see Collingwood's *The Idea of History,* Oxford University Press, New York, 1956. Collingwood actually saw the present as intruding on the study of history at two points: (1) the "facts" which make up history must be perceived in the present; (2) the present is the source of the problems which we turn to history to solve.

17. Collingwood, *Essays,* p. xxix.

18. Ibid., p. 54.

19. John Dunn, *Interpreting Political Responsibility,* Princeton University Press, Princeton, 1990, p. 3.

20. For a similar approach, though directed to a different purpose—accounting for the growth of democratic citizenship, see T. H. Marshall, "Citizenship and Social Class," in *Class, Citizenship, and Social Development,* Doubleday and Company, Inc., Garden City, New York, 1964, pp. 65–122. For a range of opinions about the process, see J. P. Kenyon, *Revolution Principles,* Cambridge University Press, London, 1977, J. A. W. Gunn, *Politics and the Public Interest in the Seventeenth Century,* Toronto University Press, Toronto, 1969, J. R. Pole, *The Seventeenth Century The Sources of Legislative Power,* Virginia University Press, Charlottesville, 1969, J. W. Gough, *Fundamental Law in English Constitutional History,* Oxford University Press, New York, 1965.

21. See especially, J. H. Plumb, *The Origins of Political Stability, England 1675–1725,* Houghton Mifflin, Boston, 1967, and William Thomas Laprade, *Public Opinion and Politics in Eighteenth Century England,* Macmillan, New York, 1936. Not all accept that change was the order of the day,

see J. C. D. Clark, *English Society 1688–1832,* Cambridge University Press, Cambridge, 1985.

22. Mark A. Kishlansky, *Parliamentary Selection,* Cambridge University Press, New York, 1986, p. 12.

23. Plumb, *Origins of Political Stability,* see esp., pp. 1–30.

24. Ian K. Steele, *The English Atlantic, 1675–1740,* Oxford University Press, New York, 1986, p. 273.

25. Jack Green, *The Quest for Power,* University of North Carolina Press, Chapel Hill, 1969.

26. Gordon S. Wood, *The Creation of the American Republic, 1776–1787,* University of North Carolina Press, Chapel Hill, 1969. See also Bernard Bailyn, *The Ideological Origins of the American Revolution,* Harvard University Press, Cambridge, 1967, and *The Origins of American Politics,* Random House, New York, 1967, Richard Hofstader, *The Idea of a Party System,* University of California Press, Los Angeles, 1969, William Chambers, *Political Parties in a New Nation,* Oxford University Press, New York, 1963, Roy F. Nichols, *The Invention of the American Political Parties,* Macmillan, New York, 1967.

27. Gordon S. Wood, *Representation in the American Revolution,* Virginia University Press, Charlottesville, 1969, especially p. 12 ff. Also see Michael Kammen, *Deputies and Liberties,* Alfred A. Knopf, New York, 1969.

28. For the Anti-federalists, see Herbert J. Storing, *What the Anti-Federalists Were For,* University of Chicago Press, Chicago, 1981, Cecelia Kenyon, *The Anti-federalists,* Bobbs-Merrill, New York, 1966 and Jackson Turner Main, *The Anti-federalists,* University of North Carolina Press, Chapel Hill, 1961.

29. John Taylor, *An Inquiry into the Principles and Policy of the Government of the United States,* Yale University Press, New Haven, 1950,p. 505.

30. Bolingbroke, "A Dissertation Upon Parties," *The Works of Lord Bolingbroke,* Vol. II, Henry G. Bohm, London, 1967, pp. 5–172, p. 165.

31. Isaiah Berlin, "Giambattisa Vico and Cultural History," *The Crooked Timber of Humanity,* Alfred A. Knopf, New York, 1991, pp. 50–51.

32. Albert O. Hirshman, *The Passions and the Interests,* Princeton University Press, Princeton, New Jersey, 1977.

33. Edmund Burke, *Reflections on the Revolution in France,* The Bobbs-Merrill Company, Inc., 1955, p. 215.

34. Edmund Burke, *The Correspondence of Edmund Burke,* 10 Vol., The University of Chicago Press, Chicago, Ill., 1963–1978. Vol. VI, To Philip Francis, 19/Nov./1790, p. 173.

35. Burke, *Reflections*, p. 69.

36. Edmund Burke, "Appeal From the New to the Old Whigs," *Works*, Vol. V, p. 165, 169.

37. Edmund Burke, "Address to the British Colonists in North America," *Works*, Vol. VI, pp. 183–196, pp. 193–194.

38. Burke, "Speech . . . on Mr. Fox's East India Bill," *Works.*, Vol. II, pp. 431–536, p. 60.

39. Burke, "Appeal," pp. 207–208.

40. Burke, "Appeal," p. 81.

41. Burke, "Thoughts . . . Discontents," p. 530.

42. See, for example, Richard H. Popkin, *The History of Scepticism From Erasmus to Spinoza*, University of California Press, Los Angeles, 1979, Barbara J. Shapiro, *Probability and Certainty in Seventeenth Century England*, Princeton University Press, Princeton, 1983, Thomas Goldstein, *Dawn of Modern Science*, Houghton Mifflin and Company, Boston, 1980, Keith Thomas, *Man and the Natural World*, Pantheon Books, New York, 1983, and Herbert Butterfield, *The Origins of Modern Science*, Macmillan Company, New York, 1957.

43. Shapiro, *Probability and Certainty*, p. 268.

44. J. R. Jones, *The First Whigs*, Oxford University Press, New York, 1966, p. 2.

45. H. T. Dickinson, *Liberty and Property*, Weidenfeld and Nicolson, London, 1977, p. 125.

46. O'Gorman, *Edmund Burke*, p. 26 ff.

47. See Ian R. Christie, *Myth and Reality in 18th Century Politics*, University of California Press, Los Angeles, 1970 and G. H. Guttridge, *English Whiggism and the American Revolution*, University of California Press, Los Angeles, 1966.

48. Frank O'Gorman, *The Rise of Party in England*, George Allen and Unwin, London, 1975, p. 415.

49. Edmund Burke, *A Philosophical Enquiry into the Origin of Our Ideas of the Sublime and Beautiful*, University of Notre Dame Press, Notre Dame, Indiana, 1968.

50. Edmund Burke, *A Vindication of Natural Society: Or, A View of the Miseries and Evils Arising to Mankind from Every Species of Artificial Society*, Liberty Classics, Indianapolis, 1982.

51. Edmund Burke, "Speech on American Taxation," *Works,* Vol. II, pp. 6–98, and "Speech on . . . Conciliation with America,"*Works,* Vol. II, pp. 99–186.

Chapter Two

1. John Locke, *Two Tracts on Government,* Philip Abrams (ed.), Cambridge University Press, Cambridge, 1967. pp. 19 ff.

2. Ibid., p. 24.

3. Ibid., p. 25.

4. John Locke, *An Essay Concerning Human Understanding,* 2 Vol., Dover Publishers, Inc., New York, 1959, Vol. I, esp. pp. 26 ff. and 64 ff.

5. Ibid., p. 93.

6. Ibid., p. 122.

7. Ibid., p. 177 ff., esp. p. 188.

8. Ibid., P. 228.

9. Ibid., p. 174.

10. Ibid., p. 64.

11. Ibid., p. 314.

12. Ibid., pp. 314–315.

13. Ibid., Vol. II, p. 436.

14. Ibid., p. 287.

15. Locke, *An Essay Concerning Human Understanding,* Vol. I, p. 78.

16. Ibid., Vol. II, p. 208

17. Ibid., pp. 325–326. An interesting theme, but one outside our immediate concern, is the development of theories of probability to deal with those areas where certain knowledge is impossible. See Ian Hacking, *The Emergence of Probability,* Cambridge University Press, Cambridge, 1975, and *The Taming of Chance,* Cambridge University Press, Cambridge, 1990, Barbara J. Shapiro, *Probability and Certainty in Seventeenth Century England,* Princeton University Press, Princeton, 1983, and Robert Brown, *The Nature of Social Laws,* Cambridge University Press, 1984.

18. Locke, *An Essay Concerning Human Understanding,* Vol. I, p. 65.

19. Ibid., p. 303.

20. Ibid., p. 348.

21. Ibid., p. 360.

22. Ibid., p. 372.

23. Samuel H. Monk, *The Sublime,* University of Michigan Press, Ann Arbor, 1960, p. 8.

24. Edmund Burke, *A Philosophical Enquiry into the Origin of Our Ideas of the Sublime and Beautiful,* University of Notre Dame Press, Notre Dame, Ind., 1958, pp. xvi–xvii. There is a confusing factor here; Burke's *Vindication of Natural Society* was published first but the *Enquiry* was written first. See the notes in Burke's *Correspondence,* Vol. I, pp. 121 and 127. Also see A. I. P. Samuels, *The Early Life, Correspondence, and Writings of the Rt. Hon. Edmund Burke,* Cambridge University Press, Cambridge, 1923, p. 203 ff.

25. Quoted in Samuels, p. 212.

26. Monk, *The Sublime,* p. 99.

27. See the introduction to Burke, *The Sublime and Beautiful,* p. lxxii.

28. Monk, *The Sublime,* p. 96 ff.

29. Burke, *The Sublime and Beautiful,* p. 32 ff.

30. Ibid., pp. 112–113.

31. Ibid., p. 92 ff.

32. Ibid., p. 57.

33. Ibid., p. 91.

34. Ibid., pp. 129–30.

35. Ibid., p. 134.

36. Ibid., pp. 133–136.

37. Ibid., pp. 149–151.

38. See the "Introduction on Taste," in Ibid., pp. 11–27.

39. Ibid., p. 11.

40. Ibid.

41. Ibid., p. 27.

42. Ibid., p. 13.

43. Ibid., p. 23.

44. Ibid., p. 13.

45. Ibid., p. 14.

46. Ibid.

47. Ibid., p. 23.

48. Edmund Burke, *A Vindication of Natural Society . . . ,* Liberty Classics, Indianapolis, 1982.

49. Ibid., p. 6.

50. Ibid., p. 11.

51. Ibid.

52. John Morley, *Burke,* p. 17.

53. Burke, *Vindication,* p. 15.

54. Ibid., p. 26.

55. Ibid., p. 51.

56. Ibid., p. 72.

57. Ibid., p. 84 ff.

58. Ibid., p. 93.

59. Ibid., p. 94.

60. Francis Hutcheson, *An Inquiry into the Origins of Our Ideas of Beauty and Virtue,* Garland Publishing, Inc., New York, 1971, p. 84.

61. Ibid., p. 3.

62. Ibid., p. 6.

63. Ibid., p. 8.

64. Ibid., pp. 9, 11.

65. Ibid., pp. 14–15.

66. Ibid., p. 17.

67. Ibid., p. 20 and pp. 30 ff.

68. See Gladys Bryson, *Man and Society: The Scottish Enquiry of the Eighteenth Century,* Princeton University Press, Princeton, New Jersey, 1945, p. 25 ff. See also, Thomas Horne, "Envy and Commercial Society: Mandeville and Smith on 'Private Vices, Public Benefits,' " *Political Theory,* Vol. 9, No. 4 (Nov. 1981) pp. 551–569 and M. M. Goldsmith, *Private Vices, Public Benefits,* Cambridge University Press, New York, 1985.

69. Bernard Mandeville, *The Fable of the Bees,* Penguin Books, Baltimore, Maryland, 1970, pp. 54–55.

70. Ibid., p. 201.

71. Ibid., p. 64.

72. Ibid., p. 69.

73. Ibid., p. 174.

74. See Ibid., p. 261 ff., for the infamous "An Essay on Charity and Charity Schools."

75. Hutcheson, "Treatise on Virtue," in *Enquiry . . . Beauty and Virtue,* p. 135.

76. Ibid., p. 119.

77. Ibid., p. 162.

78. See Ibid., pp. 266 ff. and 250 ff.

79. Ibid., p. 242 ff.

80. Ibid., p. 196 ff.

81. See Thomas Reid, *An Inquiry into the Human Mind,* The University of Chicago Press, Chicago, 1974. A useful analysis of Reid may be found in Bryson, p. 130 ff.

82. Reid, *Inquiry,* p. 16.

83. Stephen, *English Thought,* Vol. I, p. 59.

84. See Adam Smith, *The Theory of Moral Sentiments,* London, 1790. Two good commentaries on Smith's thought are T. D. Campbell, *Adam Smith's Science of Morals,* Rowman and Littlefield, Totowa, New Jersey, 1971 and Donald Winch, *Adam Smith's Politics,* Cambridge University Press, New York, 1978.

85. Campbell, p. 89.

86. For Smith on the stages of society, see Adam Smith, *An Inquiry into the Nature and Causes of the Wealth of Nations,* Random House, Inc., New York, 1937. See also Bryson, *Man and Society,* p. 148 ff. and Ronald L. Meek, *Social Science and the Ignoble Savage,* Cambridge University Press, New York, 1976.

87. Edmund Burke, *Correspondence,* Vol. I, To Adam Smith, 10/Sept./1759, p. 129.

88. Ibid., p. 130.

89. See Ibid., p. 129.

90. See Edmund Burke, *An Account of the European Settlements in America,* 2 Vol., Research Reprints Inc., New York, 1970, Vol. I, p. 31 ff. and Vol II, p. 124.

91. Ibid., pp. 167–168.

92. Edmund Burke, *Correspondence,* Vol. VI, To Claude-Francois De Rivarol, 1/June/1791, p. 266.

93. Adam Ferguson, *An Essay on the History of Civil Society,* Edinburgh University Press, Edinburgh, 1966, p. 8.

94. Peter J. Stanlis, *Edmund Burke and the Natural Law.* University of Michigan Press, Ann Arbor, 1958.

95. Ibid., p. 7.

96. Leo Strauss, *Natural Right and History,* University of Chicago Press, Chicago, 1953, p. 181.

97. Stanlis, *Edmund Burke and the Natural Law,* p. 83. Italics in original.

98. Ibid., p. 161.

99. Ibid., p. 77.

100. David Hume, *A Treatise of Human Nature,* Viking Penguin, Inc., New York, 1969, p. 515.

101. Ibid., p. 510.

102. Edmund Burke, *Reflections on the Revolution in France,* pp. 70–71.

103. Stanlis, *Edmund Burke and the Natural Law.* For Hume, see p. 6. For Burke discovering Natural Law, see p. 34 ff.

104. Richard Flathman, *The Practice of Rights,* Cambridge University Press, New York, 1976, p. 161. Wesley N. Hohfeld, *Fundamental Legal Concepts,* Yale University Press, New Haven, 1919 is the primary source for much of contemporary rights theory.

105. For rights as trumps, see Ronald Dworkin, *Taking Rights Seriously,* Harvard University Press, Cambridge, Mass., 1978, p. 81 ff. Other representative discussions may be found in Alan Gewith, *Reason and Morality,* University of Chicago Press, Chicago, 1978, Richard Flathman, *Toward a Liberalism,* Cornell University Press, Ithaca, 1989, and, of course, H. L. A. Hart, *The Concept of Law,* Clarendon Press, Oxford, 1961. A rather extreme version of the thesis is key to Robert Nozick, *Anarchy, State, and Utopia,* Basic Books, New York, 1974. Here, again, Hohfeld's work is central.

106. Flathman, *The Practice of Rights,* pp. 185–186.

107. Joseph Raz, *The Morality of Freedom,* Clarendon Press, Oxford, 1986, p. 245.

108. Flathman, *The Practice of Rights,* p. 2.

109. For Hart's minimal version of Natural Law, see H. L. A. Hart, "Are There Any Natural Rights?" *Philosophical Review* 64, 1955, pp. 175–191.

110. Flathman, *The Practice of Rights,* p. 44.

111. Edmund Burke, "Speech in Opening . . . Impeachment of Warren Hastings," *Works,* Vol. IX, p. 456.

112. Montesquieu, *The Spirit of the Laws,* Anne Cohler, Basia Miller, and Harold Stone, (ed.), Cambridge University Press, Cambridge, 1989, p. 3. A good brief discussion of Montesquieu is Judith N. Shklar, *Montesquieu,* Oxford University Press, 1987. For Montesquieu's influence on Burke, see C. B. Courtney, *Montesquieu and Burke,* Greenwood Press, Westport, Conn., 1975.

113. Montesquieu, *The Spirit of the Laws,* p. 5.

114. Ibid., p. 4.

115. Edmund Burke, "Speech in Opening the Impeachment of Warren Hastings,' *Works,* Vol. II, pp. 396–493, p. 455.

116. Burke, *Correspondence,* Vol. VI, To John Noble, 14/March/1790, p. 102.

117. Burke, "Appeal," p. 169.

118. Ibid., p. 81.

119. Ibid., pp. 108–109.

120. Edmund Burke, "Speech on the Acts of Uniformity," *Works,* Vol. VII, pp. 3–19.

121. Burke, *Correspondence,* Vol. VI, To Adrien-Jean-Francois Duport, Post 20/March/1790, p. 108.

122. Burke, *Correspondence,* Vol. VI, To Charles-Jean-Francois Depont, Nov./1789, p. 45.

123. Ibid., p. 46.

124. Burke, *Correspondence,* Vol. IX, To French Laurence, 11/Ap./1797, p. 307.

125. Burke, "Speech on . . . Conciliation with America," p. 143.

126. Edmund Burke, "Speech on Presenting to the House of Commons A Plan for the Better Security of the Independence of Parliament, and the Economical Reformation of the Civil and Other Establishments," *Works,* Vol. II, pp. 265–364, p. 305

127. Cicero, *On the Commonwealth,* Bobbs-Merrill, New York, 1929, pp. 215–216.

128. Thomas Aquinas, *The Political Ideas of Saint Thomas Aquinas,* Hafner Publishing Co., New York, 1953, p. 34.

129. Burke, "Speech on Declining the Poll at Bristol," p. 95.

130. Burke, "Letter to a Member of the National Assembly," p. 5.

131. R. R. Fennessy, *Burke, Paine, and the Rights of Man,* Martinus Nijhoff, Amsterdam, 1963, p. 68.

132. Burke, "Letter . . . Pension," p. 189.

133. Ibid.

134. See Wilkins, *Problem of Burke's Political Philosophy,* p. 122.

135. Stanlis, *Burke and the Natural Law,* p. 256. For the Appendix as a whole, see, pp. 255–258.

136. Ibid., p. 122.

137. Burke, *Appeal From the New to the Old Whigs.* p. 165.

138. Hume, *A Treatise of Human Nature,* p. 507.

139. Ibid., p. 508.

140. Ibid., p. 509.

141. Ibid., p. 510.

142. Ibid., p. 515.

143. Ibid., p. 518.

144. Ibid., pp. 520–521.

145. Ibid.

146. Hume, *A Treatise of Human Nature,* p. 138.

147. Hume, "Of the Standard of Taste," passim.

148. See Boulton's introduction to Burke, *Sublime and Beautiful,* p. xxlx.

149. Burke, *Reflections on the Revolution in France,* p. 68. For an excellent discussion of Burke on natural law, see Fennessy, *Burke, Paine, and the Rights of Man,* p. 72 ff. Fennessy's view is similar to mine but a bit more skeptical about whether Burke believed in a natural law.

150. Burke, *Reflections on the Revolution in France,* p. 69.

151. Ibid., p. 71.

152. Stephen, *English Thought,* Vol. II, p. 57.

153. Burke, "An Appeal From the New to the Old Whigs," p. 209.

154. Ibid., pp. 210–211.

Chapter Three

1. Tacitus, *The Agricola and the Germania,* Penguin Books, New York, 1982, p. 51.

2. Edmund Burke, *Correspondence,* Vol. I, To Richard Shackleton, 21/March/1746–47, p. 89.

3. Lord Bolingbroke, *Historical Writings,* University of Chicago Press, Chicago, 1972, p. 8. See also H. T. Dickinson, *Bolingbroke,* Constable and Company, Ltd., London, 1970, p. 250 ff.

4. Bolingbroke, *Historical Writings,* p. 61.

5. Ibid., p. 9.

6. Ibid., p. 28.

7. On Bolingbroke's use of Machiavelli, see Herbert Butterfield, *The Statecraft of Machiavelli,* p. 101 ff.

8. Bolingbroke, *Historical Writings,* p. 177.

9. Ibid., p. 221.

10. Ibid., p. 228.

11. H. T. Dickinson, *Bolingbroke,* p. 195.

12. For the English part of the story, see J. G. A. Pocock, *The Ancient Constitution and the Feudal Law,* W. W. Norton and Company, Inc., New York, 1967, p. 91 ff.

13. Sir Robert Filmer, "Patriarcha," in *Patriarcha and Other Political Works,* Basil Blackwell, Oxford, 1949, p. 105. A very useful description of the patriarchal style of argument may be found in Gordon T. Schochet, *Patriarchalism in Political Thought,* Basil Blackwell, Oxford, 1975.

14. Filmer, "Patriarcha," p. 106.

15. Ibid., p. 118.

16. Ibid., p. 120.

17. Peter Laslett, (ed.), *Locke's Two Treatises of Government,* Cambridge University Press, Cambridge, 1966. The range of recent commentary on Locke's political thought is broad indeed. A few of the more interesting

works are John Dunn, *The Political Thought of John Locke,* Cambridge University Press, Cambridge, 1969, Julian H. Franklin, *John Locke and the Theory of Sovereignty,* Cambridge University Press, Cambridge, 1978, James Tully, *A Discourse on Property,* Cambridge University Press, Cambridge, 1980, Neal Wood, *John Locke and Agrarian Capitalism,* University of California Press, Los Angeles, 1984, Thomas L. Pangle, *The Spirit of Modern Republicanism,* The University of Chicago Press, Chicago, 1988, and Richard Ashcraft, *Revolutionary Politics and Locke's 'Two Treatises of Government,'* Princeton University Press, 1986.

18. See Algernon Sidney, *Discourses on Government,* 3 Vol., Deare and Andrews, New York, 1805. For Sidney's significance as a Whig historian, see my "Reason and History in Early Whig Thought: The Case of Algernon Sidney," *The Journal of the History of Ideas,* Vol. XLVII, No. 1, (July–Sept. 1982), pp. 397–416.

19. Sidney, Vol. II, p. 292.

20. Ibid., p. 110.

21. Ibid., pp. 462–463.

22. Ibid., p. 463.

23. For the Walpole apologists, see Isaac Kramnick, *Bolingbroke and his Circle,* Harvard University Press, Cambridge, Mass., 1968, pp. 111–136.

24. See Gladys Bryson, *Man and Society,* A. M. Kelley, New York, 1968 and Ronald L. Meek, *Social Science and the Ignoble Savage,* Cambridge University Press, New York, 1976, for two excellent discussions of Scottish social science in the late eighteenth century.

25. Ibid., p. 2.

26. Adam Ferguson, *An Essay on the History of Civil Society,* Edinburgh University Press, Edinburgh, 1966, p. 82.

27. Ibid., pp. 218, 225.

28. Ibid., p. 230.

29. See my "Hume's Political Methodology: A Reconsideration of 'That Politics May be Reduced to a Science,'" *The Review of Politics,* Vol. 38, No. 1 (January 1976), pp. 88–108 and "Hume on Political Parties: the Case for Hume as a Whig," *Eighteenth Century Studies,* Vol. 12, No. 2 (winter 1978–79), pp. 150–173.

30. David Hume, *The History of England,* Little, Brown and Company, Boston, 1854, Vol. V, p. 275. David Fate Norton and Richard H. Popkin, (eds.), *David Hume: Philosophical Historian,* The Bobbs-Merrill Co., Inc., New York, 1965, offers both good introductory essays and a representative selection of Hume's writings on history. Two good discussions of Hume's pol-

itics are Duncan Forbes, *Hume's Philosophical Politics,* Cambridge University Press, New York, 1975, p. 260 ff. and David Miller, *Philosophy and Ideology in Hume's Political Thought,* Clarendon Press, Oxford, 1981.

31. Hume, *History,* Vol. I, p. 13.

32. Ibid., p. 179.

33. Ibid., pp. 183–184.

34. Ibid., p. 488.

35. Ibid., p. 180.

36. J. Y. T. Greig, (ed.), *The Letters of David Hume,* The Clarendon Press, Oxford, 1932, Vol. I, To James Oswald, June/28/1753, p. 179.

37. Hume, *History,* Vol. VI, pp. 258–259.

38. Ibid., Vol. V, p. 69.

39. Burke, "Abridgement of English History." The "Essay" was begun in 1763 but left unfinished. One explanation was that Burke discontinued the work when Hume's *History* began to be published. See Burke, *Correspondence,* Vol. I, notes on pages 124 and 164.

40. Burke, "Abridgement of English History," p. 159 ff.

41. Ibid., p. 166.

42. Ibid., p. 306.

43. For Burke on the ancient constitution, see J. G. A. Pocock, "Burke and the Ancient Constitution," in *Politics, Language and Time,* p. 208 ff. However, Pocock's argument should be compared to Burke, *Reflections on the Revolution in France,* p. 35 ff., and Burke's "Essay Towards an History of the Laws of England" which ends the "Abridgement," p. 475 ff, esp. p. 478.

44. To describe Burke's view of history as Whig Progressivism is not to say that his is a history of progress. In fact, Burke was not particularly interested in the concept of progress as such. For the eighteenth century view of progress, see David Spadafora, *The Idea of Progress in Eighteenth Century Britain,* Yale University Press, New Haven, 1990. Spadafora builds on an enormous body of scholarship. The central work is still J. B. Bury, *The Idea of Progress,* The Macmillan Company, New York, 1932. Other works of general interest are Morris Ginsberg, *The Idea of Progress: A Revaluation,* Beacon Press, Boston, 1953, Sidney Pollard, *The Ideas of Progress: History and Society,* Basic Books, New York, 1968, and the disappointing Robert Nisbet, *History of the Idea of Progress,* Basic Books, New York, 1980. More directly concerned with the eighteenth century and after are Charles Frankel, *The Faith of Reason: the Idea of Progress in the French Enlight-*

enment, King's Crown Press, New York, 1948, R. V. Sampson, *Progress in the Age of Reason: The Seventeenth Century to the Present Day,* Harvard University Press, Cambridge, Mass., 1956, and Peter Gay, *The Enlightenment: An Interpretation,* II Volumes, Alfred A. Knopf, New York, 1966–69. Bryson, Meek, and Lois Whitney, *Primitivism and the Idea of Progress in English Popular Literature of the Eighteenth Century,* Johns Hopkins Press, Baltimore, 1934, provide interesting discussions of the British and Scotch aspects of the debate. Bruce James Smith, *Politics and Remembrance,* Princeton University Press, Princeton, New Jersey, 1985, offers a radically different view of Burke's use of history from the one expressed here. Smith argues that Burke sought to cloak progress in a cloud of oblivion. It seems to me that this works well enough for the late works but fails to account for Burke's earlier, more reformist, works.

45. Whitney, *Primitivism,* p. 203.

46. Burke, *Correspondence,* Vol. VIII, To Edmond Malone, 5/April/1796, p. 455.

47. Edmund Burke, "Popery Tract," p. 336.

48. Edmund Burke, "Appeal From the New to the Old Whigs," pp. 162–165.

49. Edmund Burke, "Letter to William Elliot, Esq., Occasioned by a Speech Made in the House of Lords by the **** of ******, in the Debate Concerning Lord Fitzwilliam, 1795, *Works,* Vol. V, pp. 107–129, p. 124.

50. Burke, *Reflections on the Revolution in France,* p. 161.

51. Ibid., p. 110.

52. Burke, "Appeal From the New to the Old Whigs," p. 176.

53. Burke, *Reflections on the Revolution in France,* p. 186.

54. Meek, *Ignoble Savage,* esp. p. 169 ff.

55. Burke, *Reflections,* p. 90.

56. Ibid., p. 89.

57. See the "Abridgement of English History," p. 369 for Burke on the cynicism of the Crusades, p. 329 for his critique of the medieval Popes, and p. 409 for the attack on Becket.

58. Ibid., p. 239.

59. See, for example, Ibid., p. 244 ff.

60. Burke, *Reflections,* pp. 86–87.

61. Edmund Burke, "State of the Representation," p. 95.

62. Edmund Burke, "Three Letters Addressed to a Member of the Present Parliament on the Proposals for Peace with the Regicide Directory of France," *Works,* Vol. V, p. 319.

63. Ibid.

64. Burke, *Correspondence,* Vol. VI, To the Earl of Charlemont, 8/Aug./1791, p. 330. Burke, "Abridgement of English History," p. 264.

65. Burke, "Speech on a Bill for Shortening the Duration of Parliaments," *Works,* Vol. VII, pp. 69–88, p. 71.

66. Burke, "Abridgement of English History," p. 239.

67. Burke, *Correspondence,* Vol. IV, To James Boswell, 1/March/1779.

68. Burke's comment in a letter to Will Burke is typical of many: "The whole AEdifice of antient Europe is shaken by the Earthquake caused by that fire," *Correspondence,* Vol. VII, To William Burke, 3/September/1792, p. 191.

69. Burke, "Letter to the Sheriffs of Bristol," *Works,* Vol. II, p. 232.

70. Edmund Burke, "Speech on Presenting to the House of Commons A Plan for the Better Security of the Independence of Parliament, and the Economic Reformation of the Civil and Other Establishments," *Works,* Vol. II, p. 279; *Correspondence,* Vol. VI, To Unknown, 1791, pp. 479–80.

71. Burke, "Speech on . . . Economic Reformation . . . ," p. 95.

72. Burke, *Reflections,* p. 100.

73. Edmund Burke, "Fourth Letter on the Proposals for Peace with the Regicide Directory of France," *Works,* Vol. VI, pp. 1–112, p. 10.

74. Alfred Cobban, *Edmund Burke and the Revolt Against the Eighteenth Century,* p. 84.

75. Burke, *Correspondence,* Vol. V, To Sir Gilbert Elliot, Post 5/Aug./1784, pp. 166–167.

76. Burke, "Appeal From the New to the Old Whigs," *Passim.* Written in early to mid-1791 and published on August 3, the "Appeal" was Burke's response to the attacks of the Foxite Whigs, especially Fox's charge that Burke was inconsistent in opposing the French Revolution. It was the "Appeal," more than the *Reflections on the Revolution in France,* which split the Whig party.

77. Ibid., p. 68.

78. Ibid., p. 63.

79. Burke, *Correspondence,* Vol. VII, To William Weddell, 31/Jan./1792, pp. 52–53.

80. Ibid., Vol II, To Duke of Richmond, Post 15/ Nov./1772, p. 372.

81. Burke, "Observations," p. 271.

82. Burke, *Correspondence,* Vol. IX, To William Weddell, 31/ Jan./1797, p. 53.

83. Ibid., Vol. VI, To Lord Fitzwilliam, 5/June/1791, p. 274.

84. Ibid., To Lord Fitzwilliam, 21/Nov./1791, p. 450.

85. Burke, "Appeal From the Old to the New Whigs," p. 101.

86. Ibid., p. 110.

87. Ibid., p. 111.

88. Burke, *Correspondence,* Vol. IX, To William Weddell, 31/ Jan./1797, p. 56.

89. Edmund Burke, "Observations on the Conduct of the Minority, Particularly in the last Session of Parliament, 1793, *Works,* Vol. V, pp. 1–63, p. 7.

90. Burke, *Correrspondence,* Vol. VI, To Lord Fitzwilliam, 5/ June/1791, p. 273.

91. Burke, "Appeal From the New to the Old Whigs," p. 161 ff.

92. Ibid., p. 206.

93. Ibid., p. 91.

94. Ibid., p. 81.

95. Ibid., pp. 79–80.

96. Burke, *Reflections on the Revolution in France,* pp. 19–20.

97. Ibid., p. 21.

98. Ibid., p. 24.

99. Ibid., p. 36.

100. Ibid., p. 34.

101. Burke, "An Appeal From the New to the Old Whigs," p. 119 ff.

102. Ibid., pp. 133–135 ff.

103. Ibid., p. 133.

104. Burke, "An Appeal From the New to the Old Whigs," pp. 129–130.

105. Ibid., p. 119.

106. Ibid., p. 135.

107. J. H. Plumb, *Sir Robert Walpole,* II Vol., The Penguin Press, London, 1972, Vol. II, p. 280.

108. Burke, "An Appeal From the New to the Old Whigs," p. 118.

109. See Burke, "Thoughts on the Cause of the Present Discontents," *Works,* Vol. I, pp. 433–537 and "Observations on a Late Publication Entitled 'The Present State of the Nation,' " *Works,* Vol. I, pp. 269–432.

110. Burke, "Thoughts on the Cause of the Present Discontents," p. 447.

111. Ibid., pp. 531–32. For Burke's defense of the Rockingham Whigs, see "Observations on a Late Publication Entitled 'The Present State of the Nation,' " p. 379 ff.

112. Burke, "Popery Tract," p. 318 ff.

113. Burke, *Correspondence,* Vol. IX, To the Rev. Thomas Hussey, Post 9/Dec./1796, p. 171.

114. Edmund Burke, "Address to the King,' *Works,* Vol. VI, pp. 161–182, p. 178.

115. Edmund Burke, "Letter to Sir Hercules Langrishe on the Subject of the Roman Catholics of Ireland, *Works,* Vol. IV, pp. 241–306, p. 272.

116. J. P. Kenyon, *Revolution Principles,* Cambridge University Press, London, 1977, p. 10 ff.

117. Ibid., p. 45. See also H. T. Dickinson, *Liberty and Property,* Weidenfeld and Nicolson, London, 1977, pp. 57 ff.

118. See Kenyon, *Revolution Principles,* p. 19.

119. See Sidney, *Discourses on Government,* Vol. I, p. 325 and Vol. II, pp. 434–5 for two of his clearer endorsements of a right of revolution. There are, according to Sidney, things far worse that Civil War: "it is worse, to bring nations to such misery, weakness, and baseness, as to have neither strength nor courage to contend for any thing; to have left nothing worth defending, and to give the name of peace to desolation." Vol. II, p. 300.

120. William Atwood, *The Fundamental Constitution of the English Government,* Scholarly Resources, Inc., Wilmington, Del., 1973, p. 73.

121. Ibid., p. 74 ff.

122. Ibid., p. 85 ff. For Atwood's criticism of Locke, see pp. 100–101.

123. See J. R. Jones, *The First Whigs,* Oxford University Press, New York, 1966. See also, J. G. A. Pocock, "The Varieties of Whiggism from Exclusion to Reform: A History of Ideology and Discourse," in *Virtue, Commerce, and History,* pp. 215–310.

124. Jones, *First Whigs,* pp. 2–3.

125. For the *Second Treatise* as an Exclusion Tract, see Ashcraft, *Revolutionary Politics and Locke's "Two Treatises of Government",* p. 181 ff. The point has become commonplace since reasserted by Laslett in the Introduction to his edition of the *Two Treatises.* See p. 45 ff.

126. Lois G. Schwoerer, *The Declaration of Rights,* 1689, The Johns Hopkins University Press, Baltimore, 1981. See especially, p. 281 ff.

127. Burke, "An Appeal From the New to the Old Whigs," p. 128.

128. Ross J. S. Hoffman, *The Marquis A Study of Lord Rockingham 1730–1782,* Fordham University Press, New York, 1973, p. 31.

129. See, for example, G. H. Guttridge, *English Whiggism and the American Revolution,* University of California Press, Los Angeles, 1966, passim.

130. See Paul Langford, *The First Rockingham Administration 1765–1766,* Oxford University Press, New York, 1973.

131. Ibid., p. 12.

132. Burke, *Correspondence,* Vol. I, to John O'Hara, 4/July/1765, p. 208.

133. For Burke's sincerity, see *Correspondence,* Vol. II, To Lord Rockingham, 6/Nov./1769, pp. 105 and 108. Much has been said on the error of Burke's assessment. Perhaps Ian Christie says it best, see *Myth and Reality in Late Eighteenth Century British Politics,* pp. 27–54. Also see O'Gorman, *Rise of Party,* p. 258 ff. Guttridge, *The English Whigs and the American Revolution,* p. 41 ff, however, offers a much more sympathetic interpretation.

Chapter Four

1. Edmund Burke, "Speech on a Motion for a Committee to Inquire into the State of the Representation of the Commons in Parliament," *Works,* Vol. VII, pp. 89–204, p. 94.

2. Ibid., p. 94.

3. Edmund Burke, *Reflections on the Revolution in France,* The Bobbs-Merrill Company, Inc., New York, 1955, p. 201.

4. Edmund Burke, "An Appeal From the New to the Old Whigs," p. 209. See especially, p. 206 ff.

5. Edmund Burke, "Thoughts on French Affairs," *Works,* Vol. IV, pp. 313–377, p. 349.

6. Burke, *Correspondence,* Vol. IV, To Richard Shackleton, 25/May/1779, p. 79.

7. John Morley, *Edmund Burke,* p. 48.

8. Burke, *Correspondence,* Vol. VI, To Adrien-Jean-Francois DuPont, Post 20/March/1790, p. 108.

9. Edmund Burke, "Letter to the Sheriffs of Bristol, On the Affairs of America," p. 224.

10. Burke, "Regicide Peace," p. 372.

11. Burke, *Correspondence,* Vol. IX, To William Windham, 30/March/1797, p. 301.

12. Burke, "An Appeal From the New to the Old Whigs," p. 94.

13. Burke, *Correspondence,* Vol. VI, To Charles-Jean-Francois Depont, Nov./1789, p. 42.

14. Ibid., pp. 45–46.

15. See Burke, *Correspondence,* Vol. IV, To Lord Loughborough, 13/June/1780, p. 248. Also see *Correspondence,* Vol. IV, To Sir Greg Cooper, 18/July/1780, p. 257.

16. Burke, *Correspondence,* Vol. IX, To French Laurence, 13/Dec./1796, p. 173.

17. Burke, "Regicide Peace," p. 288. See also, p. 286 ff.

18. Burke, *Correspondence,* Vol. IX, To Rev. Thomas Hussey, Post 9/Dec./1796, p. 169.

19. Ibid., p. 169.

20. Burke, "An Appeal From the New to the Old Whigs," p. 165.

21. Ibid., pp. 166–167.

22. Edmund Burke, "Remarks on the Policy of the Allies with Respect to France," *Works,* Vol. IV, pp. 403–482, p. 413.

23. Burke, *Correspondence,* Vol. VI, To Lord Fitzwilliam, 5/June/1791, p. 272.

24. Edmund Burke, "An Appeal From the New to the Old Whigs," p. 165.

25. Edmund Burke, *Reflections on the Revolution in France,* pp. 16–17.

26. Edmund Burke, "Fragments of a Tract Relative to the Laws Against Popery in Ireland," p. 320.

27. For Hume, see David Hume, "Of the Original Contract," in *Essays,* p. 443 ff.

28. Burke, *Reflections on the Revolution in France,* p. 201.

29. Burke, "Appeal From the New to the Old Whigs," p. 169.

30. Ibid., p. 81.

31. Burke, *Reflections on the Revolution in France,* p. 30 ff.

32. Burke, "An Appeal From the New to the Old Whigs," p. 170.

33. Burke, *Reflections on the Revolution in France,* p. 24.

34. Ibid., p. 20.

35. Burke, "An Appeal From the New to the Old Whigs," p. 169.

36. See, for example, Richard Pares, *King George III and the Politicians,* Oxford University Press, Oxford, 1970, p. 31 ff. For an interesting account of some of the intellectual difficulties caused by the ideal of a three-way balance, see J. A. W. Gunn, "The Fourth Estate: the Language of Political Innovation," in *Beyond Liberty and Property,* McGill-Queen's University Press, Montreal, 1983, pp. 43–95.

37. Burke, "An Appeal From the New to the Old Whigs," p. 94.

38. Ibid., p. 109.

39. Ibid., p. 109–110

40. Burke, *Correspondence,* Vol. III, To Stewards of the Bell Club, 1/Nov/1777, p. 394.

41. Edmund Burke, "Letter to a Member of the National Assembly, in Answer to Some Objections to His Book on French Affairs," *Works,* Vol. IV, pp. 1–55, p. 50.

42. Burke, *Reflections on the Revolution in France,* p. 33.

43. Ibid.

44. Compare Burke, *Correspondence,* Vol. V, To William Windham, Circa 24/Jan./1789, p. 440 ff. and John W. Derry, *The Regency Crisis and the Whigs,* Cambridge University Press, New York, 1963, p. 138 ff. to the *Reflections.*

45. Edmund Burke, "Thoughts on the Causes of the Present Discontents," *Works,* Vol. I, pp. 433–537, p. 444.

46. Ibid., p. 469.

47. Burke, *Correspondence* Vol. IV, To Rockingham, 17/Oct./1779, p. 156.

48. Burke, *Correspondence,* Vol. II, To the Duke of Richmond, Post 15/ Nov./1772, p. 372 ff.

49. Burke, *Correspondence,* Vol. VII, To William Weddell, 31/Jan./1792, p. 52.

50. Too often, Burke's defense of the aristocracy is attributed to his reaction to the French Revolution. However, it is present throughout his career. The famous comparison of the nobility to the great oaks of the kingdom is, after all, to be found in a letter of 1772. For an interesting explanation of Burke's attitude toward the aristocrats, see C. B. Macpherson, *Burke,* pp. 5–6, 7–8, and passim. where it is attributed to a form of status anxiety. Isaac Kramnick, *The Rage of Edmund Burke,* sees the issue in even starker, albeit similar, terms. Frankly, I believe that a carefully nuanced reading of Burke shows that there is no glaring inconsistency in his attitude.

51. Burke, *Correspondence,* Vol. IX, To Lord Fitzwilliam, 2/Sept./1796, p. 77.

52. Burke, *Correspondence,* Vol. IV, To the Duke of Portland, 16/Oct./ 1779, p. 152.

53. Ibid., p. 159.

54. MacCunn, *The Political Philosophy of Burke,* p. 124.

55. Burke, *Correspondence,* Vol. VII, To William Weddell, 31/Jan./1792, p. 53.

56. Ibid., p. 53.

57. Edmund Burke, "Letter to Sir Hercules Langrishe on the Subject of the Roman Catholics of Ireland," p. 247.

58. Burke, "An Appeal From the New to the Old Whigs," pp. 174–175. The italics on "natural" are Burke's own.

59. Edmund Burke, "Speech on a Bill For the Repeal of the Marriage Act," *Works,* Vol. II, pp. 129–136, p. 133.

60. Burke, *Correspondence,* Vol. V, To William Windham, 14/Oct/1784, p. 177.

61. Burke, *Correspondence,* Vol. VIII, To Mrs. John Crewe, Circa 23/ March/1795, p. 216.

62. Burke, "Letter to a Noble Lord on the Attacks Made Upon Mr. Burke and His Pension, in the House of Lords, by the Duke of Bedford and the Earl of Lauderdale," *Works,* Vol. V, pp. 171–229. Usually treated as a

rather embarrassing splenetic excess, the letter actually is an impressive rhetorical exercise. The language is strong, but the argument is tightly controlled and devastating in effect.

63. Burke, *Correspondence,* Vol. II, To the Duke of Richmond, Post 15/Nov./1772, p. 372.

64. Burke, *Correspondence,* Vol. III, To Charles James Fox, 8/Oct./1777, p. 381. Also see the following letter to William Baker, pp. 388–389.

65. Burke, "Fourth Letter on a Regicide Peace," p. 99.

66. Burke, "Thought on the Causes of the Present Discontents," p. 491.

67. See Harvey C. Mansfield, Jr., *Statesmanship and Party Government,* University of Chicago Press, Chicago, 1965, p. 138 ff. Mansfield sees Burke as attempting to undercut Bolingbroke's emphasis on statesmanship by substituting party discipline for the wisdom of the statesman. While he has much to say of value on Burke on party, in my view, his argument is weakened substantially by the claim that Burke saw practical legislative politics as a means of enacting some objective political truth. For my view, see chapter 6.

68. Burke, *Correspondence,* Vol. 5, To William Lee, 6/May/1784, p. 143.

69. Burke, "Thoughts on the Causes of the Present Discontents," p. 492.

70. Edmund Burke, "Speech on Arrival at Bristol," *Works,* Vol. II, p. 96.

71. Ibid., p. 96

72. Burke, *Correspondence,* Vol. III, To Richard Champion, 26/June/1777, p. 356.

73. Burke, "Thoughts on the Causes of the Present Discontents," p. 495.

74. Edmund Burke, "Speech on a Bill for Shortening the Duration of Parliament," p. 77.

75. Burke, "Thoughts on the Causes of the Present Discontents," p. 505.

76. Ibid., p. 447.

77. Edmund Burke, "Speech on a Motion for Leave to Bring in a Bill to Repeal and Alter Certain Acts Respecting Religious Opinions, upon the Occasion of a Petition of the Unitarian Society," *Works,* Vol. VII, pp. 39–58, p. 43.

78. Burke, *Reflections on the Revolution in France,* p. 173.

79. J. C. D. Clark, *English Society 1688–1832,* Cambridge University Press, New York, 1985, p. 216 ff.

80. See Ibid., p. 246 ff.

81. Ibid., p. 249.

82. For Warburton, see John Martin Creed and John Sandwith Boys Smith, (ed.), *Religious Thought in the Eighteenth Century,* Cambridge University Press, Cambridge, 1934, pp. 268–275, and Norman Sykes, *Church and State in England in the XVIIIth Century,* Archon Books, Hamden, Connecticut, 1962, p. 318 ff.

83. Creed and Boys Smith, *Religious Thought,* p. 271.

84. Ibid., p. 273.

85. Ibid., p. 275.

86. On Tindel, see Gerald R. Cragg, *Reason and Authority in the Eighteenth Century,* Cambridge University Press, Cambridge, 1964, p. 186 ff. Stephen, *History of English Thought,* Vol. II, p. 105 ff., is an interesting account of Paley. Margaret Canovan, "The Un-Benthamite Utilitarianism of Joseph Priestley," *Journal of the History of Ideas,* July–September, Vol. XLV, No. 3, pp. 435–450, is both a useful summary of Priestley and a demonstration of the fundamental consistency of his ideas.

87. Creed and Boys Smith, *Religious Thought,* p. 276.

88. See Stephen, *History of English Thought,* Vol. II, p. 410 ff.

89. Quoted in Cragg, *Reason and Authority,* p. 215. On the Test Act, see Creed and Boys Smith, *Religious Thought,* p. 282 ff.

90. See Cragg, *Reason and Authority,* p. 187 ff, and Sykes, *Church and State,* p. 305 ff.

91. For Middleton, see Stephen, *History of English Thought,* Vol. I, p. 253 ff.

92. Ibid., p. 269.

93. Edmund Burke, "Fragment of a Tract Relative to the Laws Against Popery in Ireland."

94. Ibid., p. 318.

95. Ibid., p. 321.

96. Ibid., p. 325.

97. Ibid., p. 337.

98. Ibid., p. 334.

99. Burke, *Correspondence,* Vol. VIII, To William Smith, 29/Jan./1795, p. 131.

100. Burke, *Correspondence,* Vol. IV, To John Erskine, 12/June/1779, p. 85.

101. Edmund Burke, "An Appeal from the New to the Old Whigs," p. 162.

102. Ibid., p. 163.

103. Ibid., p. 170 ff.

104. Burke, *Reflections on the Revolution in France,* see esp. pp. 104–117.

105. Ibid., p. 112.

106. Ibid., p. 108.

107. Ibid., p. 107.

108. Ibid., p. 115.

109. Ibid., p. 186.

110. Edmund Burke, "Speech on the Acts of Uniformity," *Works,* Vo. VII, pp. 3–19.

111. Burke, "Popery Tract," p. 336.

112. Burke, *Correspondence,* Vol. IV, To James Boswell, 1/March/1779, pp. 45–46.

113. Burke, *Correspondence,* Vol. IV, To Dr. John Erskine, 12/June/1779, p. 85.

114. Burke, *Correspondence,* Vol. III, To William Burgh, 9/Feb./1775, p. 110.

115. Burke, *Correspondence,* Vol. IV, To Dr. John Erskine, 12/June/1779, p. 85.

116. Burke, "Popery Tract," p. 336.

117. Burke, *Correspondence,* Vol. IX, To Unknown, ?/Feb./1797, p. 260.

118. Edmund Burke, "Letter to Langrishe," *Works,* Vol. IV, p. 246.

119. Edmund Burke, "Speech at Bristol on Declining the Poll," *Works,* Vol. II, p. 416.

120. Burke, *Correspondence,* Vol. IV, To Dr. John Erskine, 12/June/1779, p. 84.

121. Burke, "Letter to Langrishe," p. 293.

122. Edmund Burke, "Speech on a Bill for the Relief of Protestant Dissenters," *Works,* Vol. II, pp. 21–38, p. 35.

123. Ibid., p. 30.

124. Burke, *Correspondence,* Vol. IV, To Dr. John Curry, 14/Aug./1779, p. 118.

125. Burke, *Correspondence,* Vol. VIII, To Henry Grattan, 20/March/1795, p. 207.

126. Burke, *Correspondence,* Vol. IX, to Unknown, ?/Feb./1797, p. 257.

127. Burke, "Speech at Bristol on Declining the Poll," p. 404.

128. See, for example, the "Letter to Langrishe," p. 241 ff.

129. Burke, *Correspondence,* Vol. VIII, To William Smith, 29/Jan./1795, p. 133.

130. Burke, *Correspondence,* Vol. VII, To Richard Burke, Jr., Post 21/Nov./1792, p. 300.

131. Ibid., p. 299.

132. Burke, *Correspondence,* Vol. VIII, To the Rev. Thomas Hussey, 4/Feb./1795, p. 138.

133. Burke, "Speech on a Bill for the Relief of Protestant Dissenters," p. 25.

134. Ibid., p. 26.

135. Ibid., p. 24.

136. Burke, *Correspondence,* Vol. VI, To Henry Dundas, 30/Sept./1791, pp. 419–420.

137. Burke, *Correspondence,* Vol. VII, To William Weddell, 31/Jan./1792, p. 57.

138. Burke, "Speech . . . Unitarian Society," pp. 39–58.

139. Ibid., p. 44.

140. Ibid., pp. 47–48.

141. Ibid., p. 54.

Chapter Five

1. See, for example, John Gunn's description of the difficulties involved in the acceptance of conceptions of political innovation which did not

fit the traditional scheme in "The Fourth Estate: the Language of Political Innovation," in *Beyond Liberty and Property,* McGill-Queen's University Press, Montreal, pp. 43–95.

2. Lewis Namier, *The Structure of Politics at the Accession of George III,* Macmillian and Company, New York, 1928.

3. Ian R. Christie, *Wars and Revolutions Britain, 1760–1815,* Harvard University Press, Cambridge, 1982, p. 23.

4. Alfred Cobban, *Edmund Burke and the Revolt Against the Eighteenth Century,* Barnes and Noble, New York, 1960, for example, was able to interpret Burke as a precursor of the Romantics without noting their extensive disagreement on political issues and social policy.

5. On Burke as a laissez-faire economist, see Donal Patrick Michael Barrington, "Edmund Burke as an Economist," *Economica,* New Series, 21 (1954), pp. 252–58 and Frank Petrella, Jr., "Edmund Burke: A Liberal Practitioner of Political Economy," *Modern Age* 8, (1963–1964), pp. 52–60. The Burke-Smith relationship is explored in W. L. Dunne's, "Adam Smith and Burke: Complementary Contemporaries," *Southern Economic Journal,* VII, 1941, pp. 330–346 and C. R. Fay, *The World of Adam Smith,* Cambridge University Press, Cambridge, 1950, esp. Chapter I. The case for Adam Smith as a laissez-faire thinker may be found in Jacob Vinter, "Adam Smith and *Laissez-Faire,*" in *The Long View and the Short: Studies in Economic Theory and Policy,* Glencoe, Illinois, 1958, Andrew Skinner, *Adam Smith and the Role of the State,* Glasgow, 1974, Fredrich Hayek, *Individualism and Economic Order,* London, 1948, and Joseph Cropsey, *Political Economy: An Interpretation of the Principles of Adam Smith,* The Hague, 1957.

6. Peter J. Stanlis, *Edmund Burke and the Natural Law,* University of Michigan Press, Ann Arbor, 1958.

7. Clara I. Gandy and Peter J. Stanlis, *Edmund Burke A Bibliography of Secondary Studies to 1982,* Garland Publishing, Inc., New York, 1983, p. 213.

8. Gertrude Himmelfarb, *The Idea of Poverty,* Alfred A. Knopf, New York, 1984, pp. 66–73.

9. Ibid., p. 43.

10. Ibid., p. 66 ff.

11. C. B. Macpherson, *Burke.*

12. Ibid., p. 50.

13. Ibid., p. 62.

14. See, especially, Isaac Kramnick, "The Left and Edmund Burke," *Political Theory,* Vol. 11, No. 2, (May 1983), pp. 189–214. Interestingly, Kram-

nick notes Woodrow Wilson's praise of Burke: "for Wilson, Burke was the embodiment of racial wisdom, the instinctive commonsense and practical soul of the Anglo-Saxon," p. 197. That Burke was not Anglo-Saxon does not seem to bother either Wilson or Kramnick.

15. J. G. A. Pocock, "Burke's Analysis of the French Revolution," in *Virtue, Commerce, and History,* Cambridge University Press, New York, 1985, pp. 193–212.

16. Edmund Burke, *Correspondence,* Vol. II, To Adam Smith, 10/Sept./1759, pp. 129–130.

17. Edmund Burke, "Letter to a Noble Lord," *Works,* Vol. V, p. 174 ff.

18. Ibid., p. 189.

19. Donald Winch, *Adam Smith's Politics,* Cambridge University Press, New York, 1978, p. 36 ff. Also see, T. D. Campbell, *Adam Smith's Science of Morals,* Rowman and Littlefield, Totowa, New Jersey, 1971, p. 205 ff.

20. See, for example, Gladys Bryson, *Man and Society: The Scottish Inquiry of the 18th Century.*

21. On the consistency of Smith's thought, see Winch, p. 31 ff. and Campbell, p. 16 ff. Both writers devote considerable effort—successfully in my view—to demonstrating the unity of perspective between *The Theory of Moral Sentiments* and the *Wealth of Nations.*

22. Campbell, *Adam Smith's Science of Morals,* p. 205.

23. Campbell, *Adam Smith's Science of Morals,* p. 214.

24. Winch, *Adam Smith's Politics,* p. 172.

25. Adam Smith, *An Inquiry into the Nature and Causes of the Wealth of Nations,* Random House, Inc., New York, 1937, p. 653 ff.

26. Ibid., p. 716 ff.

27. Ibid., p. 769 ff.

28. Ibid., p. 859 ff.

29. Burke, *Correspondence,* VI, To Charles-Jean-Francois DePont, Nov./1789, p. 46.

30. Edmund Burke, "An Appeal from the New to the Old Whigs," p. 81.

31. Burke, *Correspondence,* Vol. III, To Charles O'Hara, 26/July/1775, p. 182.

32. Smith, *Wealth of Nations.*, pp. 397–626.

33. Ibid., p. 420 ff.

34. Ibid., p. 493.

35. Ibid., p. 423.

36. Burke, Correspondence, Vol III, To Samuel Span, 9?/April/1778, p. 426.

37. Edmund Burke, "Letter to Society of Merchant Adventurers of Bristol," *Works,* Vol. II, pp. 249–258, p. 252.

38. Edmund Burke, "Speech to the Electors at Bristol," *Works,* Vol. II, p. 377.

39. Edmund Burke, "Letter to the Sheriffs of Bristol, On the Affairs of America," *Works,* Vol. II, p. 222.

40. Adam Smith, *Wealth of Nations,* p. 626.

41. See Ibid., Book IV, Chapter 7, pp. 523–606.

42. Ibid., p. 557 ff.

43. Ibid., p. 431.

44. Ibid., p. 896 ff.

45. Ibid., p. 900.

46. Edmund Burke, "Observations on a Late Publication Entitled 'The Present State of the Nation,' " *Works,* Vol. I, pp. 269–432, p. 394.

47. Edmund Burke, "Speech on American Taxation," *Works,* Vol. II, p. 30.

48. Ibid., p. 34.

49. Burke, "Observations . . . Nation," pp. 394–395.

50. Edmund Burke, "Thoughts and Details on Scarcity," *Works,* Vol. V, pp. 131–169.

51. Macpherson, *Burke,* p. 52 ff.

52. Ibid., p. 53.

53. Ibid.

54. Burke, *Correspondence,* Vol. VIII, To William Pitt, 7/Nov./1795, p. 337.

55. Ibid.

56. Burke, "Thoughts and Details on Scarcity," especially pp. 134–137 and 141–142.

57. Ibid., pp. 135–136.

58. Ibid., p. 134.

59. Ibid., p. 137.

60. Ibid., p. 142.

61. Ibid., p. 154.

62. Ibid., p. 157.

63. Ibid., p. 142.

64. Ibid., p. 135.

65. Ibid., p. 146.

66. Ibid.

67. Ibid., p. 166.

68. Burke, *Correspondence,* Vol. VIII, To William Windham, 9/June/1795, p. 265.

69. See Burke, *Correspondence,* Vol. IX, To William Windham 17/Nov./1795, p. 341 ff. and To Henry Dundas, 6/Dec./1795, p. 353 ff.

70. Burke, "Thoughts and Details on Scarcity," p. 164.

71. Burke, *Correspondence,* Vol. III, To John Ridge, 23/April/1763, p. 169.

72. John Townsend, *A Dissertation on the Poor Laws,* University of California Press, Los Angeles, 1971, p. 19 ff.

73. Smith, *Wealth of Nations,* p. 135 ff.

74. Ibid., p. 413.

75. Townsend, *Dissertation,* p. 24.

76. Ibid., p. 27.

77. Ibid., p. 40.

78. Smith, *Wealth of Nations,* p. 79.

79. Ibid., p. 66 and p. 87 ff.

80. Isaac Kramnick, *The Rage of Edmund Burke,* p. 161.

81. Ibid.

82. Macpherson, *Burke,* p. 29.

83. Edmund Burke, "Speech on Presenting to the House of Commons a Plan for the Better Security of the Independence of Parliament and the Economic Reformation of the Civic and Other Establishments," *Works,* Vol. II, pp. 265–364.

84. Burke, *Correspondence,* Vol. IV, To Joseph Harford, 4/April/1780, pp. 219–220.

85. Burke, "Letter to a Noble Lord . . . Pension," p. 195.

86. Ibid.

87. Burke, "Economic Reformation," pp. 286–287. If one examines Burke's seven rules of procedure, one finds extensive discussion of the importance of order and system and very little of cost-cutting.

88. Ibid., p. 334.

89. Ibid., p. 335.

90. Ibid., p. 291.

91. Ibid., p. 298.

92. Ibid., p. 310.

93. Ibid., p. 311.

94. Ibid., p. 351.

95. Edmund Burke, *An Account of the English Settlements in America,* Vol. I, pp. 167–168.

96. Ibid., Vol. II, p. 128.

97. Ibid., pp. 128–129.

98. Ibid., pp. 130–131.

99. Ibid., p. 131.

100. Edmund Burke, "Sketch of a Negro Code," *Works,* Vol. VI, pp. 262–289.

101. Ibid., p. 262.

102. Ibid., p. 263 ff.

103. Ibid., p. 265 ff.

104. Ibid., p. 273 ff.

105. Ibid., p. 275 ff.

106. Burke, *Correspondence,* Vol. VII, To Henry Dundas, 9/April/1792, p. 122.

107. Ibid., p. 123.

108. Ibid., p. 124.

109. Ibid.

110. Burkc, *Correspondence,* Vol. VIII, To William Windom, 28/March/1796, p. 451.

111. See the editorial note following the letter to Dundas, *Correspondence,* Vol VII, p. 125.

112. Burke, *Correspondence,* Vol. VII, To Henry Dundas, 9/April/1792, p. 125.

Chapter Six

1. Hanna Pitkin, *The Concept of Representation,* University of California Press, Los Angeles, 1967, p. 1.

2. Ibid., p. 168. For such an important point, Pitkin's documentation for the view that Burke believed in objective interest is quite scanty. Her argument seems to rest on such secondary sources as Samuel H. Beer, "The Representation of Interests in British Government: Historical Background," *American Political Science Review,* LI, Sept., 1957, pp. 613–650, and Ernest Barker, *Essays on Government,* Oxford University Press, 1956, p. 154 ff. For Burke's rejection of objective interest, see "An Appeal From the New to the Old Whigs," p. 208. The argument is repeated at a number of other points in Burke's writings.

3. Pitkin, *The Concept of Representation,* p. 174

4. Ibid., p. 171.

5. Ibid., p. 173.

6. Ibid., p. 180.

7. Burke, "Thoughts on the Cause of the Present Discontents," *Works,* Vol. I, p. 454. My argument here refers to the concept of "general interest," and not the related, though different, point of whether Burke believed that districts have single unitary interests. As for the latter point, it seems clear to me that he did not. In fact, he gloried in the diversity of England. Significantly, Pitkin cites Beer, not Burke himself. See *Concept of Representation,* p. 174.

8. Burke, "Thoughts on the Cause of the Present Discontents," p. 532.

9. Burke, "An Appeal From the New to the Old Whigs," p. 206.

10. Ibid., p. 206.

11. Burke, *Reflections on the Revolution in France,* Bobbs-Merrill, Co., Inc., New York, 1955, p. 40.

12. As Pitkin recognizes, pp. 180–182. Her reconciliation of freedom for the representative and ultimate popular control is unconvincing, however,

for it turns Burke into an optimistic believer in the eventual victory of truth over falsehood.

13. See Frank O'Gorman, *Edmund Burke His Political Philosophy,* and John MacCunn *The Political Philosophy of Edmund Burke.* Two of the best discussions of Burke on representation are Harvey Mansfield, Jr., *Statesmanship and Party Government,* p. 154 ff. and Gerald Chapman, *Edmund Burke The Practical Imagination,* Harvard University Press, Cambridge, 1967, p. 136 ff.

14. O'Gorman, *Edmund Burke His Political Philosophy,* p. 61.

15. MacCunn, *The Political Philosophy of Burke,* pp. 165–166.

16. Chapman, *Edmund Burke The Practical Imagination,* p. 164.

17. Edmund Burke, "Speeches on Arrival at Bristol and at the Conclusion of the Poll," *Works,* Vol. II, pp. 81–98, p. 95. For details of the story of Burke's relationship with Bristol, see Ernest Barker, "Burke and His Bristol Constituency," *Essays on Government,* pp. 154–204, p. 177, and Peter Thomas Underdown, *Bristol and Burke,* Bristol Historical Association, Bristol, 1961.

18. Burke, "Speeches on Arrival at Bristol and at the Conclusion of the Poll," pp. 95–96.

19. Edmund Burke, "Speech to the Electors at Bristol," *Works,* Vol. II, pp. 365–424, p. 373. The speech was delivered on Sept. 6, 1780.

20. Ibid., p. 385 ff.

21. Ibid., p. 381. The specter of America hangs over the Bristol speech. It seems clear that Burke's relatively progressive stands on the issues of Irish Trade and Catholic Emancipation were due in part to his belief that a hard-line approach had served only to provoke rebellion in America and might do so elsewhere as well.

22. Ibid., p. 390 ff.

23. Ibid.

24. Burke, "Speech to the Electors at Bristol," p. 370.

25. Ibid., p. 380.

26. Ibid., p. 371.

27. Edmund Burke, "Speech at Bristol on Declining the Poll," *Works,* Vol. II, pp. 425–429, There were a total of four speeches at Bristol. The first was delivered on Oct. 13, 1774, as part of Burke's successful campaign for election, and the second, on Nov. 3, was his victory statement. The second set of two accompanied his reelection campaign six years later. After arriving at Bristol and making the third speech on Sept. 6, Burke began to cam-

paign; however, it soon became obvious that he had alienated too many voters and could not win. Therefore, he conceded defeat in the fourth speech on Sept. 9, 1780.

28. Burke, "Speech to the Electors at Bristol," p. 421. This is the third, and most famous, speech.

29. Burke, 'Speeches on Arrival at Bristol and at the Conclusion of the Poll," p. 95.

30. See Lucy S. Sutherland, "Edmund Burke and the Relations between Members of Parliament and Their Constituents," *Studies in Burke and His Times,* 10 (1968), pp. 1005–1021.

31. Edmund Burke, "Two Letters to Gentlemen in the City of Bristol," *Works,* Vol. II, pp. 247–264, p. 257.

32. Burke, "Speeches on Arrival and at the Conclusion of the Polls," p. 95.

33. Burke, "An Appeal From the New to the Old Whigs," p. 164.

34. Burke, "Speech . . . Economical Reformation of the Civil and Other Establishments," *Works,* Vol. II, pp. 265–364, p. 357.

35. Burke, "Thoughts on the Cause of the Present Discontents," p. 521.

36. Burke, *Correspondence,* Vol. V, To William Baker, June/22/1784, p. 155.

37. Burke, Speech to the Electors at Bristol," p. 423.

38. Ibid., pp. 421–422.

39. Burke, *Correspondence,* Vol. III, To Richard Champion, 26/June/1777, p. 356.

40. Burke, "Thoughts on the Cause of the Present Discontents," p. 524.

41. Burke, *Correspondence,* Vol. III, To Stewards of the Bell Club, 1/Nov./1777, p. 397.

42. Burke, "Thoughts on the Cause of the Present Discontents," p. 495.

43. Burke, *Correspondence,* Vol. III, To Richard Champion, 26/June/1777, p. 356.

44. Burke, "A Representation to His Majesty," *Works.*, Vol. II, pp. 532–533.

45. Burke, *Reflections on the Revolution in France,* p. 68.

46. Ibid., p. 70. For one of Burke's infrequent citations of natural law outside of his writings on Indian politics, see "A Tract Relative to the Laws Against Popery in Ireland," *Works,* Vol. VI, pp. 299–360.

47. Burke, "Speech in Opening the Impeachment of Warren Hastings," *Works,* Vol. IX, p. 458–459.

48. Burke, "Speech on the Nabob of Arcot's Debts," *Works,* Vol. III, p. 109.

49. Burke, "Speech in Opening," *Works,* Vol. IX, p. 453.

50. Ibid., p. 476.

51. Ibid.

52. Ibid.

53. John Cannon, *The Fox-North Coalition.* Cambridge University Press, Cambridge, 1969, p. 110.

54. Lucy S. Sutherland, *The East India Company in 18th Century Politics,* Oxford University Press, Oxford. 1952, p. 265 ff. See also John Ehrman, *The Younger Pitt,* Vol. II, Constable and Co. Ltd., London, 1983, Vol. I, p. 120 ff.

55. Ibid., p. 120.

56. Burke, "Speech on Mr. Fox's East India Bill," *Works,* Vol. II, p. 519.

57. Ibid., p. 525.

58. Ibid., p. 526.

59. Ibid., p. 525.

60. Ibid., p. 441.

61. Ibid., p. 447.

62. Burke, "Speech in Opening," *Works,* Vol. IX, pp. 332–333.

63. Ibid., pp. 336–337.

64. See John Cannon, *The Fox-North Coalition,* Cambridge University Press, Cambridge, 1969, esp. p. 128 ff.

65. Ibid., p. 142.

66. Edmund Burke, "A Representation to His Majesty, Moved in the House of Commons, June 14, 1784," *Works,* Vol. II, pp. 537–576, p. 552.

67. Ibid., p. 551.

68. Ibid., pp. 552–553; see pp. 552–554 for Burke's view of the king's rights to appoint and dissolve.

69. Ibid., p. 554.

70. Ibid., p. 555 ff.

71. Burke, "Speech . . . Economical Reformation of the Civil and Other Establishments," p. 271.

72. Burke, *Correspondence,* Vol. IX, To Earl Fitzwilliam 2/Sept./1796, p. 77.

73. Burke, "An Appeal from the New to the Old Whigs," p. 116 ff. See especially, pp. 161–185.

74. Ibid., p. 163.

75. Burke, "An Appeal from the New to the Old Whigs," p. 162.

76. Ibid., p. 170.

77. Mansfield, *Statesmanship and Party Government,* p. 165 ff., especially p. 196.

78. See Burke, "Thoughts on the Cause of the Present Discontents," especially p. 525 ff. In the "Thoughts" and its companion work, the "Observations on . . . 'The Present State of the Nation,'" *Works,* Vol. I, pp. 269–432, Burke attacked on two fronts. He sought both to discredit the government and to downgrade Chatham as a leader of the opposition. The criticism of corruption was thus directed against the administration, and the praise of party was intended to prove the superiority of the Rockingham connection over Chatham.

79. See John R. Dinwiddy, "Burke and the Utilitarians: A Rejoinder," *Studies in Burke and His Times,* 19 (1978), pp. 119–126.

80. MacCunn, *The Political Philosophy of Burke,* p. 163.

81. Burke, "Observations on . . . 'The Present State of the Nation,'" pp. 370–371. A good discussion of Burke's argument linking the extension of the suffrage to greater royal power may be found in Frank O'Gorman, *Edmund Burke His Political Philosophy,* pp. 36–37. O'Gorman's general thesis is, however, subject to the same objection as Mansfield's: that it elevates Burke's stand on a single issue into a lifelong philosophy.

82. Martin Howard, Jr., "A Letter From a Gentleman at Halifax," in *Tracts of the American Revolution,* Merrill Jensen, (ed.), The Bobbs-Merrill Company, Inc., New York, 1967, pp. 63–78, For a good discussion of the general issue, see Gordon S. Wood, *Representation in the American Revolution,* Virginia University Press, Charlottesville, 1969.

83. Edmund Burke, "Letter to Sir Hercules Langrishe on the Subject of the Roman Catholics of Ireland," *Works,* Vol. IV, pp. 241–306, p. 293. Ironically, this passage, though so often quoted as a defense of virtual representation, actually is part of an argument rejecting the application of the theory of virtual representation to the case of the Irish Catholics.

84. Burke, "Thoughts on the Cause of the Present Discontents," p. 492.

85. John Dickinson, "Letters From a Farmer in Pennsylvania to the Inhabitants of the British Colonies, in *Tracts of the American Revolution,* pp. 154–155.

86. Burke, "Letter to Sir Hercules Langrishe on the Subject of the Roman Catholics of Ireland," p. 293.

87. See Burke, "Observations on . . . 'The Present State of the Nation,' " p. 372 ff.

88. Edmund Burke, "Speech on American Taxation," *Works,* Vol. II, pp. 1–80, p. 70.

89. Edmund Burke, "Letter to Sir Charles Bingham, Bart., on the Irish Absentee Tax," *Works,* Vol. VI, p. 127.

90. Ibid.

91. Edmund Burke, "Address to the King," *Works,* VoL. VI, p. 79.

Chapter Seven

1. H. T. Dickinson, *Bolingbroke,* Constable and Company Ltd., London, 1970, p. 261.

2. David Hume, "Of Parties in General," in *David Hume's Political Essays,* Charles W. Hendel, (ed.), The Liberal Arts Press, New York, p. 127.

3. Richard Pares, *King George III and the Politicians,* Oxford University Press, Oxford, p. 4.

4. See J. L. De Lolme, *The Constitution of England,* London, 1816.

5. Ross J. S. Hoffman, *The Marquis,* Fordham University Press, New York, 1973, p. 179.

6. Frank O'Gorman, *The Rise of Party in England,* George Allen & Unwin, London, 1975, pp. 28–29. In O'Gorman's view, the king was merely seeking to free himself from control by the politicians rather than attempting to become Bolingbroke's Patriot King.

7. G. H. Guttridge, *English Whiggism and the American Revolution,* passim.

8. Edmund Burke, *Correspondence,* Vol. IV, To Lord Rockingham, 17/Oct./1779, p. 156.

9. Edmund Burke, "Thoughts on the Cause of the Present Discontents," *Works,* Vol. I, pp. 433–537.

10. See Ian Christie, "Myth and Reality in 18th Century English Politics," in *Myth and Reality,* University of California Press, Los Angeles, 1970, pp. 27–54.

11. Burke, *Correspondence,* Vol. II, To Lord Rockingham, 6/Nov./1769, p. 105.

12. See *The Letters of Junius,* II Vol., Leavitt and Company, New York, 1851.

13. Richard Price, *Two Tracts on Liberty,* Da Capo Press, New York, 1972, p. 102.

14. Burke, *Correspondence,* Vol. II, to Lord Rockingham, 29/Dec./1770, pp. 175–176.

15. Hoffman, *The Marquis,* p. 37.

16. Burke, *Correspondence,* Vol. I, To Charles O'Hara, 4/July/1765, p. 208.

17. O'Gorman, *The Rise of Party in England,* p. 191.

18. Archibald Foord, *His Majesty's Opposition,* Oxford University Press, Oxford, 1964, p. 20.

19. Burke, "Thoughts on the Cause of the Present Discontents," p. 530.

20. Karl Lowenstein, *Political Power and the Governmental Process,* University of Chicago Press, Chicago, 1969, p. 75.

21. Burke, *Correspondence,* Vol. VI, to Lord Fitzwilliam, 21/Nov./1791, p. 450.

22. Burke, *Correspondence,* Vol. V, To General Burgoyne, 24/Dec./1782, p. 57.

23. Edmund Burke, "An Appeal From the New to the Old Whigs," p. 118 ff.

24. Ibid., p. 206.

25. Burke, "Speech on . . . the Economic Reformation of the Civil and Other Establishments," p. 271.

26. Burke's denial that he ever courted public opinion is at *Correspondence,* Vol. IX, To French Laurence, 7/March/1797, pp. 274–275. He did, however, make an exception of two cases. According to the editors of the *Correspondence,* these were probably the Wilkes affair and the petition movement of 1780. In the letter, pp. 274–5, Burke claimed to regret both those efforts.

27. Edmund Burke, "Observations on . . . 'State of the Nation,' " p. 419.

28. Ibid., p. 271.

29. Burke, *Correspondence,* Vol. II, To William Baker, 1/Oct./1771, p. 243.

30. See Mansfield, *Statesmanship and Party Government,* passim.

31. O'Gorman, *Edmund Burke His Political Philosophy,* p. 26 ff. Richard E. Willis, "Some Further Reflections on Burke's Discontents," *Studies in Burke and His Times,* No. 11 (1969–70), pp. 1417–1427, agrees with O'Gorman on the limitations of Burke's support for party.

32. Burke, "Thoughts on the Cause of the Present Discontents," p. 521.

33. Ibid., p. 528 ff.

34. Ibid., p. 530.

35. Ibid., p. 491 ff.

36. Ibid., p. 532.

37. Ibid., p. 526.

38. Edmund Burke, "Letter to the Sheriffs of Bristol, On the Affairs of America," p. 242.

39. Burke, "Thoughts on the Cause of the Present Discontents," p. 525.

40. Burke, "Observations on . . . 'State of the Nation,' " p. 425.

41. Burke, "Thoughts on the Cause of the Present Discontents," p. 442.

42. Ibid., p. 444.

43. Ibid., p. 461.

44. Burke, "Observations on . . . 'State of the Nation,' " pp. 370–371.

45. Burke, "Thoughts on the Cause of the Present Discontents," p. 503.

46. Ibid., p. 471. For an interesting discussion of the point, see Mansfield, *Statesmanship and Party Government,* p. 154 ff.

47. Burke, "Thoughts on the Cause of the Present Discontents," p. 523.

48. Ibid., p. 526.

49. Burke, "Observations on . . . 'State of the Nation,' " p. 388.

50. Guttridge, *English Whiggism and the American Revolution,* p. 14 ff.

51. Burke, *Correspondence,* Vol. I, To Charles O'Hara, 23/Dec./1766, p. 285. See Ross Hoffman, "Edmund Burke as a Practical Politician," In Peter

J. Stanlis, *The Relevance of Edmund Burke,* P. J. Kennedy, N.Y., 1964, pp. 109–130.

52. Burke, "Thoughts on the Cause of the Present Discontents," p. 532.

53. Burke, "Observations on . . . 'State of the Nation,' " p. 420.

54. Burke, "Letter to the Sheriffs of Bristol, On the Affairs of America," p. 241.

55. Burke, "Speech . . . Bristol," p. 421.

56. Burke, "Observations on . . . 'State of the Nation,' " p. 419.

57. Burke, *Correspondence,* Vol. VII, To Lord Fitzwilliam, 29/Nov./1792, p. 309.

58. Burke, *Correspondence,* Vol. IX, To French Laurence, 1/June/1797, pp. 364–366.

59. Burke, *Correspondence,* Vol. VIII, To William Windham, Post 21/Oct./1794, p. 62.

60. Burke, *Correspondence,* Vol. IX, To French Laurence, 23/Dec./1796, p. 196.

61. Pares, *King George III and the Politicians,* p. 112.

62. Burke, *Correspondence,* Vol. V, To Charles James Fox, 3/July/1782, p. 5.

63. Ibid., p. 5.

64. Burke, *Correspondence,* Vol. III, To Lord Rockingham, 5/Jan./1775, p. 88.

65. See Burke, "Letter to the Sheriffs of Bristol, On the Affairs of America," passim.

66. Burke, "Thoughts on the Cause of the Present Discontents," p. 495.

67. Burke, *Correspondence,* Vol. V, To Henry Dundas, 26/March/1787, p. 314.

68. Burke, "Letter to the Sheriffs of Bristol, On the Affairs of America," p. 200.

69. Hoffman, *The Marquis,* p. 339.

70. Burke, *Correspondence,* Vol. III, To Lord Rockingham, 6/Jan./1777, pp. 312–313.

71. Burke, *Correspondence,* Vol. IV, To the Duke of Portland, 3/Sept./1780, pp. 266–275.

72. Burke, *Correspondence,* Vol. V, To William Baker, 22/June/1784, p. 154.

73. Burke, *Correspondence,* Vol. V, To Sir Gilbert Elliot, 3/Sept./1788, pp. 413–415.

74. Donald E. Ginter, *Whig Organization in the General Election of 1790,* University of California Press, Los Angeles, 1967, p. xxvii.

75. Burke, "Thoughts on the Cause of the Present Discontents," p. 499. The standard work on parliamentary reform is still George Stead Veitch, *The Genesis of Parliamentary Reform,* Archon Books, Hamden, Connecticut, 1965. Among the works I have also found useful are Ian Christie, *Wilkes, Wyvill and Reform,* New York, 1962, E. C. Black, *The Association,* Harvard University Press, Cambridge, Mass., 1963, George Rude, *Wilkes and Liberty,* Clarendon Press, Oxford, 1962, E. P. Thompson, *The Making of the English Working Class,* Vintage Books, New York, 1966, and Albert Goodwin, *The Friends of Liberty,* Harvard University Press, Cambridge, Mass., 1979. For Burke's involvement, see N. C. Phillips, "Edmund Burke and the Country Movement, 1779–80," in Rosalind Mitchison (ed.), *Essays in 18th Century History,* Barnes and Noble, Inc., New York, 1966, pp. 301–325. Useful overviews may be found in Ian Christie, *Stress and Stability in Late Eighteenth Century Britain,* Oxford University Press, Oxford, 1984 and John Cannon, *Parliamentary Reform in England, 1640–1832,* Cambridge University Press, Cambridge, 1973.

76. Burke, "Thoughts on the Cause of the Present Discontents," p. 519.

77. Ibid.

78. Burke, "Observations on . . . 'The State of the Nation,'" pp. 370–371.

79. Ibid., p. 372 ff.

80. Burke, *Correspondence,* Vol. II, To Lord Rockingham, 30/July/1769, pp. 51–52.

81. See, for example, Edmund Burke, "Letter to Sir Hercules Langrishe on the Subject of the Roman Catholics of Ireland," p. 286.

82. Burke, *Correspondence,* Vol. II, To Lord Rockingham, 9/July/1769, pp. 43–46.

83. Rude, *Wilkes and Liberty,* p. 105 ff. On the role of the Whigs in the petitioning movement, also see O'Gorman, *The Rise of Party in England,* p. 242 ff., Hoffman, *The Marquis,* p. 225 ff., and Lucy S. Sutherland, "The City of London and the Opposition to Government, 1768–74," in John Stevenson, (Ed.), *London in the Age of Reform,* Basil Blackwell, Oxford, 1977, pp. 30–54. Sutherland further discusses Burke's role in "Edmund Burke and the First Rockingham Ministry."

84. See Ian Christie, *Myth and Reality,* especially p. 261 ff.

85. N. C. Phillips, "Edmund Burke and the Country Movement, 1779–80," p. 314.

86. Frank O'Gorman, *The Rise of Party in England,* London, 1975, p. 402.

87. See Ibid., p. 415 and Phillips, "Edmund Burke and the Country Movement," p. 319.

88. Veitch, *The Genesis of Parliamentary Reform,* p. 82.

89. Burke, *Correspondence,* Vol. IV, To Chairman of Burkinghamshire Meeting, 12/April/1780, pp. 226 and 228.

90. Ibid., p. 227.

91. Edmund Burke, "Speech on a Bill for Shortening the Duration of Parliaments," *Works,* Vol. VII, pp. 69–88, p. 77.

92. Edmund Burke, "Speech on a Motion for a Committee to Inquire into the State of the Representation of the Commons in Parliament," *Works,* Vol. VII, pp. 89–104, p. 101.

93. Burke, *Correspondence,* Vol. VI, To John Noble, 14/March/1790, p. 101.

94. Ibid., p. 102.

95. Ibid., p. 103.

96. See, for example, his letter to William Burke, *Correspondence,* Vol. VII, 3/Sept./1792, p. 192 ff.

97. Burke, *Correspondence,* Vol. IX, To French Laurence, 12/May/1795, p. 336.

98. Burke, *Correspondence,* Vol. VIII, To William Smith, 29/Jan./1795, p. 133.

99. Burke, "Letter to Sir Hercules Langrishe on the Subject of the Roman Catholics of Ireland," pp. 300–301.

100. Ibid., p. 291.

Chapter Eight

1. Oliver M. Dickerson, *The Navigation Acts and the American Revolution,* University of Pennsylvania Press, Philadelphia, 1951, p. 161.

2. P. D. G. Thomas, *British Politics and the Stamp Tax Crisis,* Oxford University Press, Oxford, 1975, p. 69.

3. Ibid., p. 20.

4. Ibid., p. 83.

5. Ibid., p. 139.

6. Ibid., p. 151.

7. Edmund Burke, *Correspondence,* Vol. III, To Richard Champion, 25/March/1776, p. 254. See Thomas, *British Politics and the Stamp Tax Crisis,* p. 184 for the view that the Declaratory Act was primarily a statement of principle and not intended for actual enforcement. Thomas holds, p. 249, that the Administration itself was most impressed by the impossibility of enforcing the Act without war. This is certainly consistent with Burke's argument as outlined to Dowdeswell, see note 10 below.

8. Burke, *Correspondence,* Vol. I, To Charles O'Hara, 31/Dec./1765, p. 229.

9. Ibid.

10. Burke, *Correspondence,* Vol. I, to William Dowdeswell, Circa 8/Jan./1767, p. 289.

11. Thomas, *British Politics and the Stamp Tax Crisis,* p. 198.

12. Charles R. Richardson, *British Politics and the American Revolution,* University of Oklahoma Press, Norman, 1954, pp. 110–111.

13. Lucy Sutherland, *The East India Company in Eighteenth Century Politics,* Clarendon Press, Oxford, 1952, p. 138 ff. One senses that, because India and America were both in crisis at the same time, neither received the attention from the Administration that it required.

14. Thomas, *British Politics and the Stamp Tax Crisis,* p. 299. After over two hundred years, there remain substantial differences in the assessment of the causes of the Revolution between British and American scholars. Richardson, for example, might be usefully compared with Wood, *Representation in the American Revolution,* or Bernard Bailyn, *The Ideological Origins of the American Revolution,* Harvard University Press, Cambridge, Mass., 1967.

15. See Edmund Burke, "Observations on . . . 'The State of the Nation.' "

16. Ibid., p. 380.

17. Ibid., p. 395.

18. Ibid., pp. 372–375.

19. Ibid., p. 397.

20. Ibid., p. 396.

21. Burke, *Correspondence,* Vol. II, To James DeLancy, 20/Aug./1772, p. 329.

22. Burke, *Correspondence,* Vol. II, To James DeLancy, 9/June/1771, p. 215.

23. Burke, *Correspondence,* Vol. II, To James DeLancy, 14/March/1775, p. 137.

24. Bernard Donoughue, *British Politics and the American Revolution,* Macmillan and Co., Ltd., New York, 1964, p. 280. Donoughue sees the Whigs as a faction, rather than a party, intent on putting their own interest in the East India Co. ahead of the welfare of America. His essentially Namierite discussion of the struggle blinds him to the role played by ideas. Bailyn's *Ideological Origins of the American Revolution* is a good corrective.

25. Burke, *Correspondence,* Vol. II, To the New York Assembly, 6/April/1774, p. 529.

26. Ibid., p. 528.

27. Burke, *Correspondence,* Vol. II, To the New York Assembly, 4/May/1774, p. 533.

28. Burke, *Correspondence,* Vol. III, To John Noble, 21/Feb./1775, pp. 117–118.

29. See O'Gorman, *The Rise of Party in England,* p. 327, for the Whigs' lack of concern about American affairs.

30. Burke, *Correspondence,* Vol. III, To Lord Rockingham, Sept./1774, p. 30.

31. Edmund Burke, "Speech on American Taxation," *Works,* Vol. II.

32. Ibid., p. 34.

33. Ibid., p. 41.

34. Ibid., p. 53.

35. Ibid., p. 67.

36. See, for example, Ibid., p. 6.

37. Ibid., p. 75 ff.

38. Ibid., p. 76.

39. Ibid., pp. 76–77.

40. Ibid., p. 71.

41. Ibid., p. 19.

42. Ibid., p. 73.

43. Burke, *Correspondence,* Vol. III, To Richard Champion, 9/March/1775, p. 132.

44. Burke, *Correspondence,* Vol. III, Richard Burke, Sr. to Richard Champion, 22/March/1775, p. 139.

45. Edmund Burke, "Speech on Moving Resolutions for Conciliation with America," *Works,* Vol. II, pp. 99–186.

46. Ibid., pp. 140–141.

47. Ibid., p. 135.

48. Ibid., pp. 118–119.

49. Ibid., p. 128.

50. Ibid., p. 127.

51. Ibid., p. 109 ff.

52. Ibid., p. 120.

53. Ibid., p. 120 ff.

54. Ibid., p. 130.

55. Ibid.

56. Ibid., pp. 105–106.

57. Ibid., p. 142.

58. Ibid., p. 141.

59. Ibid., see pp. 145–152.

60. Ibid., p. 154.

61. Ibid., p. 170.

62. Ibid., p. 179.

63. O'Gorman, *The Rise of Party in England,* pp. 347–348. A good example of the conservative criticism of Burke is Josiah Tucker. See, *A Series of Answers to certain Popular Objections, against separating from the Rebellious Colonies . . . ,* R. Rikes, Glochester, 1776, p. xii. For a broader view of Tucker's political opinions, see *A Treatise Concerning Civil Government,* Augustus M. Kelley, New York, 1967. An interesting secondary discussion may be found in J. G. A. Pocock, "Josiah Tucker on Burke, Locke, and Price: A study in the Varieties of Eighteenth Century Conservatism," in *Virtue, Commerce, and History,* Cambridge University Press, New York, pp. 157–192, p. 162. I cannot agree with Pocock's high regard for Tucker. To be sure,

Tucker's ideas are novel and argued with force. However, it must count for something that he is so often wrong. The prediction that a post-revolution America would collapse is, after all, only the most glaring of his errors. Similarly, the suggestion that Burke was a hypocrite, playing fast and loose with the radicals, is belied by everything Burke said and wrote during the period—as a brief review of the relevant volumes of the *Correspondence* shows.

64. Burke, "Observations on . . . 'The State of the Nation,'" p. 397.

65. Burke, *Correspondence,* Vol. III, To Citizens of Bristol, 20/Jan./1775, pp. 101–103.

66. Edmund Morgan, *The Challenge of the American Revolution,* W. W. Norton and Co., New York, 1976, p. 28 ff. Who misled the Americans? Morgan suggests that it was their English allies, seeking to obscure the gap between the American and British positions and thus to promote a compromise.

67. Burke, *Correspondence,* Vol. III, to Charles O'Hara, 26/July/1775, pp. 181–182.

68. John Derry, *English Politics and the American Revolution,* St. Martin's Press, New York, 1976, p. 4.

69. Joseph Galloway, "The Mutual Claims of Great Britain and the Colonies," in Merrill Jensen (ed.), *Tracts of the American Revolution 1763–1776,* The Bobbs-Merrill Company, Inc., New York, 1967, p. 353.

70. Ibid., p. 362.

71. Martin Howard, Jr., "A Letter From a Gentleman at Halifax," in Jensen, *Tracts of the American Revolution 1763–1776,* p. 69.

72. Bernard Bailyn, *The Ordeal of Thomas Hutchinson,* Harvard University Press, Cambridge, Mass., 1975, p. 74 ff.

73. Galloway, "The Mutual Claims of Great Britain and the Colonies," p. 391 ff.

74. Donoughue, *British Politics and the American Revolution,* p. 283.

75. G. H. Guttridge, *English Whiggism and the American Revolution,* University of California Press, Los Angeles, 1966, pp. 34–35.

76. Derry, *English Politics and the American Revolution,* p. 135.

77. Morgan, *The Challenge of the American Revolution,* pp. 40–41.

78. Ritcheson, *British Politics and the American Revolution,* pp. 182–185.

79. See Ibid., p. 185, where the proposal is praised because it "demonstrated that a great British statesman understood—albeit intuitively—that the only way Britain could maintain and keep an empire was by accepting a new imperial structure."

80. For Dickinson, see "Letters From a Farmer in Pennsylvania to the Inhabitants of the British Colonies," in Jensen, *Tracts of the American Revolution 1763–1776,* p. 127 ff. See also Ritcheson, *British Politics and the American Revolution,* p. 113.

81. Ibid., p. 225.

82. Richard Price, *Two Tracts on Liberty,* Da Capo Press, New York, 1972, p. 102.

83. Ibid., p. 3.

84. Ibid., p. 51 ff. and 73 ff.

85. See Robert E. Toohey, *Liberty and Empire,* University of Kentucky Press, Lexington, 1978, p. 176.

86. Tucker, *A Treatise Concerning Civil Government,* p. 25.

87. Tucker, *A Series of Answers,* p. ix.

88. Ibid., p. 250 ff.

89. Ibid., p. 28.

90. Donald Winch, *Adam Smith's Politics,* passim.

91. Adam Smith, *Wealth of Nations,* p. 557 ff.

92. Ibid., p. 541.

93. Ibid., pp. 581–582.

94. Ibid., p. 586.

95. Ibid., p. 588.

96. Ibid., pp. 896–897.

97. Derry, *English Politics and the American Revolution,* p. 171.

98. Richard Bland, "An Inquiry into the Rights of the British Colonies," in Jensen, *Tracts on the American Revolution 1763–1776,* pp. 108–126.

99. Ibid., p. 117.

100. Thomas Jefferson, "A Summary View of the Rights of British America," in Jensen, *Tracts on the American Revolution,* pp. 256–276.

101. Ibid., p. 263.

102. For an interesting analysis of Jefferson's argument in the Declaration, see Garry Wills, *Inventing America: Jefferson's Declaration of Independence,* Vintage Books, New York, 1979, esp. pp. 76–92. A more traditional analysis may be found in Carl L. Becker, *The Declaration of Independence,* Vintage Books, New York, 1958.

103. Burke, *Correspondence,* Vol. III, 14/March/1775, To James DeLancy, p. 137.

104. Burke, *Correspondence,* Vol. III, To Charles O'Hara, May/1775, p. 160.

105. Burke, *Correspondence,* Vol. III, To Charles O'Hara, 17/August/1775, p. 185.

106. Burke, *Correspondence,* Vol. III, To Lord Rockingham, 22,23/August/1775, p. 192.

107. See Cobbett and Wright, *Parliamentary History,* XVIII, pp. 740–757.

108. For the plan, see Ritcheson, *British Politics and the American Revolution,* pp. 205–206.

109. Burke, *Correspondence,* Vol. III, To Lord Rockingham, 6/Jan./1777, p. 308 ff.

110. Edmund Burke, "Address to the British Colonists of North America," *Works,* Vol. VI, pp. 183–196.

111. Edmund Burke, "Address to the King," *Works,* Vol. VI, pp. 161–182.

112. Ibid., pp. 164–165.

113. Ibid., p. 166.

114. Ibid., pp. 167–168.

115. Ibid., p. 179.

116. Ibid., p. 181.

117. Edmund Burke, "Letter to the Sheriffs of Bristol, On the Affairs of America," *Works,* Vol. II, pp. 187–245.

118. Ibid., p. 199.

119. Ibid., p. 223.

120. Ibid., p. 224.

121. Ibid.

122. Ibid., p. 236.

123. Ibid.

124. Ritcheson, *British Politics and the American Revolution,* pp. 232 and 249 ff. See also Guttridge, *English Whiggism and the American Revolution,* p. 97 ff.

125. Richardson, *British Politics and the American Revolution,* p. 258 ff. See page 268 ff. for the details of the plan. As most of the political nation knew that the war was lost by the end of 1778, the foolishness of fighting on for five more years almost surpasses that of provoking the rebellion in the first place.

126. Burke, *Correspondence,* Vol. III, to Richard Champion, 11/April/1778, p. 427.

127. Burke, *Correspondence,* Vol. IV, To Dr. John Erskine, 12/June/1779, p. 87.

128. Burke, *Correspondence,* Vol. IV, To Henry Laurens, 27/March/1782, p. 428.

129. Burke, *Correspondence,* Vol. IV, To Benjamin Franklin, 28/Feb./1782, p. 419.

130. Burke, "Speech on American Taxation," p. 75 ff.

131. Burke, "Address to the King," p. 176.

132. Ibid., p. 166.

133. Burke, "Observations on . . . 'The State of the Nation,' " p. 395.

134. Burke, "Letter to the Sheriffs of Bristol, On the Affairs of America," p. 236.

135. Edmund Burke, "Address to the British Colonists in North America," *Works,* Vol. VI, pp. 183–196, pp. 193–4.

136. Ibid., p. 217.

137. Edmund Burke, "Letter to Sir Charles Bingham, Bart., on the Irish Absentee Tax," *Works,* Vol. VI, pp. 121–134, p. 127.

138. See Burke, "Letter to the Sheriffs of Bristol, On the Affairs of America," p. 199 and "Speech on Conciliation with America," p. 145 ff.

139. Burke, "Speech on American Taxation," p. 74.

140. Burke, "Speech on Conciliation with America," p. 180. For a somewhat similar view, see J. G. A. Pocock, "1776: The Revolution Against Parliament," in *Virtue, Commerce, and History,* pp. 73–88.

Chapter Nine

1. Michael Freeman, *Edmund Burke and the Critique of Political Radicalism.*

2. Ibid., p. 4.

3. Ibid., p. 38.

4. See the exchange in *Political Theory,* Vol. 6, No. 3 (August 1978), between Freeman, "Edmund Burke and the Theory of Revolution," pp. 277–297, and Ted Robert Gurr, "Burke and the Modern Theory of Revolution: A Reply to Freeman," pp. 299–311.

5. C. B. Macpherson, *Burke,* Hill and Wang, New York, 1980.

6. Ibid., p. 3.

7. See Frank O'Gorman, *The Whig Party and the French Revolution,* p. 33 ff.

8. Edmund Burke, *Correspondence,* Vol. VIII, To Lord Loughborough, Circa 17/March/1796, p. 432.

9. Edmund Burke, *Reflections on the Revolution in France,* p. 11.

10. Edmund Burke, "Thoughts on French Affairs," *Works,* Vol. IV, pp. 313–377, pp. 352–353.

11. Burke, *Correspondence,* Vol. VI, To Lord Charlemont, 9/Aug./1789, p. 9.

12. Burke, *Correspondence,* Vol. VI, To Charles-Jean-Francois DePont, Nov./1789, p. 41.

13. Burke, *Correspondence,* Vol. VII, To Chevalier de Grave, 24/Aug./1792, p. 183.

14. Burke, *Correspondence,* Vol. VII, To Mrs. Crewe, Post 11/Aug./1795, p. 300.

15. James T. Boulton, *The Language of Politics in the Age of Wilkes and Burke,* University of Toronto Press, Toronto, 1963, p. 98. Olivia Smith, *The Politics of Language 1791–1819,* Clarendon Press, Oxford, 1984, takes the discussion down through the Napoleonic Wars. Two more recent works on Burke's rhetoric are Christopher Reid, *Edmund Burke and the Practice of Political Writing,* St. Martin's Press, New York, 1985 and Steven Blakemore, *Burke and the Fall of Language,* University Press of New England, Hanover, 1988. Boulton's book, however, remains the indispensible source.

16. Burke, "Three Letters on a Regicide Peace," pp. 318–319.

17. Burke, *Reflections on the Revolution in France,* p. 86.

18. Ibid., pp. 86–87.

19. Boulton, *The Language of Politics in the Age of Wilkes and Burke,* p. 131.

20. Burke, *Correspondence,* Vol. VIII, To Lord Fitzwilliam, 15/May/1795, pp. 242–243.

21. Burke, *Correspondence,* Vol. VIII, To Sir Hercules Langrishe, 26/May/1795, p. 254.

22. Edmund Burke, "Three Letters on a Regicide Peace," p. 361.

23. Burke, *Reflections on the Revolution in France,* p. 127.

24. Edmund Burke, "Letter to a Member of the National Assembly, in Answer to some Objections to His Book on French Affairs," *Works,* Vol. IV, pp. 1–55, p. 23.

25. Ibid., p. 25.

26. Ibid., pp. 27–28.

27. Edmund Burke, "Address to the King," pp. 162–163.

28. Burke, *Reflections on the Revolution in France,* p. 22.

29. Edmund Burke, "An Appeal From the New to the Old Whigs," p. 169.

30. Burke, *Reflections on the Revolution in France,* p. 290.

31. Burke, *Correspondence,* Vol. VII, To the King of Poland, 28/Feb./1792, p. 77.

32. Burke, *Reflections on the Revolution in France,* p. 145.

33. Burke, *Correspondence,* Vol. VI, To Unknown, 1791, pp. 479–480.

34. See, for example, J. M. Roberts, *The French Revolution,* Oxford University Press, New York, 1978. The nature of French society before the Revolution, the possibilities for reform, and who was to blame for the failure of reform are matters of intense controversy. What might be styled a neo-conservative school argues that the Ancien Regime was reforming itself, and the Revolution was both unjustified and, indeed, a failure. For pre-Revolutionary France, see William Doyle, *The Ancien Regime,* Macmillan Education Ltd., London, 1986, and especially the exhaustive Keith Michael Baker (ed.), *The Political Culture of the Old Regime,* Pergamon Press, New York, 1987. The latter is Volume I in a series, "The French Revolution and the Creation of Modern Political Culture." For the neo-conservative reinterpretation of the Revolution, see Doyle's *The Oxford History of the French Revolution,* Clarendon Press, Oxford, 1989 and Simon Schama, *Citizens: A*

Chronicle of the French Revolution" Alfred A. Knopf, 1989. I must admit to being unconvinced.

35. Roberts, *The French Revolution,* p. 13.

36. For Voltaire as a reformer, see Peter Gay, *Voltaire's Politics,* Princeton University Press, Princeton, 1959. Two useful biographies are Jean Orieux, *Voltaire,* Doubleday and Co., Inc., Garden City, 1979 and Haydon Mason, *Voltaire,* Johns Hopkins University Press, Baltimore, 1981. On the intellectual background, see Peter Gay, *The Enlightenment: An Interpretation,* Two Volumes, Alfred A. Knopf, New York, 1969 and especially Nannerl O. Keohane, *Philosophy and the State in France,* Princeton University Press, Princeton, New Jersey, 1980. Burke rarely commented on Voltaire, but one notable, and amusing, mention is *Correspondence,* Vol. VI, To Unknown, Jan./1790, p. 81: "Who ever dreamt of Voltaire and Rousseau as legislators? The First has the merit of writing agreeably; and nobody has ever united blasphemy and obscenity so happily together . . ."

37. Burke, "Letters on a Regicide Peace," p. 378.

38. Burke, *Correspondence,* Vol. VI, To Richard Burke, Jr., 18/Aug./1791, p. 361.

39. Burke, *Correspondence,* Vol. VI, To Richard Burke, Jr., 26/Sept./1791, p. 414.

40. Burke, *Reflections on the Revolution in France,* p. 44.

41. Ibid., p. 31.

42. Burke, "Letter to a Member of the National Assembly," pp. 15–16.

43. Burke, *Reflections on the Revolution in France,* p. 77.

44. Ibid., p. 199.

45. Burke, "Letters on a Regicide Peace," p. 375.

46. Burke, "Thoughts on French Affairs," p. 353.

47. Burke, "Fourth Letter on a Regicide Peace," p. 91.

48. Burke, *Reflections on the Revolution in France,* p. 258.

49. Freeman, *Edmund Burke and Political Radicalism,* pp. 196–197.

50. Ibid., p. 204 ff.

51. Roberts, *The French Revolution,* p. 63.

52. For a discussion of the war, see Ibid., p. 45 ff.

53. Plato, *The Republic of Plato,* F. M. Cornford, (Trans.), Oxford University Press, New York, 1945, p. 286 (VIII 562A–IX 576B).

54. Aristotle, *The Politics of Aristotle,* Ernest Barker (ED.), Oxford University Press, New York, 1946, p. 215 (1304B), p. 217 (1305A), and p. 219 (1306A).

55. David Hume, *A History of England,* Vol. V, pp. 280–281.

56. Ibid., p. 334.

57. Burke, "Letters on a Regicide Peace," p. 373.

58. J. G. A. Pocock, "Burke's Analysis of the French Revolution," in *Virtue, Commerce, and History,* pp. 193–212, p. 199.

59. Burke, *Correspondence,* Vol. IX, To French Laurence, 11/April/1797, p. 307.

60. Burke, *Reflections on the Revolution in France,* p. 86.

61. See Burke, "Letters on a Regicide Peace," p. 364 ff.

62. Ibid., p. 364.

63. Burke, "Thoughts on French Affairs," p. 319.

64. Burke, "Letters on a Regicide Peace," p. 320.

65. Ibid., p. 320.

66. Burke, "Letters on a Regicide Peace," p. 376.

67. Ibid., p. 377.

68. Ibid., pp. 380–381.

69. Burke, *Reflections on the Revolution in France,* p. 177.

70. See, Burke "Thoughts on French Affairs," p. 327 ff.

71. Ibid., p. 329.

72. Burke, *Reflections on the Revolution in France,* p. 6.

73. Burke, "Fourth Letter on a Regicide Peace," p. 99.

74. Ibid.

75. Burke, *Reflections on the Revolution in France,* p. 10.

76. Burke, "Letters on a Regicide Peace," p. 431.

77. Ibid., p. 426.

78. E. P. Thompson, *The Making of the English Working Class,* p. 102.

79. There is an extensive literature on the nature and extent of English radicalism in the era of the French Revolution. A good history of England during the years of the French Revolution may be found in Ian R.

Christie, *Wars and Revolutions Britain, 1760–1815,* Harvard University Press, Cambridge, Mass., 1982. Also helpful are several of the papers in H. T. Dickinson (ed.), *Britain and the French Revolution, 1789–1815,* Macmillan Education, Ltd., 1989. H. T. Dickinson, *British Radicalism and the French Revolution,* Basil Blackwell, Inc., New York, 1985. is a good brief introduction. George Stead Veitch, *The Genesis of Parliamentary Reform,* is the traditional standby. Other useful studies are Carl B. Cone, *The English Jacobins,* Charles Scribner's Sons, New York, 1968, Clive Emsley, *British Society and the French Wars, 1793–1815,* Rowman and Littlefield, Totowa, New Jersey, 1979, Albert Goodwin, *The Friends of Liberty,* Harvard University Press, Cambridge, Massachusetts, 1979, and, of course, Thompson's, *The Making of the English Working Class.* Ian R. Christie, *Stress and Stability in Late Eighteenth Century Britain,* Clarendon Press, Oxford, 1984, is a good counterpoint to Thompson and the others, for he sees little threat of revolution in the period. R. R. Fennessy, *Burke, Paine, and the Rights of Man,* Martinus Nijhoff, 1963, is more specialized but very good on the intellectual dimensions of the struggle. Finally, E. C. Black, *The Association,* Harvard University Press, Cambridge, Mass., 1963 and Robert R. Dozier, *For King, Constitution, and Country,* The University Press of Kentucky, Lexington, 1983, studies of the Loyalist movement, go a long way toward correcting the lack of balance which has resulted from the scholarly concentration on the radicals. A useful brief discussion of the conservatives may be found in H. T. Dickinson, "Popular Conservatism and Militant Loyalism 1789–1815," in H. T. Dickinson (ed.), *Britain and the French Revolution,* pp. 103–126.

80. Veitch, *The Genesis of Parliamentary Reform,* p. 159.

81. Edmund Burke, "Speech on a Bill for the Relief of Protestant Dissenters," *Works,* Vol. II, pp. 21–38.

82. Goodwin, *The Friends of Liberty,* p. 89.

83. Edmund Burke, "Speech on a Motion for Leave to Bring in a Bill to Repeal and Alter Certain Acts Respecting Religious Opinions, upon the Occasion of a Petition of the Unitarian Society," *Works,* Vol. VII, pp. 39–58, p. 54.

84. Ibid., p. 51.

85. Burke, *Correspondence,* Vol. VI, To John Noble, 14/March/1790, p. 103.

86. Burke, *Correspondence,* Vol. VI, To Henry Dundas, 30/Sept./1791, p. 419. Was he right? Opinions vary but see Isaac Kramnick, "Revolution and Radicalism: English Political Theory in the Age of Revolution," *Political Theory,* Vol. V, No. 4 (Nov. 1977), pp. 505–534, for a strongly argued supporting position—though one with a rather different value bias.

87. Burke, "Thoughts on French Affairs," p. 324.

88. Burke, *Correspondence,* Vol. VII, To William Weddell, 31/Jan./1792, p. 51.

89. Burke, "Letter to a Noble Lord on the Attacks Made Upon Mr. Burke and His Pension . . . ," p. 213.

90. Ibid., p. 217.

91. Ibid., p. 218.

92. Burke, "An Appeal From the New to the Old Whigs," p. 206.

93. Ibid.

94. Ibid., p. 80.

95. Burke, "Letter to a Noble Lord on the Attacks Made Upon Mr. Burke and His Pension . . . ," p. 184 ff.

96. Ibid., pp. 186–187.

97. For a good example, see Burke's "Fourth Letter on a Regicide Peace." Reid, *Edmund Burke and the Practice of Political Writing,* p. 12 ff., is a particularly good discussion of the various "voices" adopted by Burke in his polemical writings.

98. Burke, "Thoughts on the French Revolution," p. 377.

99. Edmund Burke, "Heads for Consideration on the Present State of Affairs," *Works,* Vol. IV, pp. 379–402.

100. Ermsley, *British Society and the French Revolution,* p. 20 ff.

101. Burke, "Fourth Letter on a Regicide Peace," pp. 100–101.

102. Burke, "Letters on a Regicide Peace," p. 250.

103. Ibid., p. 345.

104. Ibid., p. 347.

105. Ibid., p. 247.

106. Ibid., p. 238.

107. Ibid., p. 245.

108. Burke, *Correspondence,* Vol. VI, To John Trevor, Jan/1791, p. 217.

109. Burke, "Heads for Consideration on the Present State of Affairs," p. 401.

110. Burke, *Correspondence,* Vol. VI, To Claude-Francois De Rivarol, 1/June/1791, p. 266.

111. Edmund Burke, "Remarks on the Policy of the Allies with Respect to France," *Works,* Vol. IV, pp. 403–482, p. 433. Written in late 1793, this

work deals with the proposal to issue an allied manifesto on war policy. Burke opposed the manifesto on the grounds that it was inappropriate in a time of calamity and defeat.

112. Ibid., p. 434. The work concludes with an appendix citing examples, precedents, and authorities (out of Vattel) in support of Burke's argument that the other European nations had a right to intervene in internal French affairs if those affairs threatened their own stability.

113. Ibid., pp. 459–460.

114. Ibid., p. 421.

115. Ibid.

116. Ibid., p. 425.

117. Ibid., p. 420. See p. 452 for Burke's proposal to restore the French clergy.

118. Ibid., p. 428.

119. Ibid., p. 462, ff.

120. See, for example, Ermsley, *British Society and the French Revolution,* p. 25. Though the Burke-Paine debate sparked a great deal of interest and thus a number of commentaries, few took Burke's side. Boulton counts some seventy works spawned by the debate: the vast majority of them both polite to and critical of Burke. See *The Language of Politics in the Age of Wilkes and Burke,* pp. 185–206.

121. Fennessy, *Burke, Paine, and the Rights of Man,* p. 181 ff. For conservative thought in the period, see Thomas Philip Schofield, "Conservative Political Thought in Britain in Response to the French Revolution," *Historical Journal,* XXIX, 1986, pp. 601–622.

122. Burke, *Correspondence,* Vol. VI, From Sir Gilbert Elliot, 6/Nov./1790, p. 156.

123. See Burke, *Correspondence,* Vol. VI, p. 161, note 2.

124. Boulton, *The Language of Politics in the Age of Wilkes and Burke,* p. 84 ff.

125. Ibid., p. 255 ff.

126. Burke, *Correspondence,* Vol. VI, To William Cusal Smith, 22/July/1791, p. 303.

127. Smith, *The Politics of Language 1791–1819,* p. x. Interestingly, Burke also contributed to the formation of such a style with his intensely emotional rhetoric and his direct mode of expression. See, Ibid., p. 36 ff.

128. Ibid., p. 34.

129. Boulton, *The Language of Politics in the Age of Wilkes and Burke,* p. 147.

130. Ibid., p. 140.

131. Fennessy, *Burke, Paine, and the Rights of Man,* p. 160 ff.

132. See James MacKintosh, *Vindiciae Gallicae,* 1791. Fennessy, p. 194 ff., offers a detailed discussion of Mackintosh's argument. He sees Mackintosh as perhaps Burke's most influential moderate critic.

133. Cobban, *The Debate on the French Revolution,* p. 61.

134. Ibid., p. 165.

135. Ibid.

136. Burke, *Correspondence,* Vol. VI, From Philip Francis, 19/Feb./1790, p. 85 ff.

137. Ibid, passim.

138. Ibid., p. 86.

139. Ibid., p. 87.

140. Ibid., p. 91–92.

141. Burke, *Correspondence,* Vol. VI, From Philip Francis, 3,4/Nov./1790, p. 150 ff.

142. Ibid., p. 152.

143. Ibid.

144. Ibid., p. 153.

145. Ibid., p. 154.

146. Burke, *Correspondence,* Vol. VI, To Philip Francis, 19/Nov./1790, pp. 170–173.

147. Ibid., p. 171.

148. Ibid., p. 172.

149. Burke, *Correspondence,* Vol. VI, To Philip Francis, 4/Dec./1790, pp. 188–189. See also the note, p. 248, for a brief background.

150. For Mackintosh's admiration for Burke's principles, see *Correspondence,* Vol. IX, Headnote, p. 192.

151. Burke, *Correspondence,* Vol. VI, MacKintosh to Burke, 22/Dec./1796, p. 192 ff.

152. Burke, *Correspondence,* Vol. VI, To French Laurence, 2/Aug./1796, p. 312.

153. Burke, *Correspondence,* Vol. IX, To French Laurence, 25/Dec./1796, pp. 204–205.

154. Cobban, *The Debate on the French Revolution,* p. 377.

155. Ibid, p. 372.

156. Ermsley, *British Society and the French Revolution,* p. 15.

157. O'Gorman, *The Whig Party and the French Revoution,* pp. 10–11.

158. Burke, *Correspondence,* Vol. VII, To William Weddell, 31/Jan./1792, p. 52.

159. Edmund Burke, "Letter to William Elliot . . . in the Debate Concerning Lord Fitzwilliam," *Works,* Vol. V, p. 113 ff.

160. Burke, *Correspondence,* Vol. VII, To William Burke, 3/Sept./1792, p. 192.

161. Ibid.

162. Ibid., p. 194.

163. Burke, *Correspondence,* Vol. VII, To Lord Fitzwilliam, 29/Nov./1792, p. 306 ff.

164. Ibid., p. 308.

165. Burke, *An Appeal From the New Whigs to the Old,* p. 66.

166. L. G. Mitchell, *Charles James Fox and the Disintegration of the Whig Party 1782–1794,* Oxford University Press, London, 1971, pp. 212–213.

167. Edmund Burke, "Observation on the Conduct of the Minority . . . ," *Works,* Vol. V, pp. 1–63.

168. Ibid., p. 62.

169. Burke, *Correspondence,* Vol. VI, To Lord Fitzwilliam, 5/June/1791, p. 275.

170. See, Ibid., p. 273.

171. Burke, *Correspondence,* Vol. IX, To French Laurence, 15/Feb./1797, p. 245.

172. Burke, *Correspondence,* Vol. IX, To French Laurence, 11/March/1797, p. 264.

173. Ibid., p. 265.

174. Burke, "Letter to Elliot," p. 126.

175. Burke, *Correspondence,* Vol. IX, To French Laurence, 13/Dec./1796, p. 173 ff.

176. For Burke on the value of the coalition, see *Correspondence,* Vol. VIII, To Lord Fitzwilliam, 9/Sept./ 1794, p. 9.

177. Burke, "Letters on a Regicide Peace," p. 286.

178. Burke, *Correspondence,* Vol. IX, To William Windham, 16/ May/1797, p. 349.

179. Burke, *Correspondence,* Vol. IX, To Lord Fitzwilliam, Post 9/Dec./ 1796, p. 160.

180. For a view of the conflict which is highly critical of Fitzwilliam, see Edith M. Johnston, *Great Britain and Ireland, 1760–1800,* Oliver and Boyd, London, 1963, p. 107 ff. O'Gorman, *Whig Party and the French Revolution,* p. 218 ff., is only slightly more favorable. However, see chapter 10.

181. Burke, *Correspondence,* Vol. VIII, To William Windham, 17/Nov./ 1795, p. 343.

182. Burke, *Correspondence,* Vol. VI, To Richard Burke, Sr. 24/ July/1791, pp. 306–307. For a discussion of the riots, see Godwin, *The Friends of Liberty,* p. 180 ff.

183. Burke, *Correspondence,* Vol. IX, To Lord Fitzwilliam, 2/Sept./1796, p. 78.

184. For a good example of Burke's encouragement of Windham's efforts to build a third party, see Burke, *Correspondence,* Vol. VII, To William Windham, 24/Oct./1793, p. 460 ff.

185. Burke, *Correspondence,* Vol. IX, to French Laurence, 12/May/1797, p. 337.

Chapter Ten

1. J. C. Beckett, *The Making of Modern Ireland, 1603–1923,* Alfred A. Knopf, New York, 1966, p. 155 ff. A useful discussion of eighteenth century Irish Whig thought may be found in Caroline Robbins, *The 18th Century Commonwealthmen,* Harvard University Press, Cambridge, 1961, pp. 134–176.

2. Ibid., p. 137 ff. Only in an occasional writer, a Swift or a Berkeley, can one find any sympathy for the native Irish.

3. Edith M. Johnston, *Great Britain and Ireland, 1760–1800,* Olive and Boyd, London, 1963, p. 3.

4. W. E. H. Lecky, *A History of Ireland in the Eighteenth Century,* University of Chicago Press, Chicago, 1972, p. 184 ff., offers a positive assessment of legislative independence. Most other authorities disagree, arguing that it left the Anglo-Irish in power and even reinforced their position

by preserving the veto in the English Cabinet. See Johnston, *Great Britain and Ireland,* p. 270 ff. The disagreement may, in part, reflect Lecky's status as an Anglo-Irish reformer.

5. Thomas H. D. Mahoney, *Edmund Burke and Ireland,* Harvard University Press, Cambridge, 1960, p. 11, suggests 1761, but the editors of the *Works* say 1765. See Edmund Burke, "Fragments of a Tract Relative to the Laws Against Popery in Ireland," *Works,* Vol. VI, pp. 299–360.

6. Ibid., p. 350 ff.

7. Ibid., p. 341.

8. Ibid., p. 352.

9. Ibid., p. 337.

10. Ibid., p. 334.

11. Ibid., p. 320.

12. Ibid., p. 321.

13. Ibid., p. 322.

14. John Locke, *A Letter on Toleration.* For evidence that Burke was perfectly familiar with Locke's argument, see Edmund Burke, "Speech on the Act of Uniformity," *Works,* Vol. VII, pp. 17–18.

15. See Burke, "An Appeal From the New to the Old Whigs," p. 161 ff.

16. Burke, *Correspondence,* Vol. IV, Burke to Charles James Fox, 8/Oct./1777, p. 145.

17. Burke, *Correspondence,* Vol. IV, 18/July/1778, pp. 7–8.

18. Burke, *Works,* Vol. VI, pp. 413–429.

19. Burke, *The Correspondence,* Vol. VIII, Burke to William Smith, 29/Jan./1795, p. 128.

20. Burke, *Correspondence,* Vol. IV, To Dr. John Curry, 14/Aug./1779, p. 119.

21. Burke, *Correspondence,* Vol. IV, Burke to Viscount Kenmare, 21/Feb./1782, pp. 415–418.

22. Ibid., p. 407.

23. Ibid., p. 409.

24. Ibid., pp. 417–418.

25. Ibid., p. 406.

26. Burke, *Correspondence,* Vol. VII, To Richard Burke, Jr., 29/ Feb./1792, p. 80. For a good overview of Irish developments during the French Revolution, see Marianne Elliot, "Ireland and the French Revolution," in Dickinson (ed.), *Britain and the French Revolution,* pp. 83–101. For more detail, see Marianne Elliot, *Partners in Revolution The United Irishmen and France,* Yale University Press, New Haven, 1988.

27. Burke, "Letter to Sir Hercules Langrishe on . . . the Roman Catholics of Ireland," pp. 241–306.

28. Burke, *Correspondence,* Vol. VII, To Richard Burke, Jr., 29/ Feb./1792, p. 83.

29. Burke, *Correspondence,* Vol. VIII, To Rev. Thomas Hussey, 17/ March/1795, p. 200.

30. Burke, *Correspondence,* Vol. VII, To Richard Burke, Jr., Post 21/ Nov./1792, p. 299.

31. A good example is Burke's unsent letter to his son, "A Letter to Richard Burke, Esq., on the Protestant Ascendency," *Works,* Vol. VI, pp. 385–412. He wrote, p. 392, "new *ascendency* is the old *mastership,* it is neither more nor less than the resolution of one set of people in Ireland to consider themselves as the sole citizens in the commonwealth, and to keep a dominion over the rest by reducing them to an absolute slavery under a military power . . ."

32. Burke, *Correspondence,* Vol. IX, To Rev. Thomas Hussey, Post 9/ Dec./1796, p. 170.

33. Burke, *Correspondence,* Vol. VIII, To Sir Hercules Langrishe, 26/ May/1795, pp. 255–256.

34. Burke, "Letter to Sir Hercules Langrishe on the . . . Roman Catholics of Ireland," p. 252 ff.; p. 291.

35. Ibid., p. 283.

36. Ibid., p. 276.

37. Ibid., pp. 301–302.

38. Ibid., p. 255.

39. Beckett, *The Making of Modern Ireland,* p. 248.

40. Ibid., pp. 248–252. Along with the watering down of the original bill and the Protestant effort to frustrate its implementation, the reformers were further alienated by the concomitant enactment of measures to restrict civil liberties. Perhaps Lecky put it best, "the Catholics . . . were told on high government authority that their disqualifications were permanent and indelible, essential to the connection of their country with England, es-

sential to the maintenance of the monarchical constitution under which they lived." *A History of Ireland in the Eighteenth Century,* p. 293.

41. Burke, *Correspondence,* Vol. VIII, To William Smith, 29/Jan./1795, p. 132.

42. Quoted in Mahoney, *Edmund Burke and Ireland,* p. 189. Interestingly, Richard Burke, Jr., did not qualify under either term of the proscription, for he was neither Irish-born nor Catholic.

43. Burke, *Correspondence,* Vol. VIII, To Sir Hercules Langrishe, 26/May/1795, p. 254.

44. Frank O'Gorman, *The Whig Party and the French Revolution,* p. 209.

45. Johnston, *Great Britain and Ireland,* p. 106.

46. Burke, *Correspondence,* Vol. VIII, To Lord Fitzwilliam, 9/Sept./1794, p. 9.

47. Burke, *Correspondence,* Vol. VIII, To Lord Fitzwilliam, circa 26/Sept./1794, p. 20.

48. Ibid., p. 22.

49. Ibid.

50. Ibid.

51. Burke, *Correspondence,* Vol. VIII, To Lord Fitzwilliam, 7/Nov./1794, p. 74.

52. Ibid., p. 75.

53. Burke, *Correspondence,* Vol. VIII, To William Elliot, 24/Sept./1795, p. 158.

54. Burke, *Correspondence,* Vol. IX, To Lord Fitzwilliam, 2/Sept./1796, p. 78.

55. Burke, *Correspondence,* Vol. VIII, To William Windham, Post 21/Oct./1794, p. 62.

56. Burke, *Correspondence,* Vol. IX, To Lord Fitzwilliam, Post 9/Dec./1796, p. 158.

57. Burke, *Correspondence,* Vol. VIII, To Lord Fitzwilliam, 13/March/1795, p. 192.

58. E. A. Smith, *Whig Principles and Party Politics,* Manchester University Press, Manchester, 1975, p. 183, merely accuses Burke of inconsistency in advice, but Mahoney, *Edmund Burke and Ireland,* p. 260, suggests that Burke "clearly reveals the strain he was then experiencing. There

are places where irrationality clearly shows." Burke was certainly upset, but I see no reason to think that he was any more irrational than the other participants.

59. This is one reason why Mahoney's unqualified endorsement of Fitzwilliam won't work, see Ibid., p. 266 ff. While the precise terms of the agreement were indeed uncertain, no one shared Fitzwilliam's interpretation.

60. Burke, *Correspondence,* Vol. VIII, To Mrs. John Crewe, circa 22/Nov./1794, p. 81.

61. Burke, *Correspondence,* Vol. IX, To French Laurence, 23/Nov./1796, pp. 124–125.

62. Ibid., p. 125.

63. Burke, *Correspondence,* Vol. IX, To French Laurence, 18/Nov./1796, p. 117.

64. Burke, *Correspondence,* Vol. VIII, To Sir Hercules Langrishe, 26/May/1795, p. 255.

65. Burke, *Correspondence,* Vol. IX, To Rev. Thomas Hussey, Post 9/Dec./1796, p. 171.

66. Burke, *Correspondence,* Vol. IX, To French Laurence, 11/May/1797, pp. 332–338.

67. Ibid., p. 336.

68. Ibid.

69. Ibid.

70. Ibid., p. 337.

71. Burke, *Correspondence,* Vol. IX, To French Laurence, 11/Nov./1796, p. 116.

72. Burke, *Correspondence,* Vol. IX, To Lord Fitzwilliam, 21/Sept./1796, p. 78.

73. Ibid., pp. 77–80.

74. Burke, *Correspondence,* Vol. IX, To Lord Fitzwilliam, 7/Dec./1796, p. 149.

75. Burke, *Correspondence,* Vol. IX, To French Laurence, 1/June/1797, p. 364 ff.

76. Ibid., p. 365.

77. Smith, *Whig Principles and Party Politics,* p. 219 ff.

78. See, for example, Mahoney *Edmund Burke and Ireland,* p. 119 ff.

79. Burke, *Correspondence,* Vol. IX, To Lord Fitzwilliam, 20/Nov./1796, p. 122.

80. Burke, *Correspondence,* Vol. II, To Charles Bingham, 30/Oct./1773, p. 475.

81. Burke, *Correspondence,* Vol. IX, To Rev. Thomas Hussey, Post 9/Dec./1796, p. 166.

82. Burke's view is supported by most modern scholars. For example, both Beckett, *Making of Modern Ireland,* p. 227, and Johnston, *Great Britain and Ireland,* p. 270, argue that legislative independence benefitted the Ascendency at the expense of the reformers and the Catholics.

83. Burke, *Correspondence,* Vol. VIII, To Lord Fitzwilliam, circa 26/Sept./1794, p. 20 ff. That Burke's view was not a response to the immediate situation is shown by his expression of the same position in an earlier letter to Samuel Span. See *Works,* Vol. II, pp. 249–58.

84. Mahoney, *Edmund Burke and Ireland,* p. 142 ff.

85. Beckett, *Making of Modern Ireland,* pp. 236–240.

86. Ibid., p. 239.

87. O'Gorman, *Edmund Burke His Political Philosophy,* p. 90.

88. Mahoney, *Edmund Burke and Ireland,* p. 311.

89. Burke, "Letter to Sir Hercules Langrishe on . . . the Roman Catholics of Ireland," p. 247.

90. Smith, *Whig Principles and Party Politics,* p. 292 ff., offers a very clear statement of the thesis that Fitzwilliam and Portland sought to support the Irish aristocracy. Mahoney, *Edmund Burke and Ireland,* p. 142 ff., extends the argument to include Burke. The view is so widely accepted that it may be considered the orthodoxy. Primary responsibility for the interpretation probably lies with Lecky, *A History of Ireland in the Eighteenth Century*, passim. A unified Irish aristocracy, including both Catholic and Protestant elements, governing in the interests of the masses was Lecky's answer to Ireland's problems in his own day, and, to a considerable degree, he appears to have read his position back into Burke.

91. Burke, *Correspondence,* Vol. VIII, To Richard Burke, Jr., Post 3/Jan./1792, p. 11.

92. Edmund Burke, "An Appeal From the New to the Old Whigs," p. 215.

93. Edmund Burke, *Correspondence,* Vol. IX, Jane Burke to Charles James Fox, [Ante 9/July/1797], p. 373.

94. Burke, *Correspondence,* Vol. IX, To Earl Fitzwilliam, 2/Sept./1796, pp. 77–78.

95. Ibid., p. 78.

96. Burke, *Correspondence,* Vol. IX, To Earl Fitzwilliam, 4/[Jan.]/1797, p. 220.

97. Burke, *Correspondence,* Vol. V, To Henry Homer, Nov./1786, p. 295.

98. Burke, "Speech on Mr. Fox's East India Bill," p. 463.

99. Edmund Burke, "Speech on the Duration of Parliament," pp. 69–88, p. 74.

100. Ibid., p. 75.

101. Edmund Burke, "A Representation to His Majesty, Moved in the House of Commons, June 14, 1784," *Works,* Vol. II, pp. 537–376.

102. Ibid., p. 539.

103. Ibid., p. 552.

104. Ibid., p. 551.

105. See, for example, Ibid., p. 544.

106. Ibid., pp. 552–553 and pp. 553–554.

107. Edmund Burke, "Observations on a Late Publication Entitled 'The Present State of the Nation,' " p. 419.

108. Edmund Burke, "Three Letters Addressed to A Member of the Present Parliament on the Proposals for Peace with the Regicide Directory of France," *Works,* pp. 336–337.

109. Burke, *Correspondence,* Vol. V, To William Baker, 22/June/1784, p. 154.

110. Burke, *Correspondence,* Vol. V, To Henry Homer, Nov./1786, p. 294.

BIBLIOGRAPHY

Adams, Randolph G. *Political Ideas of the American Revolution*. New York: Barnes and Noble, Inc., 1922.

Addison, Joseph. *The Freeholder.* Oxford: Clarendon Press, 1979.

Aristotle. *The Politics of Aristotle.* Edited by Ernest Barker. New York: Oxford University Press, 1946.

Ashcraft, Richard. *Revolutionary Politics and Locke's "Two Treatises of Government."* Princeton: Princeton University Press, 1986.

Atkins, Robert. *The Power, Jurisdiction and Privilege of Parliament . . .* 1689. Wilmington, Delaware: Scholarly Resources Press, 1973.

Atwood, William. *The Fundamental Constitution of the English Government.* 1690. Wilmington, Delaware: Scholarly Resources Press, 1973.

Ayling, Stanley. *Edmund Burke.* London: John Murray, 1988.

Babbitt, Irving. *Democracy and Leadership.* 1924. Indianapolis: Liberty Classics, 1979.

Baker, Keith Michael. Editor. *The Political Culture of the Old Regime.* New York: Pergamon Press, 1987.

Barker, Ernest. "Burke and His Bristol Constituency," *Essays on Government.* Oxford: Oxford University Press, 1956: 154–204.

Bayly, C. A. *Indian Society and the Making of the British Empire.* New York: Cambridge University Press, 1989.

Beckett, J. C. *The Making of Modern Ireland, 1603–1923.* New York: Alfred A. Knopf, 1966.

Berlin, Isaiah. *The Crooked Timber of Humanity.* New York: Alfred A. Knopf, 1991.

Blake, Robert. *The Conservative Party From Peel to Thatcher.* London: Methuen, 1975.

Blakemore, Steven. *Burke and the Fall of Language.* Hanover: University Press of New England, 1988.

Bolingbroke, Viscount. *Historical Essays.* Edited by Isaac Kramnick. Chicago: University of Chicago Press, 1972.

Boulton, James T. *The Language of Politics in the Age of Wilkes and Burke.* Toronto: University of Toronto Press, 1963.

Brewer, John. "Party and the Double Cabinet: Two Facets of Burke's *Thoughts*" *Historical Journal* 14 (1971): 479–501.

Brewer, John. *Political Ideology and Popular Politics at the Accession of George III.* Cambridge: Cambridge University Press, 1976.

Browning, Reed. *Political and Constitutional Ideas of the Court Whigs.* Baton Rouge: Louisiana State University Press, 1982.

Bryson, Gladys. *Man and Society: the Scottish Inquiry of the Eighteenth Century.* Princeton: Princeton University Press, 1945.

Burke, Edmund. *The Works of the Right Honourable Edmund Burke.* 8 Volumes. Boston: Little, Brown, and Company, 1889.

Burke, Edmund. *Reflections on the Revolution in France.* (1790). New York: Bobbs-Merrill, Co., Inc., 1955.

Burke, Edmund. *A Note-Book of Edmund Burke,* Edited by H.V.F. Somerset. Cambridge: Cambridge University Press, 1957.

Burke, Edmund. *A Philosophical Enquiry into the Origin of Our Ideas of the Sublime and Beautiful.* Notre Dame: University of Notre Dame Press, 1968.

Burke, Edmund. *An Account of the European Settlements in America.* 1758. Two Volumes. New York: Research Reprints, Inc., 1970.

Burke, Edmund. *The Correspondence of Edmund Burke.* 10 Volumes. Chicago: The University of Chicago Press, 1963–78.

Burrow, J. W. *A Liberal Descent.* New York: Cambridge University Press, 1981.

Burrow, J. W. *Whigs and Liberals.* Oxford: Clarendon Press, 1988.

Bury, J. B. *The Idea of Progress.* New York: The Macmillian Company, 1932.

Butterfield, Herbert. *The Whig Interpretation of History.* 1931. London: G. Bell and Sons, Ltd., 1963.

Campbell, T. D. *Adam Smith's Science of Morals.* Totowa: Rowman and Littlefield, 1971.

Canavan, Francis. *Edmund Burke: Prescription and Providence*. Durham: Carolina Academic Press, 1987.

Cannon, John. *The Fox-North Coalition*. Cambridge: Cambridge University Press, 1969.

Chapman, Gerald. *Edmund Burke: The Practical Imagination*. Cambridge: Harvard University Press, 1967.

Christie, Ian R. *Myth and Reality*. Los Angeles: University of California Press, 1970.

Christie, Ian R. *Stress and Stability in Late Eighteenth-Century Britain*. Oxford: Clarendon Press, 1984.

Clark, J. C. D. *The Dynamics of Change: The Crisis of the 1750s and English Party Systems*. New York: Cambridge University Press, 1982.

Clark, J. C. D. *English Society: 1688–1832*. New York: Cambridge University Press, 1985.

Clark, J. C. D. *Revolution and Rebellion: State and Society in England in the Seventeenth and Eighteenth Centuries*. New York: Cambridge University Press. 1986.

Cobban, Alfred. *Edmund Burke and the Revolt Against the Eighteenth Century*. New York: Macmillan Co., 1929.

Cobban, Alfred, Editor. *The Debate on the French Revolution 1789–1800*. London: Adam and Charles Black, 1950.

Colley, Linda. *In Defiance of Oligarchy: The Tory Party, 1774–60*. New York: Cambridge University Press, 1982.

Collingwood, R. G. *Essays in the Philosophy of History*. New York: McGraw-Hill, 1965.

Cone, Carl B. *Burke and the Nature of Politics*. Two Volumes. Lexington, Kentucky: The University of Kentucky Press, 1957–64.

Conniff, James. "Hume's Political Methodology: A Reconsideration of 'That Politics May be Reduced to a Science.'" *The Review of Politics*, Vol. 38, No. 1 (January 1976). pp, 88–108.

Conniff, James. "Burke, Bristol, and the Concept of Representation." *Western Political Quarterly*, Vol. XXX, No. 3 (September 1977), pp. 329–341.

Conniff, James. "Reason and History in Early Whig Thought: The Case of Algernon Sidney." *Journal of the History of Ideas*. Vol. XLIII, No. 3 (July–September 1982), pp. 397–416.

Conniff, James. "Edmund Burke's Reflections on the Coming Revolution in Ireland." *Journal of the History of Ideas.* Vol. XLVII, No. 1 (January–March 1986), pp. 37–59.

Conniff, James. "Burke on Political Economy: The Nature and Extent of State Authority." *The Review of Politics.* Vol. 49, No. 4 (fall 1987), pp. 490–514.

Cragg, Gerald R. *Reason and Authority in the Eighteenth Century.* Cambridge: Cambridge University Press, 1964.

Cragg, Gerald R. *From Puritanism to the Age of Reason.* Cambridge: Cambridge University Press, 1966.

Creed, John Martin and Boys Smith, John Sandwith, Editors. *Religious Thought in the Eighteenth Century.* Cambridge: Cambridge University Press, 1934.

Cruickshanks, Eveline. *Political Untouchables.* New York: Holmes and Meier, 1979.

Derry, John W. *The Regency Crisis and the Whigs.* New York: Cambridge University Press, 1963.

Derry, John W. *English Politics and the American Revolution.* New York: St. Martin's Press, 1976.

Dickinson, H. T. *Bolingbroke.* Two Volumes. London: Constable and Company, 1970.

Dickinson, H. T. *Liberty and Property.* London: Weidenfeld and Nicolson, 1977.

Dickinson, H. T. *British Radicalism and the French Revolution.* New York: Basil Blackwell, Inc., 1985.

Dickinson, H. T. Editor. *Britain and the French Revolution, 1789–1815.* London: Macmillan Education, 1989.

Dickerson, Oliver M. *The Navigation Acts and the American Revolution.* Philadelphia: University of Pennsylvania Press, 1951.

Donoughue, Bernard. *British Politics and the American Revolution.* London: Macmillan and Company, 1964.

Doyle, William. *The Ancien Regime.* London: Macmillan Education, 1986.

Dozier, Robert. *For King, Constitution, and Country.* Lexington: The University of Kentucky Press, 1983.

Dunn, John. *The Political Thought of John Locke.* Cambridge: Cambridge University Press, 1969.

Dunn, John. "The Concept of 'Trust' in the Politics of John Locke.' " in Richard Rorty, J. B. Schneewind, and Quinton Skinner. Editors. *Philosophy in History.* New York: Cambridge University Press, 1984.

Dunn, John. "Trust and Political Agency," in *Interpreting Political Responsibility.* Princeton: Princeton University Press, 1990.

Dworkin, Ronald. *Taking Rights Seriously.* Cambridge: Harvard University Press, 1978.

Ehrman, John. *The Younger Pitt.* Two Volumes. New York: E.P. Dutton and Company, Inc., 1969.

Elliot, Marianne. *Partners in Revolution: The United Irishmen and France.* New Haven: Yale University Press, 1988.

Emsley, Clive. *British Society and the French Wars, 1793–1815.* Totowa: Rowman and Littlefield, 1979.

Fair, John D. and Hutcheson, John A., Jr. "British Conservatism in the Twentieth Century: An Emerging Ideological Tradition." *Albion* 19 (winter 1987), 549–578.

Feiling, Keith. *The Second Tory Party, 1714–1832.* London: Macmillan and Co., 1938.

Feiling, Keith. *Warren Hastings.* 1954. Hamden, Connecticut: Archon Books, 1967.

Fennessy, R. R. *Burke, Paine, and the Rights of Man.* The Netherlands: Martinus Nijhoff, 1963.

Ferguson, Adam. *An Essay on the History of Civil Society.* 1767. Edinburgh: Edinburgh University Press, 1966.

Fink, Zera S. *The Classical Republicans.* Evanston: Northwestern University Press, 1962.

Foord, Archibald S. *His Majesty's Opposition.* Oxford: Oxford University Press, 1964.

Forbes, Duncan. *Hume's Philosophical Politics.* New York: Cambridge University Press, 1975.

[Francis, Phillip ?]. *The Letters of Junius.* Two Volumes. New York: Leavitt and Company, 1851.

Franklin, Julian H. *John Locke and the Theory of Sovereignty.* Cambridge: Cambridge University Press, 1978.

Freeman, Michael. *Edmund Burke and the Critique of Political Radicalism.* Chicago: The University of Chicago Press, 1980.

Gay, Peter. *The Enlightenment: An Interpretation.* Two Volumes. New York: Alfred A. Knopf, 1966–69.

Gewith, Alan. *Reason and Morality.* Chicago: University of Chicago Press, 1978.

Ginther, Donald E. *Whig Organization in the General Election of 1790.* Los Angeles: University of California Press, 1967.

Goldsmith, M. M. *Private Vices, Public Benefits: Bernard Mandeville's Social and Political Thought.* New York: Cambridge University Press, 1985.

Goldsmith, M. M. "Regulating Anew the Moral and Political Sentiments of Mankind: Bernard Mandeville and the Scottish Enlightenment." *Journal of the History of Ideas,* Vol. XLIX, No. 4 (Oct.–Dec. 1988), 587–606.

Goodwin, Albert. *The Friends of Liberty.* Cambridge: Harvard University Press, 1979.

Grave, S. A. *The Scottish Philosophy of Common Sense.* Oxford: Clarendon Press, 1960.

Grean, Stanley. *Shaftesbury's Philosophy of Religion and Ethics.* Athens, Ohio: Ohio University Press, 1967.

Greene, Jack P. *The Quest for Power.* Chapel Hill: University of North Carolina Press, 1963.

Greig, J. Y. T. *The Letters of David Hume.* Oxford: Clarendon Press, 1932.

Gunn, J. A. W. *Politics and the Public Interest in the Seventeenth Century.* Toronto: University of Toronto Press, 1969.

Gunn, J. A. W. *Beyond Liberty and Property.* Montreal: McGill-Queen's University Press, 1983.

Guttridge, G. H. *English Whiggism and the American Revolution.* 1942. Los Angeles: University of California Press, 1966.

Haakonssen, Knud. *The Science of a Legislator: The Natural Jurisprudence of David Hume and Adam Smith.* New York: Cambridge University Press, 1981.

Hale, Sir Matthew. *The History of the Common Law of England.* 1713. Chicago: The University of Chicago Press, 1971.

Hanson, Donald W. *From Kingdom to Commonwealth.* Cambridge: Harvard University Press, 1970.

Harris, R. W. *Reason and Nature in the Eighteenth Century.* London: Blandford Press, 1968.

Hart, H. L. A. *The Concept of Law.* Oxford: Clarendon Press, 1961.

Hart, Jeffrey. *Viscount Bolingbroke.* Toronto: University of Toronto Press, 1965.

Hendel, Charles W. Editor. *David Hume's Political Essays.* New York: The Liberal Arts Press, 1953.

Hill, B. W. *The Growth of Parliamentary Parties 1689–1742.* London: George Allen & Unwin Ltd., 1976.

Hill, B. W. *British Political Parties, 1742–1832.* London: George Allen Unwin, Ltd., 1985.

Himmelfarb, Gertrude. *The Idea of Poverty.* New York: Alfred A. Knopf, 1984.

Hirschman, Albert O. *The Passions and the Interests.* Princeton: Princeton University Press, 1977.

Hoffman, Ross J. S., *The Marquis: A Study of Lord Rockingham, 1730–1782.* New York: Fordham University Press, 1973.

Hoffman, Ross J. S. "Edmund Burke as a Practical Politician." in Peter J. Stanlis, Editor. *The Relevance of Edmund Burke.* New York: P. J. Kenedy, 1964. 109–130.

Hohfeld, Wesley N. *Fundamental Legal Concepts.* New Haven: Yale University Press, 1919.

Holmes, Geoffrey. *British Politics in the Age of Queen Anne.* New York: St. Martin's Press, 1967.

Holmes, Geoffrey. *The Trial of Doctor Sacheverell.* London: Eyre Methuen, 1973.

Horne, Thomas A. "Envy and Commercial Society: Mandeville and Smith on 'Private Vices, Public Benefits.'" *Political Theory.* Vol. 9, No. 4 (Nov. 1981), 551–569.

Houston, Alan Craig. *Algernon Sidney and the Republican Heritage in England and America.* Princeton: Princeton University Press, 1991.

Hume, David. *The History of England.* VI Volumes. Boston: Little, Brown and Company, 1854.

Hume, David. *Essays, Moral, Political, and Literary.* Vol. II., London, 1882.

Hume, David. *Of the Standard of Taste and Other Essays.* 1757. New York: Bobbs-Merrill Co. Inc., 1965.

Hume, David. *A Treatise of Human Nature.* (1739–40). Two Volumes. New York: Viking Penguin, Inc., 1969.

Hutcheson, Francis. *An Inquiry into the Origin of Our Ideas of Beauty and Virtue*. 1726. New York: Garland Publishing Inc., 1971.

Jacobson, David L. Editor. *The English Libertarian Heritage*. New York: Bobbs-Merrill Co. Inc., 1965.

Jensen, Merrill. Editor. *Tracts of the American Revolution 1763–1776*. New York: Bobbs-Merrill, Co. Inc., 1967.

Johnston, Edith M. *Great Britain and Ireland, 1760–1800*. London: Oliver and Boyd, 1963.

Jones, J. R. *The First Whigs*. New York: Oxford University Press, 1966.

Jones, Richard Foster. *Ancients and Moderns*. 1936. New York: Dover Publishing, Inc., 1961.

Kammen, Mchael. *Deputyes and Libertyes*. New York: Alfred A. Knopf, 1969.

Kenyon, Cecelia, *The Antifederalists*. New York: Bobbs-Merrill, 1966.

Kenyon, J. P. *Revolution Principles*. London: Cambridge University Press, 1977.

Kettler, David. "History and Theory in Ferguson's Essay on the History of Civil Society: A Reconsideration." *Political Theory*. Vol. V, No. 4 (Nov. 1977), 437–460.

Kirk, Russell. *Edmund Burke: A Genius Reconsidered*. New Rochelle, New York: Arlington House, 1967.

Kirk, Russell. *The Conservative Mind*. 1953. South Bend: Gateway Editions, 1978.

Kishlansky, Mark A. *Parliamentary Selection*. New York: Cambridge University Press, 1986.

Kramnick, Isaac. *Bolingbroke and His Circle*. Cambridge: Harvard University Press, 1968.

Kramnick, Isaac. *The Rage of Edmund Burke*. New York: Basic Books, 1977.

Kramnick, Isaac. "The Left and Edmund Burke." *Political Theory*, Vol. 11, No. 2 (May 1983), 189–214.

Kramnick, Isaac. *Repulicanism and Bourgeois Radicalism*. Ithaca: Cornell University Press, 1990.

Langford, Paul. *The First Rockingham Administration 1765–1766*. New York: Oxford University Press, 1973.

Laprade, William Thomas. *Public Opinion and Politics in Eighteenth Century England*. New York: The Macmillan Company, 1936.

Laslett, Peter. Editor. *Patriarcha and Other Political Works of Sir Robert Filmer.* Oxford: Oxford University Press, 1949.

Laslett, Peter. Editor. *Locke's Two Treatises of Government.* Cambridge: Cambridge University Press, 1966.

Law, William, "Three Letters to the Bishop of Bangor." *The Works,* IX Volumes. Vol. I. New York: Georg Olms Verland, 1974, 1–203.

Lecky, W. E. H. *A History of Ireland in the Eighteenth Century.* Chicago: The University of Chicago Press, 1972.

Lenzer, Steven J. "Strauss' Three Burke's: The Problem of Edmund Burke in Natural Right and History." *Political Theory.* Vol. 19, No. 3 (August 1991), 364–390.

Locke, John. *An Essay Concerning Human Understanding.* 1690. Two Volumes. New York: Dover Publications, Inc., 1959.

Locke, John. *Essays on the Law of Nature.* Edited by W. von Leyden. Oxford: Oxford University Press, 1954.

Macaulay, T. B. *Warren Hastings.* New York: Chautauqua Press, 1886.

MacCunn, John. *The Political Philkosophy of Burke.* New York: Russell and Russell, Inc., 1965.

Macpherson, C. B. *Burke.* New York: Hill and Wang, 1980.

Mahoney, Thomas H. D. *Edmund Burke and Ireland.* Cambridge: Harvard University Press, 1960.

Main, Jackson Turner. *The Antifederalists.* Chapel Hill: North Carolina Press, 1961.

Mandeville, Bernard. *The Fable of the Bees.* 1724. Baltimore: Penguin Books, 1970.

Mansfield, Harvey C. Jr. *Statesmanship and Party Government.* Chicago: University of Chicago Press, 1965.

Marshall, P. T. *The Impeachment of Warren Hastings.* Oxford: Oxford University Press, 1965.

Meek, Ronald L. *Social Science and the Ignoble Savage.* New York: Cambridge University Press, 1976.

Miller, David. *Philosophy and Ideology in Hume's Political Thought.* Oxford: Clarendon Press, 1981.

Mitchell, Austin. *The Whigs in Opposition, 1815–1830.* Oxford: Clarendon Press, 1967.

Mitchell, L. G. *Charles James Fox and the Disintegration of the Whig Party 1782–1794.* London: Oxford University Press, 1971.

Mitchison, Rosalind. Editor. *Essays in Eighteenth Century History.* New York: Barnes and Noble, Inc., 1966.

Monk, Samuel H. *The Sublime.* Ann Arbor: University of Michigan Press, 1960.

Monod, Paul Kleber. *Jacobitism and the English People 1688–1788.* New York: Cambridge University Press, 1989.

Montesquieu, Baron de. *The Spirit of the Laws.* 1748. Cambridge: Cambridge University Press, 1989.

Moon, Penderel. *Warren Hastings and British India.* London: Hodder and Stoughton, 1947.

Morley, Johm. *Edmund Burke: A Historical Study.* London: Macmillan, 1867.

Morley, John. *Burke.* New York: Harper and Brothers, 1879.

Mosher, Michael. "The Skeptic's Burke: *Reflections on the Revolution in France.*" *Political Theory,* Vol. 19, No. 3 (August 1991), 391–418.

Namier, Lewis. *The Structure of Politics at the Accession of George III.* 1928. New York: Macmillan and Co., 1957.

Norton, David Fate, and Richard H. Popkin. Editors. *David Hume: Philosophical Historian.* New York: Bobbs-Merrill, 1965.

O'Gorman, Frank. *The Whig Party and the French Revolution.* New York: St. Martin's Press, 1967.

O'Gorman, Frank. *Edmund Burke: His Political Philosophy.* Bloomington: Indiana University Press, 1973.

O'Gorman, Frank. *The Rise of Party in England.* London: George Allen Unwin Ltd., 1975.

Pangle, Thomas L. *The Spirit of Modern Republicanism.* Chicago: The University of Chicago Press, 1988.

Pares, Richard. *King George III and the Politicians.* Oxford: Oxford University Press, 1970.

Phillips, N. C. "Edmund Burke and the County Movement, 1779–80," in Rosiland Mitchison. Editor. *Essays in 18th Century History.* New York: Barnes and Noble, Inc., 1966, pp. 301–325.

Phillipson, N. T. and Rosalind Mitchison. Editor. *Scotland in the Age of Improvement.* Edinburgh: Edinburgh University Press, 1970.

Pitkin, Hanna. *The Concept of Representation.* Los Angeles: University of California Press, 1967.

Plato. *The Republic of Plato*. F.M. Cornford. Translator and Editor. Oxford: Oxford University Press, 1945.

Plumb, J. H. *The Origins of Political Stability, England 1675–1725*. Boston: Houghton Mifflin, 1967.

Plumb, J. H. *Sir Robert Walpole*. Two Volumes. London: the Penguin Press, 1972.

Pocock, J. G. A. *The Ancient Constitution and the Feudal Law*. New York: W. W. Norton and Co., 1967.

Pocock, J. G. A. *Politics, Language and Time*. New York: Atheneum, 1971.

Pocock, J. G. A. *The Machiavellian Moment*. Princeton: Princeton University Press, 1975.

Pocock, J. G. A. *Virtue, Commerce, and History*. New York: Cambridge University Press, 1985.

Pole, J. P. *The Seveenth Century: The Sources of Legislative Power*. Charlottesville: Virginia University Press, 1969.

Polybius. *The Histories*. New York, Washington Square Press, Inc., 1966.

Popkin, Richard H., *The History of Scepticism From Erasmus to Spinoza*. Los Angeles: University of California Press, 1979.

Price, Richard. *Two Tracts on Liberty*. 1777. New York: Da Capo Press, 1972.

Quinton, Anthony. *The Politics of Imperfection*. Boston: Faber and Faber, 1978.

Reid, Christopher. *Edmund Burke and the Practice of Political Writing*. New York: St. Martin's Press, 1985.

Reid, Loren. *Charles Jame Fox*. Columbia, Missouri: The University of Missouri Press, 1969.

Reid, Thomas. *An Inquiry into the Human Mind*. Chicago: The University of Chicago Press, 1974.

Richeson, Charles R. *British Politics and the American Revolution*. Norman: University of Oklahoma Press, 1854.

Richie, Daniel E. Editor. *Edmund Burke: Appraisals and Applications*. New Brunswick, New Jersey: Transaction Publishers, 1990.

Roberts, J. M. *The French Revolution*. Oxford: Oxford University Press, 1978.

Robbins, Caroline. *The 18th Century Commonwealthman*. Cambridge: Harvard University Press, 1961.

Robbins, Caroline. Editor. *Two English Republic Tracts*. Cambridge: Cambridge University Press, 1969.

Rude, George. *Wilkes and Liberty*. Oxford: Clarendon Press, 1962.

Samuels, Arthur P. I. *The Early Life, Correspondence, and Writings of the Rt. Hon. Edmund Burke*. Cambridge: Cambridge University Press, 1923.

Schochet, Gordon. *Patriarchalism in Political Thought*. Oxford: Basil Blackwell Press, 1975.

Schwoerer, Lois G. *The Declaration of Rights, 1689*. Baltimore: The Johns Hopkins University Press, 1981.

Shapiro, Barbara J. *Probability and Certainty in Seventeenth-Century England*. Princeton: Princeton University Press, 1983.

Sher, Richard. *Church and University in the Scottish Enlightenment*. Edinburgh: Edinburgh University Press, 1985.

Shklar, Judith N. *Montesquieu*. Oxford: Oxford University Press, 1987.

Sidney, Algernon. *Discourses on Government*. Three Volmes. New York: Deare and Andrews, 1805.

Smith, Adam. *An Inquiry into the Nature and Causes of the Wealth of Nations*. 1776. New York: Random House, 1937.

Smith, Bruce James. *Politics and Remembrance: Republican Themes in Machiavelli, Burke, and Tocqueville*. Princeton: Princeton University Press, 1985.

Smith, E. A. *Whig Principles and Party Politics*. Manchester: Manchester University Press, 1975.

Smith, Olivia. *The Politics of Language, 1791–1819*. Oxford: Clarendon Press, 1984.

Spadafora, David. *The Idea of Progress in Eighteenth-Century Britain*. New Haven: Yale University Press, 1990.

Stanlis, Peter J. *Edmund Burke and the Natural Law*. Ann Arbor: University of Michigan Press, 1958.

Stanlis, Peter J. Editor. *Edmund Burke*. New York: P. J. Kenedy, 1964.

Stanlis, Peter J. *Edmund Burke: The Enlightenment and the Modern World*. Detroit: University of Detroit Press, 1967.

Stanlis, Peter J. *Edmund Burke: The Enlightment and Revolution*. New Brunswick, New Jersey: Transaction Publishers, 1991.

Steele, Ian K. *The English Atlantic, 1675–1740*. New York: Oxford University Press, 1986.

Stephen, Leslie. *History of English Thought in the Eighteenth Century.* Two Volumes. New York: G.P. Putnam's Sons, 1927.

Stevenson, John. Editor. *London in the Age of Reform.* Oxford: Basil Blackwell, 1977.

Storing, Herbert J. *What the Anti-Federalists Were For.* Chicago: University of Chicago Press, 1981.

Strauss, Leo. *Natural Right and History.* Chicago: University of Chicago Press, 1953.

Stromberg, Ronald N. *Religious Liberalism in Eighteenth-Century England.* Oxford: Oxford Unversity Press, 1954.

Sykes, Norman. *Church and State in the XVIIIth Century.* Hamden, Connecticut: Archon Books, 1962.

Sutheland, Lucy. *The East India Company in Eighteenth-Century Politics.* Oxford: Clarendon Press, 1952.

Tacitus. *The Agricola and the Germania.* New York: Penguin Books, 1982.

Thomas, P. D. G. *British Politics and the Stamp Act Crisis.* Oxford: Oxford University Press, 1975.

Thompson, E. P. *The Making of the English Working Class.* New York: Vintage Books, 1966.

Toohey, Robert E. *Liberty and Empire.* Lexington: University of Kentucky Press, 1978.

Townsend, Joseph. *A Dissertation on the Poor Laws.* 1786. Berkeley: University of California Press, 1971.

Tuck, Richard. *Natural Rights Theories.* New York: Cambridge University Press, 1979.

Tucker, Josiah. *A Series of Answers to Certain Popular Objections, Against Separating from the Rebellious Colonies.* Glochester, R. Raikes, 1776.

Tucker, Josiah. *A Treatise Concerning Civil Government.* 1781. New York: Augustus M. Kelley, 1967.

Tully, James. *A Discourse on Property.* Cambridge: Cambridge University Press, 1980.

Underdown, Peter Thomas. *Bristol and Burke.* Bristol: Bristol Historical Society, 1961.

Veitch, George Stead. *The Genesis of Parliamentary Reform.* 1913. Hamden, Connecticut: Archon Books, 1965.

Westfall, Richard. *Science and Religion in Seventeenth-Century England.* New Haven: Yale University Press, 1958.

Weston, John C., Jr. "Edmund Burke's View of History." *Review of Politics* 23 (1961), 203–229.

Whitney, Lois. *Primitivism and the Idea of Progress in English Popular Literature of the Eighteenth Century.* Baltimore: The Johns Hopkins Press, 1934.

Wilkins, Burleigh T. *The Problem of Burke's Political Philosophy.* Oxford: Oxford University Press, 1967.

Winch, Donald. *Adam Smith's Politics.* New York: Cambridge University Press, 1978.

Winstanley, D. A. *Lord Chatham and the Whig Opposition.* 1912. New York: Barnes and Noble, Inc., 1966.

Wolpert, Stanley. *A New History of India.* New York: Oxford University Press, 1989.

Wood, Gordon S. *The Creation of the American Republic, 1776–1787.* Chapel Hill: University of North Carolina Press, 1969.

Wood, Gordon S. *Representation in the American Revolution.* Charlottesville: University of Virginia Press, 1969.

Wood, Neal. *The Politics of Locke's Philosophy.* Los Angeles: University of California, 1983.

Wood, Neal. *John Locke and Agrarian Capitalism.* Los Angeles: University of California Press, 1984.

INDEX